Candlestick Charting

Candlestick Charting

3rd Edition

by Larissa J. Adamiec, PhD, and
Russell Rhoads, PhD

Candlestick Charting For Dummies®, 3rd Edition

Published by: **John Wiley & Sons, Inc.**, 111 River Street, Hoboken, NJ 07030-5774, www.wiley.com

For general information on our other products and services, please contact our Customer Care Department within the U.S. at 877-762-2974, outside the U.S. at 317-572-3993, or fax 317-572-4002. For technical support, please visit https://hub.wiley.com/community/support/dummies.

Wiley publishes in a variety of print and electronic formats and by print-on-demand. Some material included with standard print versions of this book may not be included in e-books or in print-on-demand. If this book refers to media that is not included in the version you purchased, you may download this material at http://booksupport.wiley.com. For more information about Wiley products, visit www.wiley.com.

Library of Congress Control Number: 2026938839

ISBN 978-1-394-39815-7 (pbk); ISBN 978-1-394-39822-5 (ebk); ISBN 978-1-394-39823-2 (ebk)

SKY10153595_041426

Contents at a Glance

Introduction 1

Part 1: Getting Familiar with Candlestick Charting and Technical Analysis 5

CHAPTER 1: Understanding Charting and Where Candlesticks Fit In 7
CHAPTER 2: Getting to Know Candlestick Charts 17
CHAPTER 3: Building a Base of Candlestick Chart Knowledge 31
CHAPTER 4: Using Artificial Intelligence with Candlestick Charting 49

Part 2: Working with Simple Candlestick Patterns 61

CHAPTER 5: Working with Straightforward Single-Stick Patterns 63
CHAPTER 6: Single-Stick Patterns That Depend on Market Context 85
CHAPTER 7: Working with Bullish Double-Stick Patterns 109
CHAPTER 8: Using Bearish Double-Stick Patterns 137

Part 3: Making the Most of Complex Patterns 165

CHAPTER 9: Getting the Hang of Bullish Three-Stick Patterns 167
CHAPTER 10: Trading with Bearish Three-Stick Patterns 197

Part 4: Combining Patterns and Indicators 225

CHAPTER 11: Using Technical Indicators to Complement Your
Candlestick Charts 227
CHAPTER 12: Buy Indicators and Bullish Reversal Candlestick Patterns 247
CHAPTER 13: Sell Indicators and Bearish Reversal Candlestick Patterns 257
CHAPTER 14: Using Technical Indicators Alongside Bullish-Trending
Candlestick Patterns 267
CHAPTER 15: Combining Technical Indicators and Bearish-Trending
Candlestick Patterns 279
CHAPTER 16: Combining Economic Indicators and Bullish-Trending
Candlestick Patterns 289
CHAPTER 17: Combining Economic Indicators and Bearish-Trending
Candlestick Patterns 299

Part 5: The Part of Tens 309

CHAPTER 18: Ten Myths about Charting, Trading, and Candlesticks 311
CHAPTER 19: Ten Tips to Remember about Technical Analysis 317

Index 323

Table of Contents

INTRODUCTION 1
About This Book. 1
Foolish Assumptions. 2
Icons Used in This Book 2
Beyond the Book. 3
Where to Go from Here 3

PART 1: GETTING FAMILIAR WITH CANDLESTICK
CHARTING AND TECHNICAL ANALYSIS 5

CHAPTER 1: **Understanding Charting and Where
Candlesticks Fit In** 7
Considering Charting Methods and the Role of Candlesticks. 8
Getting a feel for your options for charting. 8
Realizing the advantages of candlestick charting 9
Differentiating Candlestick Components. 9
Working with Candlestick Patterns 11
Simple patterns 11
Complex patterns 12
Making Technical Analysis Part of Your Candlestick Charting
Strategy. 12
Trading Wisely: What You Must Know Before Working
the Markets 13
Trading can be an expensive endeavor 13
Paper trading costs you nothing but time 14
Develop rules, and stick to them. 14

CHAPTER 2: **Getting to Know Candlestick Charts** 17
Recognizing the Many Benefits of Candlestick Charting 18
Seeing is believing: Candlesticks are easy to read 19
Spotting bears and bulls quickly. 20
Seeing into the future (sort of) 22
Showing price patterns. 23
Admitting Potential Candlestick Charting Risks 25
Comparing Candlestick Charts with Alternative Charting
Methods 26
Line charts 26
Bar charts 27
Point and figure charts 28

CHAPTER 3: **Building a Base of Candlestick Chart Knowledge** 31

Constructing a Candlestick: A Core of Four 32
    Price on the open 32
    High and low prices for the session 35
    Price on the close 37
Considering Additional Information Included in
Candlestick Charts 39
    Volume 39
    Open interest 40
    Technical indicators 42
    Fundamental information 43

CHAPTER 4: **Using Artificial Intelligence with Candlestick Charting** 49

Retracing the History of ChatGPT 50
Taking ChatGPT for a Spin 51
Opting for Other AI Software 56
Exploring Trading Platforms 59

PART 2: WORKING WITH SIMPLE CANDLESTICK PATTERNS 61

CHAPTER 5: **Working with Straightforward Single-Stick Patterns** 63

The Bullish Long White Candle 64
    Taking a look at long white candles 64
    Identifying the three variations of the long white candle 68
The Bullish Dragonfly Doji 70
    Recognizing a dragonfly doji 71
    Trading based on a dragonfly doji 73
The Bearish Long Black Candle 75
    Taking a look at long black candles 75
    Identifying the three variations of the long black candle 77
    Trading based on long black candles 78
The Bearish Gravestone Doji 81
    Identifying the gravestone doji 81
    Trading based on gravestone dojis 83

CHAPTER 6: **Single-Stick Patterns That Depend on Market Context** 85

Sorting Out Market Environments 86
    Recognizing the three market states 86
    Identifying the market trend 86

Delving into Dojis. 88
The long-legged doji 88
Other dojis 93
Looking at Other Patterns: Spinning Tops. .96
Identifying spinning tops 97
Using spinning tops for profitable trading. 97
Discovering More about Belt Holds 100
Spotting belt holds on a chart 100
Buckling down for some belt hold-based trading. 102
Deciphering the Hanging Man and the Hammer 105
Spotting the hanging man and the hammer. 105
Trading on the hanging man and the hammer. 106

CHAPTER 7: **Working with Bullish Double-Stick Patterns**. 109
Bullish Reversal Patterns 110
Bullish engulfing pattern 110
Bullish harami 114
Bullish harami cross 117
Bullish inverted hammer 119
Bullish doji star 122
Bullish meeting line. 123
Bullish piercing line 126
Bullish Trend-Confirming Patterns 129
Bullish thrusting lines 129
Bullish separating lines. 131
Bullish necklines 134

CHAPTER 8: **Using Bearish Double-Stick Patterns**. 137
Working with Bearish Reversal Patterns 137
The bearish engulfing pattern. 138
The bearish harami pattern. 141
The bearish harami cross pattern. 143
The bearish inverted hammer pattern. 145
The bearish doji star 147
The bearish meeting line 150
The bearish piercing line (or dark cloud cover pattern). 152
Making a Profit with Bearish Trend Patterns 155
The bearish thrusting lines. 156
The bearish separating lines 158
The bearish neck lines 161

PART 3: MAKING THE MOST OF COMPLEX PATTERNS 165

CHAPTER 9: Getting the Hang of Bullish Three-Stick Patterns 167

Understanding Bullish Three-Stick Trend Reversal Patterns 168
The three inside up pattern 168
The three outside up pattern 171
The three white soldiers pattern 173
The morning star and bullish doji star patterns 176
The bullish abandoned baby pattern 179
The bullish squeeze alert pattern 181
Working with Bullish Three-Stick Trending Patterns 184
The bullish side-by-side white lines pattern 185
The bullish side-by-side black lines pattern 187
The upside tasuki gap pattern 190
The upside gap-filled pattern 193

CHAPTER 10: Trading with Bearish Three-Stick Patterns 197

Understanding Bearish Three-Stick Trend Reversal Patterns 198
The three inside down pattern 198
The three outside down pattern 201
The three black crows pattern 203
The evening star and bearish doji star patterns 206
The bearish abandoned baby pattern 209
The bearish squeeze alert pattern 210
Forecasting with Bullish Three-Stick Trending Patterns 213
The bearish side-by-side black lines pattern 214
The bearish side-by-side white lines pattern 216
The downside tasuki gap pattern 218
The downside gap-filled pattern 221

PART 4: COMBINING PATTERNS AND INDICATORS 225

CHAPTER 11: Using Technical Indicators to Complement Your Candlestick Charts 227

Using Trend Lines 228
Drawing trend lines 229
Considering trend line direction 230
Taking advantage of automated trend lines 230
Using Moving Averages 231
Selecting appropriate moving average periods 231
Using simple moving averages 232

Using other types of moving averages: What have
you done for me lately? 233
Combining two moving averages 236
Combining three moving averages. 237
Examining the Relative Strength Index 239
Calculating the RSI. 239
Reading an RSI chart 240
Cashing In on Stochastics. 242
Grasping the math behind the stochastic oscillator. 242
Interpreting the stochastic oscillator 242
Buddying Up with Bollinger Bands 244

CHAPTER 12: **Buy Indicators and Bullish Reversal
Candlestick Patterns**. 247

Buying with the RSI and Bullish Reversal Candlestick Patterns 248
Using the RSI to pick a long entry point 248
Using the RSI to pick long exits 250
Buying with the Stochastic Indicator and a Bullish
Reversal Candlestick Pattern 252
Using the stochastic indicator to pick a long entry point. 252
Using the stochastic indicator to pick long exits. 254

CHAPTER 13: **Sell Indicators and Bearish Reversal
Candlestick Patterns**. 257

Shorting with the RSI and Bearish Candlestick Patterns 258
Picking short entry points with the RSI and candlesticks 258
Using the RSI to help pick short entry and exit points. 260
Using the Stochastic Indicator and Bearish Candlestick
Patterns for Shorting 262
Picking short entry points. 263
Deciding when to get in and out of shorts. 264

CHAPTER 14: **Using Technical Indicators Alongside
Bullish-Trending Candlestick Patterns** 267

Using Trending Patterns for Buying and Confirmation 268
Buying trend lines with bullish candlestick patterns 268
Determining sales and stop levels with trend lines 270
Combining Moving Averages and Bullish-Trending
Candlestick Patterns 273
Using moving averages with bullish-trending
candlestick patterns to confirm trends .273
Setting stops with the moving average and
bullish-trending candlestick patterns 275

CHAPTER 15: **Combining Technical Indicators and Bearish-Trending Candlestick Patterns** 279
Combining Lines with Candles for Confirmation 280
Analyzing short trades with trend lines and
bearish patterns 280
Bearish trend lines and candlestick patterns leading
to short entries and exits 282
Combining Moving Averages and Bearish Patterns for Shorts......284
Pinning down short entry points and confirming trends 285
Picking shorts with moving averages and candlesticks.........287

CHAPTER 16: **Combining Economic Indicators and Bullish-Trending Candlestick Patterns** 289
Gross Domestic Product...................................290
Interest Rates...292
Unemployment Rate.......................................293
Consumer Price Index.....................................295
Volatility Index 296

CHAPTER 17: **Combining Economic Indicators and Bearish-Trending Candlestick Patterns** 299
Gross Domestic Product...................................300
Interest Rates...301
Unemployment...303
Consumer Price Index.....................................305
Volatility Index 307

PART 5: THE PART OF TENS 309

CHAPTER 18: **Ten Myths about Charting, Trading, and Candlesticks**..................................311
There's No Difference between Candlesticks and Bar Charts 312
Market Efficiency Makes It Impossible to Beat the
Market over the Long Run 312
Only a Full-Time Professional Can Make Money in the Markets 313
Technical Analysis Is Nothing More than Reading Tea Leaves......313
Charting Is for Short-Term Traders Only 314
You Must Be Rich to Start Trading 314
Trading Is an Easy Way to Get Rich Quick 315
Candlestick Charts Require In-Depth Data and Are Difficult to
Create 315
The Trading Game Is Stacked against the Small Trader 315
Selling Short Is for Professional Traders Only.................316

CHAPTER 19: **Ten Tips to Remember about Technical Analysis** 317

Charts Can Give False Signals 317
You Will Run into Skeptics 318
There's No Definite Right or Wrong Opinion of a Chart 318
A Single Chart Doesn't Tell a Whole Story 318
Charting Is Part Science, Part Art 319
You Can Overanalyze 319
Develop a Backup System 320
Error-Free Data Doesn't Exist. 320
No System Is Silly as Long as It Works 321
Past Results Don't Always Predict Future Performance. 321

INDEX 323

Introduction

When Russell wrote the first version of this book, candlestick charts were a known method of displaying and analyzing price data, but weren't the default charting method for most traders. Now, more than ten years later, the charts shown in the business media are often candlestick charts. This situation is fully understandable because candlestick charts are better visuals than line charts or bar charts. But even though candlestick charts are common nowadays, most traders still don't understand candlestick patterns, much less use them in day-to-day trading.

After the first edition of this book was published, Russell received some criticism that he had spent too much time discussing instances in which candlestick patterns didn't work out. One main reason traders fail, however, is that they don't take losses even when it makes sense. Whenever a trader enters a trade, they should have an exit plan that involves taking either losses or profits. This book sticks with the format of showing both profitable and losing trades for each pattern.

About This Book

This book isn't intended to be an end-all-and-be-all guide to profitable trading. It's meant to provide readers with some insight into how candlesticks are created and how they can be used to analyze the psychology behind what happens over the course of trading days. (When we say *psychology*, we aren't trying to conjure up images of Freud and Rorschach tests; we're talking about the motivating factors that determine how the market behaves.)

We made an effort to use as many examples as possible in the text, and every example comes from actual charts, showing you not only how common candlestick patterns are in everyday trading but also how they're used in live trades. They're waiting for you to harness their power!

Also, for each new candlestick pattern we introduce, we present at least one case that produces a useful signal and one that produces a dud. Candlesticks are terrific, but they're not perfect, and recognizing the failure of a signal is just as important as picking up on a valid signal.

We hope the candlestick methods described in this book help you make trading and investment decisions that lead to solid profits, but unfortunately, we can't guarantee those profits. What we *can* guarantee is that after reading this book, you'll understand what candlesticks are, what they represent, and how to use them effectively in trading.

Foolish Assumptions

Knowledge of candlesticks varies widely from trader to trader. Even traders with the same amount of trading experience can differ quite a bit in their candlestick know-how. So we've made these assumptions about you:

>> You have at most only a basic understanding of what comprises a candlestick chart. (Our apologies if you already know a little about candlesticks, but hey, it never hurts to review and hone essential candlestick skills.)

>> You have some sort of experience in trading a stock or at least a mutual fund.

>> You've spent some time looking over stock charts.

Icons Used in This Book

We used the following icons throughout this book to point out various types of information:

When you see this icon, you should store the accompanying nugget of candlestick or trading wisdom somewhere safe in your brain.

This icon offers hands-on advice that you can put into practice as you trade. In many cases, the information next to this icon tells you directly how to conduct a trade on a pattern or technical analysis method.

If you ignore this information, you might wake up one day in a den full of writhing, angry pit vipers. Okay, things won't get *that* bad, but this icon can help you avoid making costly trading mistakes.

This icon flags places where we get truly technical about charting. Although the information is useful, you can safely skip it without missing out on the discussion at hand.

Beyond the Book

In addition to the scintillating text in your hands, this book comes with a free access-anywhere Cheat Sheet that you can use whenever you need a quick refresher on common candlestick patterns or trading tips. To get this Cheat Sheet, simply go to www.dummies.com and type **Candlestick Charting For Dummies Cheat Sheet** in the Search box.

Where to Go from Here

To figure out which area of this book to dive into first, think hard about what facet of candlestick charting you want to understand. Do you want to get grounded in the basics or polish up on a few candlestick fundamentals that you've forgotten since you read that online article about candlestick charting months ago? Check out Part 1.

If you want to get cracking by finding out about a few real candlestick patterns and seeing how they can tell you what a market or security will do next, check out one of the chapters in Part 2 or Part 3. We cover many candlestick patterns in those chapters — enough to give you plenty to look for as you pore over charts on the web or in a charting software package.

You may have been exposed to other technical indicators, and it's possible that reading about candlesticks alongside some of that familiar material may help you get your feet wet. If so, make a beeline for Part 4, and enjoy! We've also added some quick summaries and resources in Part 5, so check it out, too.

The water's fine no matter where you choose to dive in, and you're just a few page-turns away from adding a powerful weapon to your trading arsenal.

1

Getting Familiar with Candlestick Charting and Technical Analysis

Get familiar with the mechanics of candlestick charting and how it contrasts with other methods of charting security prices.

Discover how powerful candlestick charting is relative to other, less-illustrative types of charting.

See what price activity creates candlesticks.

Understand the mind of the market based on individual candlesticks.

Explore electronic resources for creating candlestick charts and even some for identifying bullish and bearish patterns.

Chapter **1**

Understanding Charting and Where Candlesticks Fit In

The advent of the Internet has leveled the playing field for securities traders. Access to markets once meant placing orders by way of a broker; now it takes little more than a couple of mouse clicks. Commission rates are dramatically lower, and sometimes even free. Additionally, access to market information is free in many cases. Breaking into securities trading is easier than ever, and the result is that a whole generation of investors and traders handles their finances without professional help. Technology allows these people to enjoy many new types of market information, and one of the best tools available is candlestick charting.

Candlestick charting methods have been around for hundreds of years, but candlesticks have caught on over the past couple of decades or so as a charting standard in the United States. *Candlestick charts* allow for an easy way to visualize market information, which has created a fierce loyalty among traders who use them. We think you'll feel the same way, and this book is the first step on your path to conquering candlesticks.

The material we spell out in this chapter exposes you to many of the facets of candlestick charting that continue to fuel its rise as one of the most popular charting techniques. We begin with the overall role of candlesticks within the context of charting. We cover the advantages of candlestick charting and the basics of candlestick construction. We also take the opportunity at the end of this chapter to discuss how to get started and then give you some insight into the characteristics and habits that successful traders employ in their pursuit of profits. Enjoy, and happy charting!

Considering Charting Methods and the Role of Candlesticks

With advances in technology and the growing availability of trading and investing resources available to traders, many options exist for the charting of securities. Several types of charts and dozens of variations and features can be configured for each type. It's important that you're clear on what other charting options are out there and — perhaps more important — on why candlestick charting is at the top of the heap. We provide answers to both questions.

Getting a feel for your options for charting

When it comes to alternatives to candlestick charting, these are the three main charting contenders:

» **Line charts:** These charts are simple and helpful for short-term decisions, but they're quite limited when it comes to the amount of data presented.

» **Bar charts:** These charts, the most common type, are much more useful than line charts, but they're not as versatile as candlestick charts.

» **Point and figure charts (also known as P&F charts):** These tried-and-true charting methods are helpful for recognizing support and resistance levels, but they're far less dynamic than candlestick charts. These charts, discussed in Chapter 2, have been around since the 19th century as a way of tracking price movements. The Xs and Os were incorporated in the 1930s as a way of standardizing the price movement.

Each one of these charting methods can be used effectively to ratchet up the effectiveness of your trading strategy, but, for several reasons, they pale in comparison with candlestick charts, a few of which we describe in the next section.

Realizing the advantages of candlestick charting

You'd be hard-pressed to find people who are more enthusiastic about candlestick charting than we are. We can go on and on about the benefits that candlesticks afford. If you want to read more of our gushing about the many fantastic features of candlestick charting, turn to Chapter 2, but for now, here are our top three reasons:

>> **Two of the best features of candlestick charting in general are visual appeal and readability.** You can glance at a candlestick chart and quickly gain an understanding of what's going on with the price of a security. You can also tell whether sellers or buyers have dominated a given day and gain a sense of how the price is trending. This isn't easily seen in the other types of charting, such as line charts, bar charts, and point and figure charts.

>> **Even after reading up on the most rudimentary candlestick basics, you can easily spot on a candlestick chart the opening and closing price of a security.** These price levels can be vital areas of support and resistance from day to day, and knowing where they are can be extremely helpful, especially for short-term traders. Support and resistance are, in essence, the floor and ceiling of pricing: The level at which the price naturally doesn't fall below is the *support;* on the other hand, the price level at which the asset doesn't break through, like a glass ceiling, is the *resistance.* Asset prices can, of course, break through either the support or resistance level; they usually don't, however.

>> Candlesticks aren't just pretty faces — candlestick charts also feature specific patterns you can identify and use to determine when it's time to buy, sell, or wait on a trade or an investment. These patterns can be a true boon to your work with securities, and you can combine them with other technical and economic indicators for even more reliable results.

Differentiating Candlestick Components

You can't trade and invest effectively by using candlestick charts unless you understand candlestick patterns, and you may have difficulty understanding those patterns if you aren't familiar with basic candlestick construction. Candlestick charting starts with the knowledge of what it takes to make a candlestick and how changes in that basic information affect a candlestick's appearance and what it means. For starters, you need to know what goes into creating a candlestick's *wick* (the thin vertical line) and its *candle* (the thick part in the middle).

The following four pieces of information are combined to create a candlestick:

>> **Price on the open:** The price at which a security opens in a given period is the first piece of information used in creating a candlestick. Depending on whether the security's performance is bullish or bearish, the opening price corresponds to either the bottom edge of a candlestick's candle or its top edge.

Candlesticks that represent *bullish* price action appear white on a chart in this book, but green in many charting packages, and candlesticks that represent *bearish* price action appear black (or red, when color is available).

>> **High price:** The highest price a security reaches during a given period corresponds to the top of a candlestick's wick. If a security opens at a certain price and then trades consistently lower than that price throughout the period, no wick appears above the candle.

>> **Low price:** The lowest price a security reaches during a period corresponds to the bottom of a candlestick's wick. If the price action for that period is extremely bullish and prices trade higher than the open, no wick appears below the candle.

>> **Price on the close:** When a security finishes trading during a given period, its closing price is the last piece of information used to create a candlestick. Depending on the security's performance during that period, the closing price can correspond to either the top edge of a candlestick's candle (if the period was bullish) or the bottom edge (if the period was bearish).

As true candlestick devotees, we believe that you can gain far more insight into a period's trading by looking at a candlestick than you can by looking at any other type of charting tool. Want proof? Take a look at Figure 1-1.

You can tell right away that the up day has a white candle and the down day has a black candle. That simple difference alone clearly reveals the nature of the price action that took place during that period. In the case of the candlestick with the black candle, there was more selling pressure than desire to buy. And the candlestick with the white candle indicates that there was more buying pressure than desire to sell.

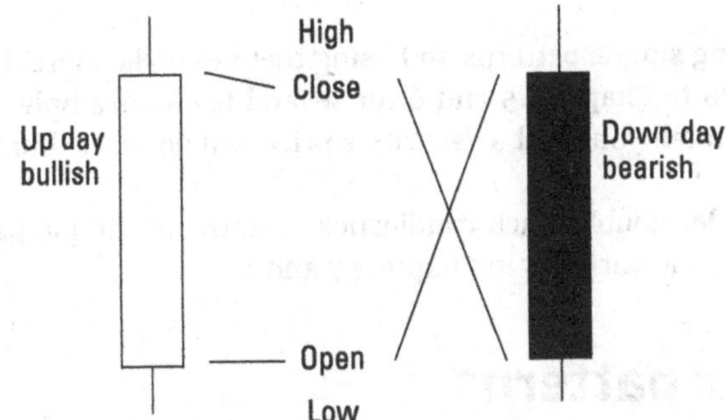

FIGURE 1-1: Bullish and bearish candlesticks, side by side.

Why are these details important? Candlestick charts quickly clue you in on the type of buying and selling that has been going on during a given period and where it may occur again. In many cases, the buyers continue to buy and the sellers continue to sell during subsequent periods or when the price reaches a level that spurred them to action in the past. This activity describes momentum or trends, which is a large part of short-term trading.

For more information on candlestick construction, see Chapter 3.

Working with Candlestick Patterns

The components of a candlestick may form the bones of candlestick charting, but candlestick patterns are its heart and soul. Patterns appear on candlestick charts as simple, single-stick occurrences or complex, multistick formations, and many types of patterns can tell you what may be in store for a security you've had your eye on for trading or investing. Knowing what may lie ahead can mean the difference between a profitable trade and a flop.

REMEMBER

Candlestick patterns indicate when prevailing trends reverse or continue. Both types of patterns are quite useful because they tell you when to jump into a trade, when to jump out of a trade, when a trade you're in may make no sense, and even when to hang on to a trade you're already in. Check out Parts 2 and 3 of this book for more info on identifying and trading on a wide variety of candlestick patterns.

Simple patterns

Some candlestick patterns are simple: A single candlestick on a chart can serve as a candlestick pattern. A single candlestick that signifies time to buy or sell is appealing to traders who are just starting to work with candlestick charts because, after you understand the basics of candlestick construction, you can immediately start identifying simple patterns and using them to make more-informed trading decisions. Turn to Chapters 5 and 6 for several useful examples of how just one candlestick can tell you what a security's price will do in the immediate future.

We also consider double-stick candlestick patterns as simple patterns, and you can explore several varieties in Chapters 7 and 8.

Complex patterns

When a candlestick pattern includes three periods' worth of price action (three candlesticks), we consider it to be a *complex* pattern. Many complex candlestick patterns require specific price activity over the course of three days for the pattern to be considered valid, and we discuss a range of them in Part 3.

Complex candlestick patterns can be frustrating at times because you may watch with anticipation as a pattern develops nicely for the first two days, only to fizzle out on the third. With all trading, patience is the key.

Complex candlestick patterns are rarer than their simple counterparts, but they can be worth the wait. Because the conditions and criteria for a complex pattern are so specific, it's more likely that the signals they offer will be good ones.

Making Technical Analysis Part of Your Candlestick Charting Strategy

A stunning amount of mathematical ingenuity is applied to security-trading analysis. The options for technical analysis can be as simple as the average of a few days of closing prices and as complex as applying calculus to price action to indicate the momentum of prices. The possibilities are endless, and you shouldn't be shy about including some of them in your trading strategy alongside candlestick charts.

Take the time to get familiar with an array of technical indicators to make yourself a versatile trader and enrich your work with candlestick charts. It's helpful when you spot a candlestick pattern indicating that it's time to buy while your favorite technical indicator is also flashing a buy signal. Combining trading tools helps build your confidence and can help you determine quickly when a trade won't work out, allowing you to exit with minimal losses.

We explore several types of technical and economic indicators in Chapter 11 and clue you in on a few ways you can combine these indicators with candlestick patterns in Chapters 11–15. Find a few technical indicators that match up with the type of trading you want to pursue, and add them to your candlestick charts. Read up on the choices, and if Chapter 11 doesn't hold enough information, you can always turn to *Technical Analysis For Dummies*, 4th Edition, by Barbara Rockefeller (Wiley). Added understanding of technical and economic indicators can truly aid you in your candlestick charting efforts.

Trading Wisely: What You Must Know Before Working the Markets

Security trading and investing can be a financially rewarding and fulfilling experience, but it's far from a risk- and stress-free undertaking. We want to make clear to you a few key points and concerns before we dive into our candlestick charting discussion so that you're fully aware of what you're up against and what you can do to maximize rewards and minimize risks.

Trading can be an expensive endeavor

There's money to be made on the security markets, but don't be fooled into thinking that earning profits is easy or effortless. Do your homework, and practice wise money management.

By "do your homework," we mean look at charts and develop a trading plan. The more you prepare (much as you would for a test), the better your trading results should be. We've seen a direct correlation between the level of trading success we've achieved and how much time we put into preparing for trading situations. As far as wise money management goes, the key is making sure to take a loss when it becomes apparent that a trade won't work. Take the loss and move on. More importantly, take this loss early and quickly before it becomes a much bigger loss. As the old Wall Street saying goes, "Your first loss is often your best loss."

Here's the most important rule for managing your trading and investing funds: Do not risk money you can't afford to lose. The financial markets have many obvious and unforeseen risks. If your lifestyle has changed dramatically because a trade or an investment wiped out your account, you have probably put too much of your personal net worth on the line.

Paper trading costs you nothing but time

Paper trading refers to the practice of tracking trades on paper that haven't been traded in an account. Professional traders tell you that paper trading isn't the same as putting real money at risk on the markets. As professional traders, we totally agree. The emotional roller coaster involved with making and losing money can't be matched in a dry run. But if you're a novice who's just starting to understand the ways of the market, we think that paper trading is a useful idea. The risks are nil, and the educational benefits are outstanding. We still tend to paper-trade new ideas or systems for a while before putting real-life money to work.

If you try paper trading but lose interest because you have no skin in the game, make just a small trade in a live account. The size of your trade and the risk you're taking to try out a new strategy should be inconsequential relative to your net worth.

If you're new to trading, test your trading ideas and refine your trading strategy by signing up for a trial account online with an electronic broker. (You can read all about electronic trading resources in Chapter 4.) All you stand to lose is a little time and some pride. But that's better than jumping directly into a live trading scenario and getting taken to the cleaners!

Develop rules, and stick to them

Throughout this book, we stress the importance of setting rules for yourself and sticking to those rules. We just can't stress enough what a good practice that is for any trader. Making and losing money on the market is an *emotional* experience. One main reason that some traders lose big when they should lose (or even win) just a little is that they let their emotions take control of their trading. You can take emotions out of the equation if you develop trading rules and adhere to them no matter what happens.

Create a set of trading rules for yourself and stick to them. Include rules such as these:

>> When to get into trades

>> Where to place stops in various trading situations

>> What amount of money to risk on trades and investments

>> When to get out of trades, with either a loss or profit

Write down your rules and keep them handy for a quick review when you're in the midst of a trade and having second thoughts about what action to take. This strategy is imperative because it removes the emotional element from trading.

We've been trading for a long time, and we can say without reservation that creating and adhering to a set of trading rules is the best way to reward yourself, both personally and financially, for the effort you put into the markets. We *always* follow the rules we've set for ourselves, and although it may sound crazy, at this point we're prouder of our rules than we are of our profits. Every trader has to come up with their own set of rules that talk to their trading style and comfort with risk — you should keep that fact in mind and jot down potential rules as you explore the content of this book.

Chapter **2**

Getting to Know Candlestick Charts

Ever wonder why a trader or an investor would choose candlestick charts over other types of charts when analyzing the price action of investments or markets? Well, this chapter provides some answers.

Trading and investing aren't easy undertakings, and they certainly aren't easy professions. Most traders — professional and amateur alike — and investors struggle just to keep up with the market's performance as measured by the Standard & Poor's 500 index (S&P 500), which is considered to be representative of the stock market as a whole.

REMEMBER

To be one of the successful few who beat the market and other market participants, strive to develop a competitive advantage or a unique insight, commonly referred to as your *edge,* that you believe most market participants aren't using or considering. We can't say that using candlestick charting provides an edge by itself — and we have to say that it does come with a couple of potential problems. But when you combine it with recurring patterns, other technical indicators, and economic indicators, you can find your edge!

In this chapter, we cover the good, the bad, and the ugly of candlestick charts, and we review a handful of alternative charting methods. If you read to the end, you'll understand why candlestick charting is the way to go.

The history of candlestick charting stretches back to Japanese rice traders in the 17th or 18th century, which is why candlestick charts are frequently referred to as *Japanese candlestick charts*. A man named Munehisa Homma developed the methodology of monitoring the price of daily rice trading, and his methods eventually evolved into what traders now call candlestick charting.

Homma found that having a visual representation of daily rice trading allowed him to make more informed buy-and-sell decisions during the hectic trading day. It's said that Homma once had a streak of more than 100 winning trades!

Fast-forward to the early 1990s, when Steve Nison published a book and a magazine article on candlestick charting. Until then, candlestick charting wasn't widely used. Nison's first book, *Japanese Candlestick Charting Techniques* (Prentice Hall Press), served as an introduction to candlestick charting methods for many traders and investors in the United States, including this edition's author team. In the years that followed, the acceptance and use of candlestick charting became widespread, and the use of computer software for analyzing recurring patterns proved to be profitable for many traders.

Recognizing the Many Benefits of Candlestick Charting

Trading, investing, and charting styles are plentiful. You can spend hours debating what type of approach to the markets is best. For us (and for a growing number of other traders), the benefits of a candlestick chart versus other types of charts aren't really debatable. Let us tell you why.

Changes and developments in the way stocks and other securities are traded (and *when* they're traded) have made trading an increasingly complex undertaking. (For more info, see the nearby sidebar "What makes up a day?") Because trading is becoming more complex, the need for a consistent, dynamic charting method is more important than ever. Traders need easy-to-read charts that allow them to make quick decisions and analyze patterns efficiently. Candlesticks offer those benefits and many more, all of which are covered in this section.

The definition of a trading "day" used to be simple: Trading was done on a central exchange with specific opening and closing times. Trading on stocks listed on the New York Stock Exchange (NYSE) or Nasdaq, for example, began at 9:30 A.M. and ceased at 4 P.M. These days, trading in these stocks commences on some ECNs hours before the open hours of the formal listed exchanges. (An *ECN*, or *electronic communication network*, is a network of brokerage firms and traders that allows for trading directly between the brokerage firms and traders.) A "day," therefore, is much different from what it was in the past. Throw in futures exchanges and currency markets that trade almost 24 hours a day, and this issue becomes even more confusing. With all that trading going on outside exchange hours, what constitutes an actual day for data purposes?

In the case of stocks, the official open and close are now based on the primary exchange they trade on, but in this world of expanding electronic trading, the actual open and close are becoming more blurred. With respect to futures markets that trade almost 24 hours a day, it's almost impossible to pin down a day. For daily testing, we use data between 7 A.M. Eastern time and the close at 3 P.M. to constitute a day.

Seeing is believing: Candlesticks are easy to read

It sounds simplistic, but one noteworthy advantage candlesticks have over other charts is readability. Consider Figure 2-1, which compares a bar and a candlestick.

Figure 2-1 gives you a basic idea why candlesticks are easier to read, but it doesn't provide a full picture of why they're also much better at helping traders visually interpret *price action* (how the stock or market traded during the day relative to the opening price), which is an essential skill for successful trading. Figure 2-1 shows how a single day would be displayed on a bar chart and a candlestick chart.

Notice the dramatic difference between the bar chart and the candlestick chart. By comparing them, you can clearly interpret what occurred from day to day, including the openings and closings and how they change from day to day. The candlestick chart is superior to a bar chart for interpreting price action from day to day. Don't worry: We cover extensively in several other chapters how to read candlestick charts. But even in this simplistic example, you can see that knowing where a stock closed relative to its open on a given day is a powerful piece of information that you can glean quickly from a candlestick chart.

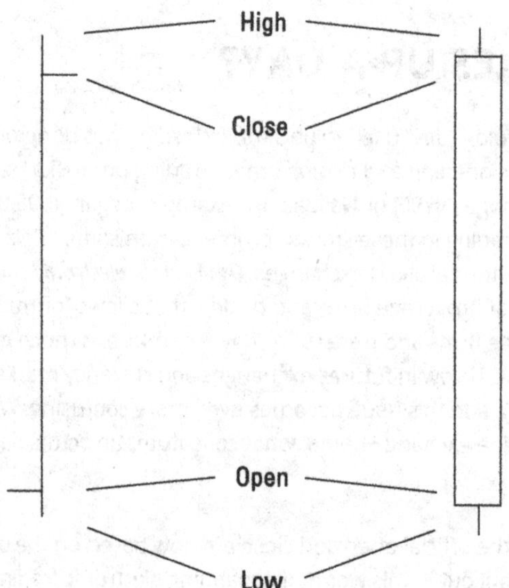

FIGURE 2-1:
A bar versus a
candlestick.

Spotting bears and bulls quickly

Knowing a security's closing price relative to its opening price during a certain period is vital information. Candlestick charts allow you to quickly identify the days when a closing price is higher than an opening price, and vice versa.

REMEMBER

We like to think of the daily price action as a battle between bears and bulls. Bears win when the price of a security closes lower than its open, and bulls win on the days when the close settles higher than the open.

Figure 2-2 shows a helpful example of bearish and bullish days on a candlestick chart. Although the two candlesticks are the same size and shape, you can tell the difference between a bear and a bull:

>> **The bear:** The black, filled-in candlestick indicates a bearish performance by the security because the close is much lower than the opening price.

>> **The bull:** The hollow white candlestick indicates a bullish performance, meaning that the opening is lower than the close.

Figure 1-1 in Chapter 1 displays "hollow" candlesticks that show a higher close than open and a "filled-in" candlestick that shows a lower close than open.

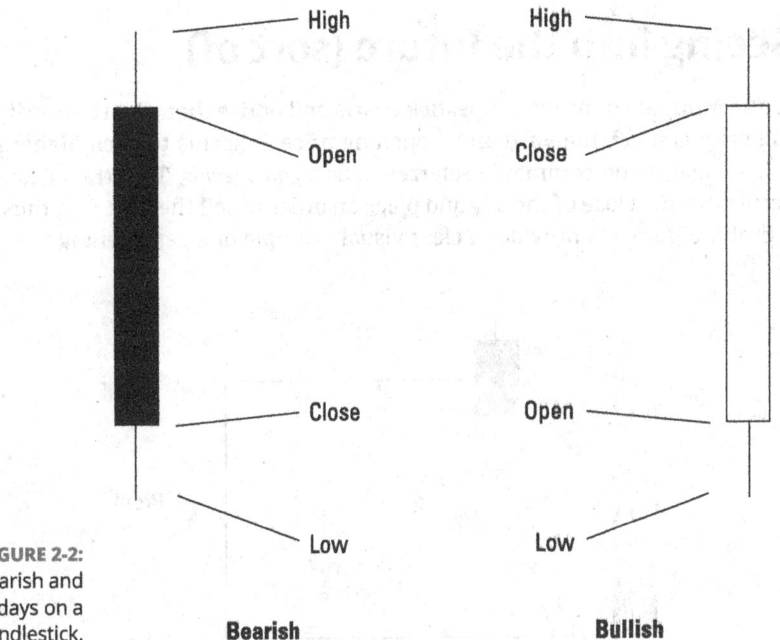

FIGURE 2-2: Bearish and bullish days on a candlestick.

REMEMBER

Understanding the ways that prices are trending is useful information in making buy-or-sell decisions. The old saying "The trend is your friend" is a reminder that you always want to be on the dominant side of price action. By recognizing whether the bulls or bears (see the nearby sidebar "Bulls and bears") are the dominant group, you can be conscious of the trend and better prepared to stay on the right side of the market.

BULLS AND BEARS

The terms *bull* and *bear* have been in the trading lexicon for many years. Both terms apply to people and market trends. A *bull* is a market participant who expects or wants the market to move higher, but it's also part of an expression that explains an up market (a *bullish* market). A *bear,* on the other hand, is a person who expects the market to decline, so *bearish* indicates a declining market.

Seeing into the future (sort of)

A trader might study old candlestick charts and notice that when a security's closing price is much higher than its opening price, it seems to open higher the next day — a situation commonly referred to as a *gap opening*. That trader can buy the security at the close of the day and place an order to sell the next day, thus making a profit. Figure 2-3 provides a clear visual example of a gap opening.

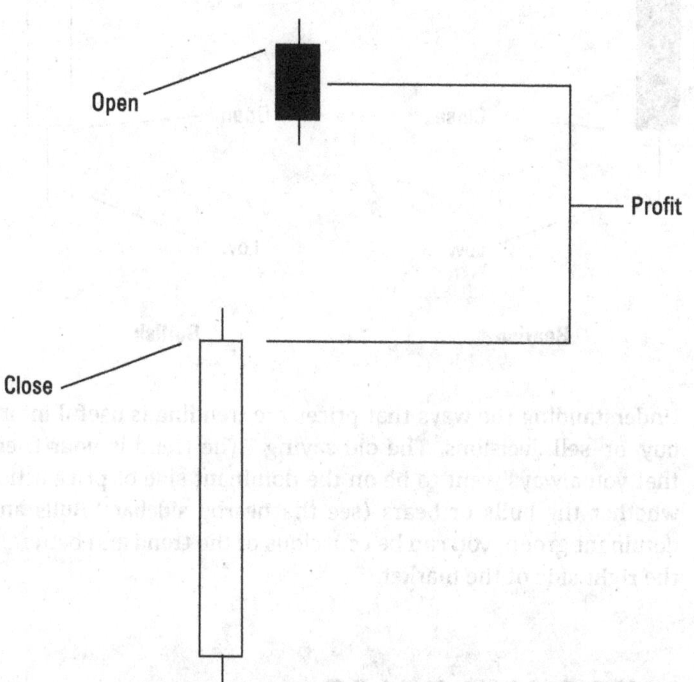

FIGURE 2-3: Two candles showing a classic gap opening.

REMEMBER

Just by studying past price action on old candlestick charts, the trader in this section's example can predict a small piece of the future and use it to turn a profit. History does repeat itself in markets and trading, and you can use this repetition to your advantage by considering past candlestick charts, which can be a cinch to read. But keep in mind that, as with all aspects of technical analysis and investing, past results don't ensure future returns.

TIP

At the very least, pay attention to price gaps because they indicate an increase in volatility in the price of a security. When there's an increase in volatility, there's an increase in trading opportunity. Many other types of patterns, including those that incorporate candlesticks, reappear and may be profited from.

EXAMINING PRICE GAPS

Price gaps, which are common in the financial markets, occur on charts when no overlap exists between consecutive period highs and lows. If XYZ stock's high is 81 and its low is 80 on a given day, for example, and the next day it opens higher than 81 — let's say 83 — and trades in a range between 82 and 84, a gap with no trading exists between 81 and 82. That stock *gapped higher* and never closed the gap. If the stock had opened much lower — 77 or 78, for example — and never reached the previous day's low, it would have *gapped lower*.

What causes price gaps? These gaps are usually the result of news about a certain security being released outside market hours. This situation isn't uncommon: Most companies release their quarterly earnings or other big news either after the market closes or before it opens. The market adjustment to that news causes price gaps. Also, a gap may occur on specific stocks just because they're moving up or down due to a gap in the overall market. The gap may occur because of the release of certain economic news before the market opens or possibly a macro event, such as a terrorist attack.

Remember that gaps always get filled when the high-to-low price action of a future day covers the price range where no trades occurred. But you can't always tell when gaps will be filled. When the dot . com bubble was building, some Internet stocks had several price gaps on their way up to stratospheric valuations. These gaps were eventually filled, but anyone who was trying to short these stocks for the gap being filled would have ended up in the poorhouse before any gap-filling took place.

Showing price patterns

Recognizing patterns on candlestick charts is easy, and you can combine two or more candlestick charts to flesh out a reliable pattern that can lead you to profitable trading. Figure 2-4 depicts a common price pattern that serves as a good sell signal.

The pattern is a two-day pattern, and the third day is a common reaction to the first two days. Here's the typical progression:

1. The first day is a strong open-to-close day. The closing price is considerably higher than the opening price. The first day is a victory for the bulls.

2. The second day reveals very little price action because the close is very near the open. The second day is a wash because higher prices entice more bears to be sellers.

3. After this shift from bullish to neutral price action, the following day is a down day. The third day is a winning day for the bears!

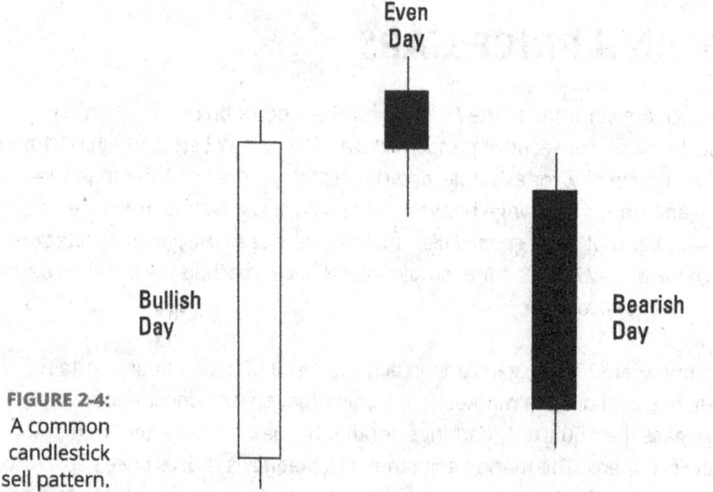

FIGURE 2-4: A common candlestick sell pattern.

Once again, a trader who studies candlestick charts and patterns can easily spot this change. This type of momentum shift is useful to someone who owns a security and is considering selling it or to a trader who has the ability to sell short. (See the nearby sidebar, "Selling short, in short," for more information.)

SELLING SHORT, IN SHORT

Possibly the best-known trading adage is "Buy low, sell high" — the simplest way to turn a profit in a market. But other ways exist, including *short selling,* or *shorting,* a security: This somewhat counterintuitive process involves selling a security and buying it back later. Traders who practice this strategy are known as *shorts.*

The mechanics of selling short can be fairly complex, but we'll sum them up in this list:

1. A short borrows a stock from a bank that holds it for the owners, expecting the price of the stock to go down.

2. The short sells the borrowed stock to a buyer.

3. When the stock price drops, the short buys back the stock, returns it to the bank at the original (higher) price, and pockets the difference.

Shorts get a bum rap and are often accused of being responsible when a stock trades lower. Companies have even sued shorts on claims that they spread negative rumors to drive down the company's stock price. But short sellers are really just part of the overall market mechanism, and they can even help keep companies honest because they're constantly on the lookout for companies with deteriorating fundamentals, or the quality of their earnings, or evidence of suspicious accounting. The fundamentals of a firm became a big question during the dot-com crash in 2000. Many firms were "cooking the books" by using unethical accounting metrics that deviated from the fundamentals of the firm.

Admitting Potential Candlestick Charting Risks

Candlesticks are helpful tools that can easily capture information — we think they're wonderful!

However, you should exercise some caution when using candlesticks, for these reasons:

>> **They don't work in the *very* short term.** Candlestick charts are an excellent way to display price action, but for some extremely short-term trading strategies, such as holding for a matter of minutes, the patterns that reveal themselves on a daily candlestick chart may not develop on a much shorter time frame — fewer than 5 minutes, for example.

We like to think of candlestick charts as visual representations of the battle between the bulls and bears, which is played out in the price action of a stock. That battle takes some time to play out, so patterns on a very short-term chart may not produce signals that can be interpreted properly and traded on.

Candlesticks aren't as useful in intraday *scalping* (buying or selling in a matter of seconds) or day-trading strategies in which hold periods are generally shorter. Candlesticks are a bit more useful for periods where behavior is developing over time versus the reactionary trading of day traders. A *reactionary* trading day is one in which traders move the market by reacting to news as opposed to the firms' ability to generate revenue.

>> **They don't reflect trade volume outside regular market hours.** The advent of increased electronic trading means that significant volume is sometimes traded outside regular market hours. This trading can cause patterns that keep the full picture from appearing on a candlestick chart.

If a stock officially opened at 9:30 A.M. at a price of $50 but traded as low as $49 during the premarket hours (on an electronic trading network), the open may not be a true reflection of where the stock initially traded on the day.

As a result, the open recorded on the candlestick is somewhat inaccurate. Also, if the stock never trades down to $49 during the day, the low on the chart may not be an accurate depiction of the day's price action.

Comparing Candlestick Charts with Alternative Charting Methods

Knowing a bit about alternatives to candlestick charts serves as a point of reference and makes clear the benefits of using candlestick charts for analyzing price data.

Although these alternative charts aren't as versatile and useful as candlesticks, each one has its benefits:

>> **Line charts** are simple and straightforward.

>> **Bar charts** are important to understand because they're still relatively prevalent and often the default setting in a charting package.

>> **Point and figure charts** are helpful for revealing support and resistance levels.

We're confident you'll be a believer in candlesticks when everything is said and done, but evaluating the alternatives is certainly worth your time.

Line charts

A *line chart* is a line on a chart that displays security prices over time. A line chart represents the price — usually, the closing price — of a security from one period to the next.

On a very short-term basis, a line chart is definitely a proper choice for decision-making. Because no other information is displayed, however, attempting to formulate any sort of trading strategy from a line chart of price action wouldn't be a worthwhile venture.

Figure 2-5 shows a line chart displaying three months of daily closing prices for a stock.

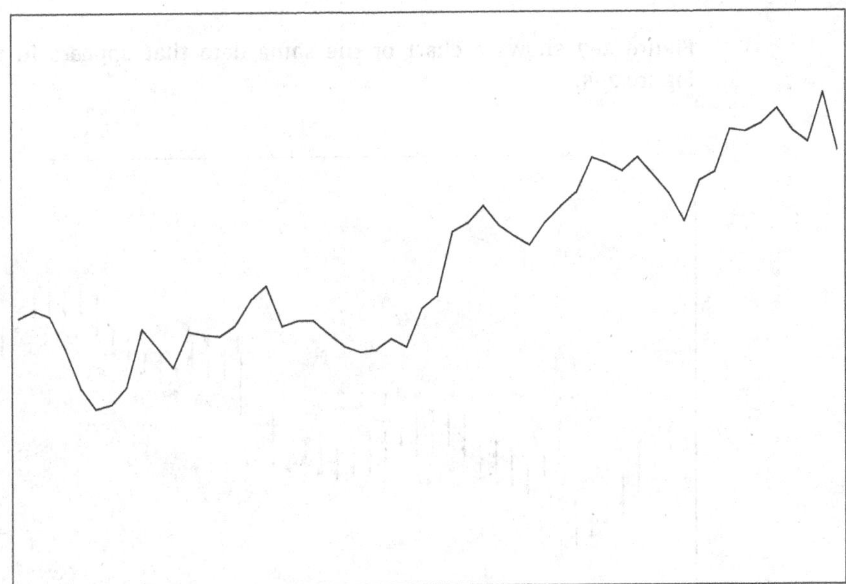

Bar charts

A traditional *bar chart* contains bars that represent price action from period to period. Each bar is a vertical line that shows the difference between the high and the low of the period. The top of the bar is the high, and the bottom is the low. The distance between the top and bottom is similar to the wick of a candle on a candlestick chart. (The wick is discussed more fully in Chapter 1.) The finishing touch on a bar chart is a little notch on the right side of the bar that's made to indicate where the security closed. Figure 2-6 shows a single bar taken from a bar chart.

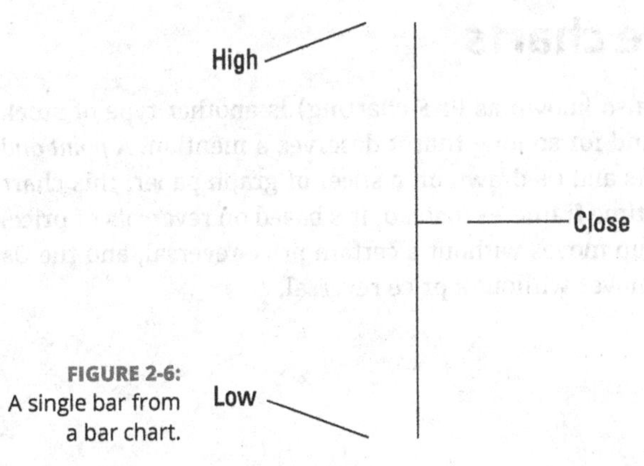

Figure 2-7 shows a chart of the same data that appears in the line chart in Figure 2-5.

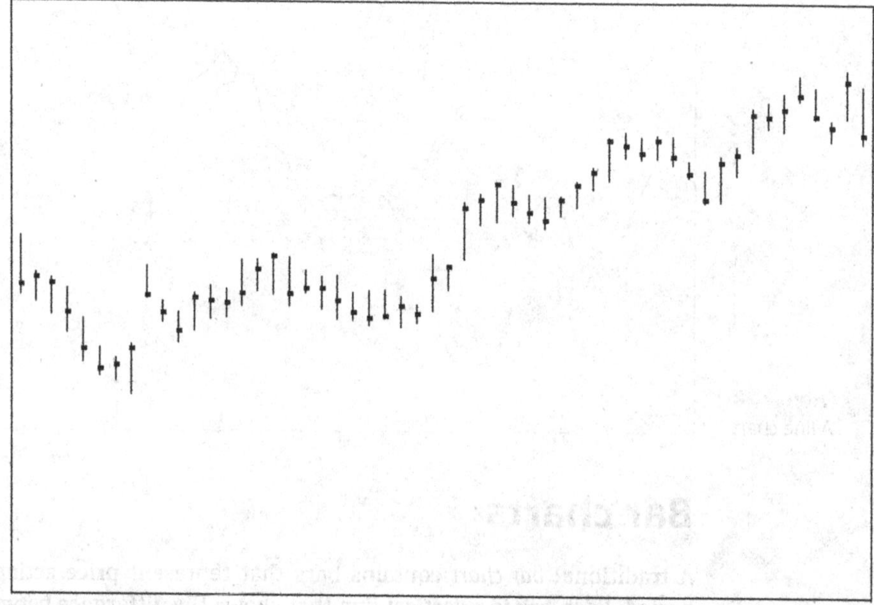

Bar charts have been the industry standard for some time but are quickly being replaced by candlestick charts. When *The Wall Street Journal* starts using a new charting convention (as it has with candlestick charts), the convention is considered to be the industry standard.

Point and figure charts

Point and figure charting (also known as P&F charting) is another type of stock charting that has been around for so long that it deserves a mention. A *point and figure chart* is composed of Xs and Os drawn on a sheet of graph paper; this chart isn't constructed with a set time frame — instead, it's based on reversals of price. The Xs make up a series of up moves without a certain price reversal, and the Os represent a series of down moves without a price reversal.

Figure 2-8 shows a point and figure depiction of the same data that comprises the line and bar charts in Figures 2-5 through 2-7. The figure values each square with one point and adds a new column with a change of direction of at least two points based on the close. If day one has a closing price of 75 and day two has a closing price of 78, you draw Xs from 75 to 78. If on day three the closing price is 76 (a 2-point reversal), a new column is added, and Os are placed in the 76 and 77 squares. If the price stays in the 76 to 77 range for a few days, no changes are made to the chart.

						X						
						X						
				X		X						
				X	O	X						
				X	O							
				X								
		X		X								
	O	X	O	X								
	O	X	O									
	O	X										
	O											

FIGURE 2-8: A point and figure chart.

Point and figure charts are unique because they purely reflect price moves. Because time isn't factored in, you don't need to update the chart if a stock stays at a certain price for some time. On the other hand, when a price trades between two prices several times — bouncing between 50 and 55, for example — a point and figure chart offers a clear display of the support levels and resistance levels described earlier in this chapter. In this case, 50 is the support level, and 55 is the resistance level.

If you can recognize support and resistance levels, you can potentially use that knowledge to make a tidy profit. Using the example in the previous paragraph, if you can buy at 50 and sell at 55 several times over, the returns can be astounding because you know the range of the price movement.

So why aren't point and figure charts right up there with candlesticks in terms of usefulness? The answer is simple: Support and resistance levels show up well on candlestick charts, too, and candlesticks also contain a variety of other information.

Although the point and figure charting technique is interesting and unique, it's a throwback to a time when stock prices were charted based on the daily closing prices published in the financial press and were meticulously maintained by hand. Its use has fallen by the wayside with the advent of modern technology.

Chapter **3**

Building a Base of Candlestick Chart Knowledge

To fully benefit from candlestick charts, you must understand how they're constructed. From the basic pieces of information used to generate a candlestick to the various additions and extra pieces of data that can be tacked onto a chart, you need to know just what you're looking at before you can make wise trading decisions. You need to be familiar with the candlestick nuts and bolts before delving into their interpretations and uses.

In this chapter, we provide a solid foundation in candlestick knowledge, and we start with the data that goes into constructing individual candlesticks. Although candlesticks can represent the action of a security over a wide variety of time periods, the basic information used to build them is the same. We also cover the other pieces of data that are commonly included in a candlestick chart — added features that enhance the usefulness and readability of the chart.

Constructing a Candlestick: A Core of Four

For any security, each day of trading includes four key components in terms of data: opening price, closing price, highest price traded on the day, and lowest price traded on the day. These four pieces of data are required to construct the individual bars that make up candlestick charts. Several bars, created by using the data from several days or periods, are generated in succession to produce a full candlestick chart.

Candlestick charts may be applied to the performance of securities over a variety of time periods. We use them on charts from as short-term as five minutes per bar to as long-term as a week per bar. A five-minute chart might be applied to a day or two of activity, whereas the weekly chart might be applied to a period of several years. Although those time frames are vastly different, a candlestick chart is appropriate for both, and candlesticks would work for any time periods in between.

Price on the open

The first piece of data used to construct a candlestick is the opening price for the day. For stocks, in most cases, that price is the official opening price on a specified primary exchange.

Recording an opening price on a candlestick

On a single candlestick, the thin vertical line is the *wick*, and the thick part in the middle is the *candle*. The opening price on a single candlestick is always either the top or bottom of the candle, and it's created on the chart by using the price scale on the chart's vertical axis. A hollow (white) candle is bullish, meaning that the opening price is lower than the closing price (see Chapter 2). If you see a hollow candle, the bottom of the candle is the opening price. Conversely, a filled-in (black) candle is bearish, meaning that the opening price is higher than the closing price. In that case, the top of the candle is the opening price.

WHAT'S THE STOCK MARKET?

When most people think of the stock market, they picture stock traders in bright-colored jackets shouting and hand-signaling orders in a giant room. This picture is accurate; it's how the commodity markets function. The stock market, or at least the floor of the New York Stock Exchange, is more like a giant bank lobby, with each stock having a particular place, or post, where transactions for that stock take place.

Dealing with the challenges of pinning down an opening price

Because many securities now trade on multiple exchanges or electronic trading networks, pinning down an exact opening price can be difficult, which makes constructing a candle a difficult endeavor.

Recently, Russell was trying to trade a stock for which significant — and misinterpreted — news came out before the opening of the trading day. The stock had closed the day before at $48 per share, but was trading on one of the electronic communication networks (ECNs) two hours before it was to open on the New York Stock Exchange (NYSE) at $45 per share. Over the next two hours, the breaking news was better understood, and the stock started to trade higher. It actually opened at about $51 per share. Despite already trading between $45 and $51 in the two hours leading up to the open, the open for the day that showed up on most charts was $51.

For futures contracts on commodities — agreements between two parties to buy or sell a certain product on a predefined date (see the nearby sidebar "Focus on futures" for details) — attempting to determine the opening price for a day can be even more difficult. Many futures markets now have trading hours that match up with business hours in their home market and trading hours outside the normal trading day. A perfect example is the Japanese yen.

Japanese yen futures trade electronically on the CME Group's Globex platform. During a nonholiday week, the yen futures market opens on Sundays at 5 P.M. central time and closes at 4 P.M. Monday through Thursday, with a one-hour break at 4 P.M. central time. With trading occurring practically 24 hours a day, five days a week (closed from Friday afternoon through Sunday afternoon), patterns are difficult to determine from a candlestick chart that doesn't adjust for hours.

For such a convoluted situation, we divide the day into non-US and US sessions for analysis purposes. Because the greatest volume is traded during non-US hours, we always have to reevaluate what we consider to be the open. For other examples of futures contracts that trade almost 24 hours a day, see Figure 3-1.

Futures Contract	Trading Hours (Chicago Time)
Corn	19:00 - 7:45 (break) 8:30 - 13.20
Soybeans	19:00 - 7:45 (break) 8:30 - 13.20
Wheat	19:00 - 7:45 (break) 8:30 - 13.20
Crude Oil	18:00 - 17:00
RBOB Gasoline	18:00 - 17:00
Gold	18:00 - 17:00
Silver	18:00 - 17:00
S&P 500	17:00 - 16:00
Nasdaq-100	17:00 - 16:00
Russell 2000	17:00 - 16:00
British Pound	17:00 - 16:00
Euro Currency	17:00 - 16:00
Japanese Yen	17:00 - 16:00
Euro Dollars	17:00 - 16:00
10 Year Notes	17:00 - 16:00
Treasury Bonds	17:00 - 16:00

FIGURE 3-1: Futures contracts that trade almost around the clock.

In Figure 3-1, you see that for futures contracts, the actual opening price for a session can be hard to determine.

FOCUS ON FUTURES

When explaining how futures contracts work, we love to use an example about buying a lawn mower at a home improvement superstore.

Suppose that it's December 15, and you know that when spring rolls around in May, your rusty old lawn mower just won't cut it, so to speak. You need a new mower. The one you want is expected to cost $500 on May 1, which will be the first day you need to cut the grass. You don't want to pay that much for a mower, and you're in luck because your home improvement superstore is the only one in the world that offers lawn mower futures, and May 1 just so happens to be the day when May lawn mower futures expire. The price of a May lawn mower futures contract is $400, so you make a small deposit — maybe 10 percent of the mower contract size of $400 — and buy one futures contract by way of your mower futures broker. When May 1 rolls around, you'll be able to pay $400 for your new lawn mower, even though the market price is $500. But who would offer such an attractive deal?

The seller of the futures contract can be a lawn mower dealer who's more than happy to lock in a price of $400 to sell a lawn mower on May 1. After all, it would help that dealer plan production by locking in a guaranteed number of mower sales at a set price. Or the seller could be a speculator who thinks that mowers will be on sale at the home improvement superstore for $300 at some point before May 1, which would allow them to buy the mower at a discount and then sell it to you for $400 on May 1, generating a $100 profit.

The futures markets were created to give farmers a mechanism for locking in the price of their crops and eliminating the risk that when their crops were ready to be sold, the selling price wouldn't be enough to cover their costs and provide a profit. For farmers, whose livelihood is dependent on factors out of their control, this method was extremely helpful in eliminating selling price as one of the major risks.

High and low prices for the session

The second and third pieces of data that are essential for constructing a candlestick are the high and low prices for a session. No tricks here — the *high* price is the highest point the security's price reaches during the session, and the *low* is the lowest point reached during the same session. Because there may be some flexibility in what you consider to be a trading session, it may be the high and low that have traded between 6:30 A.M. and 2 P.M., so your session would be 6:30 A.M. to 2 P.M.

Incorporating high and low prices into a candlestick

The high and low prices for a session or day are used to make the thin vertical line, or *wick*, of the candlestick. (See Chapter 1 for an illustration of a basic candlestick.) The top of the wick represents the high price for the session, and the bottom of the wick represents the session's low price.

You need to define what your trading session is, and the wick represents the range from the high to the low. How you define a trading session can be for the formal exchange floor or pit trading times or, as discussed earlier, for a period you decide to use to represent a trading session.

If a security opens at a certain price and it drops steadily throughout the session, you don't see any wick extending above the candle. If, on the other hand, the security opens at a certain price and it increases during the session without dropping below the open, you don't see any wick extending below the candle.

How low (or high) can you go? Deciding on a high and low price

Like opening prices, high and low prices can be tough to nail down because of the various electronic trading venues operating today. If big news on a particular security breaks before the official open or after the close, it may well trade higher or lower on an electronic trading venue than it does on its primary exchange.

The futures contracts are even more likely to trade at prices above the exchange session high or below the exchange session low because the electronic futures markets are active 24 hours a day. In no area is this likelihood more evident than in currency futures. The currency market is a true 24-hour market, and news across the globe constantly affects currency movements. Because of that volatility, it's quite possible that lots of price action will take place outside normal exchange pit-trading hours that may not show up on a chart.

For more insight into the dramatic difference between 24-hour activity and US market-hour activity, see Figure 3-2, which shows charts of futures contracts on the Swiss franc price and the US dollar. These contracts used to trade from 7:20 A.M. to 2 P.M. central time on the floor of the CME Group, and they trade up to 23 hours a day between Sunday evening and Friday afternoon on the CME Group's Globex system. The chart on the left in Figure 3-3 shows a chart of the price action over the course of a couple of months using *only* data from the old pit-trading hours. The chart on the right in Figure 3-2 uses the same time period but takes all trading hours into account.

Frankly <ahem>, the franc chart has so many gaps that it's not even worth trying to analyze. It's highly unlikely that you'd work out a profitable method of trading based on this chart. There's little opportunity to catch the many dramatic price moves that occur in the hours outside normal or exchange trading hours. You just don't have enough information to make smart (and profitable) moves. The chart on the right in Figure 3-2, on the other hand, gives you a fuller picture of the price moves of the futures and allows you to make well-informed decisions about buying and selling.

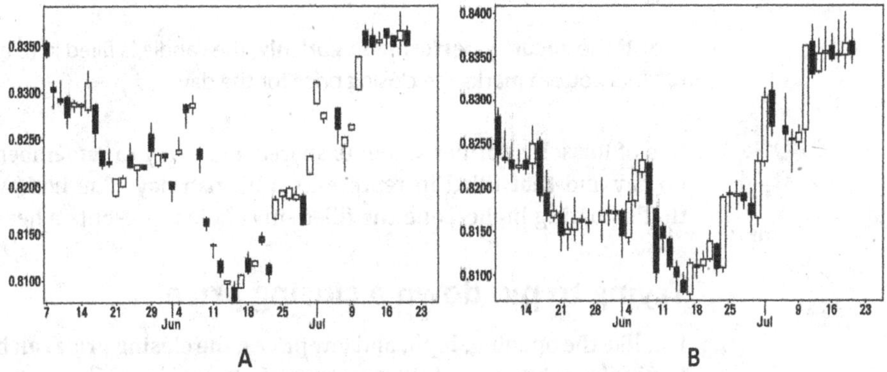

TECHNICAL STUFF

REMEMBER

FIGURE 3-2: Daily chart of Swiss franc futures using only pit trading data (A) and data from all trading hours (B).

Currencies aren't the only futures contracts that experience these types of overnight moves. Bond futures and stock index futures, such as 10-year government bond futures contracts or S&P 500 futures, experience significant price action in the overnight session, while the underlying bond and stock markets are closed. Traders are even starting to see price moves for true commodity futures trading overnight — moves that aren't caught in charts properly.

The choice of what to use for a day is up to the individual trader. If you're looking to make longer-term trades, for example, the prices that trade outside of normal trading hours may not mean as much to you as they would to a trader who's trying to catch very short-term moves (as short as a few minutes). Also, what you use for a day may depend on how much time you can devote to watching the markets.

Price on the close

The fourth and final piece of data used to build a candlestick is a security's *closing price*: the final price that's traded on a security during the day. These prices are the closing numbers that appear in the stock tables in newspapers and the ones that investment professionals use to monitor their day-to-day performance. Like the other data used in creating a candlestick, closing prices are becoming tougher to pin down.

Recording a closing price on a candlestick

Depending on the performance of a security, its closing price may appear in either of two places on a candlestick:

>> **If the security had a bullish performance on a given day,** the candle part of the candlestick is hollow (white) or green. In that case, the closing price is represented by the top of the candle.

>> **If the security performed bearishly,** the candle is filled in (black) or red, and its bottom marks the closing price for the day.

One of Russell's former students shared a fun way to remember that hollow is an up day and that filled in represents a bearish day: The hollow is like a balloon that's floating higher, and the filled-in candle represents a heavier trading day.

Trying to pin down a closing price

Just like the opening, high, and low prices, the closing price can be a true challenge to pin down because of the presence of electronic trading networks. Also, stocks and futures stay open for some time after their official exchanges close, so pinpointing what the market believes the true value for a stock or futures contract is at the end of the day is difficult.

Although trading continues beyond the primary market's hours, stocks generally trade for an hour or so after the exchanges close. Usually, trading in stocks after 4 P.M. Eastern time on the electronic trading networks is pretty light in volume, but on days with significant earnings announcements or other news, several million shares of a stock may trade after the close.

One example of after-close trading is what's referred to as *earnings season:* This time period is when many companies report their quarterly financial results to the financial and investing communities. During a recent earnings season, both Microsoft (MSFT) and Alphabet (GOOG), the parent company of Google, reported their earnings. Both stocks traded millions of shares after the 4 P.M. official close of the Nasdaq, their primary trading market. With such a high volume of trading, this price action is significant enough to be included in charts.

For the earnings season in question, the investment community ("the street") wasn't terribly impressed by either company's results, and the stocks traded off pretty significantly as a result. Microsoft's official closing share price at 4 P.M. Eastern was $31.51, but in the "after hours," the stock traded down to $30.90, which is a nearly 2 percent drop from the closing price at 4 P.M. and 0.02 percent below the official low for the day of $30.93 per share.

The difference in Alphabet's stock was even greater: The official 4 P.M. close was $548.59 per share, but after checking, the post-market trading revealed a final price of $508.70 per share — more than 7 percent lower than the 4 P.M. close and quite a bit lower than even the official low of the day, which was $542.24 per share.

Considering Additional Information Included in Candlestick Charts

In addition to the basic information described in the earlier sections of this chapter, most candlestick charts automatically include other pieces of data. This added data allows you to quickly digest how the stock has traded in the past and includes some fundamental activities, such as dates of earnings releases or dividend payments, that may also appear in charts.

In this section, we discuss a few pieces of information that may be included in your candlestick charts.

Volume

In trading lingo, *volume* is the number of shares traded during a certain period. A volume measurement usually appears in the bottom quarter to bottom third of a chart. Figure 3-3 is a chart of Alphabet stock, showing roughly the 50 days leading up to September 19, 2025.

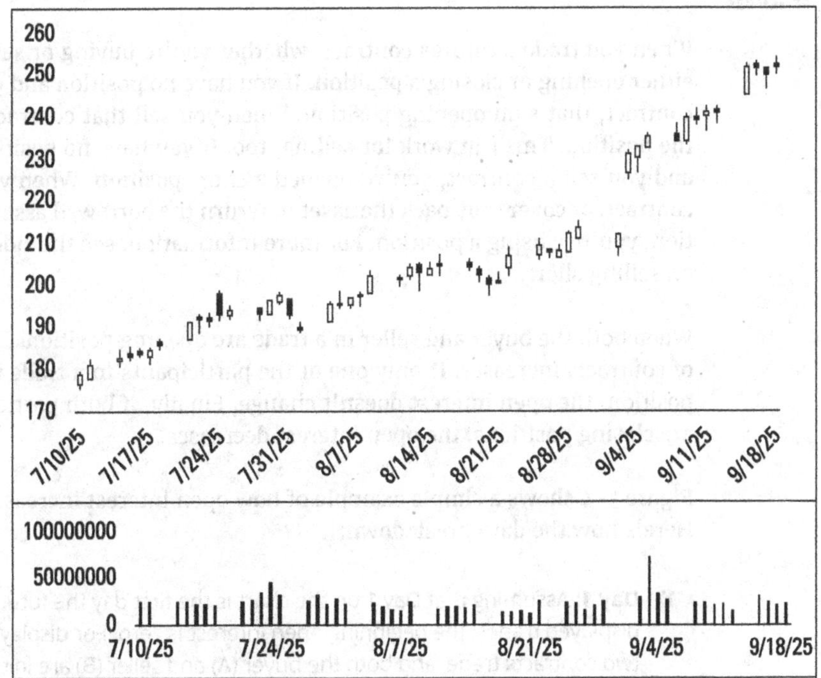

FIGURE 3-3: Daily candlestick chart of Alphabet, with volume information included.

The bottom of the chart in Figure 3-3 shows daily volume for Alphabet's stock. On a few days, volume was excessive. Combining strong volume with a reversal pattern, which is demonstrated by changing direction of the price, is one of the most powerful combinations of information for traders who use candlestick charts.

Many technical analysts put quite a bit of emphasis on volume as it relates to certain chart patterns. If a stock trades down to what's considered to be a support level (see Chapter 2 for more info on support levels) on a day with significant volume, many traders may give this support level more credence and consider buying. The reason is that the increase in volume indicates a high level of buy or sell interest emerging at this level.

Open interest

In the case of futures charts, open interest takes the place of volume. Before we discuss open interest on a chart, we'll explain how it's determined and what it means.

Put simply, *open interest* is the number of outstanding futures contracts. When a buyer and a seller in a futures contract initiate new positions, the open interest increases by one contract.

When you trade a futures contract, whether you're buying or selling, you're also either opening or closing a position. If you have no position and you buy a futures contract, that's an opening position. When you sell that contract, you're closing the position. This can work for selling, too. If you have no position to begin with and you sell a contract, you've opened a short position. When you buy back this contract, or cover (buy back the asset to return the borrowed asset) the short position, you're closing a position. For more information, see the sidebar in Chapter 2 on selling short.

When both the buyer and seller in a trade are opening positions, the open interest of contracts increases. If only one of the participants in a trade is opening a new position, the open interest doesn't change. Finally, if both participants in a trade are closing positions, the open interest decreases.

Figure 3-4 shows a simple example of how open interest increases and decreases. Here's how the days break down:

>> **Day 1:** Assuming that Day 1 on the chart is the first day the futures contract displayed trades, the beginning open interest is zero. For display purposes, two contracts trade, and both the buyer (A) and seller (B) are initiating new positions. These new positions create two new contracts.

>> **Day 2:** Four more contracts are initiated by both the buyer (C) and seller (D), and the open interest increases to six contracts.

>> **Day 3:** The situation gets a little trickier. Person A decides to sell two contracts, and Person D decides to buy back (or *cover*) two of the contracts they previously sold short, reducing the open interest by two contracts.

>> **Day 4:** Finally, Person C sells their four contracts, but Person A buys these open contracts, which are transferred, so no new contracts are created. The open interest doesn't change.

Open Interest

Day	Action	Open Interest
Day 1	A buys 2 contracts and B sell 2 contracts	2
Day 2	C buys 4 contracts and D sells 4 contracts	6
Day 3	A sells 2 contracts and D covers 2 contracts	4
Day 4	C sells 4 contracts and A buys 4 contracts	4

Figure 3-5 is a chart of soybean futures. The open interest appears in the same area on the chart as the volume in Figure 3-3. Notice the increase in open interest during the life of this contract moving from left to right on the chart. This increase is caused by the approaching expiration date, but also the fact that the summer market was volatile (although all summers are volatile in the wild world of beans).

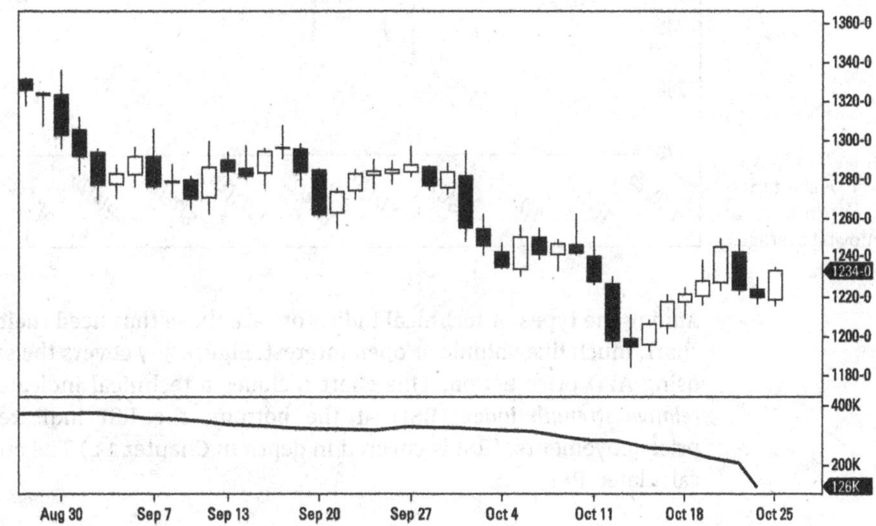

FIGURE 3-5: A candlestick chart of the soybean market futures with open interest.

As beans bottomed out, open interest started to drop. That drop would have sparked some traders to buy beans because fewer new participants were coming into the market to sell, and the next few days experienced bullish price action as open interest continued to decrease.

Technical indicators

Numerous technical indicators may automatically appear in the charts you generate. *Technical indicators* are ways of analyzing current trends in the market in the hope of being able to predict future trends. You can usually expect to see some sort of average of closing prices (a moving average), and possibly another basic technical indicator in a chart. Don't let those indicators rattle you — you can remove them or, better, alter them to your personal preferences. (We discuss a variety of technical indicators in detail in Part 4.) Take a look at Figure 3-6, which depicts daily APD stock trading for the past 50 days in the late summer of 2025. This chart includes a 10-day moving average — one common type of technical indicator.

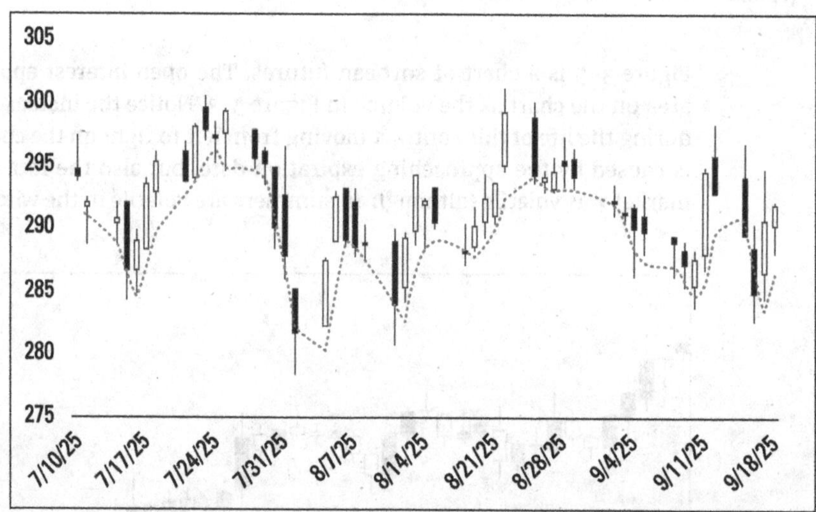

FIGURE 3-6: A chart that includes a moving average.

Among the types of technical indicators are those that need their own space on a chart, much like volume or open interest. Figure 3-7 covers the same time frame, using APD price action. This chart includes a technical indicator known as the *relative strength index* (RSI) at the bottom; the RSI indicates the trend of price movements. (RSI is covered in depth in Chapter 13.) The crooked line is the calculated RSI.

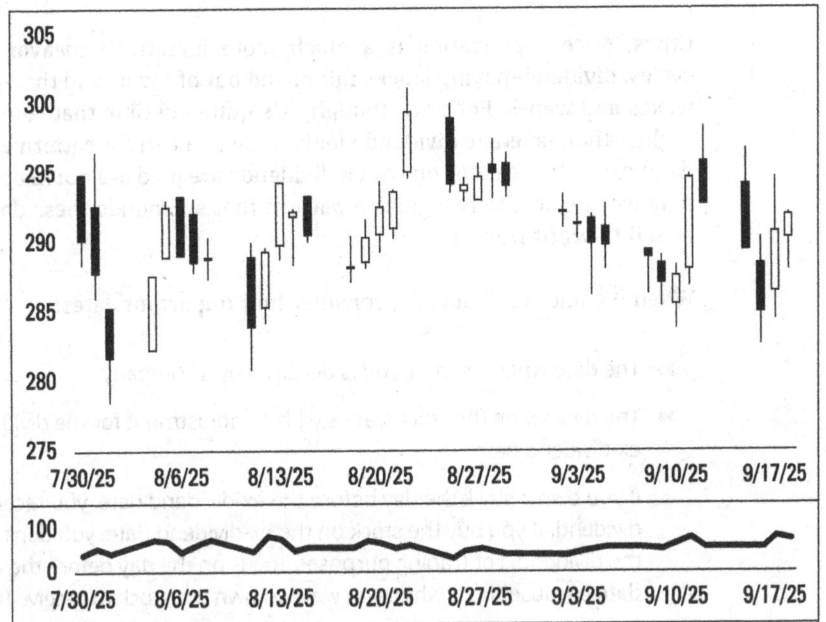

FIGURE 3-7: A chart that includes RSI.

As you can see, the RSI takes nothing away from the rest of the chart and actually provides some useful additional information that you can consider when making chart-based decisions.

Fundamental information

Charts containing fundamental information aren't particularly common, but the addition of that information can be extremely useful. Fundamental information can include dividend dates, earnings release dates, stock splits, and the number of days when people who have inside information (*legal* inside information) may have bought or sold stock. This info relates almost exclusively to charts of stocks, so we stick to stocks in this section's discussion.

Needless to say, monitoring how a stock performs around the time dividends are paid or earnings are reported is helpful. If some patterns tend to repeat, trying to trade around these dates may be a profitable strategy. Also, keep an eye on how stocks are bought and sold by company officials, who have intimate knowledge of their company's business activities.

Dividend dates

The utility of dividends as a way of making a profit on the market comes and goes. Sometimes, investors focus on buying stocks for their dividend yields; at other times, price appreciation is a much more lucrative endeavor. Like all market cycles, dividend-paying stocks fall in and out of favor, and the focus on dividends waxes and wanes. For now, though, it's quite possible that some stocks that pay higher-than-average dividend yields trade in a certain pattern around their dividend dates. If the dates on which dividends are paid are noted on your charts, you may well be able to recognize a pattern that surrounds these dates and then buy or sell to profit from it.

When it comes to dividends, consider four important dates:

» The date when the dividend is declared by a company.

» The date when the stock trades with an adjustment for the dividend, or the ex-dividend date.

   If you own a stock the day before the ex-dividend date, you receive the dividend. If you buy the stock on the ex-dividend date, you don't receive the dividend. For trading purposes, focus on the day before the ex-dividend date because that's when you want to own the stock to receive the dividend.

» The *record* date, or the trading date after the ex-dividend date, which is the date on which the owners of a stock are identified as eligible to receive a dividend.

» The *payable* date, when you receive your dividend check.

Earnings dates

During each quarter of the year, companies are required to release a summary of their earnings for the previous quarter. These numbers are usually distributed via press releases, which are quickly picked up by news services and the financial press. Traders react to the resulting news. The press releases are usually followed an hour or two later by conference calls in which members of the companies' management teams answer questions from industry analysts regarding the recently released earnings. These calls are important because the outlook for the company is typically discussed in detail.

These earnings release dates are by far the most important four days of the year for many companies, and their stocks are usually at their most volatile just before and after the conference calls. At the very least, if you're interested in trading a particular stock, be aware of when the company is scheduled to release its next earnings report.

In a charting capacity, seeing how the stock trades before and after earnings dates can be useful for trading decisions. If a company generally trades higher going into its earnings release, buying a week before the earnings date and selling the day before may be a profitable strategy. Also, if a company usually reacts strongly to its earnings announcements (either good or bad) but seems to reverse this move a few days later, this information can lead to a good short-term trading strategy. Either way, it should be clear that having earnings date info on the charts you use isn't a bad thing, and it can set you on the path to making a nice profit if you can spot a usable pattern.

You can find numerous sources for earnings dates or earnings calendars on the Internet. Check out these good (and free) sources:

>> Earnings calendar at Yahoo! Finance:

   https://finance.yahoo.com/calendar/earnings

>> The MarketWatch.com earnings calendar:

   www.marketwatch.com/tools/calendars/earnings.asp

>> Nasdaq's earnings calendar:

   www.nasdaq.com/market-activity/earnings

Stock splits

Sometimes, when the price for a stock reaches a high level, a company announces that it's either paying a stock dividend or splitting the shares in two. The timeline for a stock split is similar to that of a dividend, and split information is sometimes included in charts. A company will announce a split, which is usually considered to be a positive event for the stock. The announcement indicates what type of split it is (2 for 1 or 3 for 1, for example) and the date when the split will be effective.

That date is the day when shareholders own more shares at a lower price, and it's the date that's noted on a chart — typically, with a big letter S or a note about the type of split.

How does splitting work for you? If you own 10 shares of that stock, you own 20 on the split date. The price of the stock is usually adjusted accordingly. If a stock is trading at $100 and the stock splits so that each share held becomes two shares, that's considered to be a 2-for-1 split, and the price of each new share becomes $50. The dollar amount is the same, but the number of shares increases.

Splitting shares allows for broader ownership of a stock. Many people can afford to buy 100 shares of a stock that trades for $15 per share ($1,500); few people can afford 100 shares of a stock that trades for $200 per share ($20,000). The idea is that the broader the ownership, the better the performance of shares.

Stock-split information on a chart is useful when a company's stock has had recurring reactions to stock splits. Generally, a stock rallies after news of a split, although whether this fact is logical is debatable because a stock split doesn't necessarily mean that something has changed fundamentally within the company. Unfortunately, the announcement of a split isn't common on a chart. But because the date when the split is effective is generally available, you can easily focus on how the stock trades leading up to the split and afterward and then make appropriate trading decisions.

Insider trading: The legal kind

Legal insider trading — not the kind of insider trading that results in executives wearing handcuffs on the evening news — is the trading activity of company executives in their company's stock. In this context, an *insider* is anyone who's officially associated with a company or even an owner of 10 percent or more of a company's stock.

The option to buy stock can be a major part of the compensation package for employees of public companies; this aligns management goals with shareholder goals. From the company's standpoint, it makes sense to offer employees another incentive to work hard for the financial well-being of the company and the strength of its stock. Employees of a company may also buy stock in the open market when they believe that the company's prospects are bright.

Owners of 10 percent or more of stock may have access to certain information you may not have. You can't blame them if they make decisions on buying or selling that stock based on their insider information. By law, however, they must report this trading activity within a few days of making such transactions; the resulting data is public and sometimes ends up in charts!

On the flip side, employees who own shares sometimes choose to sell. It's a bit tricky to automatically assume that an inside sale is an indication of lack of confidence in a company. The stock may be sold for personal reasons — a major purchase such as a home or a child's college education, for example — or it can be a signal that an employee believes a stock's price has reached a level at which it's prudent to sell shares. Or the employee might be required to sell the shares as indicated in their contract. In this case, following an insider's lead and selling that stock may prove to be profitable or help you avoid a loss.

To see what insider trading information looks like in a chart, take a gander at Figure 3-8.

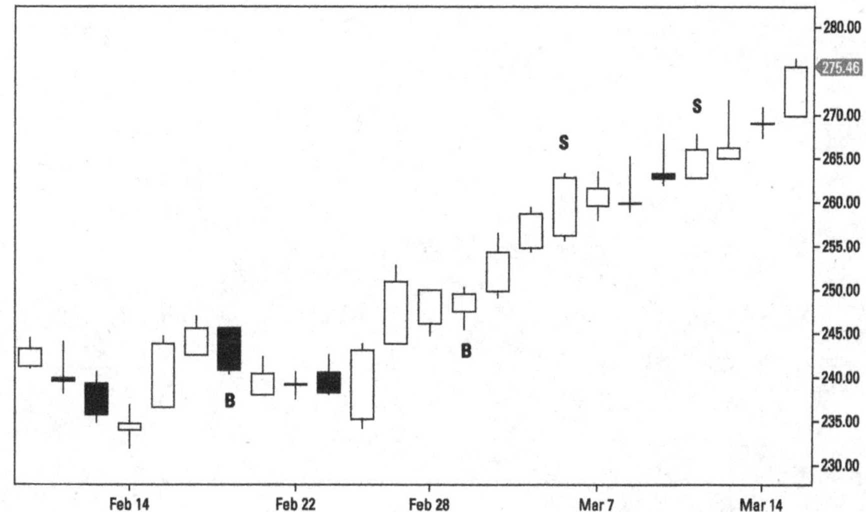

FIGURE 3-8: Insider trading activity included on a candlestick chart.

When insider trading information is included in candlestick charts, the indications of insider activity are usually easy to read. In Figure 3-8, the *B* indicates insider buying, and the *S* indicates insider selling. (Splits also use the *S*, but splits normally have 2 for 1 or some numbers along with the split. The format varies from chart service to chart service.) Some other charts use up arrows to indicate buying and down arrows to indicate selling. This chart includes buying in February and selling in March. It appears that the insiders in this company do a good job of trading their own stock!

Trying to trade along with insiders is so popular that not only does insider trading information appear on some charts, but you'll also find services and newsletters devoted to disseminating this information. One service, InsiderScore, even ranks individual insiders by how well they bought and sold shares in the past!

Search the Internet for *insider trading newsletter* and you'll see more results than you'll know what to do with.

Chapter 4

Using Artificial Intelligence with Candlestick Charting

The advancement of artificial intelligence (AI) has made certain aspects of the trading world easier; however, understanding and interpreting the results will always remain the trader's responsibility. The technology behind AI allows traders to quickly see a market's behavior, possibly create a trading strategy, and then execute the trading strategy by way of an online broker.

Candlestick charts were initially created to allow traders to quickly see information regarding the market. The candlestick demonstrated the high, the low, the open price, and the closing price, all in one candlestick. This information is now readily available via financial data providers, which can then be incorporated into trading models.

A challenge with AI is the blind faith that some might place in the technology. Traders need to be able to understand the inputs into the model that AI generates, the model itself, and the results. Traders also need to be able to understand the limitations of the model — limitations that can be revealed only by systematic testing of the system by way of *back testing,* or testing the data to ensure the system works, and paper trading. AI is a tool that can be employed by traders to generate ideas, understanding, and, potentially, trading with the use of candlestick charts.

Traders can now use AI to find the kinds of patterns we describe in Chapters 5–11. These patterns previously had to be read by the trader, almost like tea leaves. The trader then was charged with being able to see the leaves clearly and being able to make a quick decision on those leaves. In some instances, traders looked at the patterns *intraday,* meaning they were evaluating price movement throughout the day as opposed to looking at price movement at the end of the day. The ability to quickly find the patterns allows the trader to be able to make a snap decision about whether to buy a security, sell a security, wait on selling a security, or wait on buying a security.

ChatGPT is one of the most popular AI tools used by traders, so we start our investigation of trading the AI way with this particular tool. (It helps that the software is free to use.) The flexibility offered to users when it comes to how someone interacts with the software system has made the system quite popular. (Users can interact with the platform via text, audio, or image prompts, for example.) Being able to supply the software platform with an idea of what you're looking for makes it easier for the trader to generate better and more concrete ideas.

Retracing the History of ChatGPT

The software was introduced relatively recently — in November of 2022, to be precise. The software platform was an immediate hit, as evidenced by the fact that it was quickly featured in the *New York Times.* Individual traders now had access to sophisticated modeling and analysis for free. By February of 2023, ChatGPT was able to gain more than a million users in just a few days, eventually growing to 100 million users in two months. This has made ChatGPT now one of the top five most-used websites on the Internet. Since the initial launch of the software, numerous new versions have been released, each one more accurate and popular.

In December 2024, a version of ChatGPT was released that allowed for more thoughtful and meaningful responses.

When using AI, you need to remember that you're smarter than the software. We'll say it again: You are smarter than the software. The software is a tool you can use to enhance something you're doing, but it's only a tool. Keeping this in mind lets you better embrace what ChatGPT can do for you while still recognizing what it cannot do for you.

The software system can make errors regarding inaccurate information. Both authors of this book have used the kind of AI software that kindly makes grammar suggestions and word use suggestions — and we have both personally experienced times when the software AI system makes a suggestion that completely changes the overall meaning of the passage. Keeping track of what you're trying to communicate and the information you need from AI is important because AI might not always get it right. If you blindly accept what AI is giving you, you could easily make a trade you really do not want to make.

Another issue with AI is the list of challenges for real-time information. Without a proper feed of data going into ChatGPT, the software system cannot make recommendations for you (and really, you don't want it to do so, either). You want something that has fresh, up-to-date information so that you can make the best decisions you can make.

Taking ChatGPT for a Spin

ChatGPT is essentially a software system that lets the end user create a conversation between themselves and the software system itself. (The technical term for such a system is "a conversational chatbot based on large language models.") A discussion of the many different uses for the software is outside the scope of this book, so, in line with the title of this book, we focus on ChatGPT and candlestick charting. However, you should note the origins of ChatGPT to fully understand the capabilities and limitations of what the software can do for a trader.

The conversations with the AI system let you work with ChatGPT to better understand what you're looking for in terms of recommendations. Perhaps you're interested in whether you see a bullish or bearish pattern, a specific pattern, or simply an overall direction in the market. The software system can give you the information you need based on your prompts.

When you're more confident with candlestick charting, you can begin to ask the AI software to evaluate your candlesticks. Then it can be of value to you for one of two reasons:

>> You might simply want the system to tell you what the pattern is from your data.

>> You might be looking for the system to confirm what you have already seen.

If you're new to candlestick charting, this strategy can be quite valuable to you, because you might not feel confident in what you're seeing in the charts.

When you have created your own account for ChatGPT, you'll see that the software system not only remembers you personally but also remembers portions of your previous conversations, just as though AI were a real person. (Well, maybe a real person with a fantastic memory, because no one we know can remember everything they may have ever said to another person!) This is a tremendous help to novice and experienced traders alike. The system now will have a better sense of who you are and your trading style. This style you create will become your overall methodology for making decisions on whether to get into a trade, when to take profits, and when to take losses. Having a systematic approach when it comes to making these decisions is critical because it removes emotion from the trading equation.

Trading can become quite emotional. Traders take losses *seriously*, often losing sleep, growing anxious, and feeling agitated. Conversely, traders are thrilled with gains! (One of us authors often even *struts* after a particularly good trade.) Some traders may even begin to mentally spend this money. They often see this money as "house" money — excess disposable money as opposed to money needed to pay down the mortgage, in other words. Traders don't feel these things the same way. The level of happiness someone feels from a gain is much lower than the level of unhappiness they feel from a loss. They have a disproportionate response in terms of feelings.

Because of how feelings are inextricably tied to trades, some traders are too cautious to get into a trade and then miss out on the opportunity. Other traders jump into a trade before they should because they lack the information required to make an informed decision. Once the trade is in play, the next question is when to get out of a trade. If the trade is losing money, how do you know when to cut your losses or to hold out, hoping that the trade goes in your favor? On the other side, if the trade is making money, when do you know how to take your gains from the table? Or do you wait, hoping for higher returns, which also can lead to the trade being wiped out?

Creating a systematic approach to when you get into a trade and when you get out of a trade is critical for your financial stability. The systematic approach is even good for your mental well-being. If you have a systematic approach, you won't second-guess yourself during every decision over what needs to happen to get into (and out of) a trade.

The conversational aspect of ChatGPT can help you not only find and verify patterns but also help you find your natural rhythm around trading using candlestick charting. As we noted, this openness can help you find your way of evaluating candlestick patterns and determine how you will trade using those candlestick charts.

With all the Thrill of Victory, Agony of Defeat stuff out of the way, it's time to get you started using ChatGPT. The process is straightforward:

1. Create a ChatGPT account.

2. Log in to the ChatGPT account.

3. Ask your first question!

4. Continue the conversation with ChatGPT.

Here's a more detailed account of what you need to do:

1. **Create a ChatGPT account.**

   Creating a ChatGPT account is straightforward: Go to the ChatGPT site at https://chatgpt.com and click the Sign Up for Free link.

   The software platform allows you to create an account using your email address, your Google account, your Apple account, or your Microsoft account. We chose to create accounts using our email accounts. The preference is completely yours.

2. **Log in to ChatGPT.**

   Once you have established that you have an account, you need to log in to the account. The system will most likely request that you verify your account with a password. (That's pretty much what you'd expect, given how online systems are set up these days.) Once you enter the temporary passcode and then create a permanent passcode, you're all set to begin working with ChatGPT.

   We're assuming you have no history with ChatGPT, but if you do, the program may offer to describe you based on your past chats. (See Figure 4-1, which shows what it had to say about Larissa.) She's not sure whether the description it came up with is *entirely* accurate, but based on her chats with ChatGPT, she feels it's not too far off from who she really is!

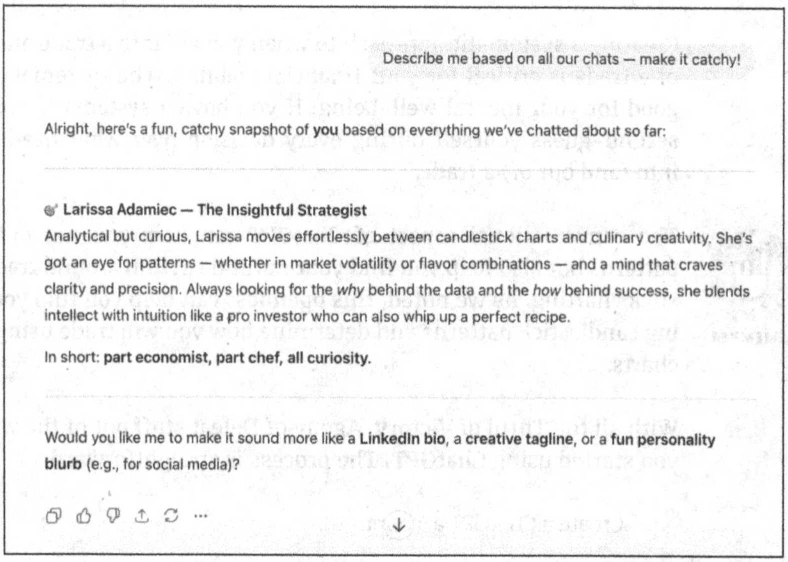

Describe me based on all our chats — make it catchy!

Alright, here's a fun, catchy snapshot of **you** based on everything we've chatted about so far:

Larissa Adamiec — The Insightful Strategist
Analytical but curious, Larissa moves effortlessly between candlestick charts and culinary creativity. She's got an eye for patterns — whether in market volatility or flavor combinations — and a mind that craves clarity and precision. Always looking for the *why* behind the data and the *how* behind success, she blends intellect with intuition like a pro investor who can also whip up a perfect recipe.

In short: **part economist, part chef, all curiosity.**

Would you like me to make it sound more like a **LinkedIn bio**, a **creative tagline**, or a **fun personality blurb** (e.g., for social media)?

FIGURE 4-1:
ChatGPT describing Larissa Adamiec, an "analytical but curious" author.

The account Larissa is using to help write this chapter has dealt only with her desire to learn how artificial intelligence can be used for traders who use candlestick charting to help make informed decisions. (She also got a kick out of reading this description about herself!)

3. **Ask your first question.**

   An AI session is a conversation, so you need to either ask an initial question or start the conversation another way. Larissa, for example, wanted to gain a sense of what ChatGPT knows about candlestick charting.

REMEMBER

As we discuss earlier in this chapter, ChatGPT has its limitations. You *have* to remember that the system is flawed and will make mistakes from time to time. Also, because Larissa is someone who teaches topics in the financial markets and who has also worked in the financial markets, she noticed that ChatGPT came up with things she simply doesn't agree with. (And she could say the same thing about what she found in some of the textbooks she has used in the past.) Trusting your source is vital if you'll be using it to help you make decisions, especially if you're trusting it with decisions around your financial well-being.

This is the first question Larissa asked: What is a candlestick chart?

The response from ChatGPT (see Figure 4-2) is spot-on. Woo-hoo! We are beginning to be able to trust the information. (You can, if you want, verify this information from Chapters 1–3 in this book.) ChatGPT also has learned that we are interested in candlestick charting, which, as you can see in its description of Larissa, makes sense. They are learning about each other.

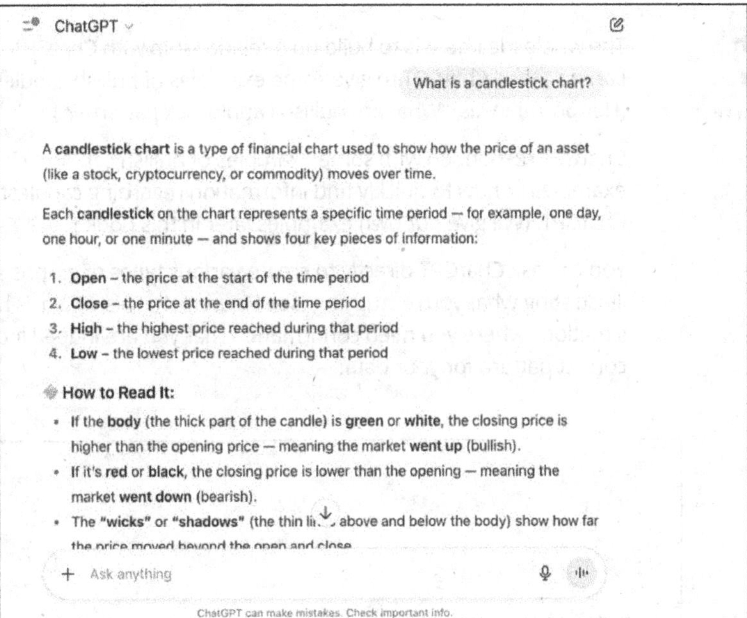

FIGURE 4-2: ChatGPT defining a candlestick chart.

Encouraged, Larissa asked another question (see Figure 4-3).

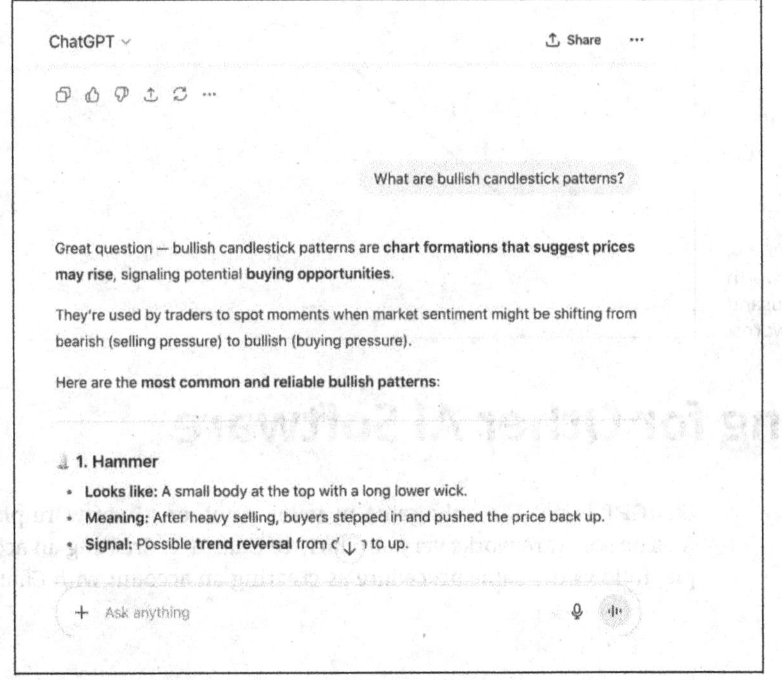

FIGURE 4-3: Continuing the conversation.

The whole idea here is to build up a relationship with ChatGPT. This time, Larissa asked ChatGPT to give some examples of bullish candlestick patterns. (Her prompt was, "What are bullish candlestick patterns?")

ChatGPT responded with some examples of bullish candlestick patterns — examples of how to quickly find information regarding candlestick charts using ChatGPT. (We give our own examples later in this book.)

You can ask ChatGPT directly to create various types of graphs and patterns illustrating what you're studying (see Figure 4-4). This, again, is helpful in situations where you need confirmation that you are indeed looking at the correct pattern for your data.

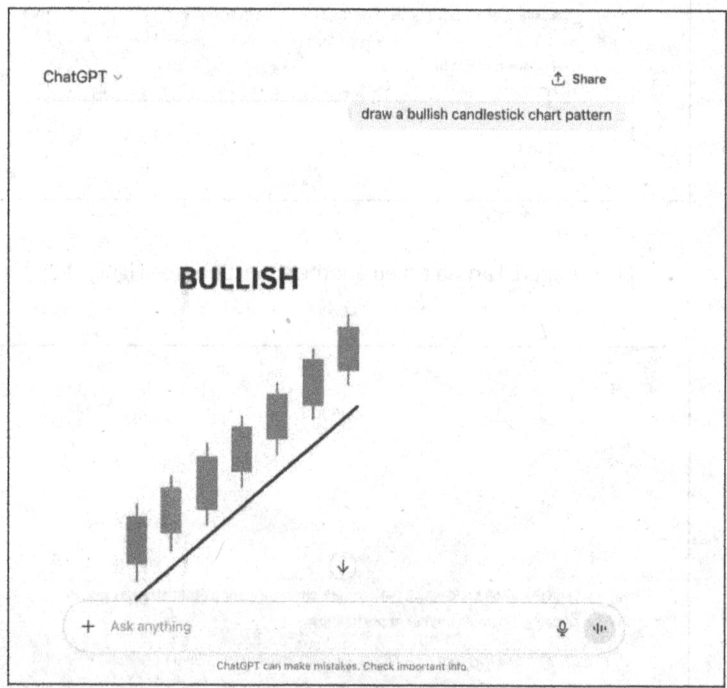

FIGURE 4-4:
A picture is worth a thousand words.

Opting for Other AI Software

ChatGPT is not the only game in town. Another AI software platform is Claude AI. The software works very similarly to ChatGPT. Creating an account, for example, follows the same procedure as creating an account with ChatGPT.

Claude allows users to work with their own code base. If you're someone who employs algorithmic trading using a programming platform in conjunction with your trading algorithm, this might be a good choice for you. We, however, focus on using the AI software platform to better understand (and better use) candlestick charting.

Similar to using ChatGPT, we chose to start our conversation with a simple question: What is a candlestick chart? Figure 4-5 shows Claude's response.

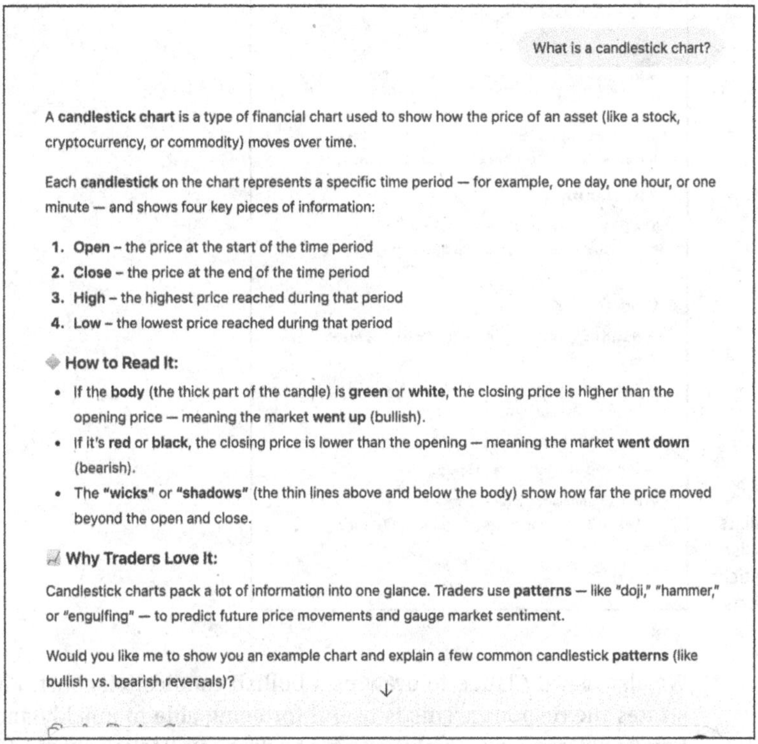

FIGURE 4-5: Claude answers a question.

Notice how both Claude and ChatGPT provide information similar to one another. (And, yes, please note that this information can be verified for accuracy with the help of our excellent book.) By starting the conversation with our candlestick question, the software platform is beginning to understand the types of topics we are interested in exploring. The software will also have a recommendation algorithm embedded that allows the software to make suggestions on where to pivot the conversation.

We're interested in seeing our conversation with Claude go further. We will ask the same question we asked ChatGPT, which is to name some bullish candlestick chart patterns.

Figure 4-6 demonstrates what Claude will tell you. Again, note the similarity between ChatGPT and Claude. Both AI software systems generate a hammer as the first example of a bullish candlestick pattern.

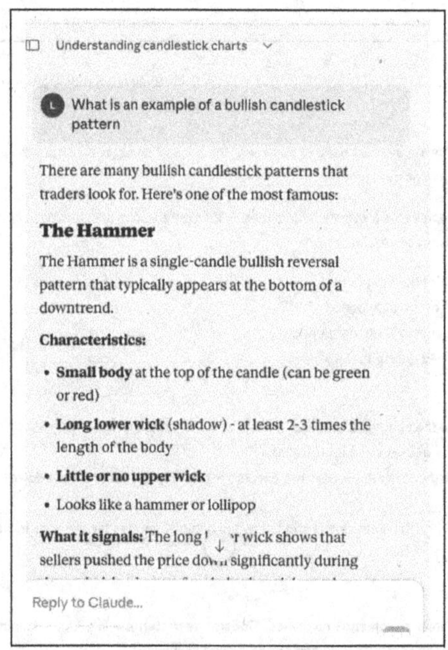

FIGURE 4-6: Claude lists some bullish candlestick patterns.

We also asked Claude to draw us a bullish candlestick chart. Figure 4-7 demonstrates the response. This is useful for being able to quickly and easily verify the type of pattern we're evaluating for trading candlestick charts. Claude also has the ability to read into the AI software platform data that can then be used as a tool for evaluating the data for trends. This further gives the trader more confidence when it comes to whether they should get into the trade or leave the trade alone. By being able to add data, you would have the ability to put in past data of a trade in process to better assist the decision-making for the best point to exit the trade.

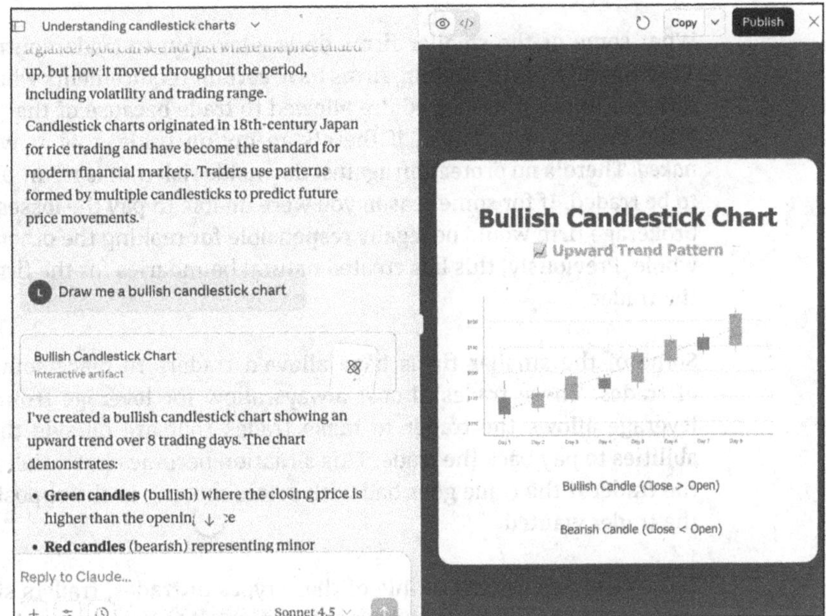

FIGURE 4-7: Testing Claude's artistic side.

Exploring Trading Platforms

Lots of different platforms allow people to trade easily and cheaply. Trading has significantly changed from what was standard practice just a few short years ago. Previously, people had to call to the exchange to make an order. Every trade had two associated trade fees: into the trade and out of the trade. Electronic trading made trades cheaper, but definitely not free. In the first fund that Larissa ran, the broker gave her a discount on trades by giving her 50 free trades and then $20 per side, in and out. Now trades can be traded for free. Many platforms provide free trades because the costs associated with trading have been vastly reduced.

REMEMBER

Don't lose any sleep worrying that the trading platforms aren't making any money. The platforms make money from the interest they receive when you deposit your money on the platform. As a result, they are quite interested in you shifting some of your cash to their site. They will make money as long as you have money deposited with them.

Due to the increased competition among the various platforms, the fees of trading have declined, so much so that there's no longer any fee associated with trading. Certain well-known firms allow you to set up a trading account, such as JPMorgan, Charles Schwab, and Fidelity. Some smaller firms, such as RobinHood, allow you to trade on their sites.

What some of the smaller firms do is allow you to trade nontraditional trades. Traditionally, when trading, firms have certain requirements when it comes to the different types of trades you're allowed to trade because of the risk profile of the trade itself. For example, if there's an option trade, that is what's considered *naked:* There's no protection against downside risk that is traditionally not allowed to be traded. If for some reason you were unable to pay the losses of the trade, the brokerage firm would be legally responsible for making the other side of the trade whole. Previously, this has created natural boundaries for the firm with respect to the trader.

Some of the smaller firms have allowed traders to place some of these types of trades. These trades almost always allow for leverage from the trader. The leverage allows the trader to make trades that are outside the scope of their abilities to pay back the trade. This situation becomes potentially problematic for the trader if the trade goes bad with prices moving in the opposite direction that the trader wanted.

Due to the risk-return profile of these types of trades, traders should be wary of trades that have unlimited downside potential. Just because things don't seem to be able to fall apart doesn't mean that they can't fall apart.

When you look at the return risk profile or the break-even graph that the platform provides and you see unlimited downside risk, it's a sign that the trade might not be right for you.

And if for some reason you find yourself in a pickle with substantial losses, please relax and reach out to your broker or the trading platform. They're willing to work with you if there's a possibility that you might not be able to pay back the lost amount.

2
Working with Simple Candlestick Patterns

Discover signals garnered from individual candlesticks as well as patterns that emerge as a result of a combination of candlesticks.

Recognize signals in candlestick charts.

See how market context contributes to the decision about whether a candlestick is bullish or bearish.

Apply your knowledge of patterns in a trading context, making both buying and short-selling decisions.

Chapter 5

Working with Straightforward Single-Stick Patterns

t's time to begin diving into individual- and multiperiod candlestick patterns. Many patterns give buy and sell signals, and some serve as a heads-up that a big move is on the horizon (although it's not always clear just what that big move will be!).

Most candlestick patterns are valid based only on the market activity of the previous few days. Some patterns indicate a change in trend, for example, and using one of them without knowing about the previous trend wouldn't be useful. Usually, the context in which you find a pattern tells you a great deal about what you should do based on that pattern. Some single-stick patterns, however, are considered to be either bullish or bearish regardless of the context, and those patterns are what we focus on in this chapter.

This chapter explores the signals that single-stick candlestick patterns may send, some bearish and some bullish. (The constructions of these patterns are covered in Chapter 3.) We demonstrate what may have happened during a particular day, trading-wise, to result in the formation of a significant single candlestick on your chart. (We say "significant" because candlestick patterns are often used to fore-cast price action.) We give examples of a candlestick signal working well and cases in which the pattern may not give such a positive signal. If you know how to rec-ognize and trade on these examples, they should provide some reliable tools that you can add to your trading toolbox.

The Bullish Long White Candle

The most bullish of patterns is the *long white candle*, which represents a day during which the bulls controlled trading and pushed prices higher from the opening all the way to the closing. As the price moves up, sellers come in, but not enough to keep the price from continuing its rise. Any time sellers show up during this day, the buyers buy from them, and prices move higher. With the long white candle closing near the high, odds are good that the bulls aren't done with their buying and will return for more on the following day. There just wasn't enough supply of stock by sellers to keep the buyers from pushing up the price.

You can find several specific types of long white candles (see the section "Identi-fying the three variations of the long white candle," later in this chapter). All of them depict bullishness during the day, but each has unique characteristics.

Taking a look at long white candles

One common feature of the *long white candle* (see Figure 5-1) is an open near the low of the day and a close near the high of the day, indicating that buying has taken place throughout the day.

Figure 5-2 is an intraday chart of the price action that results in a long white candle on a daily chart. An *intraday chart* depicts the price action during a period less than a day, such as 5 minutes or 30 minutes. Each candlestick represents the price action for this subperiod. For the day that corresponds to Figure 5-2 — a figure depicting the price action of a single day made up of 30-minute pricing periods — you can see that the opening price was very near the low of the day and the closing price was near the high of the day.

A textbook long white candlestick has a long candle with no wick, but that doesn't happen often, and long candles that have a little wick on either or both ends are still considered to be long white candles.

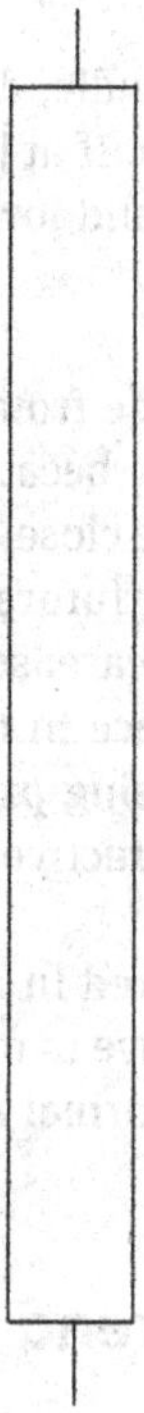

FIGURE 5-1:
A long
white candle.

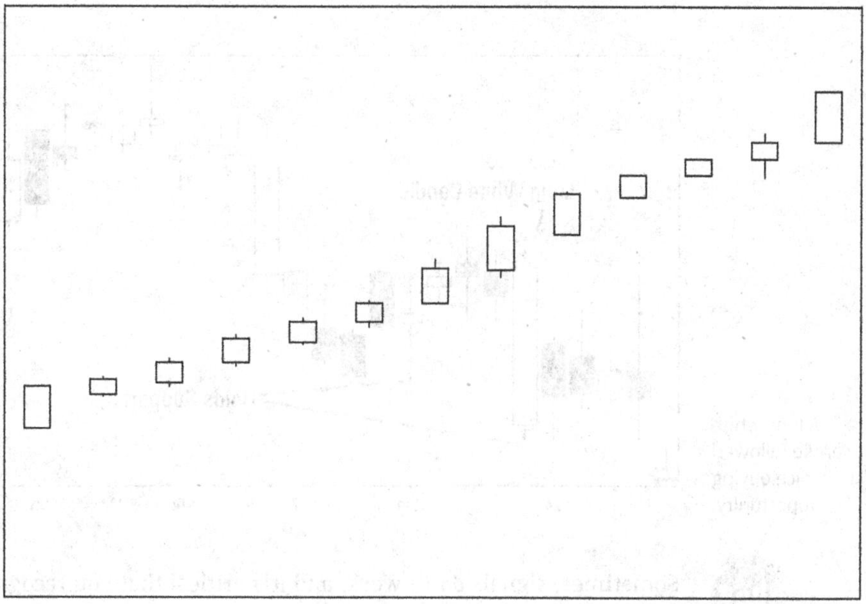

FIGURE 5-2:
A 30-minute chart
that produces a
long white candle
on a daily chart.

To figure out whether you're looking at a long white candle, determine the area covered by the difference between the close and the open. If at least 90 percent of the area is covered by the difference between the high and low, you have a long white candle.

For the day shown in Figure 5-2, the bulls were in charge from the beginning of the day to the end. There's just no disputing this fact, because the price does nothing but go higher over the course of the day, and the close is near the high of the day; the bulls will probably stay in charge for the near future. The signal is just that bullish. You usually have the chance to act in such a case; some trading below the closing price of the long white candle may take place in the next couple of days, and you can place a buy order lower than the closing price but within the range of the long white candle to try to determine an attractive entry point.

On a long white candle day, lots of price action is covered in a short amount of time. Stocks — and markets, for that matter — don't move in one direction without some sort of move in the opposite direction. This normal retracing of prices gives you a chance to act on this bullish signal.

The long white candle signaling an uptrend

Figure 5-3 shows a few days in which the price action is lower than the high of the long white candle. After seeing this bullish signal, you have several days to buy.

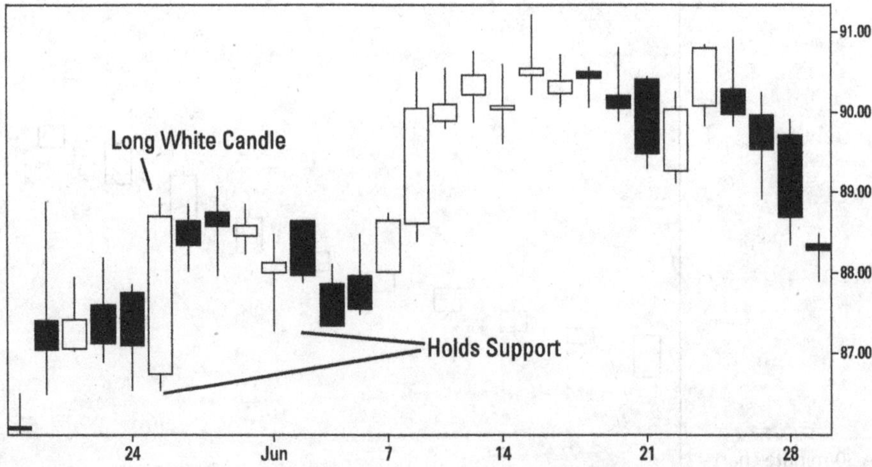

FIGURE 5-3:
A long white candle followed by a nice buying opportunity.

Sometimes, signals don't work, and it's critical that you recognize this fact. With long white candlesticks, the low price on the candlestick is a good support level.

Support is a level at which buyers are expected to maintain the price of a security if market conditions are consistent. If this support doesn't hold, whatever buy signal you're dealing with has changed, and you shouldn't act on the signal. In that case, you should exit your position fairly quickly. You may take a small loss, but getting out before prices fall even lower prevents you from taking a much larger loss later.

Look again at Figure 5-3, where we point out the low of the day on the long white candle; also note that the price doesn't trade below that support level over the next few days. If you watch that stock and see that the support level is broken, the bullish signal has failed and is no longer valid. When a signal is no longer valid, you should get out of a trade. The biggest mistake traders of all experience levels make is ignoring what the market is telling them when they're in a failing trade. There's a saying on Wall Street that your first sell is often your best sell.

We can't stress enough that when a signal is no longer valid, you should exit any trades based on that signal and take no new positions based on it. Many small losers turn into big losers when the small loss isn't realized and corrected quickly.

The long white candle failing as a long signal

What happens when the support level revealed by a long white candle is broken? Take a look at Figure 5-4. This chart shows a nice long white candle and then a quick violation of its support level. Despite the long white candle on the chart, the bullish action won't continue!

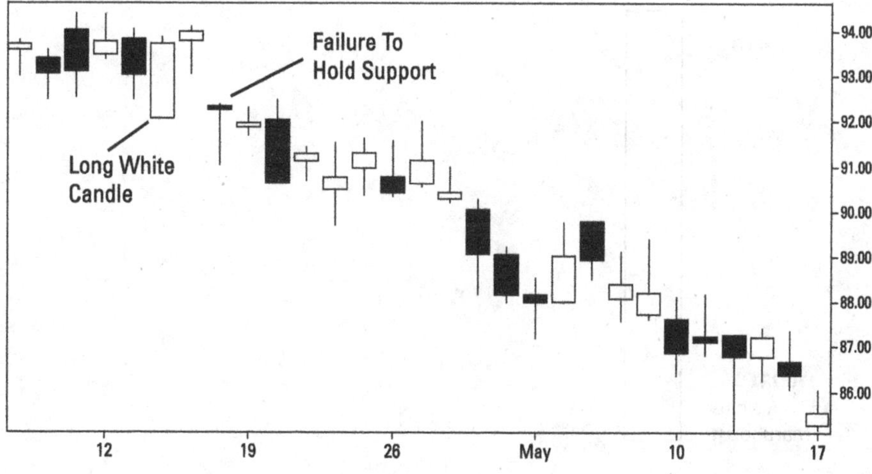

FIGURE 5-4:
A chart showing the failure of a long white candle to hold support and the resulting price action.

How do you cope with a failed signal? You should have made that decision when you first got into the trade. Take preemptive action. Place an order that triggers whenever a signal fails. This process is known as a *stop order*. When you're trading long, stop orders are known as *sell stop orders* or *sell stops*. A sell stop is placed below the current market price of a stock and triggered when the price reaches this level. If a stock is trading at 51, for example, you can place your sell stop order at 50. As long as trading stays over 50, nothing happens. When the price hits 50, however, a sell order is executed, protecting you from further drops in price. Use stops when initiating positions to minimize the damage caused when a signal turns bad.

Identifying the three variations of the long white candle

The long white candle has three variations. All of these are single-day patterns during which the bulls were in control from the open to the close.

The white marubozu

The first variation, the *white marubozu*, is the most bullish of them all: a long white candle with no wicks. (Loosely translated from Japanese, *marubozu* means "bald" or "little hair.") The day begins on the low and finishes on the high, meaning that the market opened and moved higher only over the course of a trading day (see Figure 5-5).

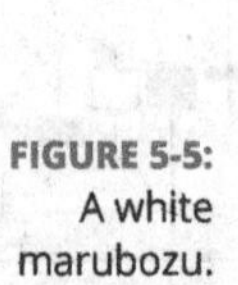

FIGURE 5-5:
A white marubozu.

The closing long white candle

The second version of the long white candle is the *closing long white candle*. On this single-stick pattern, the close is equal to the high, so there's no wick at the top of the stick. The wick at the bottom means that there may have been some early selling, but the selling didn't last when the sellers recognized strong buying. It's also called the *closing white marubozu*, even though it has a tiny wick. Figure 5-6 shows a closing long white candle.

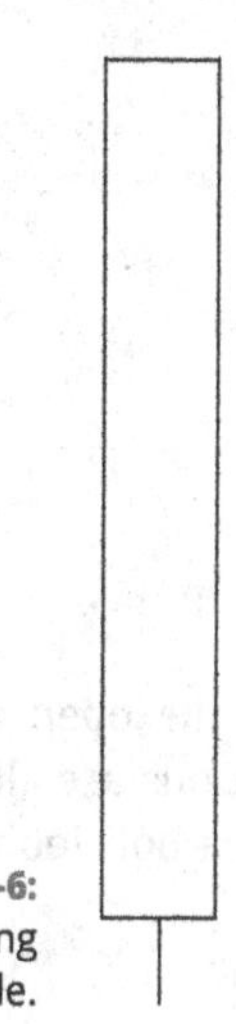

The opening long white candle

The third variation of the long white candle is the *opening long white candle*. This pattern's opening price is equal to the low of the day, and as a result, there's no wick at the bottom. The wick at the top means that a high was reached before the end of the day, and some selling came in. This is also known as a *closing white candle*. Figure 5-7 shows an opening long white candle.

TIP

This variation is one to keep a close eye on for potential failure as a bullish signal.

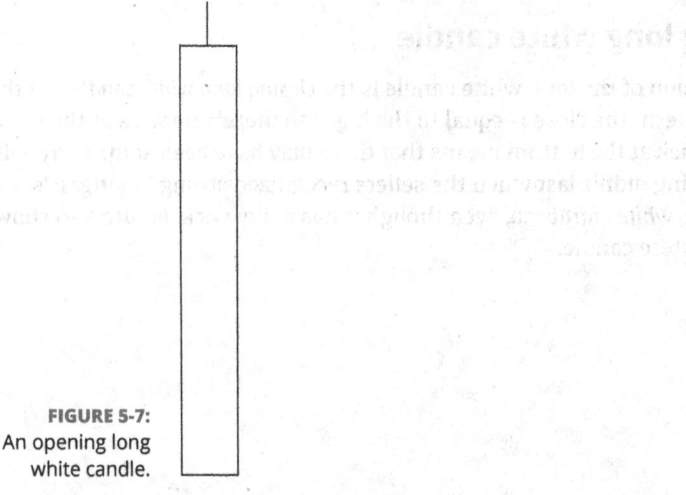

The opening long white candle

FIGURE 5-7:
An opening long
white candle.

The Bullish Dragonfly Doji

The *doji* is a candlestick pattern that's created when the open and close are equal, so there's essentially no stick to the candlestick. Dojis are almost all wick. Figure 5-8 shows a few types of dojis. As you can see, a doji looks more like a cross or a *T* than a pattern on a candlestick chart.

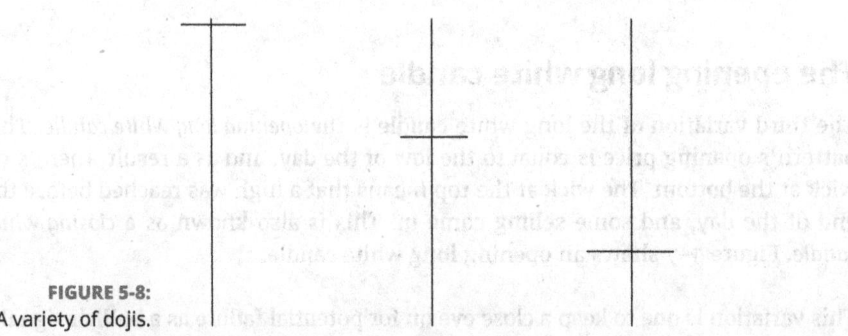

FIGURE 5-8:
A variety of dojis.

TECHNICAL
STUFF

Loosely translated, *doji* means "blunder" or "mistake." It's said that the pattern earned its name because having a whole day's worth of trading end up back at the starting point seems like a goof, but price action is never a mistake, so we're not crazy about that explanation.

Although several varieties of dojis exist, you can count on all of them to be fairly frustrating for traders. For a doji to be created, a day must begin and end with the same price, so lots of trading takes place, but when it's all said and done, the price is back where it started. Dojis are differentiated by the locations of the open and close on the wick — where trading begins and ends on a given day.

At first glance, dojis may not seem to be very exciting, but don't be fooled: Doji patterns are usually associated with a change in market trend, even though they depict a day on which the battle between bulls and bears is fairly equal. Even though the battle for the day is a draw, one side soon overpowers the other. The situation is like a prolonged tug-of-war that ends when one team is violently yanked into the mud. For the tug-of-war that's a doji pattern, that yank in price action usually occurs in the next few days, or even on the following day.

Recognizing a dragonfly doji

Although dojis indicate some indecision, in some instances, a doji is more bullish or bearish, depending on the price action. A *dragonfly doji* is one of those cases; this pattern is fairly bullish due to the price action behind it.

The dragonfly doji is unique in that three of the four candlestick components — the open, high, and close — are equal. A dragonfly doji comes from a day when a stock opens, trades down during the first part the day and then starts to trade back up, eventually closing on the high (which is also the open). In terms of bears and bulls, on a dragonfly-doji day, the bears initially decide that they're going to rule the day, and the resulting lower prices lead the bulls to decide that it's time to buy. The bulls take over and push up the price as they dominate the rest of the day until the price is back where it started. Figure 5-9 shows a classic example of a dragonfly doji.

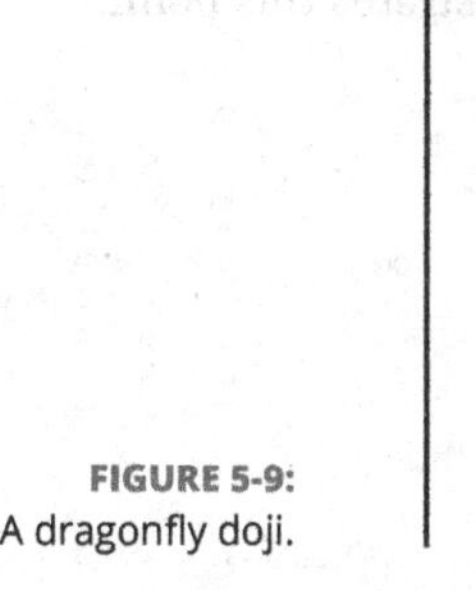

For an illustration of the inner workings of a day that results in a dragonfly doji, check out Figure 5-10. This figure features a 30-minute chart of the price action that occurs over the course of a day to cause a dragonfly doji. The bears dominate the first half of the day, but the bulls take over in the afternoon, and the result is a close equal to the open. All that struggle during the day came to nothing.

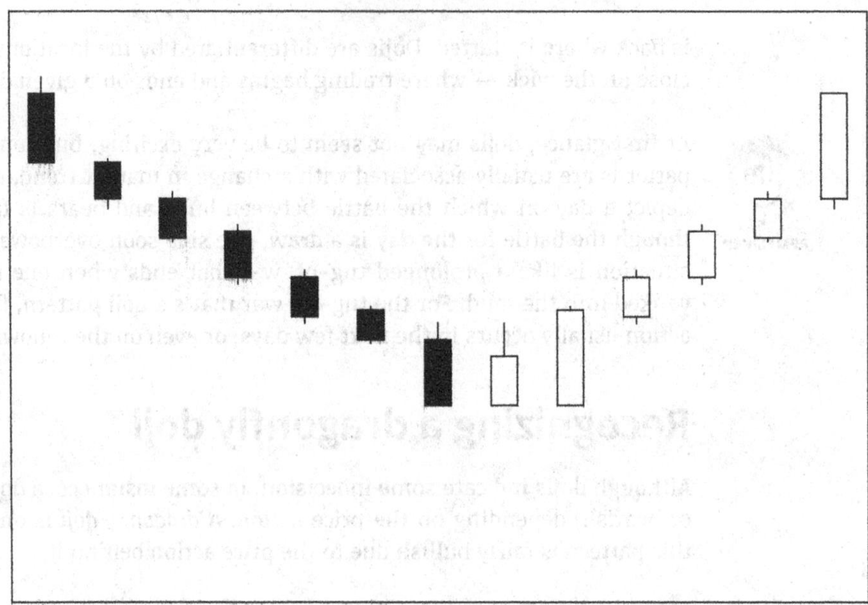

REMEMBER

The price action behind a dragonfly doji bodes well for those who hope that prices go higher, because a price at which people buy aggressively has been set at the low end of the wick. The low of a dragonfly doji day is considered to be a near-term support level because it's clear that buyers came in at that level and turned the trend from down to up.

The length of a wick from the high to low doesn't have to be any specific distance to qualify as a dragonfly. But the wick length can signify the amount of bullish significance that a dragonfly doji has for future price action. Put simply, the longer the wick, the more bullish the pattern. Figure 5-11 illustrates this point.

Dragonfly dojis appear when the open and close are very near or equal to the high, so the beginning and ending of this chart are equal. The price action during this day is interesting: The bears take over from the open and push the price down. Eventually, though, lower prices entice buyers, who get aggressive, pushing the price back up to the open and settling on the high of the day.

Trading based on a dragonfly doji

You can make smart trades based on the dragonfly dojis you see in your charts. Two charts can help:

>> One in which a dragonfly doji indicates a nice buying opportunity

>> One in which a dragonfly doji fails badly

First, the good chart. Much like the long white candle we discuss earlier in this chapter, the dragonfly doji helps you establish a solid support level to buy with confidence. In Figure 5-12, notice that the bottom end of the dragonfly doji wick works as a support level, which is held as the security remains bullish for several days. The dragonfly doji appears after some *range trading*, or trading between prices, and it's followed by a quick breakout of prices that reach new highs. Although the first day following the dragonfly doji shows an opening price lower than the previous close, the dragonfly's low price isn't violated, and the signal remains valid. Sticking with this valid signal leads to some nice profits!

Now for a dragonfly doji that doesn't work out well. The dragonfly that appears in Figure 5-13 looks promising, but it's followed the next day by a low that's lower than the bottom of the dragonfly's wick. As you can see, the next moves are even lower.

The low of the dragonfly doji is a significant support level, but when that level is violated, it negates the dragonfly's buy signal. Whenever a level is violated, get out of your position as soon as possible. Counter-trend trading can be dangerous to your wealth.

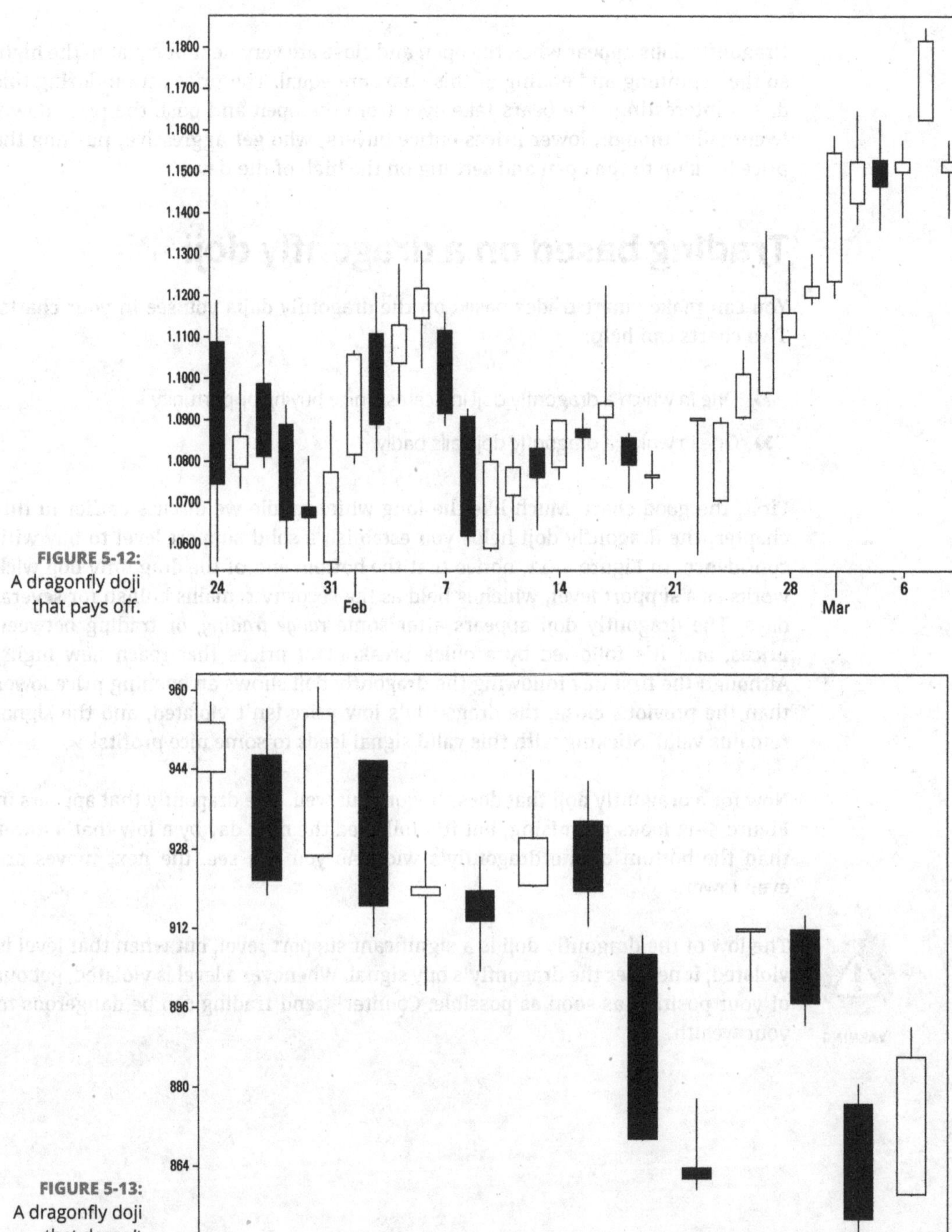

FIGURE 5-12:
A dragonfly doji
that pays off.

FIGURE 5-13:
A dragonfly doji
that doesn't
work out well.

The Bearish Long Black Candle

The long black candle is a direct counterpart of the long white candle, discussed earlier in this chapter. It's a long candlestick compared with other candlesticks on the same chart, and most or all of it is made up of a solid candle.

The long black candle is as bearish as it gets. When you see one of these candles, it means that sellers took over at the beginning of the day and pushed prices lower until the end of the day. Typically, these sellers are selling just to get out, and their price sensitivity is low. Seeing this type of enthusiastic selling should give you confidence that the bears will be in control for a few more days, and you can capitalize on that opportunity.

Taking a look at long black candles

A long black candle is created when the bears seize control at the start of a day and push prices down until day's end. Figure 5-14 shows a typical long black candle.

FIGURE 5-14:
A long black candle.

For some quick insight on the numbers involved, take a look at Figure 5-15, which is an intraday chart of price action that creates a long black candle. (Keep in mind that the figure is just one example; several other intraday patterns can produce a long black candle on a daily chart.) Basically, any pattern that begins near the high of the day and ends near the low of the day results in a long black candle, even if the action that got the price to the low occurred in only a couple of the 30-minute bars.

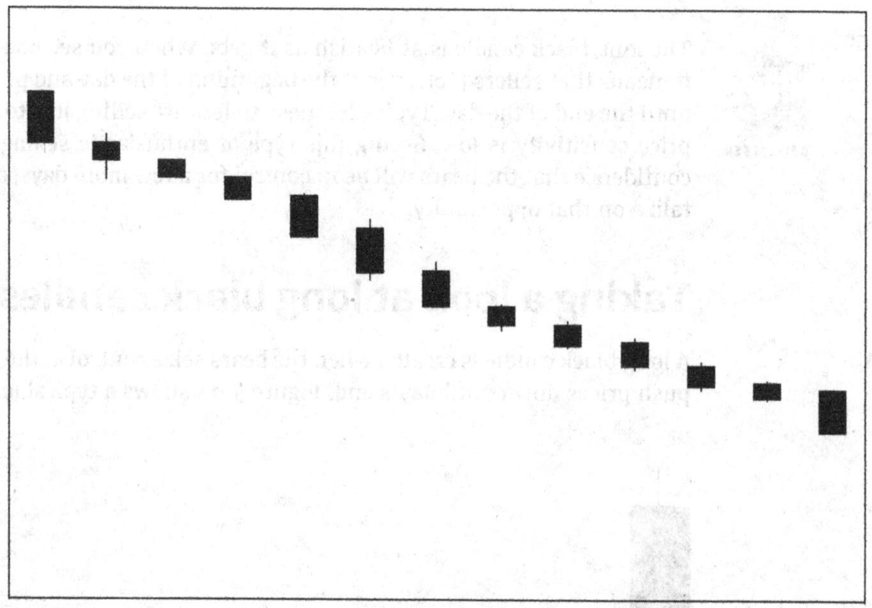

REMEMBER

The potential intraday action is limitless; the important things to know are that the bears pushed hard and down and that the bulls weren't able to hold up the price.

TIP

A useful rule of thumb for the long black candle is that the candle section should cover at least 90 percent of the candlestick. The wicks should be barely visible or missing.

The long black candle usually indicates that many price levels have been covered over the course of one day. A reversal is possible in the short term, but the long black candle shows that the bears are being aggressive and suggests that this aggression will continue.

Identifying the three variations of the long black candle

Like the long white candle, described earlier in this chapter, the long black candle has several variations:

>> **Black marubozu:** The *black marubozu,* shown in Figure 5-16, opens on its high and closes on its low. It has no wicks.

>> **Closing long black candle:** Also known as *closing black marubozu,* you can spot it by recognizing that there's no wick at the bottom (closing) end of the candlestick. The close is equal to the low, whereas the open is a little lower than the high for the day. Figure 5-17 shows a closing black candle.

>> **Opening long black candle:** Also known as an *opening black marubozu,* it is created when the open is equal to the high of a day and the close is just above the day's low. A small wick appears only at the bottom of this candlestick.

Figure 5-18 shows a typical opening long black candle. The small wick at the bottom of this candlestick indicates that some late-day buying occurred or that the low price of the day enticed some buyers. This type of speculation leads some people to regard the opening long black candle as being the least reliable of the three long-black-candle variations.

FIGURE 5-16: A black marubozu.

FIGURE 5-17:
A closing long
black candle.

FIGURE 5-18:
An opening long
black candle.

Trading based on long black candles

Now it's time to see how you can trade with long black candles in the real world. Figure 5-19 is near and dear to Russell's heart because it represents a trade he actually executed while writing the first edition of this book. This figure is a chart of a November soybean futures contract that traded at the Chicago Board of Trade. At the time, Russell wanted to take a short position in the soybean contract but was waiting for a confirming trading signal or bearish chart pattern before executing his position. The long black candle highlighted in Figure 5-19 provided the short signal he sought.

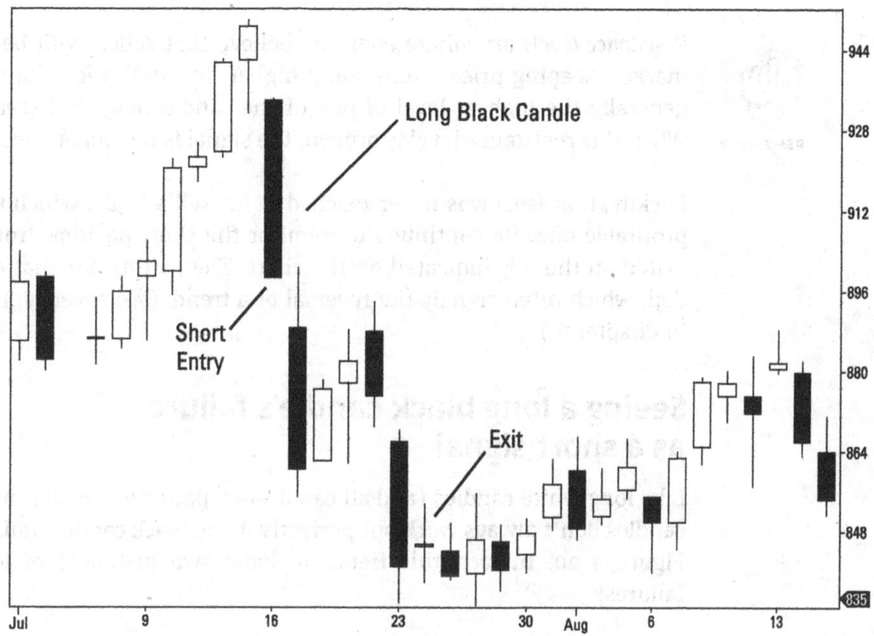

FIGURE 5-19: A long black candle that provided a nice sell signal.

Getting a good bearish signal from a long black candle

TIP

We've noticed in the past that long white or black candlesticks are generally followed by continuations of their up or down moves, more often with commodities than with stocks. Futures in commodities — such as gold, soybeans, and oil — tend to trend more than stocks do. This tendency makes us quicker to initiate a position in futures than in stocks when a trend signal like the marubozu shows up on a chart. By the same token, we're usually quicker to concede that we're wrong on a futures trade than on a stock trade when a trend is broken. Keep these differences in mind and use them to your advantage. (Chapter 11 covers trends in detail.)

To return to the example of Russell's soybean trade, for fundamental reasons, he was looking for a signal that told him to short the soybean futures contract. When he saw the long black candlestick on a particular day, he put on a short near the close of that day. He was quickly rewarded when another bearish day followed.

If things hadn't worked out as he'd planned, he still wouldn't have suffered big losses, because he also entered a protective order called a *buy stop*, which is the opposite of the sell stop mentioned earlier in this chapter. (See the earlier section "Taking a look at long white candles.") His buy stop level was the high of the long black candle — the resistance level that, if broken, would negate the sell signal given by the long black candle.

Resistance levels are where chartists believe that sellers will be brought into the market, keeping prices from going higher. In candlestick charting, resistance is generally the highest level of one of the candlesticks that created a sell signal. When this resistance level is broken, the signal is no longer considered to be valid.

Luckily, that level was never reached in Russell's trade, which turned out to be a profitable one. He continued to monitor the short position from day to day and exited on the day indicated on the chart. The pattern for that day was a regular doji, which often signals the reversal of a trend. (We cover regular dojis in detail in Chapter 6.)

Seeing a long black candle's failure as a short signal

Like long white candles (and all candlestick patterns, for that matter), long black candles don't always work out perfectly. Long black candles fail, as you can see in Figure 5-20. In fact, this figure includes two instances of long-black-candle failures!

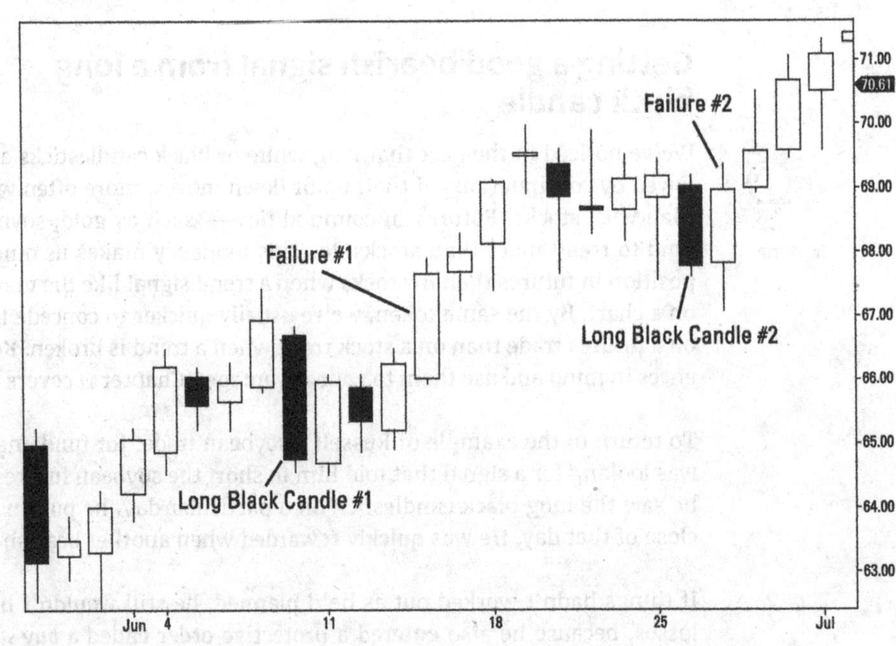

FIGURE 5-20: A long black candle as a failing sell signal.

Figure 5-20 shows a chart of the futures contract trading on crude oil from the summer of 2007. If you were involved with any oil or other energy-related commodity trading during that time, you'll remember that shorting was a hard row to hoe then.

Both long black candles in Figure 5-20 failed. One crashed and burned after a few days, and the other followed suit the next day. For clarity's sake, we've labeled them #1 and #2 in the figure:

>> Long black candle #1 was followed by an up day, but this up day didn't break resistance or the high of the signal candle. It managed to stay below resistance for a few days before breaking out and then trading higher for several days in a row. Note that if you didn't get out of a short position on the day that resistance was broken, you never had a shot to get out at that level again. Without a protective buy stop at the failure level, your losses would have continued to pile up.

>> Long black candle #2 didn't work out well, either, but at least it failed quickly. The possibility of a successful trade was clearly over at that point, and if you were involved, you could have moved on to the next trade. The trait that #2 shares with #1 is that if you didn't exit when the resistance level was violated, you didn't have a chance to get out at a lower level to limit your losses. Your losing trade would only have gotten worse. Getting out of trades quickly is just as important as finding and executing winning trades.

The Bearish Gravestone Doji

The doji is one of the most significant candlestick formations and is created when the open and close for a day are equal. It doesn't matter where the candle occurs on a wick for a candlestick to be classified as a doji, but the location dictates what kind of doji it is.

Identifying the gravestone doji

When the open and close are equal to the low of the day, the result is the most bearish of doji: the *gravestone doji*. Figure 5-21 is a good example of a bearish gravestone doji.

The price activity that creates a gravestone doji begins and ends at the low of a day. This step list shows the progression for the day:

1. A security opens and trades up during the day as the bulls dominate the activity.

2. Higher prices attract sellers, and the selling becomes strong enough to overwhelm the bulls.

3. As the bears take over, the price moves back down to the open, which was also the low of the day.

Closing at this level after trading up during a day doesn't bode well for the bulls in the near term. Figure 5-22 shows an example of such a day, which would be a fearful one for the bulls.

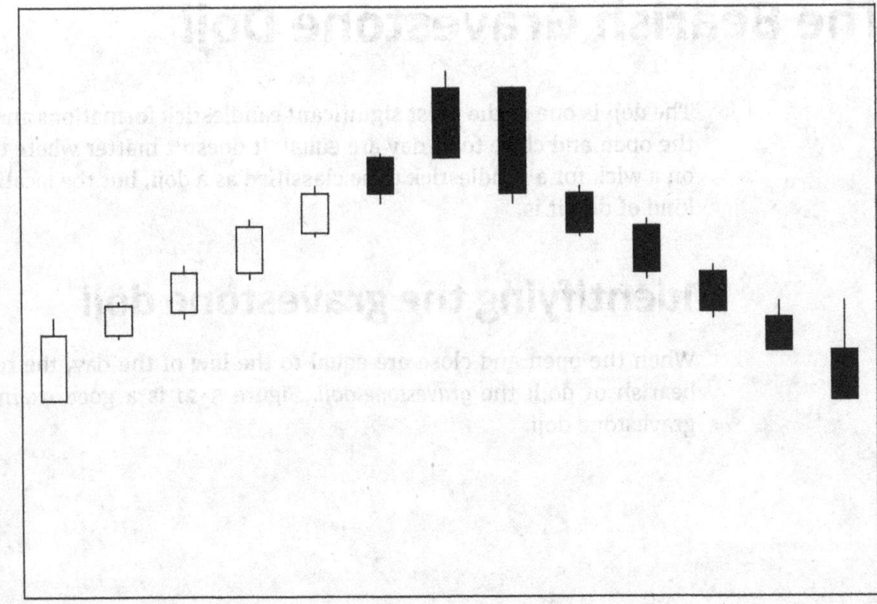

Trading based on gravestone dojis

This section describes a couple of gravestone dojis that popped up in the real world and what happened afterward. The two examples involve stocks, not commodities. The first example, which you can see clearly in Figure 5-23, is a gravestone doji that offered a useful sell signal followed by lower prices.

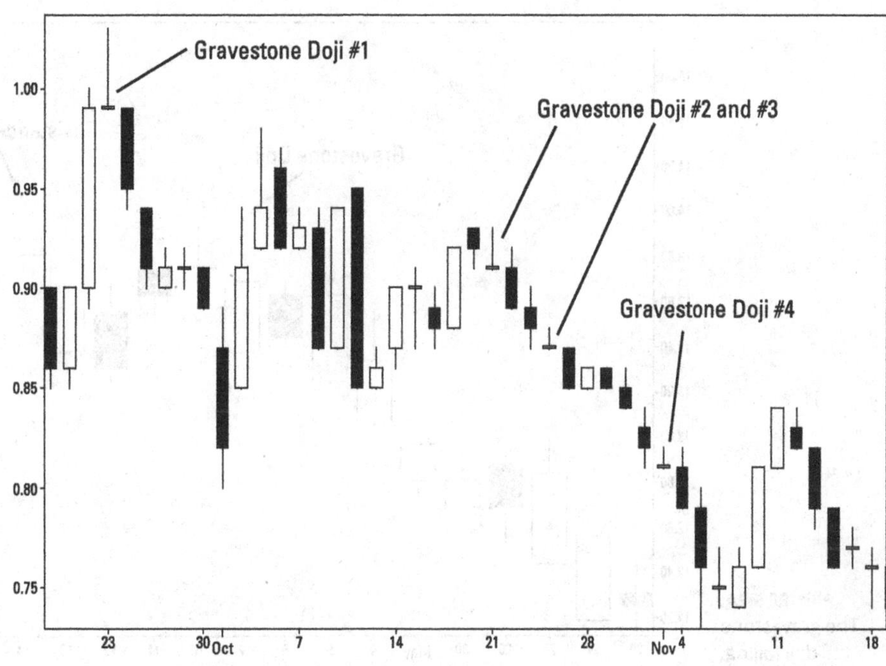

FIGURE 5-23: An excellent example of the gravestone doji working as a sell signal.

We included several days of price action in the figure to show a combination of interesting factors:

>> This gravestone doji signals the beginning of a prolonged downtrend in the stock.

>> During the downtrend, a couple of small gravestone dojis appear. If you'd shorted on the first gravestone doji and kept on the short position, you would have been pretty happy with the result. The appearance of a couple more bearish formations would have given you the confidence to maintain your short position.

>> A fourth gravestone doji appears toward the end of the downtrend. Notice that it fails fairly quickly, as the following day has a high equal to the original gravestone doji's high. If you'd ridden the stock price down to this level and seen a sell signal fail, it would have been time to buy the stock back, take your profit, and move on to the next trade — a profitable outcome for you.

The next example shows what can happen if you're not as fortunate. Figure 5-24 is a chart of Apple Computer (AAPL) stock. A gravestone doji appears in the middle of the chart and during an uptrend. Dojis are often associated with a trend change, and seeing the bearish doji in an uptrend may be a signal of a trend change to the downside. Unfortunately for anyone who was trading this sell signal, things didn't work out well.

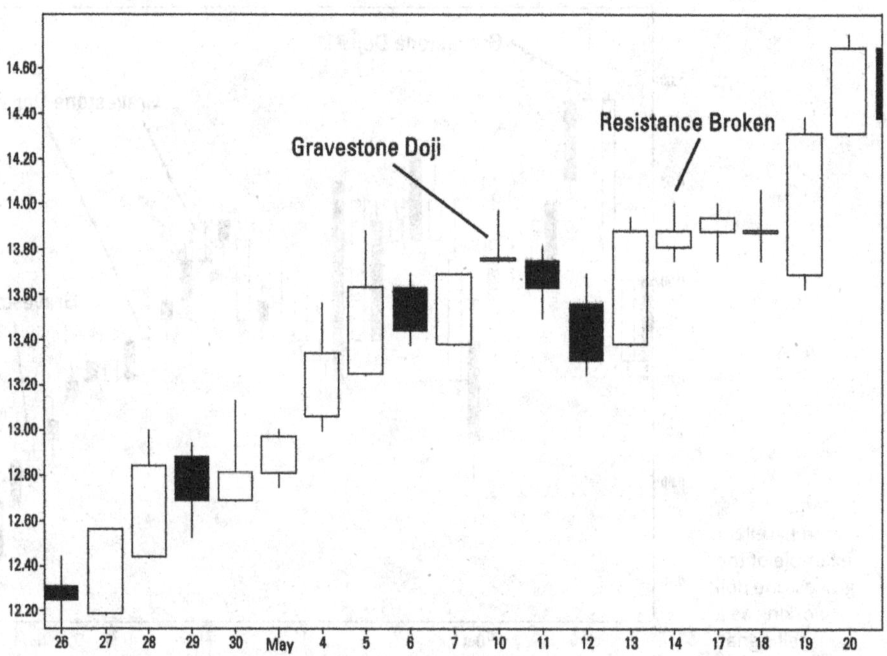

FIGURE 5-24: The gravestone doji failing.

The gravestone doji was followed by a couple of down days, and it did appear that the trend might have been changing. But a couple of positive days put this trend change in doubt. A couple of days later, resistance was tested and broken, and the uptrend continued. The sell signal failed, but a nimble trader would have placed a buy stop to limit the losses on this failure.

Chapter **6**

Single-Stick Patterns That Depend on Market Context

I n Chapter 5, we cover a few of the most basic, most easily defined single-stick candlestick patterns, ones that are either bullish or bearish indicators regardless of their location on a chart. For those patterns, the price action that occurs during the previous few days isn't too significant.

But not all single-stick patterns are straightforward. Some extremely useful single-stick patterns rely heavily on their location on a chart as much as the shape they form, because the signal depends on the trading activity that occurred before the single-stick pattern appears. Being familiar with these patterns and knowing how to identify and trade based on them adds a versatile weapon to your trading arsenal. That skill is what this chapter is about.

Context is essential to the single-stick patterns that are covered in this chapter. This isn't always the case, but for this chapter, you need to know the market environment before deciding whether a signal or pattern is valid.

REMEMBER

A variety of single-stick patterns can provide some terrific trading opportunities if you spot them in the right market environment. We begin this chapter by touching on how you can define a market environment; then we cover some of the most significant single-stick patterns you can exploit for profitable trading.

Sorting Out Market Environments

To take full advantage of single-stick patterns that rely heavily on the market context in which they appear, you need to know how to determine the market environment quickly and effectively. Being aware of the current market environment is the key to using most candlestick patterns properly, especially the ones we describe in this chapter.

Recognizing the three market states

A market or stock is usually defined as being in one of three states:

>> **Bullish:** Price behavior trending up

>> **Bearish:** Price behavior trending down

>> **Range-bound:** No discernable trend

REMEMBER

Deciding which of the three states a market is in can be as easy as looking back a few weeks or even a few days on a chart and spotting a general direction or drawing a line that shows the market's trend. Or the process may be as complicated as using a technical indicator to reveal the direction of the market. (These indicators are covered extensively in Chapter 11.) In the examples in this chapter, however, the market trends are easy to decipher.

Identifying the market trend

For a visual representation of what an uptrend or downtrend looks like on a chart, check out a few figures. Figure 6-1 shows an uptrend using the daily chart of Alphabet (GOOG) in 2025.

Figure 6-2 conversely shows a downtrend, using a daily chart of price action for Alphabet (GOOG) earlier in the year.

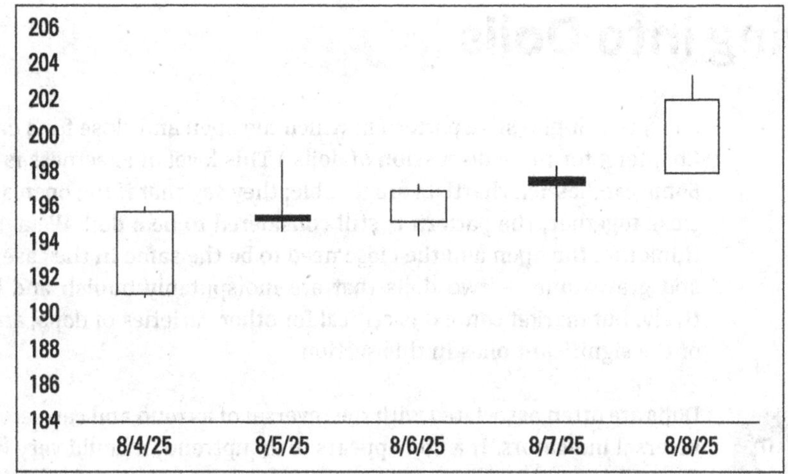

FIGURE 6-1:
A GOOG chart with a nice uptrend.

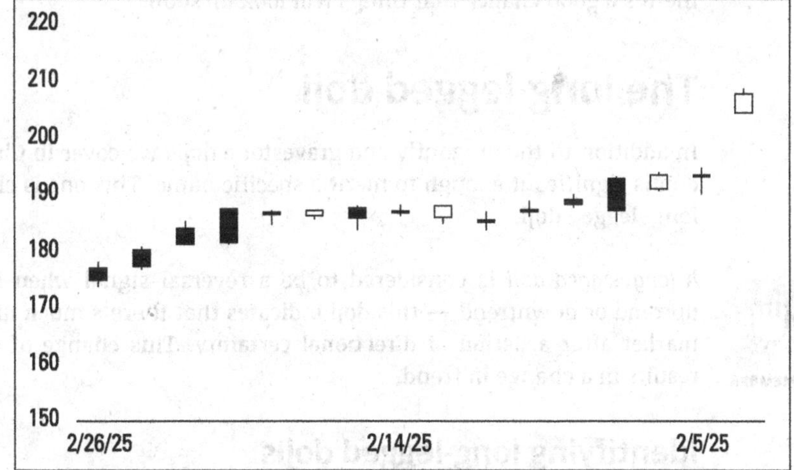

FIGURE 6-2:
A GOOG chart with a nice downtrend.

WARNING

At times, the market environment may not be apparent or obvious. People may see the trend (or lack of trend) in different ways, or the time frames that participants are using may cause traders to have differing views of the trend (or lack of trend). In such cases, pass on any trades you're considering. The uncertainty is too high, and you will always have another trading opportunity in the future.

Delving into Dojis

A *doji* is a single-stick pattern in which the open and close for a day are equal. (See Chapter 5 for more discussion of dojis.) This level of exactness is a rarity, though. Some candlestick chartists are flexible; they say that if the open and close are very close together, the pattern is still considered to be a doji. We agree, although we think that the open and the close need to be the same in the case of the dragonfly and gravestone — two dojis that are indisputably bullish and bearish, respectively. But market context is critical for other varieties of dojis, and we cover a few of the significant ones in this section.

REMEMBER

Dojis are often associated with the reversal of a trend and can serve as outstanding reversal indicators. If a doji appears in an uptrend, it could very well indicate that the trend may be changing to a downtrend, especially if the doji is a gravestone doji. Likewise, if a doji (especially a dragonfly doji) appears during a downtrend, there's a good chance that things will look up soon.

The long-legged doji

In addition to the dragonfly and gravestone dojis we cover in Chapter 5, one last doji is significant enough to merit a specific name. This one is cleverly called the long-legged doji.

REMEMBER

A *long-legged doji* is considered to be a reversal signal when it appears in an uptrend or downtrend — this doji indicates that there's much uncertainty in the market after a period of directional certainty. This change of conviction often results in a change in trend.

Identifying long-legged dojis

The long-legged doji has a fitting name: It features a small stick with a long wick (or leg) at each end. The small candle on a long-legged doji is normally located close to the center of the candlestick. Figure 6-3 shows a classic example of a long-legged doji.

In addition to its unique appearance, the long-legged doji is singled out due to the unusual price action that causes the formation of this candlestick pattern on a daily chart. Figure 6-4 provides a look at a 30-minute chart that translates into a long-legged doji.

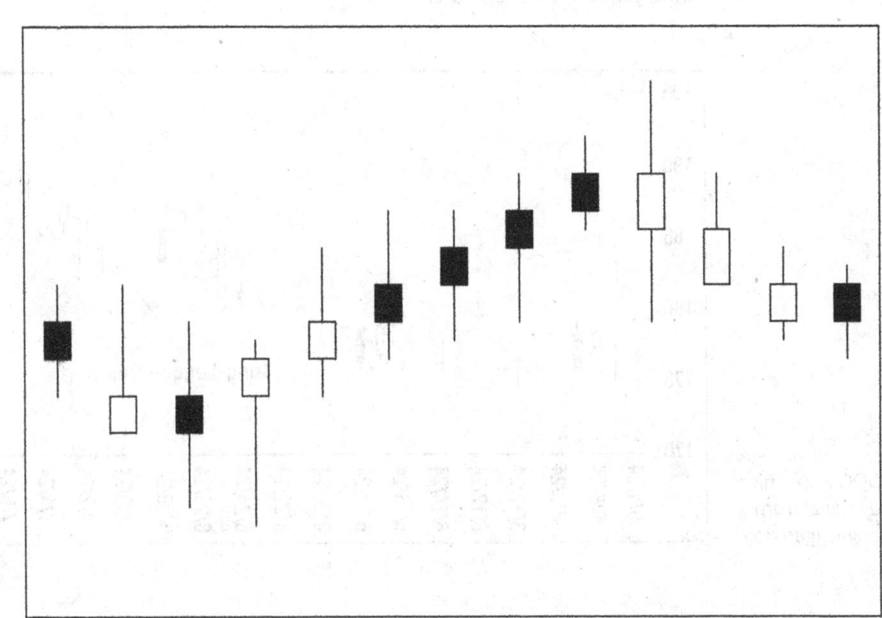

FIGURE 6-3:
A long-
legged doji.

FIGURE 6-4:
A 30-minute chart
that creates a
long-legged doji
in a daily chart.

Figure 6-4 looks like a roller-coaster ride. Imagine trying to trade during a day like that and ending up where you started. You can really lose (or win) big on such a day because the long-legged doji represents a possible reversed trend. Time will tell whether the signal is valid.

If you've just started trading or don't feel quite comfortable with your trading abilities yet, it's probably best to steer clear of day trading on extremely volatile days. We've been trading for years, and we've taught ourselves to lay off the day trading when things are particularly hairy.

Using long-legged dojis as buy signals

As we mention earlier in this section, the long-legged doji may be a buy or sell signal depending on previous price action. In a downtrend, the signal can forecast a change to an uptrend and act as a buy signal; in an uptrend, the long-legged doji can indicate that the uptrend is coming to an end and serve as a sell signal. The following sections provide a couple of examples.

The long-legged doji giving a good buy signal

Figure 6-5 shows a long-legged doji on a daily GOOG chart. The trend reversed, and the following five days resulted in bullish price action. This example shows how a long-legged doji works when it signals the end of a down move. Unfortunately, we didn't trade this particular scenario, but we definitely will if we see the same pattern in the future!

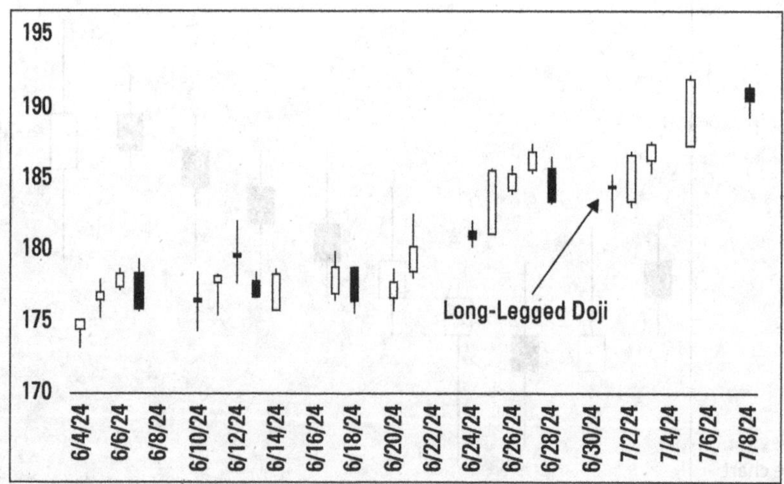

FIGURE 6-5: GOOG with a nice buy signal from a long-legged doji.

Notice that the doji buy signal in Figure 6-5 works almost immediately — which is what's to be expected of a trend changing signal. If the signal doesn't seem to be working quickly, beware.

Trading against a trend is a dangerous prospect. You need to be prepared to take a loss and move quickly to the next trade if things go sour.

A failing long-legged doji

This section discusses a bullish long-legged doji that didn't work well. In all honesty, it was difficult to find a good real-world example. The long-legged doji is fairly rare, and when it shows up during a trend, it usually signals an impending trend change. But Figure 6-6 shows a long-legged doji that didn't signal a change in trend.

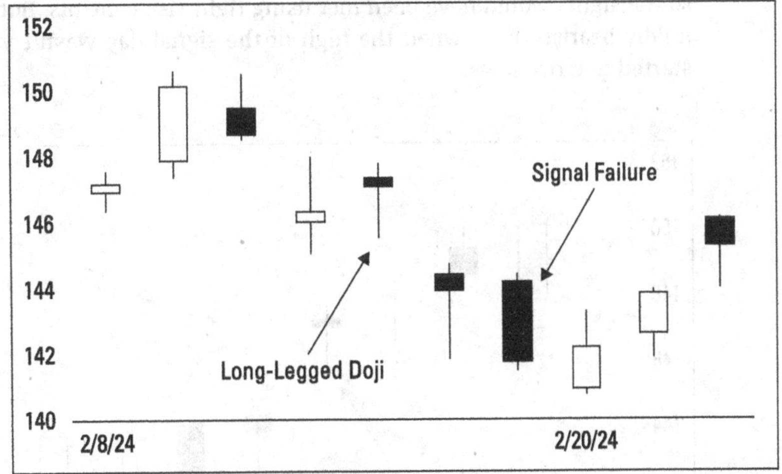

FIGURE 6-6:
A long-legged doji buy signal in Alphabet that failed quickly.

Figure 6-6 features price action for Alphabet. The price trends up for the next day or two, and things look fine, but then the long-legged doji's low is broken, and the signal is no longer valid. If you were trading this signal and didn't get out at that critical point, where you should have placed a stop order or executed an exit trade, you would have endured some painful losses.

Be sure that you're prepared to get out of a trade immediately when the signal you're trading goes bad. Follow that rule regardless of how much it hurts. To remember the importance of the rule, Larissa taped the following quote from *Zen in the Markets,* by Edward A. Toppel (Grand Central), to the monitor on her trading desk: "You can break the rules and get away with it. Eventually the rules break you for not respecting them."

Using long-legged dojis as sell signals

Just as a long-legged doji that appears during a downtrend can be considered to be a buy signal or the end of the downtrend, a long-legged doji that appears in an uptrend may be considered to be an uptrend reversal or sell signal — extremely helpful if you're looking to short a security.

REMEMBER

Sometimes, no trend is obvious, or no trend exists. If you see a long-legged doji during one of these times, do nothing. The long-legged doji is useful as a signal only when it appears during a trend.

Seeing a good short signal on the long-legged doji

Figure 6-7 shows a long-legged doji that provides a useful signal for selling short. Again, the stock is Alphabet, and the chart is a daily chart. The long-legged doji appears in the middle of an uptrend. This doji followed two strong uptrend days, so the signal would have been met using tight risk controls. But after a couple of mildly bearish days, when the high of the signal day wasn't violated, Alphabet started to move lower.

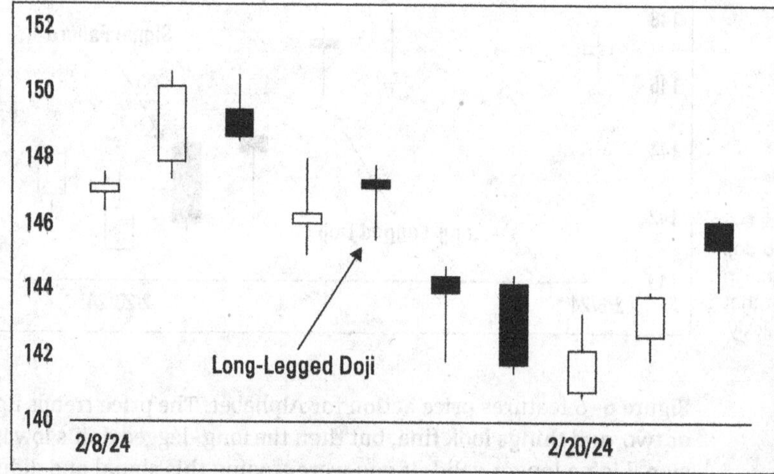

FIGURE 6-7:
A long-legged doji sell signal on Alphabet that worked out quite well.

The long-legged doji sells signal failing

As always, an example that didn't work is in order. Figure 6-8 shows how prices can quickly fluctuate. In the center of the chart is a nice long-legged doji that appears in an uptrend and may seem to be rolling over. (*Rolling over* means that the price action on a chart has been strong but is starting to top out.) Toward the right side of this rolling price action, a long-legged doji appears. Things look good for a while. Then the high of the doji is overtaken a few days later and the price is off to the races yet again.

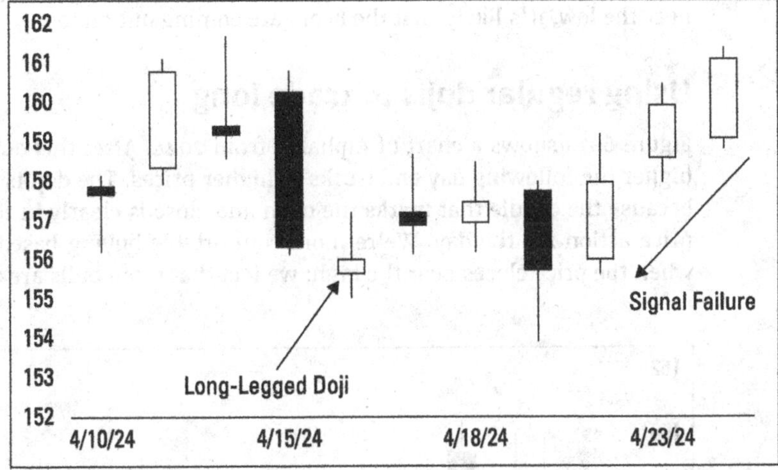

FIGURE 6-8: A long-legged doji sell signal on Bitcoin futures that failed.

Other dojis

The long-legged doji, bullish dragonfly doji, and gravestone dojis are powerful but rare. You're more likely to see a doji with an open and close that appear somewhere other than the center or one of the ends of a wick. These dojis are useful as reversal indicators when a trend is in place and, because they appear more often than the named dojis, they offer more trading opportunities. Figure 6-9 shows a variety of dojis, all of which look like Ts or upside-down Ts.

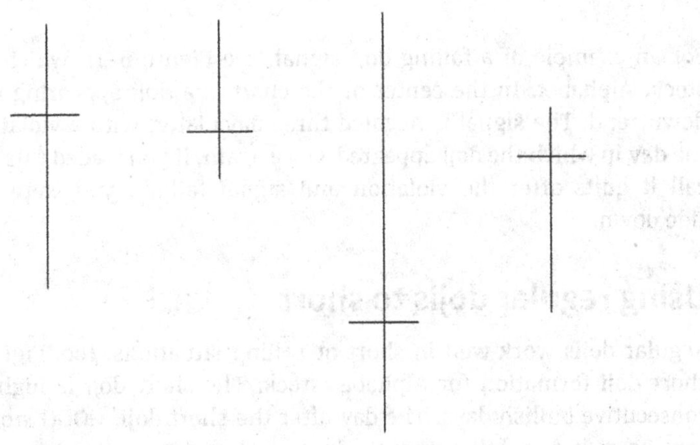

FIGURE 6-9: A variety of dojis.

When evaluating a doji, you should look for the candle to appear on the top half of the wick if you're using the doji as a buy signal or on the bottom half of the wick if you're using it as a sell signal. When the open and close are near the high, you should assume that the bulls are winning the day, and if the open and close are near the low, it's likely that the bears are coming out on top.

Using regular dojis to trade long

Figure 6-10 shows a chart of Alphabet from 2024. After this doji, the stock gaps higher the following day and works to higher prices. The doji is a useful example because the candle that marks the open and close is clearly in the top half of the price action for the day. We're more comfortable buying based on a doji signal when the price closes near the high; we feel that more bulls are on our side.

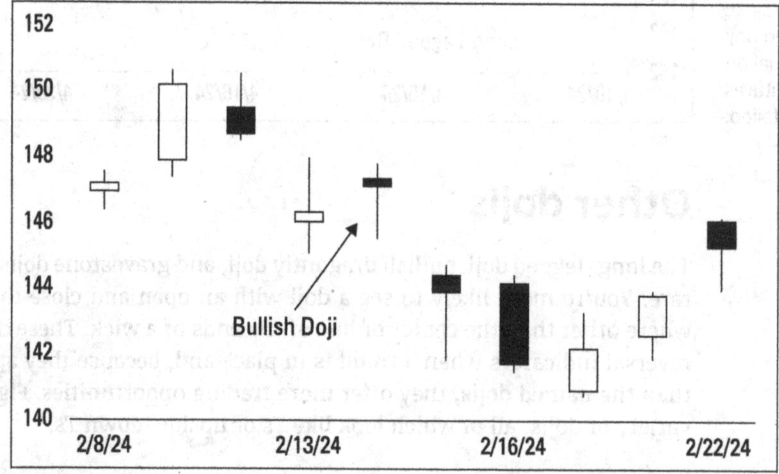

FIGURE 6-10: A regular long doji, appearing in a chart of GOOG stock.

For an example of a failing doji signal, see Figure 6-11, which shows the same stock, Alphabet. In the center of the chart is a doji appearing during a definite downtrend. The signal is negated three days later, with a violation of the low of the day in which the doji appeared. Once again, if you traded this signal and didn't call it quits after the violation and signal failure, you were in for a painful ride down.

Using regular dojis to short

Regular dojis work well in short or selling situations, too. Figure 6-12 shows a short doji formation for Alphabet stock. The short doji is highlighted after six consecutive bullish days. The day after the short doji, GOOG stock experienced a very bearish day, followed by a drop of almost 20 percent from the signal day, which is a very large drop.

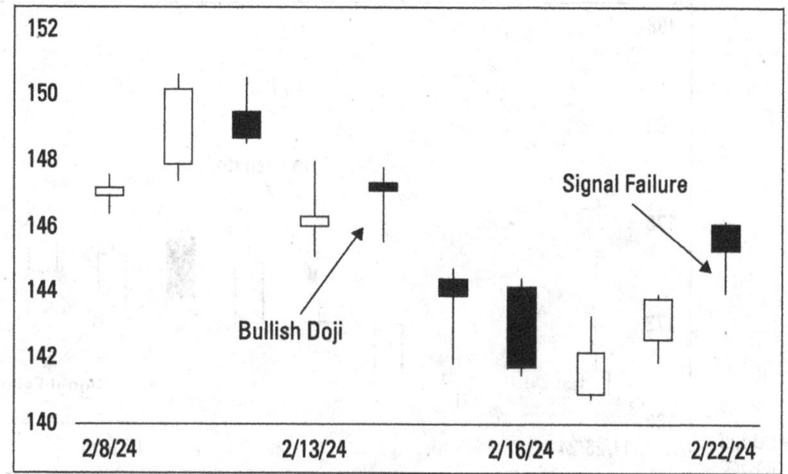

FIGURE 6-11: A regular long doji, appearing (and failing) in a chart of GOOG stock.

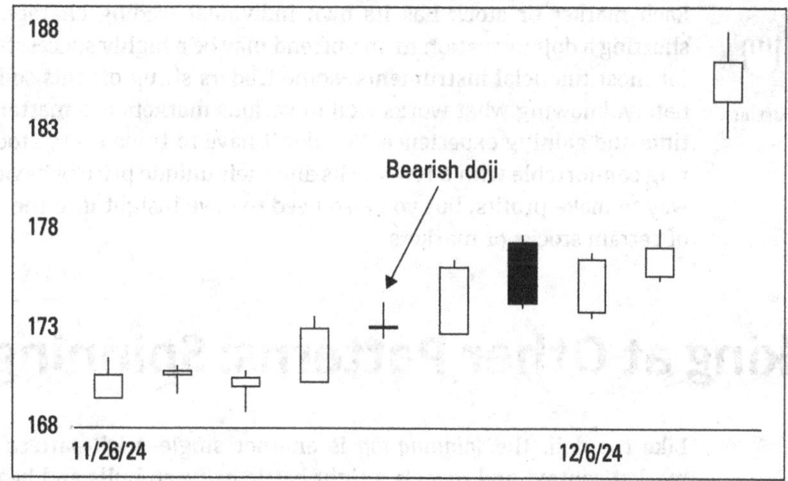

FIGURE 6-12: A short doji in a chart of GOOG stock.

The signal doji in Figure 6-12 meets the buying criterion of appearing in an uptrend and also appears to have the open and close near the bottom half of the day's price action. No violation negates the signal, and the signal is quickly followed by a downtrend lasting several days. (Don't you wish that all your trades were so easy to identify and profit from?)

Like all other signals, short dojis aren't perfect. Take a look at Figure 6-13, a chart of the same stock. This figure shows a bearish doji signal following a very strong uptrend. The single is followed by a bearish day, but then the uptrend resumes. Five trading days later, the signal is no good, and any short trade should be abandoned.

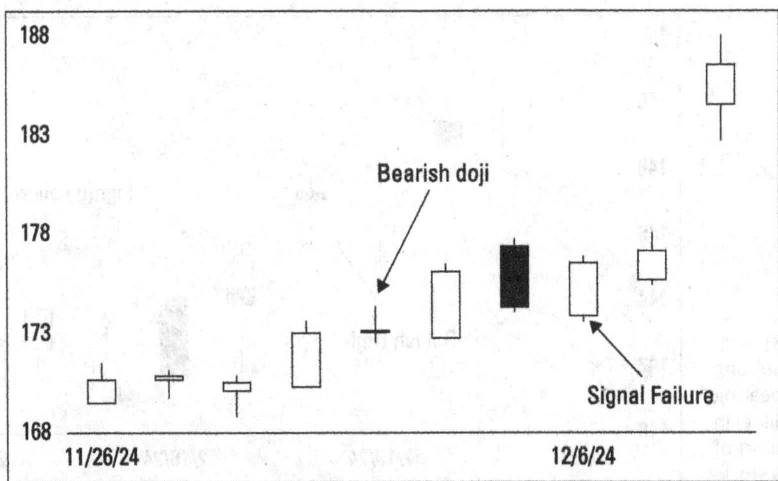

Each market or stock has its own individual trading characteristics. Although shorting a doji formation in an uptrend may be a highly successful trading method for most financial instruments, some traders shrug off this sell signal. Unfortunately, knowing what works well in various markets is a matter of putting in the time and gaining experience. You don't have to trade every stock out there. Getting comfortable with a few stocks and their unique price behaviors is an excellent way to make profits, but you also need to have insight into the specific behaviors of certain stocks or markets.

Looking at Other Patterns: Spinning Tops

Like the doji, the *spinning top* is another single-stick pattern that depends on market context and reveals a tight battle between bulls and bears. Whenever the bulls-versus-bears battle is close, eventually one side has to give, and when this happens, an explosive move in one direction is possible. Our favorite analogy for that scenario is a coiled spring being pushed hard on both sides. Eventually one side gives in, and that's the direction in which the spring flies. On the high side of the spring are sellers, and on the low side are buyers. If the sellers start to get out of the way of the buyers, the spring moves to the up side. Conversely, if the buyers get out of the way, the sellers win, and prices move lower.

The key is picking the right direction or determining the market environment in which you can find a pattern that helps you make the right pick. For spinning tops or any other patterns that indicate a tight battle between bulls and bears, if the bulls have been in charge for some time leading up to the pattern, the pattern usually indicates that the bears are starting to gain some strength. The reverse is also true: If the pattern appears during a bearish trend, it generally indicates that the bulls will make a run (and you don't have to be in Pamplona to run with them).

Identifying spinning tops

To qualify as a spinning top, a candlestick should have a small body and wicks that stick out on both ends. The body should appear close to the center of the range of the day's price action. Also, both the wicks should be at least as wide as the candle section of the candlestick. For a clear picture of what a spinning top looks like, check out Figure 6-14.

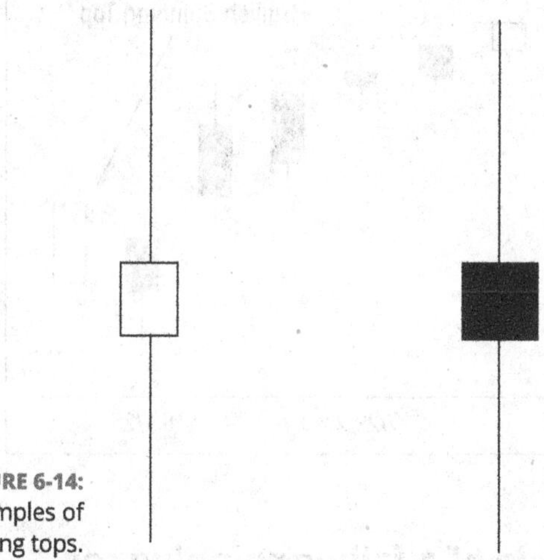

FIGURE 6-14: Examples of spinning tops.

The color of a spinning top's candle isn't terribly important, although it's nice to see a dark body if you're expecting a reversal of an uptrend (sell signal) or a white body if you're expecting a reversal of a downtrend (buy signal).

One advantage of spinning tops compared with dojis is that spinning tops appear much more frequently. Dojis are powerful signals, but they can be rare. We scanned many charts to come up with the examples for this book, and it was much, much easier to find good examples of spinning tops than it was to track down dojis — and with more appearances come more chances to trade and make profits!

Using spinning tops for profitable trading

Like dojis, spinning tops are nice indicators that a trend may be about to change direction. Catching an early trend change can be quite a profitable endeavor. In the following sections, we give you an idea of how you can execute some fruitful trades by using spinning tops.

Recognizing a buy signal with a spinning top

Figure 6-15 is a chart of Air Products stock. The low of a downtrend culminates with a spinning top, and a trader who recognizes this signal is rewarded with a nice up move. The following day is a choppy but solid uptrend.

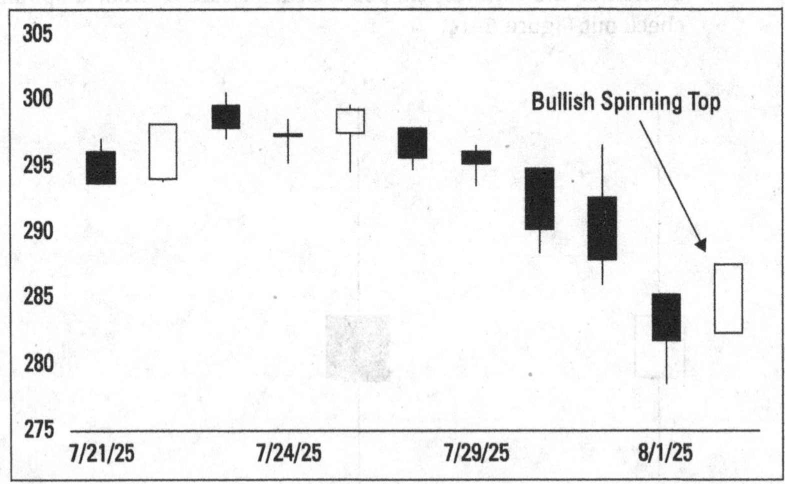

FIGURE 6-15:
A long spinning top in a chart of APD stock.

Looking at an example of a failing spinning top

On the flip side, take a look at Figure 6-16, which is a chart of the Air Products stock. We've highlighted a spinning top that appears after a break in trading that formed a gap and resumed at a lower price level. The next few days are pretty encouraging, but the uptrend doesn't gain much steam, and a resumed downtrend is confirmed a few days later.

Getting a nice short signal from a spinning top

Spinning tops may also be used quite effectively to recognize a shift from an uptrend to a downtrend. Figure 6-17 holds yet another chart showing the price action for Air Products stock. A spinning top appears just as an uptrend is rolling over, which is a favorite situation of ours. The next day's price action is a big gap lower, confirming the reversal signal. The result is a downtrend that lasts almost a month.

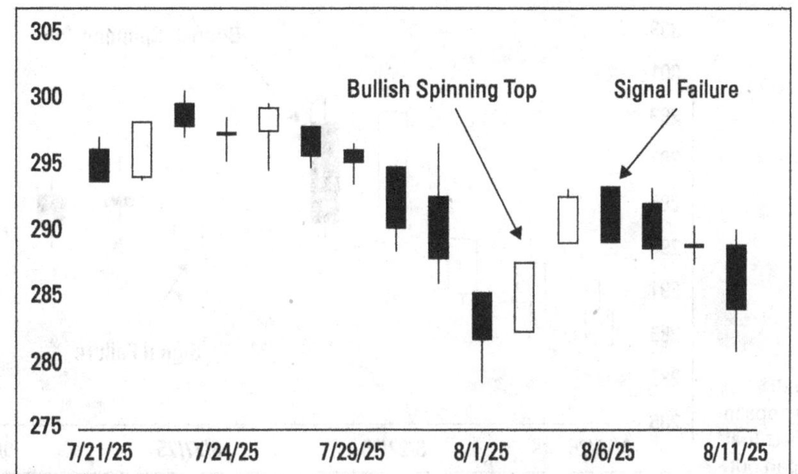

FIGURE 6-16: A long spinning top in the APD stock that failed.

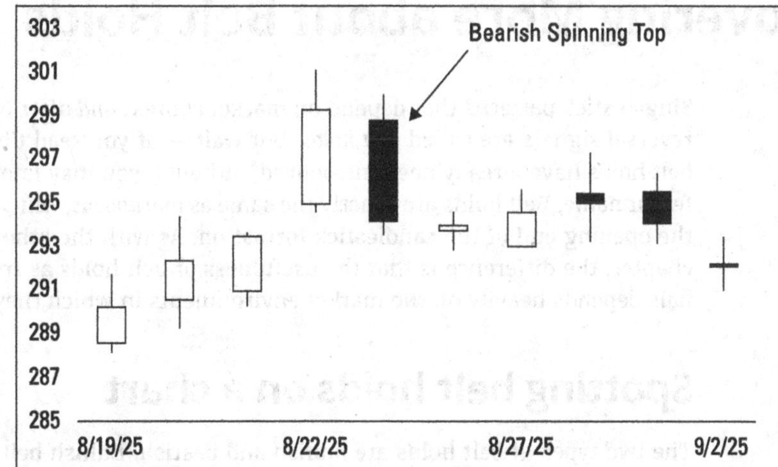

FIGURE 6-17: A short spinning top in a chart of APD stock.

Seeing a failing spinning top short

Figure 6-18 shows a chart in which spinning tops keep failing. This chart is of APD stock, and the bearish reversal signal occurs after three strong market days. The following day, APD closes lower, but the intraday price action was bullish, as indicated by the white candle body. Each day, GOOG shares move a bit higher, and the signal fails four days later.

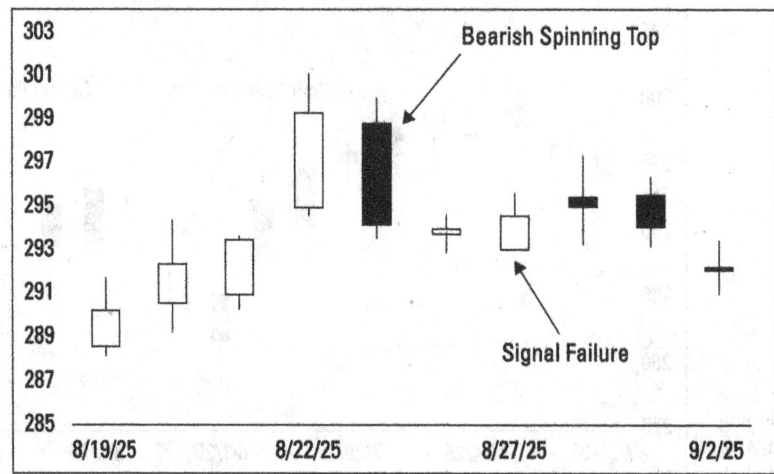

FIGURE 6-18: Spinning tops in an APD chart that didn't pan out.

Discovering More about Belt Holds

Single-stick patterns that depend on market context *and* offer outstanding trend reversal signals are called *belt holds.* But wait — if you read Chapter 5, you and belt holds have already been introduced, although you may know them by a different name. Belt holds are exactly the same as *marubozus,* which have no wick on the opening end of the candlestick formation. As with the other patterns in this chapter, the difference is that the usefulness of belt holds as trend reversal signals depends heavily on the market environments in which they appear.

Spotting belt holds on a chart

The two types of belt holds are bullish and bearish. Bullish belt holds feature an open equal to the low and a close near the high, which leaves a small wick on the top of the candle. Bullish belt holds appear during downtrends. For an ideal example of a bullish (long) belt hold, take a peek at Figure 6-19.

Bearish belt holds, on the other hand, open on their highs and close near their lows, leaving a small wick on the bottom of the candle. Bearish belt holds show up in the midst of uptrends. You can find a picture-perfect version of a bearish (short) belt hold in Figure 6-20.

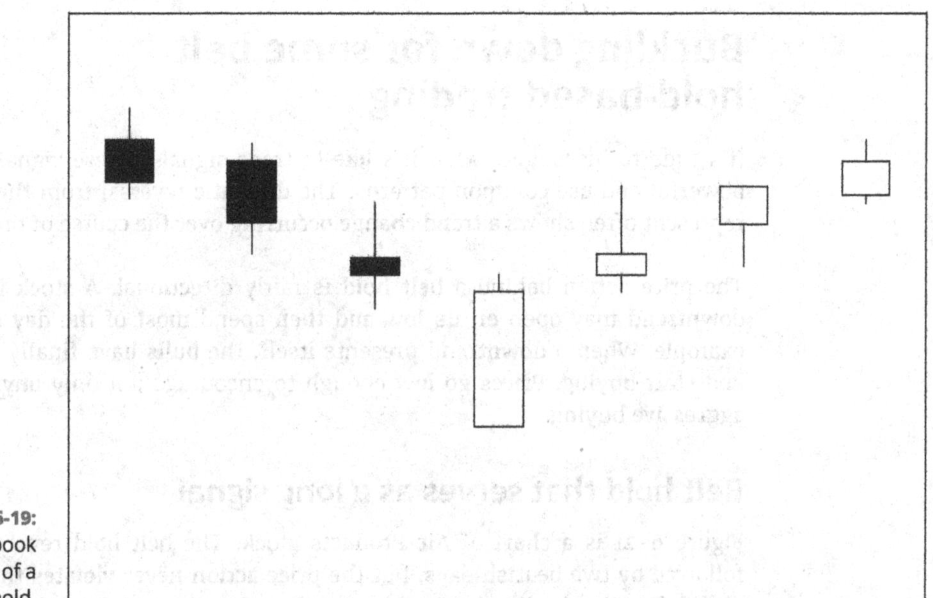

FIGURE 6-19:
Textbook
example of a
long belt hold.

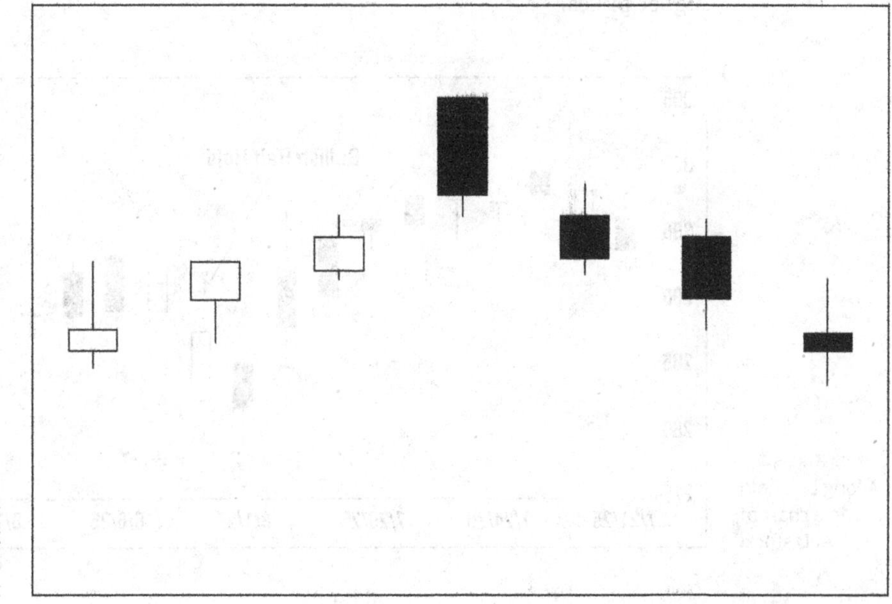

FIGURE 6-20:
Textbook
example of a
short belt hold.

Buckling down for some belt hold-based trading

It's time to investigate what it's like to trade signals. These signals are pretty powerful and use common patterns. The dramatic reversal from the opens they represent often shows a trend change occurring over the course of one day.

The price action behind a belt hold is fairly directional. A stock in a defined downtrend may open on its low and then spend most of the day rallying, for example. When a downtrend presents itself, the bulls have finally had enough and start buying. Prices go low enough to encourage not only buying but also aggressive buying.

Belt hold that serves as a long signal

Figure 6-21 is a chart of Air Products stock. The belt hold reversal signal is followed by two bearish days, but the price action never violates the low of the signal day. Eventually, the stock starts to work its way higher. This signal probably tested some traders' patience, but those who held on were rewarded with higher prices.

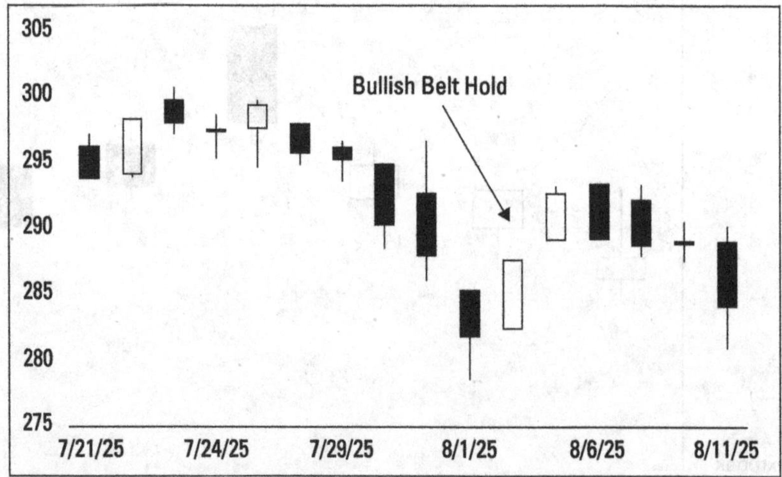

FIGURE 6-21: A long belt hold in a chart of APD stock.

Two factors contribute to the strength of this long belt hold:

>> **The sheer length of the candlestick:** Very aggressive buying is exhibited by the size of the candle and overall candlestick.

Belt hold that fails on the long side

Want to know what happens when bullish belt holds go bad? Look at Figure 6-22, which shows a chart of APD stock. The bullish belt hold comes on the heels of some bearish trading that occurred over the course of a few days. This signal is attractive because the low of the previous day wasn't tested and shares closed near the high of the day. After a few days of trendless price action, however, the signal failed.

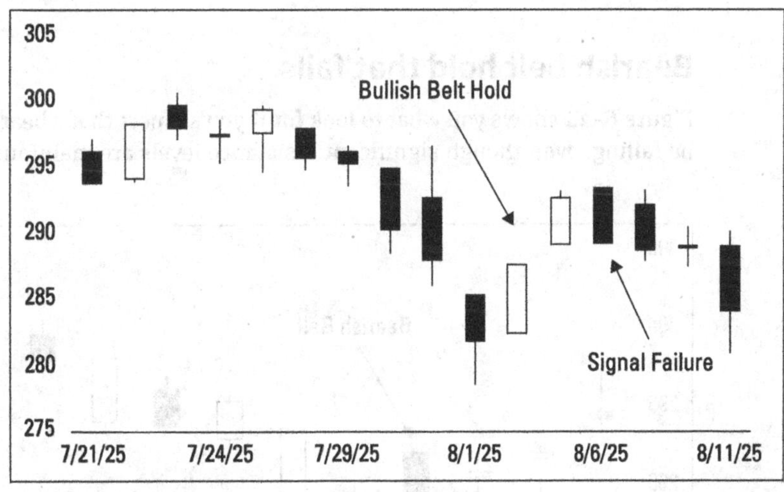

FIGURE 6-22: A failing bullish (long) belt hold in a chart of APD stock.

Bearish belt hold signals occur during an obvious uptrend, with a day that opens on its high and closes very near its low. This signal appears as a dark candle with a small part of the wick appearing at the bottom. It's a day when the bears rule after being pushed around by the bulls for several days.

Bearish belt hold that works out

For a nice bearish belt hold scenario, look at Figure 6-23, which turns back to shares of Air Products (APD). Before the signal, APD shares were in a moderate uptrend, with mixed trading each day. The day after the signal, however, the shares experienced a significant price drop, moving about 10 percent lower over a couple of weeks.

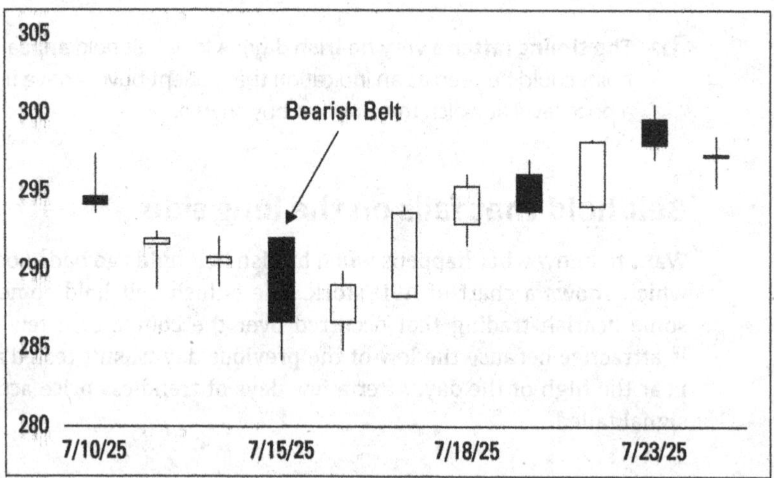

FIGURE 6-23:
A nice short belt hold signal in a chart of APD stock.

Bearish belt hold that fails

Figure 6-24 shows you what to look for if you suspect that a bearish belt hold may be failing, even though significant resistance levels are maintained.

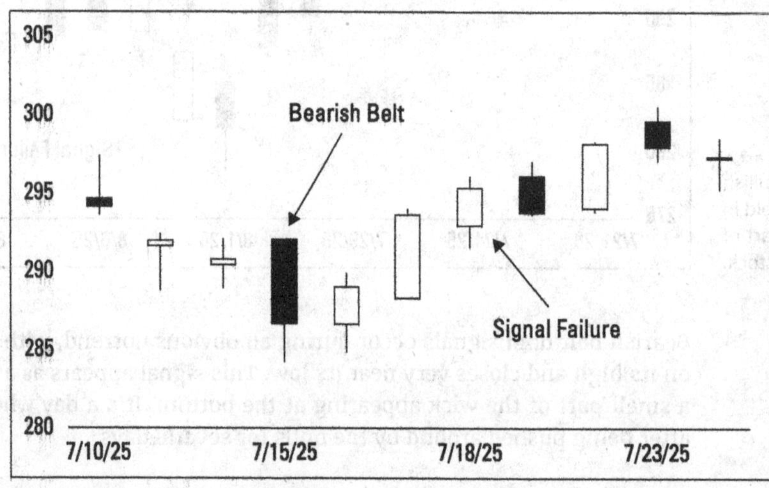

FIGURE 6-24:
A bearish belt hold in the APD chart.

The figure shows a nice bearish belt hold pattern, but it just doesn't work out. Rather than violate a significant price level, this chart puts up price action in a nontrending manner. If a signal isn't confirmed in short order, the signal may not be valid.

Sometimes signals take a few days to fail, so stay on your toes and watch for signs of trouble. Complacent price behavior may lull you into believing that the signal is still valid, but after a few days, it may be time to reassess.

Deciphering the Hanging Man and the Hammer

Two other single-stick patterns that rely on a specific market environment are the hanging man and the hammer. We paired them in this section because they have a similar appearance. Don't be fooled, though: The two patterns aren't identical. The hanging man is considered to be bearish, and the hammer is considered to be bullish. The difference is where they appear in a chart.

Spotting the hanging man and the hammer

The first step in working with the hanging man and the hammer is recognizing how to spot them. The patterns are fairly distinctive, so identifying them usually isn't a problem.

The hammer and the hanging man are represented by a small candle that appears at the top or the bottom of a pattern. Usually, the bottom of the candle has a fairly long wick. If you see this pattern at the bottom of a downtrend, you're looking at a hammer; if it appears at the top of an uptrend, it's considered to be a hanging man. (The patterns are good signals, of course.) In less-than-ideal cases, it's possible for a small wick to stick out of the top of the candle. For a classic example, see Figure 6-25.

Although the hammer and the hanging man are individual patterns, they have one extra step: the confirmation of the pattern. The confirmation comes on the following day's opening price. If the opening price on the next day is in the direction of the signal, you're working with a true hammer or a true hanging man. If you think that you have a hanging man appearing in an uptrend, you wouldn't trade on it unless it's confirmed the next day by an opening price lower than the previous close. By the same token, if a hammer appears during a downtrend, you need to confirm it with an opening price on the next day that's higher than the hammer's close.

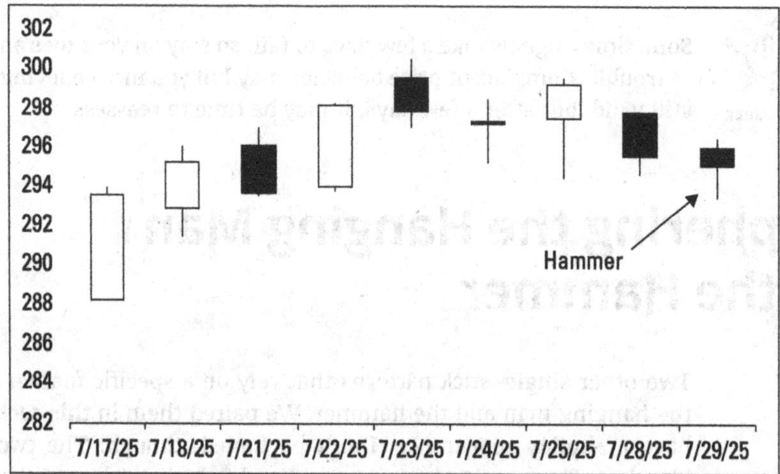

FIGURE 6-25:
A hammer or hanging man, depending on the market context.

Trading on the hanging man and the hammer

To better illustrate the intricacies of the hanging man and the hammer, this section shows examples of both patterns that were confirmed the next day — or not. (If you're planning to dig into later chapters and read more about complex patterns, get used to the idea of confirming patterns, because it pops up continually throughout the rest of the book.)

Going long with a hammer pattern

Figure 6-26 is a chart of Air Products with a hammer that pops up during a downtrend. The following day, the stock trades higher — confirmation that the hammer is a good long signal and that you'd be wise to wait for it before buying. Be patient and wait for the confirmation, even if you're convinced that it's hammer time!

The confirmation may cost you a little in profits because you pay a slightly higher price, but Figure 6-27 shows what not waiting for confirmation might cost you.

Figure 6-27 is also a chart of APD. This chart contains a potential buy hammer that isn't confirmed on the next day. In fact, the opening the next day is lower than the high on the day when the hammer appeared. You'd have saved yourself the effort of trading in and out of this stock by waiting for confirmation, and you'd also have saved some losses.

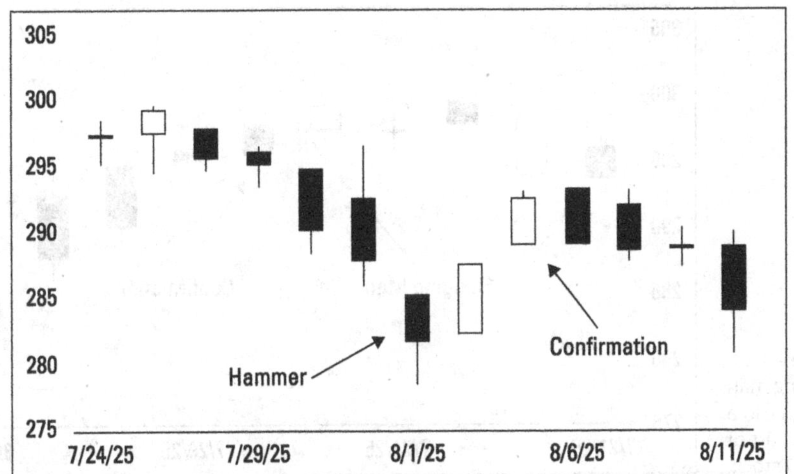

FIGURE 6-26: A hammer with confirmation in a chart of APD stock.

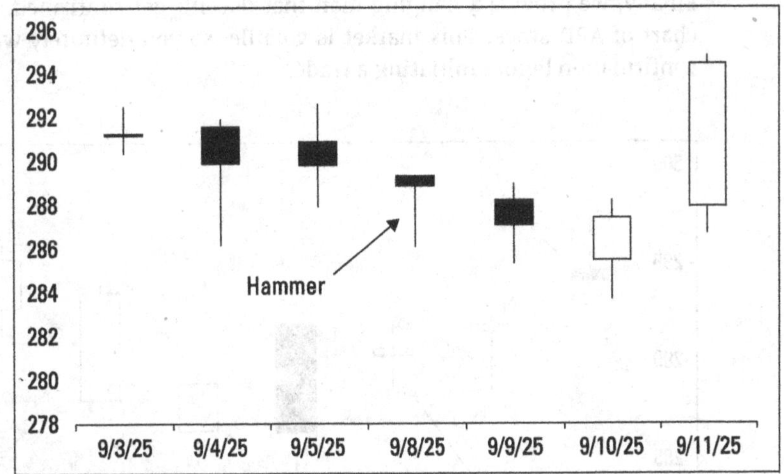

FIGURE 6-27: A hammer with no confirmation in a chart of APD stock.

REMEMBER

If a candlestick signal calls for some sort of confirmation, always wait for the confirmation. Don't try to get ahead of confirmation day by trading in early. In the long run, early trading catches up with you.

Shorting with a hanging man pattern

Now take a look at a successful hanging man. Figure 6-28 is a chart of APD stock. The hanging man signal is fairly obvious but, as with the hammer, confirmation is a helpful sign when you're trading this pattern. The following day is a down day, and the high of the hammer day is never violated, offering a confirmation of the bearish signal.

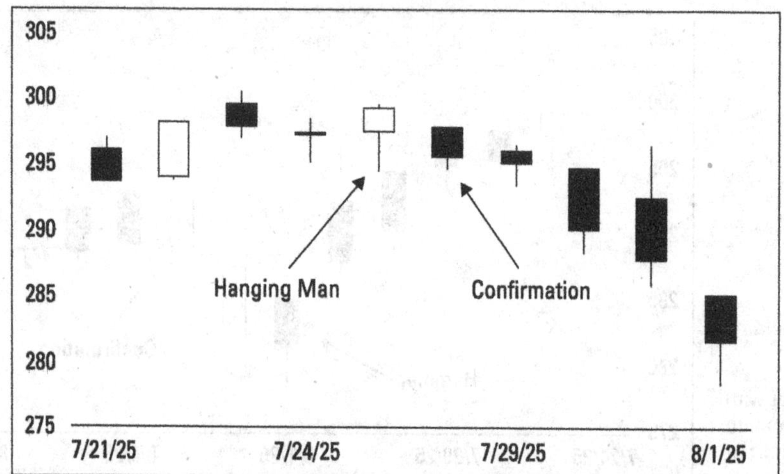

FIGURE 6-28:
A hanging man short signal in a chart of APD stock.

Finally, we provide a hanging man that doesn't get confirmed. Figure 6-29 is a chart of APD stock. This market is volatile, so you definitely want to see signal confirmation before initiating a trade.

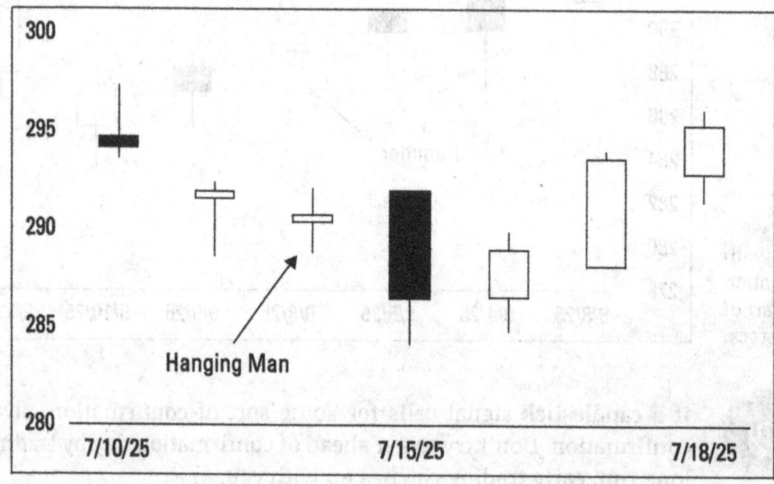

FIGURE 6-29:
A failing hanging man short signal on APD stock.

An encouraging hanging man appears in the chart in a flattening uptrend. After waiting patiently overnight for confirmation of the end of the uptrend and a shorting opportunity, however, a trader is surprised to see a gap opening and a continuation of the uptrend. Even if the trader is following the rules and waiting for the confirmation of the hanging man, disappointment is the result. But something could be worse: Had the trader jumped the gun and sold, that move would have cost them even more.

Chapter **7**

Working with Bullish Double-Stick Patterns

ompared with the single-stick patterns we discuss in Chapters 5 and 6, double-stick patterns are difficult to come by. But these patterns can be quite powerful and profitable if you put in the time and effort to monitor them.

We tackle several double-stick patterns in this chapter, each of them consisting of two days. We refer to the first day as the *setup day*, and we call the second day the *signal day*. When you're looking for double-stick patterns, you'll have to start paying attention to the possibility that a pattern will develop on the setup day, and you'll react (trade) if you see what you need to see on the signal day.

In this chapter, some of the double-stick patterns we cover signal a trend reversal, and a few signal a trend continuation. The reversal signals are more fun because they help you outsmart the crowd and buy near the end of a trend. The trend-confirming signals are useful if you're already on the right side of a trend or if you're considering going against a trend and looking for a signal that can kindly tell you to reconsider.

If you want to go hunting for double-stick patterns, we must warn you that you're bound to suffer some disappointments. Often, you see the beginnings of a double-stick pattern on the first day, but you can get discouraged when the pattern doesn't shape up correctly on the second day. Your patience may be tested, and you may want to give up and work with only single-stick patterns, but doing so is like playing a game without all the equipment you need to play it well.

Bullish Reversal Patterns

Various two-day patterns signal the end of a downtrend and the beginning of an uptrend; those patterns are the focus of this section. There's an old saying in trading: "The trend is your friend." This saying is based on the idea that getting (and staying) on the right side of the trend is the best way to make a profit in the market. We don't disagree with that sentiment, but plenty of traders make a good living catching changes in trend. This type of trading, which involves trying to pick the top or bottom of a trending move, isn't the easiest, but it can be rewarding. Just keep in mind that, because it involves going against the current type of market and against the majority of participants, the process is a difficult one.

If your trading strategy depends on catching trend changes, make sure you're humble and quick to acknowledge when you're wrong about a trade. Use orders that force you to take a small loss before you rack up big losses.

Throughout this section, we include patterns that work and ones that fail, and we point out where a trade starts to go wrong. In these examples, you can see how bad a trade can get if you don't play it safe and take a small loss to prevent losing big.

Bullish engulfing pattern

The first double-stick pattern is the *bullish engulfing pattern*. The pattern's name comes from the fact that the signal day engulfs the setup day. Both the wick and the body of the second day completely cover the same ground as the first day and then some. Also, the first day of this bullish pattern is a down day, and the second day starts out looking like a day of more bearish trading, but this selling is reversed by the emergence of buying — so much buying that both the previous day's open and highs are surpassed. (The bearish version of this pattern is covered in Chapter 8. In fact, most of the bullish double-stick patterns we discuss in this chapter have bearish counterparts.)

Spotting the bullish engulfing pattern

To find the bullish engulfing pattern, take these steps:

1. **Look for a setup day with a dark candle.**

2. **See whether the signal day is bullish.**

   If so, you're on the right track, but the following statements must also be true for your pattern to be a full-fledged bullish engulfing pattern:

   - The wick of the signal day is longer than the wick of the setup day.

   - The high of the signal day is higher than the high of the setup day.

   - The low of the signal day is lower than the low of the setup day.

   - The candle of the signal day is longer than the candle of the setup day. (In this case, the signal day's close is higher than the setup day's open, and the open of the signal day is lower than the close of the setup day.)

Figure 7-1 includes two days that create a bullish engulfing pattern.

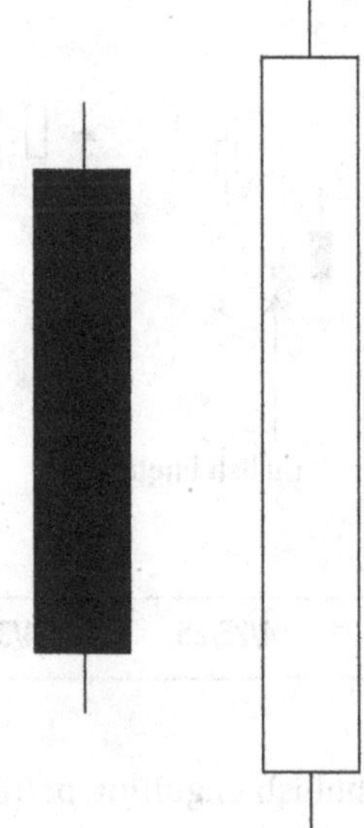

FIGURE 7-1:
A bullish
engulfing pattern.

The trading activity that creates this pattern is extremely bullish:

>> **Day 1:** On the first day (the setup day), the bears dominate.

   The open is near the high, and the bears push the price down all day until the close ends up near the low.

>> **Day 2:** On the second day (the signal day), the bears are at it again; they move the price a bit lower before the bulls come roaring in.

When the bulls arrive on the scene, they immediately start pushing prices up, and they don't stop. Prices exceed those of the previous day, and even the closing price is higher than when trading commenced the previous day.

When a bullish engulfing pattern occurs in a downtrend, it indicates that the bulls were pushed around for some time before the pattern developed and that they're geared up to continue their buying assault on the bears for days.

Using the bullish engulfing pattern for savvy trading

If you're vigilant and lucky enough to spot a bullish engulfing pattern, trading on it can yield some appealing results. Figure 7-2 shows a real-world example of the bullish engulfing pattern in a chart of the SPY ETF, representing the S&P 500 index.

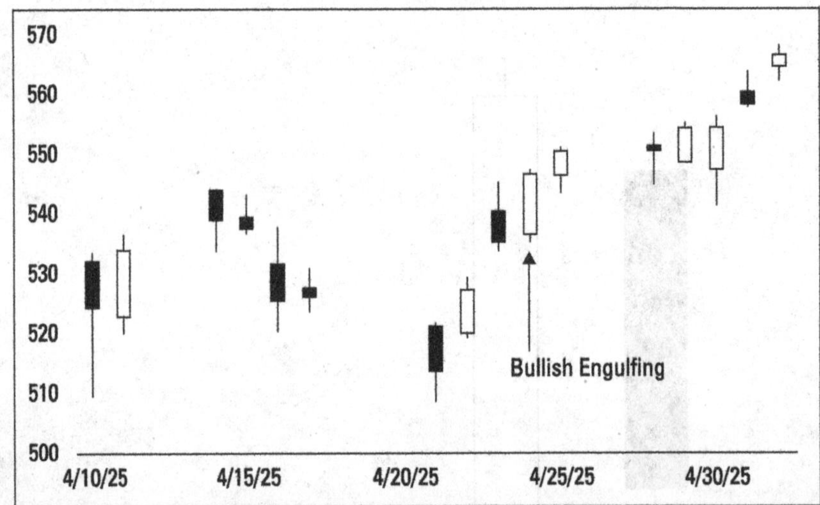

FIGURE 7-2:
A bullish engulfing pattern developing in a chart of SPY.

Figure 7-2 is a useful example of how the bullish engulfing pattern develops and how it can work out profitably. The bears dominate the setup day, leaving the close near the low. On the signal day, the SPY ETF opens lower than the previous day's low, which also turns out to be the low of the day. From that moment, the bulls are in control of the day. The following day brings a bit of selling, but the resulting price action includes several days in which the bulls are firmly in the driver's seat.

That situation leads to an important question: How do you know when the bullish engulfing pattern's signal is no longer valid? Our rule of thumb is that if the low of the setup day is violated, the signal is no longer good. To work this rule into your trading strategy, place a sell stop on the low of the setup day, not the signal day. Other traders may suggest placing the sell stop on the closing price of the setup day or even the opening price of the signal day, and you may want to consider those options as you get comfortable trading on the bullish engulfing pattern. Keep in mind, though, that things can get pretty miserable if you hold on to this trade too long.

A failing bullish engulfing pattern

Figure 7-3 is an example of what happens when good bullish engulfing patterns go bad, using our handy SPY ETF example to show the price action when the setup day's low is violated a few days after the pattern arises.

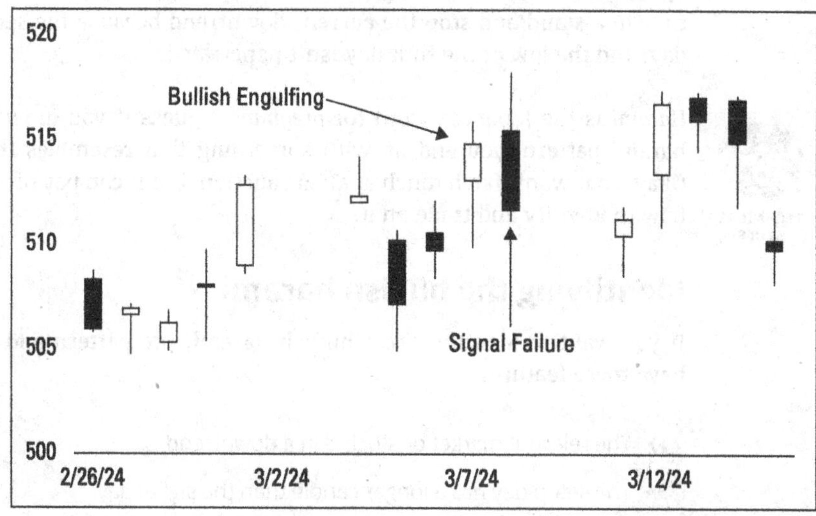

FIGURE 7-3:
A bullish engulfing pattern that fails in SPY ETF.

The setup day in this example is encouraging. There's a definite downtrend, and all the other bullish engulfing pattern criteria check out. But things sour quickly. The bulls lose the fight the following day, and the result is a slightly bearish day. Although the first day following the signal is only moderately bearish, the low violates the low of the setup day. The downtrend that was in place resumes with much lower prices.

As we were compiling real-world examples for this book, we had an extremely tough time finding a bullish engulfing pattern that didn't work out profitably if it was traded correctly. Bullish engulfing patterns don't *always* work, but finding one is an exciting prospect, and the chances are good that if you trade on it wisely, the result will be bright.

Bullish harami

In general, a *harami* is a two-day pattern in which the candle of the setup day is longer than the candle of the signal day. This pattern is almost the opposite of the bullish outside day and can be called a bullish inside day.

The first day is bearish, occurring in a downtrend. On the second day, the bulls take a shot at moving prices higher. The bulls don't have much success because, although the second day closes up slightly, it closes lower than the first day's open, and the first day's high is never surpassed. But the bulls may have started to take a stand and stop the current downtrend because the second day is an up day, and the low of the first day isn't penetrated.

Harami is the Japanese word for *pregnant*. I guess if you draw an outline of the harami pattern, you end up with something that resembles the outline of. . . . Okay, so it won't fetch much at an art auction, but it can pay off if you understand how to identify and trade on it.

Identifying the bullish harami

If you want to identify a true bullish harami, the pattern and the market must have these features:

>> The relevant market or stock is in a downtrend.

>> The setup day has a longer candle than the signal day.

>> The setup day has a black candle, with the open greater than the close, and that candle is fairly long.

>> The signal day's candle has an open lower than its close.

>> The open of the signal day is higher than the close of the setup day.

>> The low of the setup day is lower than the signal day's low, and the high of the setup day is higher than the high of the signal day.

>> The signal day's open is higher than the setup day's close.

>> The signal day's close is lower than the setup day's open.

Figure 7-4 is a picture of two days that create a bullish harami. *Note:* The high and low of both days don't come into play in this pattern — only the open and close.

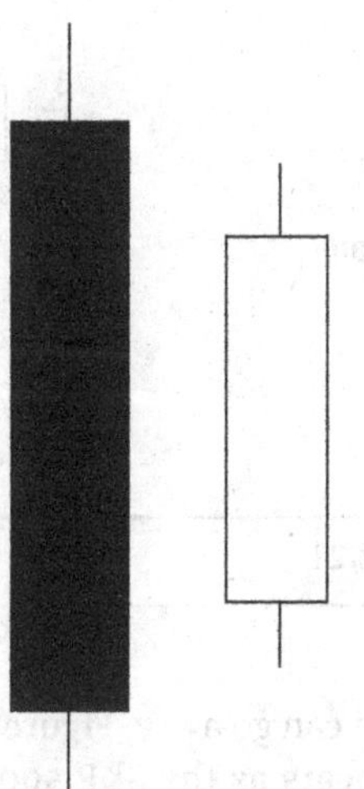

FIGURE 7-4: A bullish harami pattern.

The setup day of the harami is a down day that follows a bearish trend. On the signal day, the open is up from the first day's close, and the bulls rule the day because the close is higher than the open. Because there's been a downtrend, the bulls may be a bit timid, worried that the bears will return and push to new lows. The confidence that the bulls gain when the lows don't occur should translate to more buying and a reversal of the downtrend that culminated in the bullish harami.

Trading based on the bullish harami

This section provides a couple of examples of the bullish harami that help you figure out what to do (or not do) when you spot one on your own. We start with a successful appearance of the pattern at the end of a downtrend. The result is an attractive trend reversal.

Figure 7-5 is a chart of the SPY ETF. The bears push down the price from the open until the close for two days in a row. Finally, on the signal day of the bullish harami, the bulls find a level at which they're ready to start buying. This day is the first of many on which the bulls push prices back up from the depths where the bears pushed them.

With a bullish engulfing pattern, all four price components of the candlestick are involved, but only the open and close matter when you're working with a harami.

REMEMBER

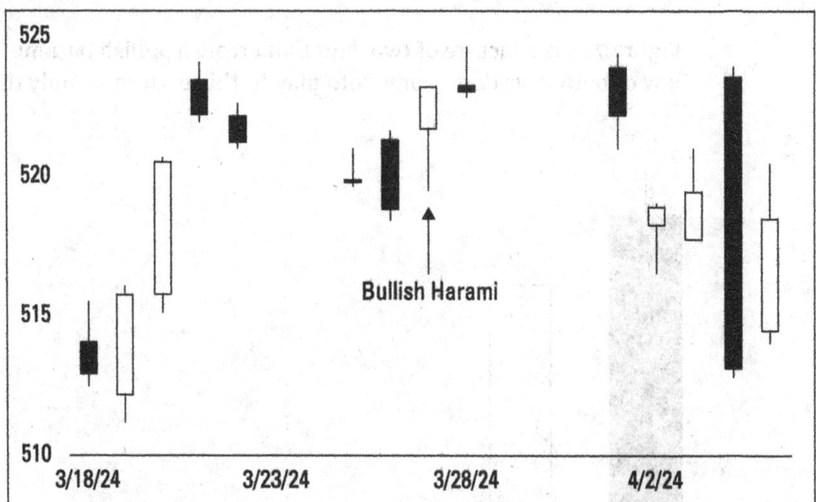

Like most other patterns, the bullish harami can go awry. Figure 7-6 is yet another chart of the SPY ETF. A bullish harami appears as the S&P 500 steadily trending lower. Some up days exist, but most days are down for a few sessions leading up to the harami pattern. Any bullish inklings from the harami don't last long.

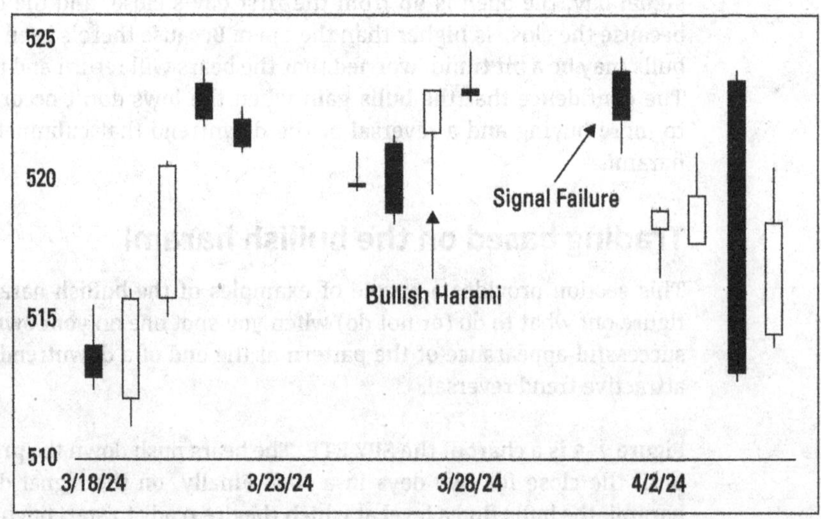

The failure level of a bullish harami can vary, depending on your preference. We use the open of the signal day as our stop level, and we suggest that you use the same level in your trading efforts. In Figure 7-6, this level holds up for less than a day, and the downtrend that was in place continues lower.

Bullish harami cross

Much like the doji with all its variations, the harami has more than one version. A doji pattern has an open that's higher than the close of the setup day and a close that's lower than the open of the setup day. This section covers the bullish harami cross — a special variety of harami that involves a doji pattern (see Chapter 6) but should always be considered to be an indicator of a potential reversal.

Recognizing the bullish harami cross

The bullish harami cross starts like its cousin, the bullish harami (covered earlier in this chapter), and it must contain these characteristics:

>> It appears during a downtrend.

>> Its setup day is a long black candle.

>> Its signal day is a doji.

It's much easier to understand the specifics of the bullish harami cross if you see a good example, so check out Figure 7-7.

FIGURE 7-7: A bullish harami cross pattern.

Using the bullish harami cross for profitable trading

The bullish harami cross isn't a common pattern, but when it appears, the trend reversal may be abrupt. Also, if the pattern doesn't hold and the downtrend continues, this failure usually happens quickly.

A nice buy signal from the bullish harami cross

To get an idea of how you can trade to turn a profit with the bullish harami cross, look at Figure 7-8. The figure shows a chart of Target (TGT) stock with a bullish harami cross that successfully signals a trend reversal.

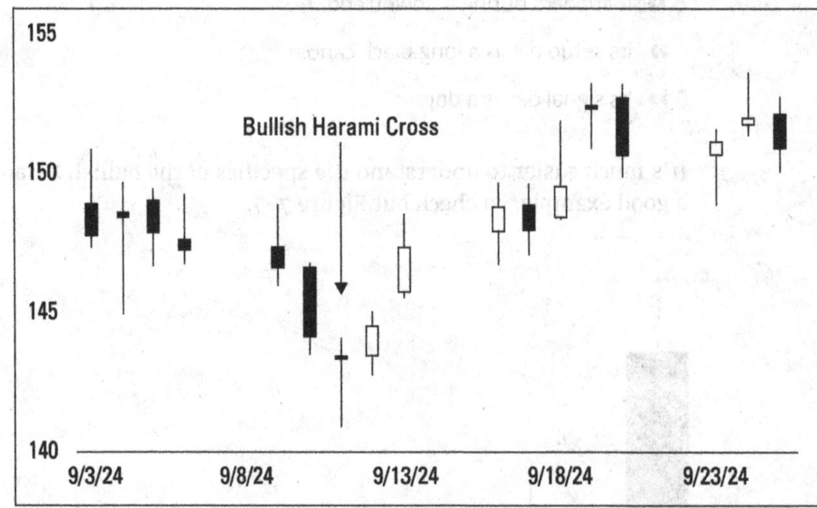

FIGURE 7-8: A bullish harami cross in a chart of TGT stock.

When this pattern reared its head, we were looking for an entry point to buy shares of TGT. We'd been monitoring TGT for a while, and we bought near the close of the bullish harami cross's signal day. This pattern adheres to the rules for a buy signal because it's at the bottom of a downtrend and the doji's open and close fall within the setup day's open and close. Soon after we got in, we were rewarded by an uptrend that lasted for several weeks. You can enjoy the same kind of results if you spot the bullish harami cross in a similar environment.

Failing to give a good buy signal

Figure 7-9 is an example of the bullish harami cross giving a signal that doesn't work out. This chart shows the daily price action for Target.

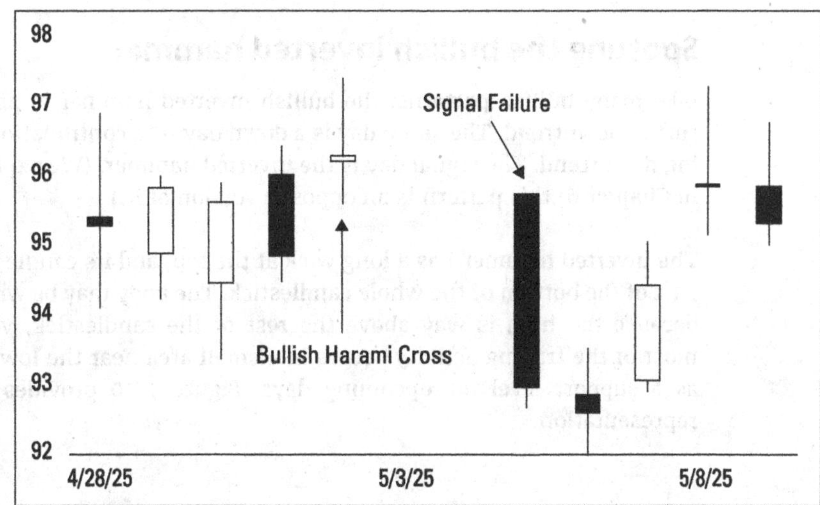

The first trading day after this signal was slightly encouraging, as the stock closed higher and the low of the signal day wasn't violated. The following day, the bears took over; the day after that, the price broke through both the low of the signal and setup day. Either low price would work as sufficient stop-loss prices, and both were violated in the same day.

Sometimes, stops that don't allow for some market fluctuation get you out of a successful trade too quickly. On the other hand, placing a stop with too much wiggle room can get you out of a bad trade long after exiting it would have been prudent. Placing stops is as much an art as a science and one of the most difficult parts of trading. Refer to Chapter 5 for details on stops.

Bullish inverted hammer

The bullish inverted hammer is fairly rare. This pattern occurs in a downtrend and the setup day is a bearish candle — usually, a long bearish candle. The signal day is actually the inverted hammer, which is the rare part, because the price action that creates an inverted hammer is fairly rare.

To get the inverted hammer as the signal day, you should start with a price gap down and end with a close near the opening gap price. Usually, when lots of volatility is associated with a gap opening, the open and close prices are rarely in the same proximity.

In this section, we demonstrate what the two days that create the bullish inverted hammer look like.

Spotting the bullish inverted hammer

Like many bullish patterns, the bullish inverted hammer is preceded by some sort of downtrend. The setup day is a down day — a continuation of the prevailing downtrend. The signal day is the inverted hammer. (We explain the hammer in Chapter 6; this pattern is an opposite version of it.)

The inverted hammer has a long wick at the top, and its candle takes up a small part of the bottom of the whole candlestick. The body may be white or black, but because the high is way above the rest of the candlestick, you can tell that most of the trading activity occurs in a small area near the low. The low serves as a support level for upcoming days. Figure 7-10 provides a handy visual representation.

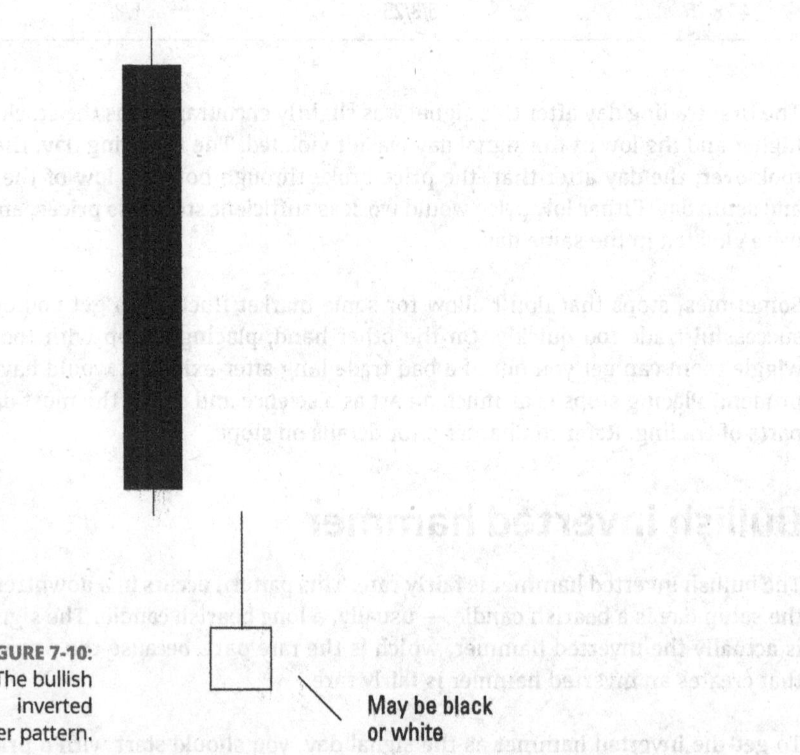

FIGURE 7-10:
The bullish inverted hammer pattern.

Evaluating how to trade on the bullish inverted hammer

To initiate a trade by using the bullish inverted hammer, wait until the open of the subsequent day. Initiate a position only if the open of that day is higher than the low of the inverted hammer day.

Think of the signal this way: For the bullish inverted hammer to be valid, it needs to be confirmed by the open of the day immediately after its appearance. If that open is higher than the signal day's low, you're clear to buy, and you should put your stop in at the same time.

Checking out a successful bullish inverted hammer

Figure 7-11 is another Target chart. The inverted hammer appears after a down day and is confirmed by a higher opening. We chose this chart because there's no question that the open on the day after the pattern confirms the bullish signal. If you see a bullish inverted hammer confirmed this way, you should enter a long trade quickly because an uptrend is likely on the way.

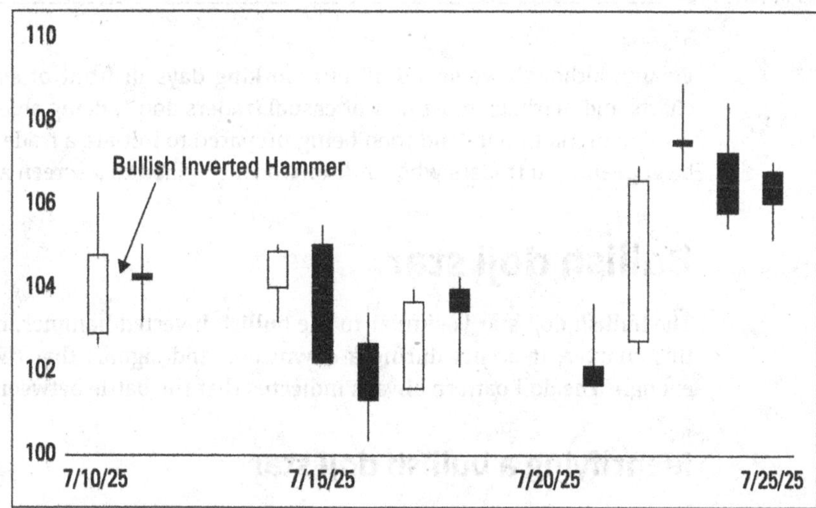

FIGURE 7-11: The bullish inverted hammer, confirmed in a chart of TGT.

REMEMBER

The bullish inverted hammer appears often — and then the following day's open won't confirm the bullish signal. If you see that pattern develop, immediately wash your hands of any trades involving the pattern.

A failed inverted hammer on confirmation day

Figure 7-12 is a chart of a bullish inverted hammer for TGT. With a downtrend in place, and after a down day, a bullish inverted hammer appears. On the following day, the opening price is higher than the previous low or the low of the inverted hammer. But by the end of the day, the signal was negated by a violation of the low of the inverted hammer day.

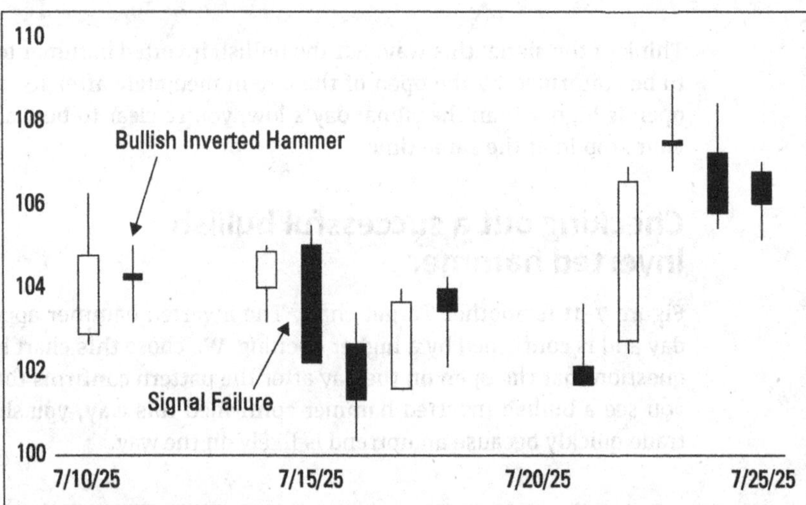

FIGURE 7-12:
A failed bullish inverted hammer in TGT.

Finally, although we spend all our working days in front of screens looking at charts and markets, most new or casual traders don't. Being able to look at charts outside market hours and then being prepared to initiate a trade the next day can be appealing to traders who can't or won't be glued to a screen all day.

Bullish doji star

The bullish doji star is similar to the bullish inverted hammer, covered earlier in this chapter. It occurs during a downtrend and signals that the bulls have had enough. The doji pattern always indicates that the battle between bulls and bears.

Identifying a bullish doji star

A genuine bullish doji star must also include these features:

>> A down setup day, preferably with a long black candle.

>> A signal day that includes an open and close that are equal or nearly equal, preferably in the middle of a trading day.

   This pattern indicates an almost equal battle between the bulls and bears, in which neither faction can claim victory.

>> A gap down opening, longer candlestick, between the long black candle of the setup day and the doji of the signal day.

   This feature shows that a gap down is met with buying, but only enough buying to keep the price stable.

A gap occurs when a stock opens at a lower level than the previous day's low or a higher level than the previous day's high.

Figure 7-13 shows two days of trading activity that creates the bullish doji star.

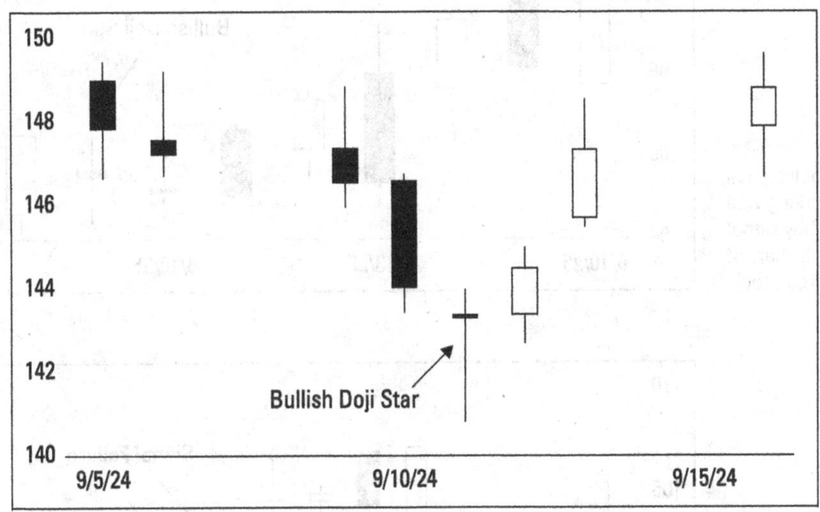

FIGURE 7-13: The bullish doji star.

Wishing (and trading) on a bullish doji star

Figure 7-14 shows a bullish doji star working out in a downtrend reversal for the Target stock. Notice the doji that appears after the gap from the lower open from the previous day, which was a down day. The low of the doji is never violated, and a buyer is handsomely rewarded by a huge day for the bulls three days after the pattern appears. If only all buy signals resulted in a 10 percent up day!

Failing on a long signal

Unfortunately, some bullish doji stars are more like falling stars than shooting stars. Check out Figure 7-15 for an example; it's another Target chart. A doji star appears after an up day and in the midst of a small move up during a downtrend. But this signal is a bust, as TGT gaps lower the following day, with all price action below the low of the signal day.

Bullish meeting line

The bullish meeting line is another helpful example of a pattern that offers a heads-up that a trend reversal is on the way. This pattern is an interesting (and rare) one.

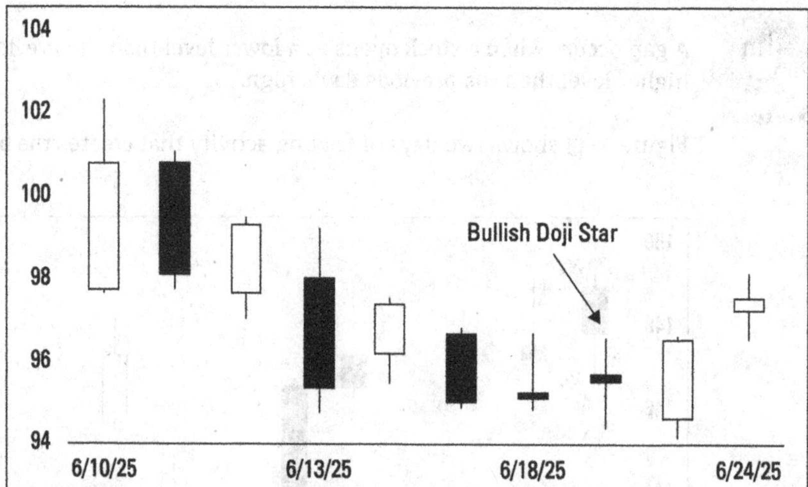

FIGURE 7-14: The bullish doji star working well as a buy signal in a chart of TGT stock.

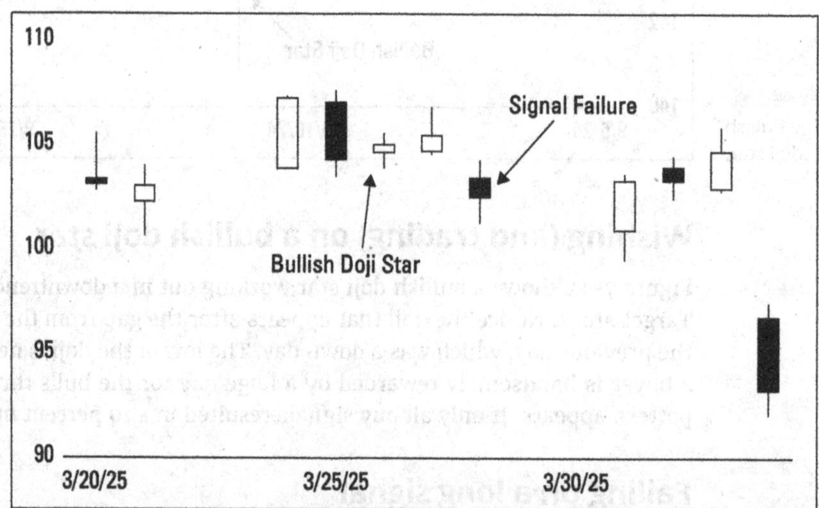

FIGURE 7-15: The bullish doji star failing in a chart of the TGT.

Recognizing a bullish meeting line pattern

The setup day of this pattern is a long black candle, and the signal day is a long white candle. The closing prices of the two days are equal or nearly equal, indicating that the bears controlled the setup day. There's also a gap down opening, which shows that the bears are still in control at the beginning of the signal day, but the bulls soon arrive on the scene. As the signal day progresses, the low opening price brings in buying activity; the close reaches the previous day's close and eliminates the gap opening.

Figure 7-16 shows how bullish meeting lines appear in a chart.

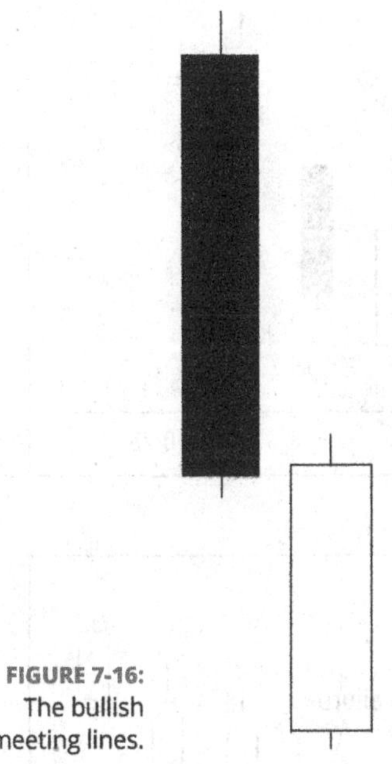

Making a successful trade using bullish meeting lines

For a successful example of trading on the bullish meeting line pattern, we use an example of a stock that everyone should be familiar with: Apple (AAPL). The chart in Figure 7-17 reveals a pattern that shows up during a downtrend and when the setup day is bearish. The signal day opens below the low of the setup day and then recovers to close near the previous day's close, completing a bullish meeting line pattern. The following day threatens to break the support as the stock trades lower than the signal day's close, but the low of that day holds. The result is a few days of bullish trading. Spotting the bullish meeting lines and getting in at the right time would yield some substantial profits.

To give you an idea of what failing bullish meeting lines look like, look at another chart of WMT (see Figure 7-18). True to form, the stock is in a downtrend, and the pattern shows up where indicated in the chart. The pattern appears to be validated, as the next few days trend slightly higher but aren't very bullish. The low of the signal day isn't violated for several days, however. Putting a wise sell stop in place at either the low or the open of the signal day would serve as a nice tourniquet.

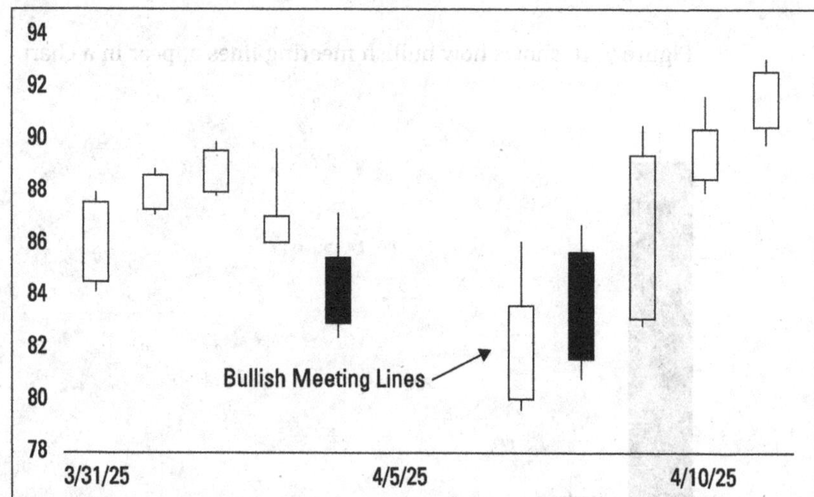

FIGURE 7-17: The bullish meeting line pattern in a chart of WMT.

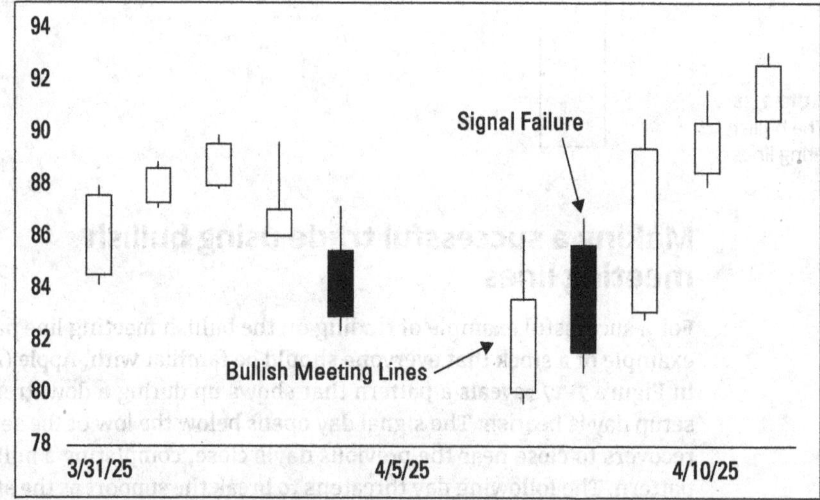

FIGURE 7-18: A failing bullish meeting line pattern in a chart of WMT stock.

Bullish piercing line

The bullish piercing line is one more bullish double-stick pattern that signals a trend reversal. As with the patterns discussed earlier in this chapter, the bullish piercing line must appear during a downtrend to be considered valid.

Identifying a bullish piercing line pattern

Like the bullish meeting line pattern (covered earlier in this chapter), the bullish piercing line consists of a long black candle on the setup day and a long white candle on the signal day. The open of the signal day should be lower than the low of the setup day, which means that bearishness persists on the setup day and the open of the signal day reveals more selling because the open is lower than the setup day's low. The signal day's close is much higher than the open, which means that the bulls came in as a reaction to the lower opening price and pushed prices higher. Therefore, the tide has turned in favor of the bulls. Figure 7-19 shows a good example of a bullish piercing line.

Trading on the bullish piercing line

The bullish piercing line pattern emerges when you have a setup day marked by a long black candle. The signal day is a bullish candlestick that opens with a gap down but closes well within the range covered by the first day. In this case, the bulls show up after a bearish open and decide that it's time to take charge and push prices up.

Figure 7-20 is an example of a bullish piercing line appearing in a Walmart chart. You can't beat this example for a clear representation of the bullish piercing line pattern signaling the end of a downtrend. The setup day is a long black candle, and the signal day has a gap opening that's lower than the previous day's low before the bulls show up and make a solid bullish run. Notice that the signal day doesn't have a high that exceeds the high of the first day. If it did, and if its close exceeded the setup day's open, this pattern would be a bullish engulfing pattern. (We cover the bullish engulfing pattern earlier in this chapter.)

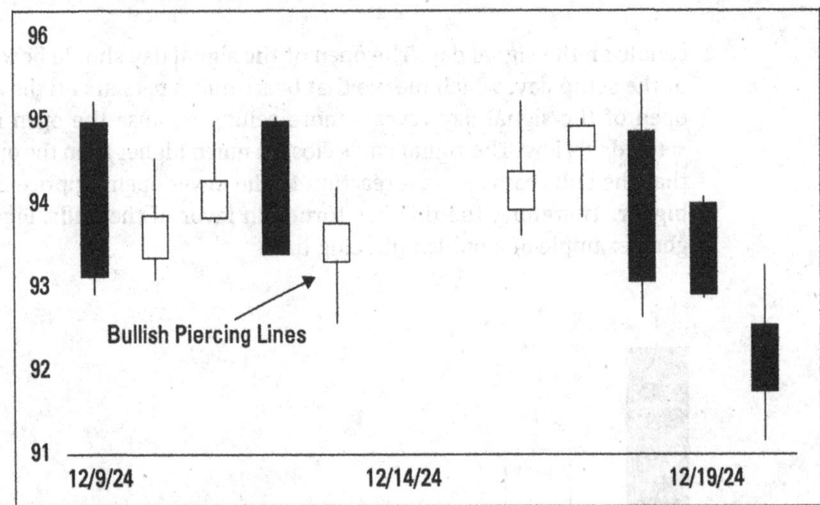

FIGURE 7-20: The bullish piercing line appearing in a chart of WMT stock.

As an example of a bullish piercing line failure, we provide yet another Walmart chart. In this case, the bullish piercing line doesn't deliver. As you can see in Figure 7-21, in the midst of a small downtrend, a bullish piercing line appears. The following day, the stock gaps on the open with a price above the previous day's high, but that price level is violated along with the previous day's close. Price action on that day is discouraging, and the signal is negated on day two with a violation of the signal day's open and low.

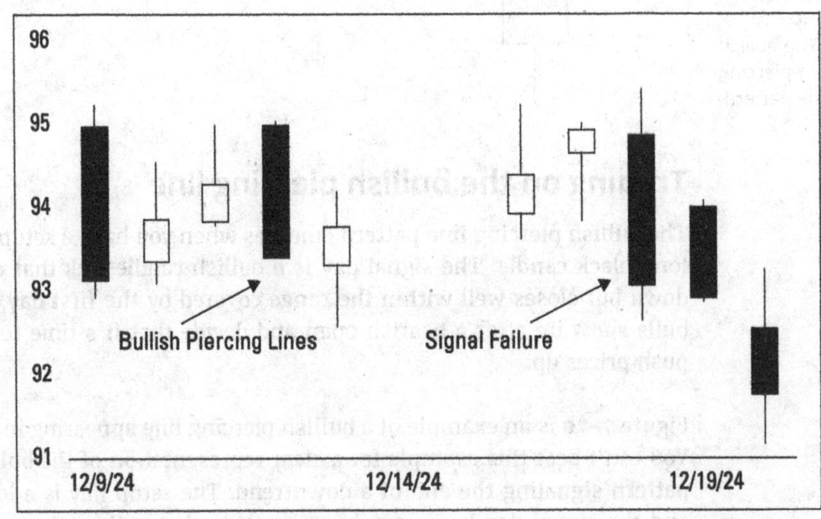

FIGURE 7-21: A failing bullish piercing line in a chart of WMT stock.

Bullish Trend-Confirming Patterns

Not all double-stick patterns indicate that a trend reversal is forthcoming; some of them tell you that the market will continue in the direction in which it's going. Seeing signs of a continuation may not sound exciting, but you can sometimes benefit from confirming that a trend will stay in place.

If you're considering selling a stock because you believe the price is close to peaking, the appearance of a pattern showing that the trend is still in place may help you improve your exit price. After all, it's always frustrating to sell and then watch as a stock continues to climb in value.

Also, everyone has heard that the way to make money buying securities is to buy low and sell high, but plenty of traders buy high and sell higher. These people are known as *trend followers*, and they can embrace these trend confirmation signals to the tune of some outstanding returns. Do you think you may want to join their ranks? If so, read on for a few examples of bullish double-stick patterns that do a terrific job of confirming the continuation of a trend.

Bullish thrusting lines

The first trend confirming pattern we cover in this section may be a bit difficult to pick out of a chart at first glance, but it's worth recognizing and looking out for. Unlike the double-stick patterns described earlier in this chapter, the bullish thrusting line pattern appears during an uptrend, not a downtrend; this pattern would be confirming the direction of an uptrend but wouldn't have much significance during a downtrend.

Recognizing a bullish thrusting line pattern

The setup day of a bullish thrusting line is a long white candle, which is bullish in pretty much any market. The signal day is a black candle. This black candle should have a gap opening higher than the high of the setup day and a close near the day's low. The close of the signal day, however, should be above the midpoint of the first day. To see a bona fide bullish thrusting line, check out Figure 7-22.

Trading on a bullish thrusting line

On the setup day of a bullish thrusting line (and for several days before that), the bulls have been in charge of the price action. On the signal day, the bulls push a stock to a gap opening, which does bring in some sellers — but the sellers don't push hard enough to move the closing price below the midpoint of the previous day. This situation means that the bulls are still around and poised to take control, which can be a big help if you're considering buying, because the bullish signal from this pattern can give you a chance to get on board at a reasonable price before the stock goes up.

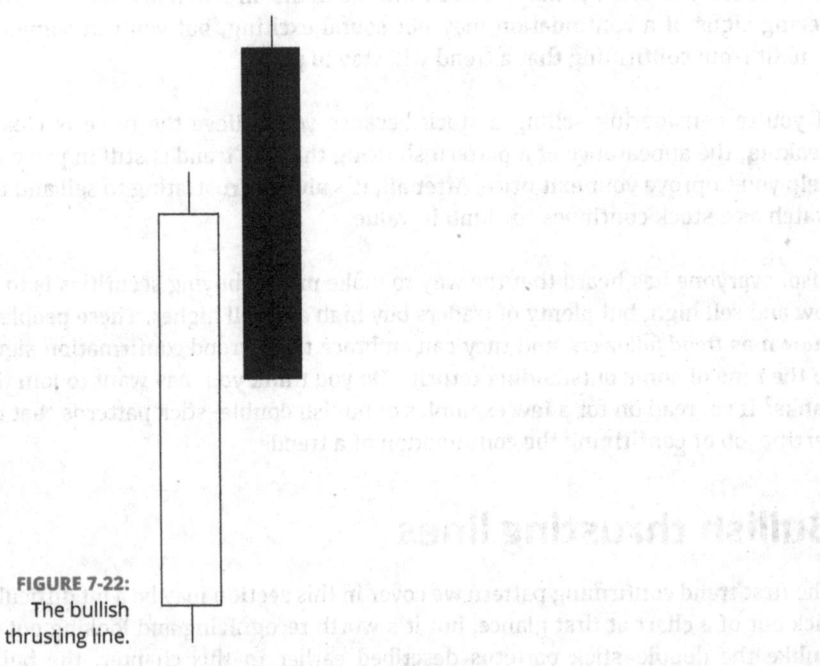

Figure 7-23 is an example of the bullish thrusting line in another chart of JPMorgan Chase (JPM) stock. The setup day is an up day, followed by a gap opening. The stock trades off a bit on the signal day after opening higher, but it manages to close above the midpoint of the first day of the pattern. (Hooray!) For a few days after this signal, the stock trades sideways; then the uptrend resumes.

Notice that the stock doesn't violate the low of the first day of the pattern; that's the stop level we use when trading on this pattern. We suggest that you use the same stop level, and you can see why in the next example.

Failing to indicate the continuation of an uptrend

Figure 7-24 is another JPMorgan Chase (JPM) chart. The figure shows two bullish thrusting line patterns, both of which fail, with the second one a disaster as the market gapped lower on the open the day after the second signal.

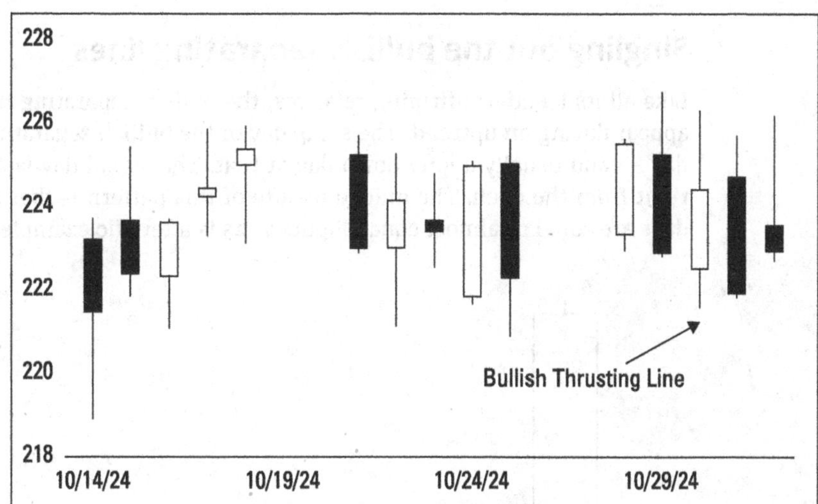

FIGURE 7-23: The bullish thrusting line in a chart of JPM.

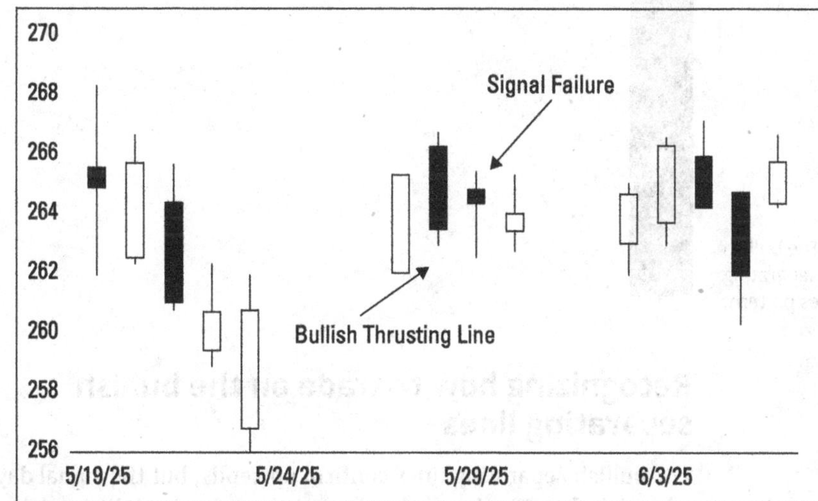

FIGURE 7-24: The bullish thrusting line failing twice in a chart of the JPM stock.

If you bought JPM stock based on that bullish thrusting line and failed to put a stop at the low of the setup day, you lost more than you could bear. A failing trade like that one makes even the most grizzled traders want to curl up and hibernate.

Bullish separating lines

For another double-stick pattern that confirms a trend, consider a bullish separating line. The pattern isn't exactly what it sounds like, because the lines involved may overlap a bit, but it's useful and certainly worth understanding in depth.

Singling out the bullish separating lines

Like all its trend-confirming relatives, the bullish separating lines pattern must appear during an uptrend. The setup day of the bullish separating lines is a down day — and usually a long down day at that. The signal day is an up day, bullish right from the open. The unique feature of this pattern is that the opens of both days are equal or almost equal. Figure 7-25 is a terrific example.

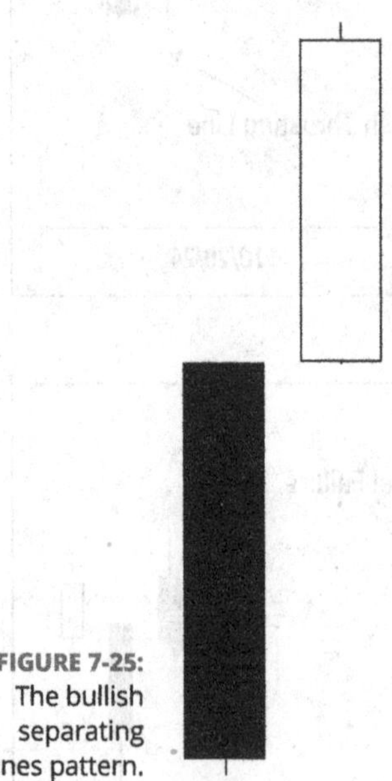

FIGURE 7-25: The bullish separating lines pattern.

Recognizing how to trade on the bullish separating lines

The bullish separating lines confirm uptrends, but the signal day of the pattern is a bearish day. The bears decide that the price is right to start selling, and they dominate the bulls, pushing prices lower throughout the day. On the signal day, the bulls come in, ready to start buying again. There's so much bullishness that the opening price of the signal day is equal to the opening price of the setup day, and from that point on, the bulls dominate the day; the uptrend remains intact.

The bullish thrusting lines and a trend that comes to an end

Figure 7-26 is yet another chart of JPM Stock. We've highlighted the pattern that forms at the beginning of an uptrend.

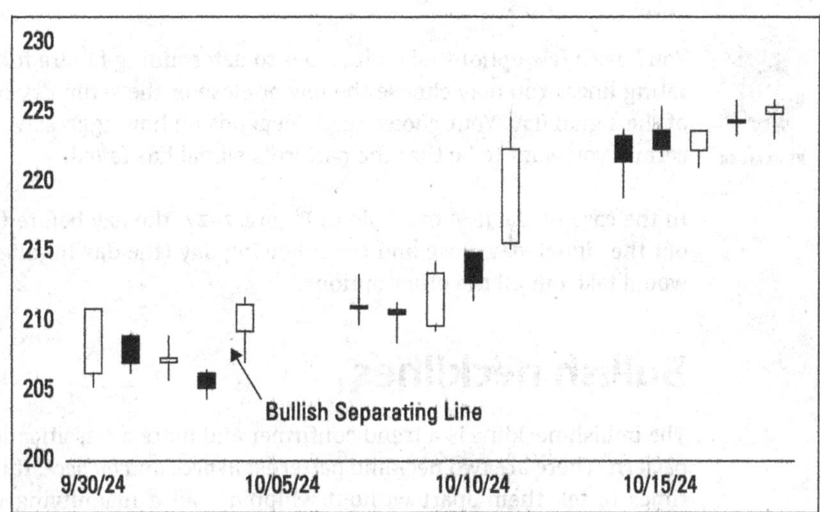

FIGURE 7-26: The bullish separating lines in a chart of JPM stock.

We love this example because the pattern occurs early in an uptrend, so a trader may feel that they haven't missed the bull run when using this signal as an entry point. If a trader missed a buy at a lower price but still has some interest in getting in on a trade, this pattern may give them the confidence to step up to the plate and buy the stock.

Figure 7-27 shows another example of JPM, this one not as successful. This signal comes after a handful of higher moves but is met with resistance each day after the signal, with no trading activity above the high of the signal day. The fund doesn't break through the highs and the signal is done.

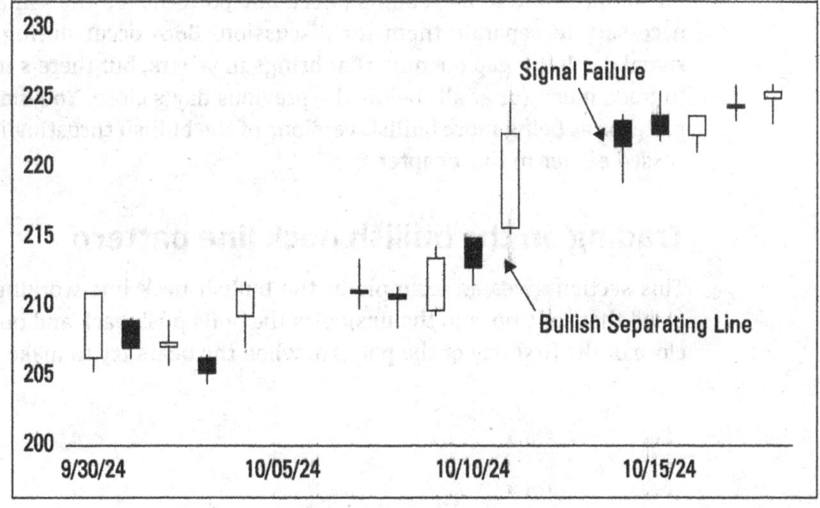

FIGURE 7-27: The bullish separating lines failing in a chart of the JPM.

You have a few options when it comes to determining failure for the bullish separating lines: You may choose the low or close of the setup day or the open or low of the signal day. Your choice really depends on how aggressive you feel and how certain you want to be that the pattern's signal has failed.

In the case of the JPM example in Figure 7-27, the day before failure would take out the signal-day close and the following day (the day highlighted as a failure) would take out all the other options.

Bullish necklines

The bullish neckline is a trend confirmer and more a classification than a distinct pattern. There are two neckline patterns: *in neck* and *on neck*. It may be difficult at times to tell them apart without whipping out a magnifying glass to look at a chart, but because they look very much alike, we decided to discuss them together in this section. Keep in mind that the bullish neck lines we describe must occur during an uptrend to have any real significance.

Identifying bullish neck lines

The setup day of the bullish neck line pattern is a long white candle that indicates lots of buying, and the signal day is a black candle that may be long or short. The close of the signal day will be near the close of the setup day. In that case, the pattern is said to be *on neck*. If the close of the signal day is a little lower than the close of the setup day, the pattern is said to be *in neck*. You can see examples of both patterns in Figure 7-28.

The on neck and in neck bullish neck line patterns tell the same story, so it's not necessary to separate them for discussion. Both occur during an uptrend. The signal day has a gap opening that brings in sellers, but there's not enough selling to trade much (or at all) below the previous day's close. You may recognize these patterns as being more bullish versions of the bullish thrusting lines pattern, discussed earlier in this chapter.

Trading on the bullish neck line pattern

This section gives an example of the bullish neck line working well to signal a trend that continues to the upside as the bulls push back and hold prices near the close of the first day of the pattern, when the bears try to make a push.

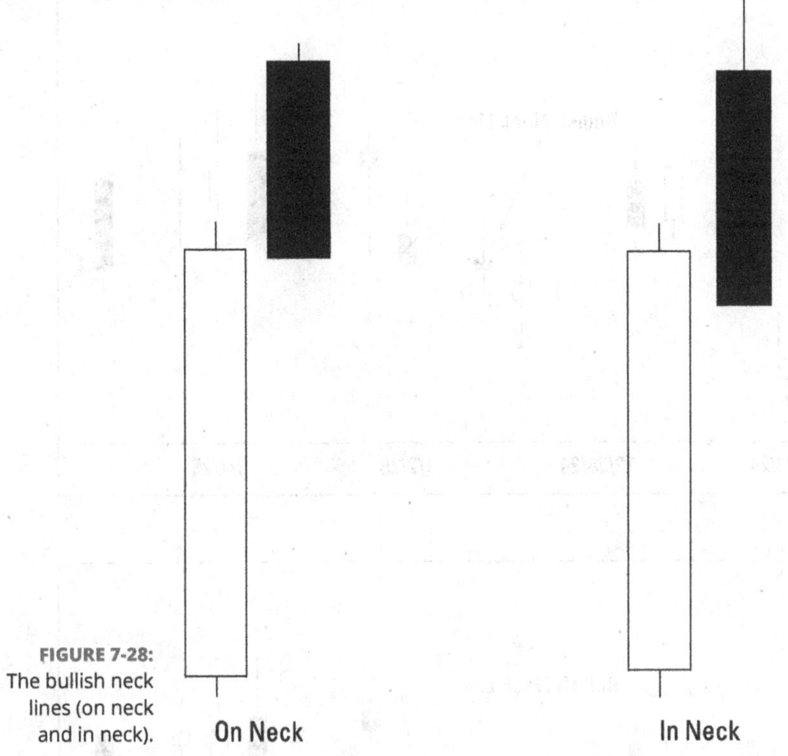

Figure 7-29 is one more JPM stock chart, with this one showing daily close data. The bullish neck line appears during a small pullback during a longer-term uptrend. The pattern is slightly in neck, almost to the point that it may not qualify as a bullish signal. But a trader who takes this pattern as a buy signal and places a stop at any appropriate level would be handsomely rewarded by a continuation of the uptrend. In this case, the potential stop level would be the low of the setup day, which holds on despite being tested a couple of times after the signal day.

Bullish neck line fails to signal a trend continuation

We hate to end this chapter on a down note, but we need to show you what a failing bullish neck line pattern looks like. Figure 7-30 is another JPM chart. A bullish neck line appears near the top of this bullish move. The signal fails quickly as the JPM trend turns from positive to negative quickly. The only positive thing we can say about this scenario is that it happened quickly, so traders were able to move on to the next trade without a long and painful failure.

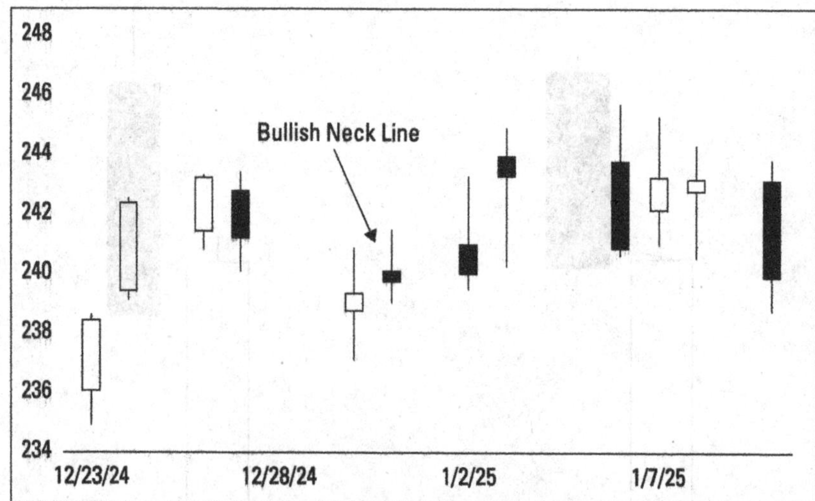

FIGURE 7-29:
The bullish neck line working well in a chart of JPM.

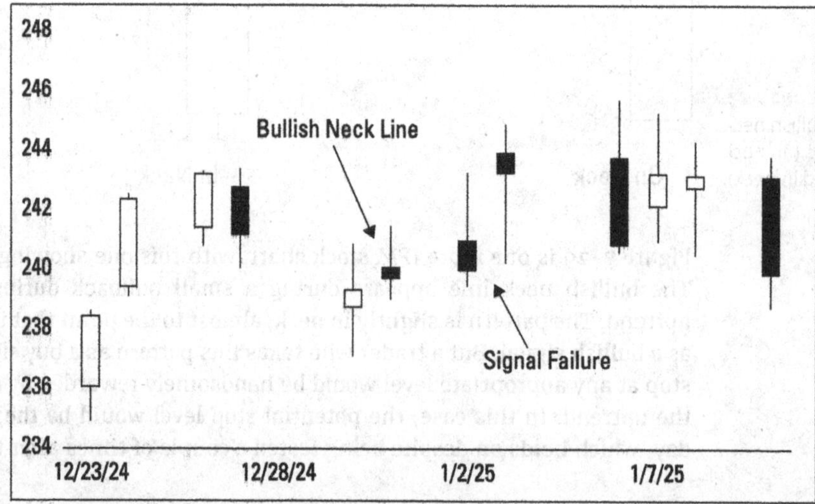

FIGURE 7-30:
The bullish neck line failing in a chart of the JPM.

That's it for bullish double-stick patterns for now. In later chapters, they come back, teamed up with technical indicators that may signal a reversal or a strong trend.

Chapter **8**

Using Bearish Double-Stick Patterns

In Chapter 7, we discuss the nature and usefulness of bullish double-stick patterns, but they aren't the only double-stick show in town. As with most bullish patterns, bearish two-day counterparts exist, and you should know how to recognize and trade them because these patterns work as effective sell signals. When a sell signal pops up, even if you don't own any securities, you can use the opportunity to initiate a successful short position.

Like the bullish patterns in Chapter 7, the bearish double-stick patterns in this chapter may appear as *reversal patterns* (signaling that an uptrend is coming to an end) or as *continuation patterns* (telling you that a prevailing downtrend will continue). These bearish examples have two parts: the first day, which we refer to as the *setup day*, and the second day, which we call the *signal day*.

REMEMBER

Working with Bearish Reversal Patterns

We're definitely biased toward bearish reversal patterns. We've always been a bit of a countertrend trader, and because many candlestick patterns signal trend reversals, we've always found plenty to use in our trading. But trading in anticipation of trend reversals isn't always a cakewalk. In fact, it almost put us out of the business during the strong bullish markets that became known as the dot.com bubble. We managed to keep from going broke during that period, and we learned some expensive lessons about managing money and using stops — lessons we describe throughout this chapter.

WARNING

Here's a bit of a warning about using short reversal patterns: In theory, a short has an unlimited loss. Also, keep in mind that when you're shorting stocks, you're working against a general long-term uptrend in stock prices. Some successful traders are exclusive shorts, but they're rare. Don't get us wrong: We do believe that shorting should be part of any trading or investing program. But please use shorting as part of a larger trading strategy, not as your primary way of working the markets.

You can use many extremely useful patterns for shorting, as signals for exiting from a long or as exercises in patience before buying. This section covers those patterns.

The bearish engulfing pattern

The bearish engulfing pattern is one of the best patterns to start with because of the dramatic nature of the bearish second day. The pattern involves the bears taking control after an extended period of bullishness, and the trend is definitely one to watch.

Identifying the bearish engulfing pattern

Check out Figure 8-1 for an example of the bearish engulfing pattern.

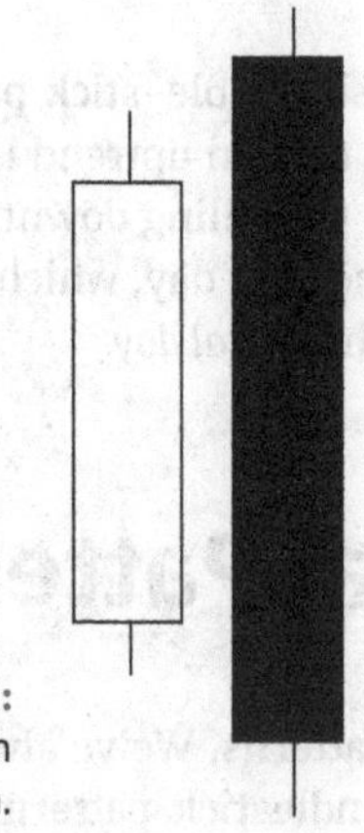

FIGURE 8-1:
The bearish engulfing pattern.

Up to and including the setup day of this pattern, the bulls are in the driver's seat. On the open of the signal day, the sellers or shorts have finally had enough; they decide that the price has gone up enough to bring them into the action, so they push the price down dramatically and quickly (in one day). But these bears aren't finished with their selling and the close of the signal day is near that day's low. That trend will most likely continue, to the point where a downtrend develops because the sellers aren't done putting pressure on the stock or market.

Trading on the bearish engulfing pattern

For a real-world example of a bearish engulfing pattern that can be used for profitable trades, have a look at Figure 8-2. Here, the pattern appears in a chart of the SPY, an exchange-traded fund (ETF) that represents Standard & Poor's (S&P) 500.

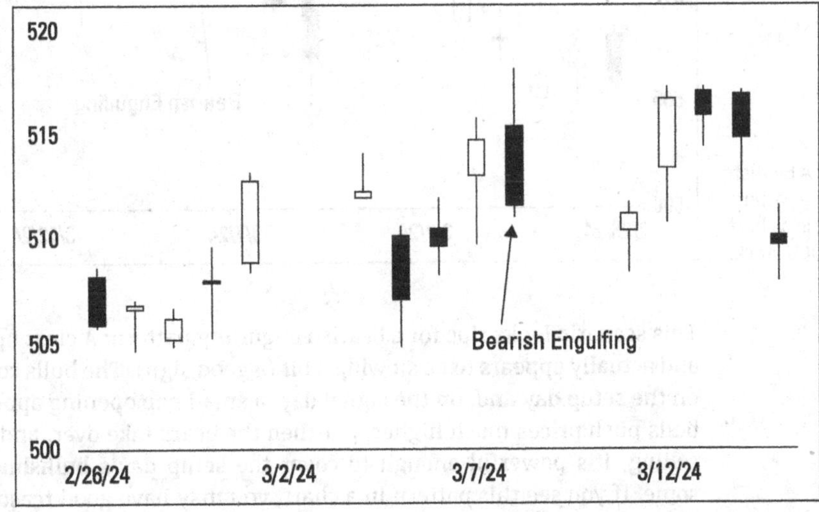

FIGURE 8-2: Two bearish engulfing patterns in a chart of the SPY ETF.

This chart shows two bearish engulfing patterns. The first one occurs just after a small uptrend and results in a reversal and steady downtrend for a few days. The trend reverses back to the upside and the price levels where the first bearish engulfing pattern showed up. A second bearish engulfing pattern results in another reversal to the downside.

The overwhelming push by the bears that stops an uptrend dead in its tracks is the key to the bearish engulfing pattern. The SPY chart in Figure 8-2 is a useful example of a bearish engulfing pattern scenario that can lead you to profitable results. After the bears reverse the uptrend, the signal holds and, in both instances, the next day's trading doesn't come near the pre-reversal prices. If you short at the end of the pattern and ride the downtrend for a while before buying back, you have a profitable trade.

Recognizing a failing bearish engulfing pattern

We provide an example of a failing pattern for every successful pattern in this book, and in Figure 8-3, we highlight what can happen when a bearish engulfing pattern goes wrong. This unfortunate outcome occurs in a chart showing price action for the SPY ETF.

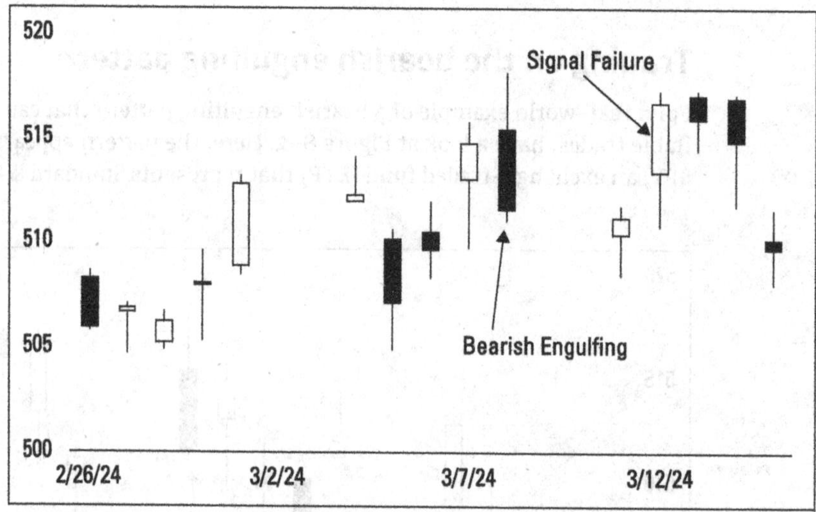

FIGURE 8-3: A bearish engulfing pattern failing in a chart of DOCU stock.

This scenario looks ripe for a bearish engulfing pattern: A clear uptrend is in place and actually appears to be slowing a bit (a good sign). The bulls continue the trend on the setup day and, on the signal day, a small gap opening appears. At first, the bulls push prices much higher, but then the bears take over, and when they start selling, it's powerful enough to cover the setup day's bullishness — and then some. If you see this pattern in a chart, you may have good reason to get excited, but a move to lower prices will be short-lived.

A few days after the pattern appears, the bulls get back in on the action, and the price closes higher than the opening of the signal day. The pattern clearly fails, but if you trade on it, you can avoid heavy losses if you place a stop at the right level.

TIP

When working with bearish engulfing patterns, we place our stops at the open of the second day. That's when we can tell that the bulls have seized control of the price action again and we know the bullish action can continue for some time. It's always prudent to have a stop in place, and that level may be a good one to choose for your stop. We advise you to place your stops at the same level.

The bearish harami pattern

The bearish harami pattern can tip you off that an uptrend is about to be reversed. Loosely translated from the Japanese, *harami* means *pregnant*. If you use your imagination and squint a little, you can see in Figure 8-4 how the pattern got its name.

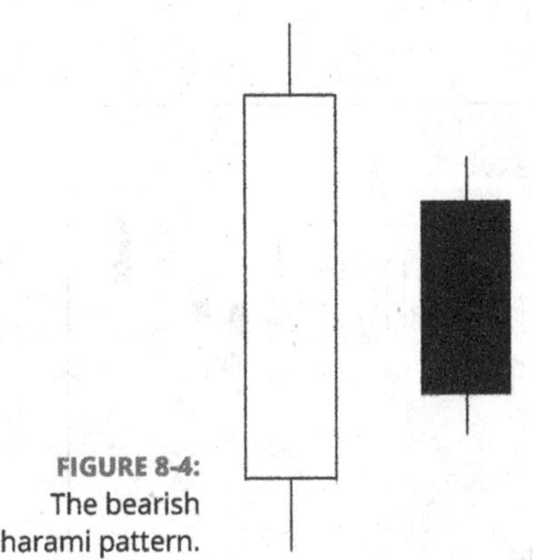

Spotting a bearish harami

The setup day of a bearish harami pattern is a continuation of a prevailing uptrend — a strong up day. At first glance, the signal day isn't much to jump up and shout about, either. It's a day on which the price action doesn't stray outside the high and low of the setup day; the bears take over on the open, and neither side makes much progress in pushing around the price action. But because this trend occurs after a bullish day and during a marked bullish trend, it can very well serve as a sign that the bears are starting to take control of the price action. Figure 8-4 shows an extremely straightforward illustration of the bearish harami pattern.

Another name for the signal day in this pattern is an *inside day* — a day when the high is lower than the previous high, and the low is lower than the previous low. When they occur on their own, inside days indicate a lack of conviction by both the bulls and the bears. But combine an inside day with a preceding bullish day and a bullish trend in place, and the combination can show you that the bull run is coming to an end.

When a prevailing trend starts to fade into indecision, the next dominant trend is likely to go in the opposite direction.

REMEMBER

Using the bearish harami pattern for a clever trade

For a good look at what the bearish harami looks like in a real-life chart, check out Figure 8-5. We like this particular ETF as a trading vehicle because its performance is closely linked to the state of the economy. With fluctuations in economic opinion come volatility in these stocks, and with volatility come trading opportunities!

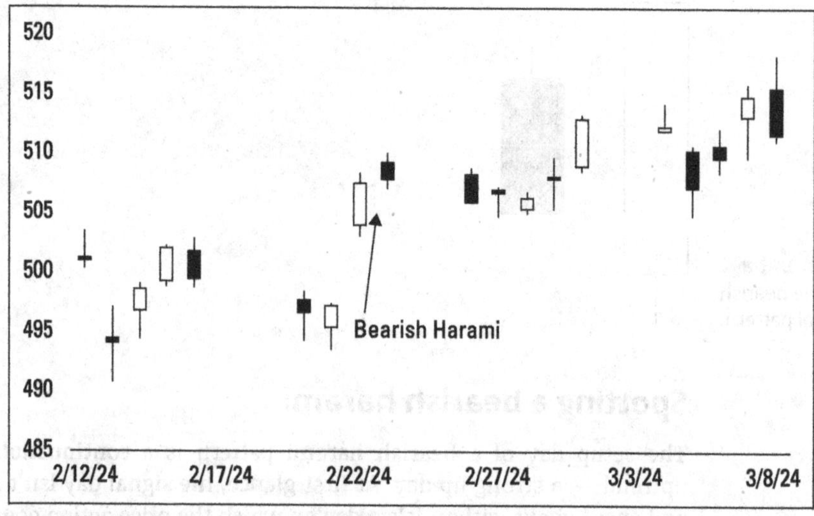

FIGURE 8-5:
A bearish harami working in a chart of the SPY ETF.

The setup day of this two-day bearish harami pattern is a strong up day that occurs in the midst of an uptrend that's been in place for several days. The signal day is an inside day that's a little on the bearish side. The next day, the SPY ETF gaps lower and remains at lower levels in a narrow range for the next few days.

Recognizing a failing bearish harami pattern

Figure 8-6 provides a solid example of how the bearish harami can fail. Even with good signals, you need to have stops in place so that you don't lose big when the bearish harami doesn't play out favorably.

Figure 8-6 is yet another chart of the SPY ETF. This signal occurs in the midst of an uptrend, but with the exception of a single day, this signal isn't valid, and it fails as the SPY resumes marching higher. The failure of a bearish harami may involve moving higher than the signal — or setup-day high. Two days after the signal day, the SPY manages to trade higher than the high of both days — a distinct indication that this signal is a bust.

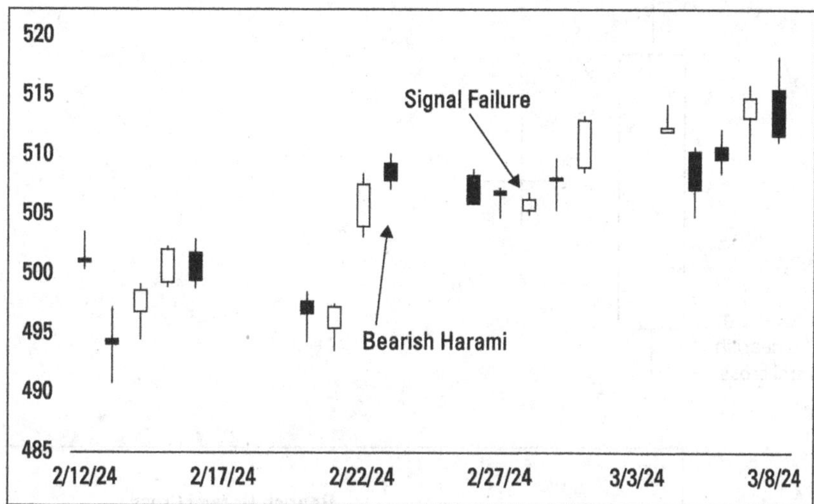

FIGURE 8-6:
A bearish harami
pattern failing in
a chart of
the SPY ETF.

The bearish harami cross pattern

The next bearish two-day pattern is closely related to the pattern we discussed in the preceding section and can be used in a similar manner. This pattern — the bearish harami cross — also marks the return of the doji in this chapter. A *doji* is a candlestick pattern that looks like a cross and usually indicates some sort of indecision in the market. (Dojis are covered in Chapter 6.) When this indecision occurs in a trend, it may signal that the trend is preparing to reverse.

Recognizing the bearish harami cross

The bearish harami cross occurs in an uptrend and consists of an up setup day followed by a doji for the signal day. The signal-day doji must be both a cross and an inside day. Figure 8-7 illustrates the bearish harami cross.

TIP

Because the doji indicates that indecision ruled the day, we actually prefer the bearish harami cross to the plain old harami reversal pattern. Dojis are rare, and the occurrence of a bearish harami cross pattern is a bigger event than the appearance of the bearish harami.

Trading on the bearish harami cross

Figure 8-8 is a chart of Target (TGT) which gives you an idea of how the bearish harami cross can spell market success for you. This chart shows trading activity for Target.

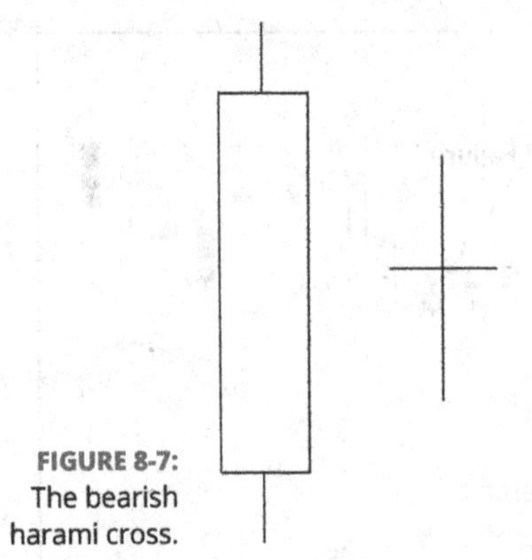

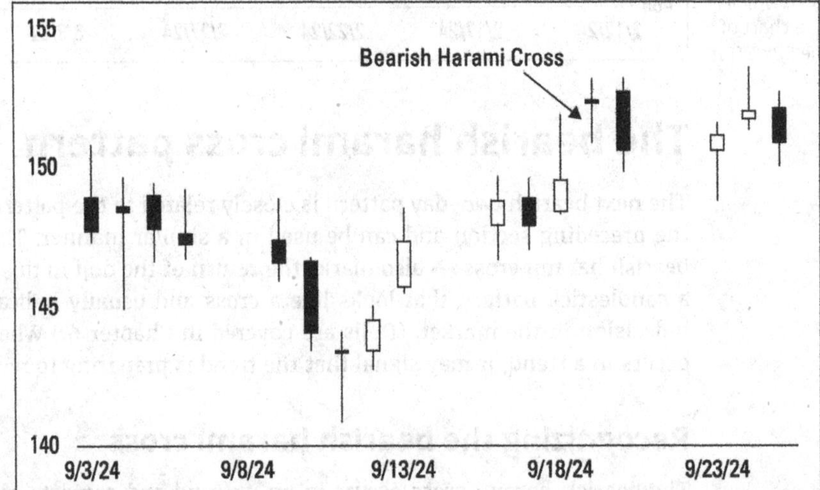

This signal occurs in the midst of a strong uptrend for TGT, with the setup day consisting of bullish trading activity. The next day, trading falls within the high and low of the setup day, and the close is near where TGT opened for the day. This activity is followed a lower price and two consecutive days on which the bears rule the trading activity. TGT does manage to trade up to the low of the signal day a couple of days later, but it never breaches any significant levels, continuing to put in lower prices.

Signaling a losing trade

To illustrate a failing bearish harami cross, we'll use Target again, one of the most familiar companies in the world. In Figure 8-9, you can see that during a slight uptrend, a little cross appears after a bullish day. This cross or doji is actually a slight up day, but it's a doji just the same in our book. This bearish harami fails pretty quickly, and the uptrend stays intact.

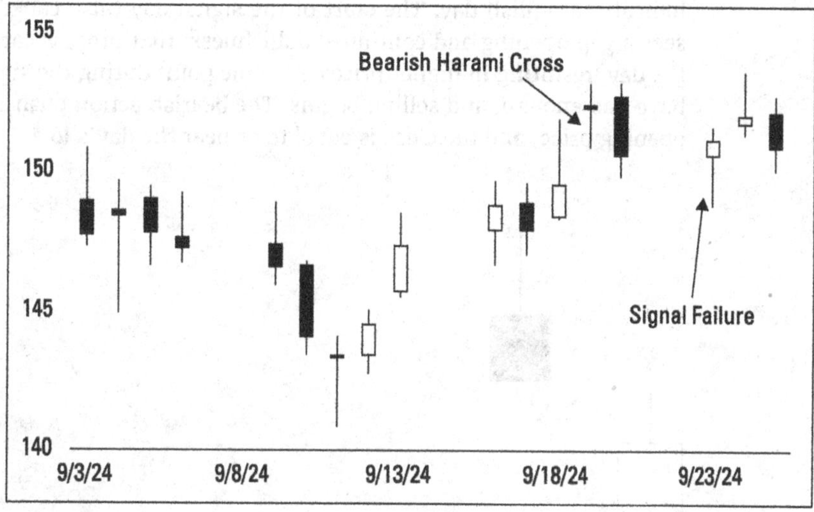

FIGURE 8-9: A bearish harami cross pattern failing in a chart of TGT stock.

REMEMBER

Signals sometimes fail, and trades sold by the exchange temporarily, only to reveal price action that could have produced profitable results. These occurrences are frustrating, but we've never been upset with ourselves for following trading rules or signals, even when it's clear a few hours or days later that we could have made money by overriding a stop or ignoring a failure signal. When we consistently follow the rules, we can't second-guess ourselves, but if we don't follow the rules and a trade fails, we can only blame ourselves. We suggest that you adopt the same philosophy, especially if you're just starting to trade.

TIP

We can't emphasize enough that sticking with a trading plan and following your rules may be the key to becoming a successful trader.

The bearish inverted hammer pattern

Like many of the bearish reversal patterns described in this chapter, the bearish inverted hammer is set up with a long white candle that occurs during an uptrend, followed by a gap opening and even more buying to start the signal day. But at some point, the bears are called to action and start to push prices lower — if you keep your eyes peeled for that move and trade accordingly, you should be able to turn a profit.

Identifying the bearish inverted hammer

Figure 8-10 depicts the bearish inverted hammer. The inverted hammer is actually the second day of the pattern. The setup day is a long white candle, which indicates a bullish day. The start of the signal day (also called the *hammer day*) sees a gap opening and continued bullishness; that process carries on for part of the day, resulting in higher prices. At some point during the signal day, the bears have had enough, and selling begins. The bearish action pushes prices below the opening price, and the close is equal to or near the day's low.

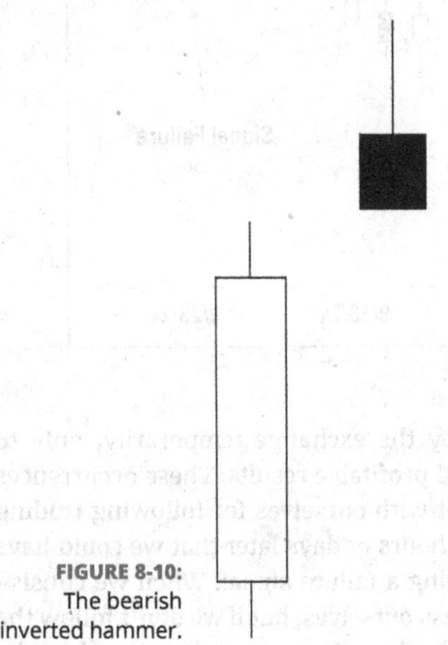

FIGURE 8-10:
The bearish inverted hammer.

Using the bearish inverted hammer in your trades

To provide a winning scenario for the bearish inverted hammer (see Figure 8-11), for Target.

Recognizing a losing trade

On a somewhat gloomier note, Figure 8-12 shows a couple of failing bearish inverted hammers; this example revisits the TGT Stock. Luckily, we didn't have a real-life trade for this example, because the signal failed twice in a short period.

Both patterns appear in an uptrend and both feature an up setup day followed by a gap opening and strong activity during the signal day that reverses with a lower close. Although these signals usually indicate a reversal, both times they proved to be false fairly quickly. In both cases, the high of the signal day was violated the day after the signal.

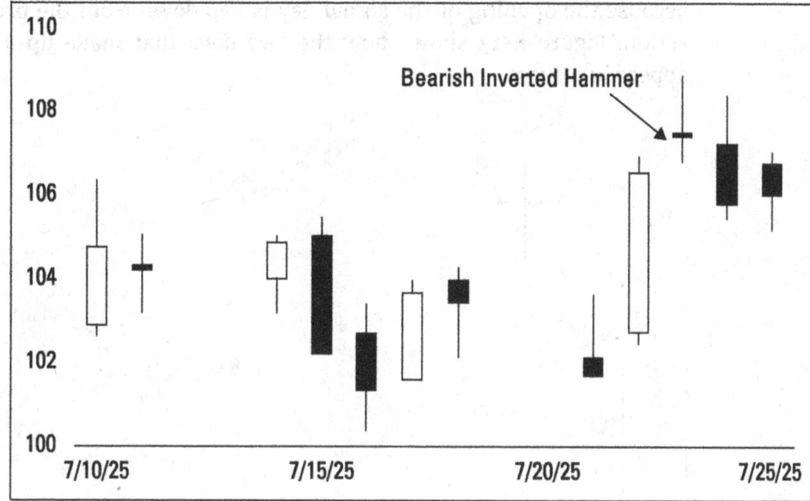

FIGURE 8-11: A bearish inverted hammer working in a chart of TGT stock.

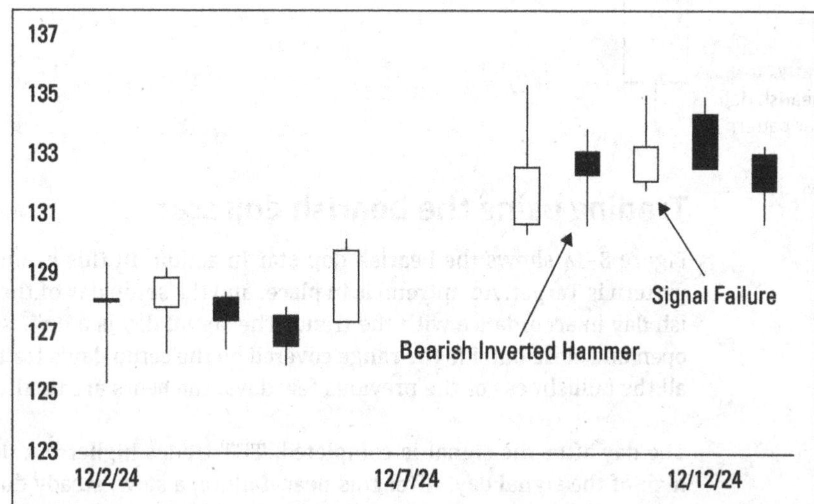

FIGURE 8-12: Two bearish inverted hammer failures in a chart of the TGT stock.

The bearish doji star

The bearish doji star is another bearish reversal pattern that contains — you guessed it — a doji. This pattern is also an extension of the bearish inverted hammer, which we discuss in the preceding section.

Spotting the bearish doji star

The bearish doji star always occurs when you have an uptrend and the setup day is an up day. The signal day is a doji that's sort of hanging out there by itself, because the opening of the signal day is gap down from the previous day's price action. Figure 8-13 shows how the two days that make up a bearish doji star appear in a chart.

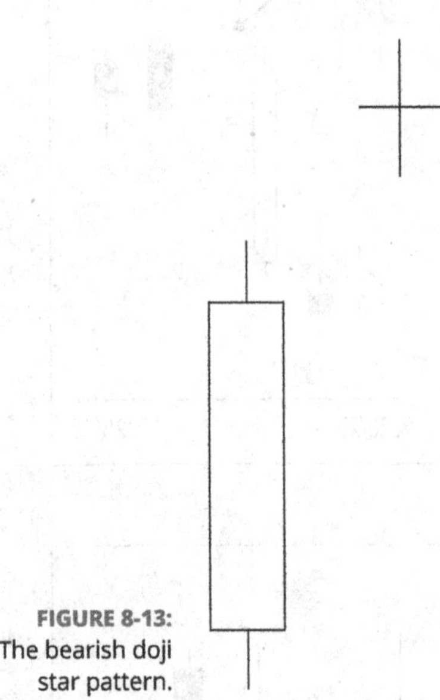

FIGURE 8-13: The bearish doji star pattern.

Trading using the bearish doji star

Figure 8-14 shows the bearish doji star in action. In this example, this doji star pattern is Target. An uptrend is in place, and the setup day of the pattern is a bullish day in accordance with the trend. The signal day is a doji, with the combined open and close outside the range covered by the setup day's trading activity. After all the bullishness of the previous few days, the bears are finally making a stand.

The day after the signal is completed, TGT trades higher but doesn't breach the high of the signal day. After this near-failure, a slow, steady downtrend favoring the bears takes over.

Failing to give a good short signal

For the losing example of a bearish doji star, we'll stick with TGT stock. In Figure 8-15, the bearish doji star highlighted in the figure showed up during a bullish trend; you can see that this chart includes a nice up day followed by a doji.

All the bearish doji star criteria are in place, but the pattern fails swiftly and mercilessly, and the trend continues with a strong up day directly after the pattern.

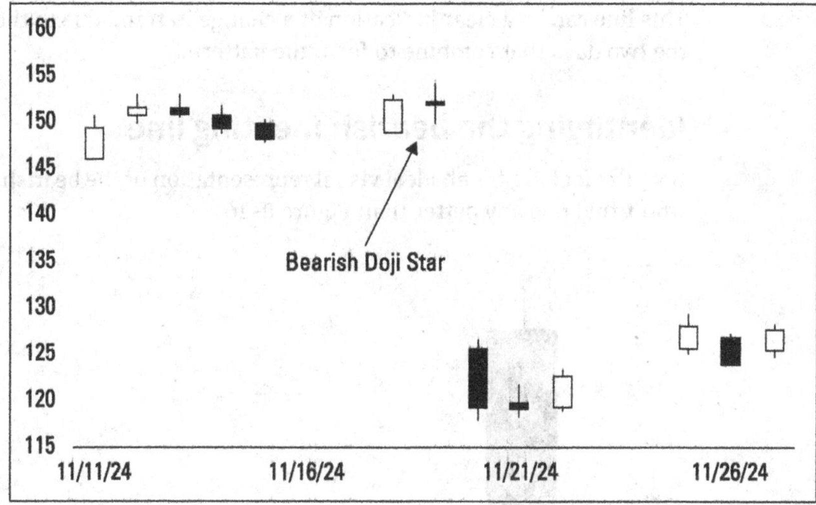

FIGURE 8-14: A bearish doji star pattern working in a chart of TGT stock.

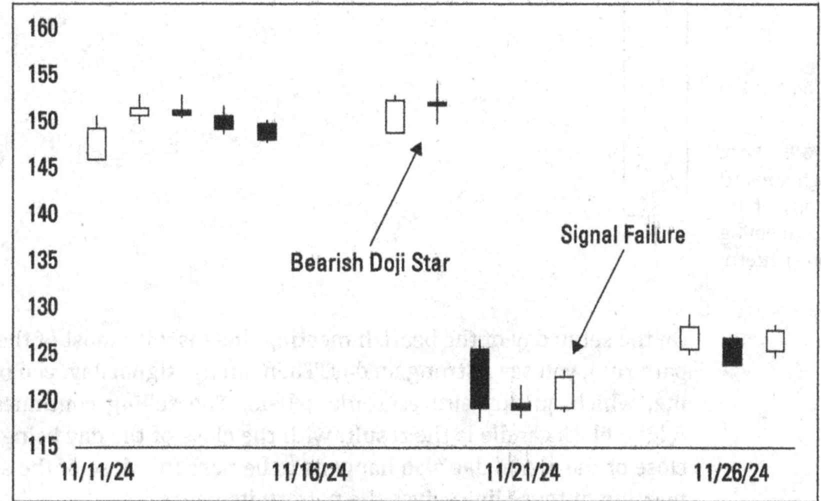

FIGURE 8-15: The bearish doji star pattern failing in a chart of the TGT.

REMEMBER

Our failure level for a bearish doji star is the high of the signal day, as opposed to that day's open or close. Using the combined open and close area of the doji doesn't provide much room for volatility on a stop. If the stock opens just slightly up the next day, it will hit the buy stop, which is likely to happen even in the case of a trend reversal. To avoid being forced out of a trade by regular market noise, we prefer to rely on the high of the signal day as our stop exit.

The bearish meeting line

Although rare, the bearish meeting line pattern is worth understanding as you build your arsenal of double-stick bearish patterns that signal a trend reversal. This line can be a clear indication of a change in trend due to the stark contrast of the two days that combine to form the pattern.

Identifying the bearish meeting line

If you're looking for an ideal visual representation of the bearish meeting line, you won't find one any better than Figure 8-16.

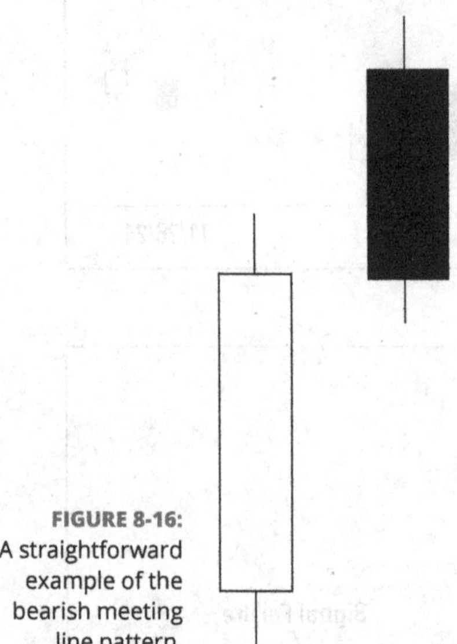

On the setup day of the bearish meeting line (as with most of the two-day bearish patterns), you see a strong up day. Then, on the signal day, you notice a gap opening, which quickly entices some sellers. The selling continues until the close. A long black candle is the result, with the close of the day being near its low. The close of the signal day also happens to be near the close of the setup day, and the meeting of these lines gives the pattern its name.

Trading on the bearish meeting line

For an example of the bearish meeting line pattern producing a scenario that's ripe for a successful trade, see Figure 8-17. It's a chart of Walmart (WMT), which you (and many others) may have used to purchase this book. As a seller of just about anything you can imagine (except cars), WMT is another stock that has strong ties to the overall economy.

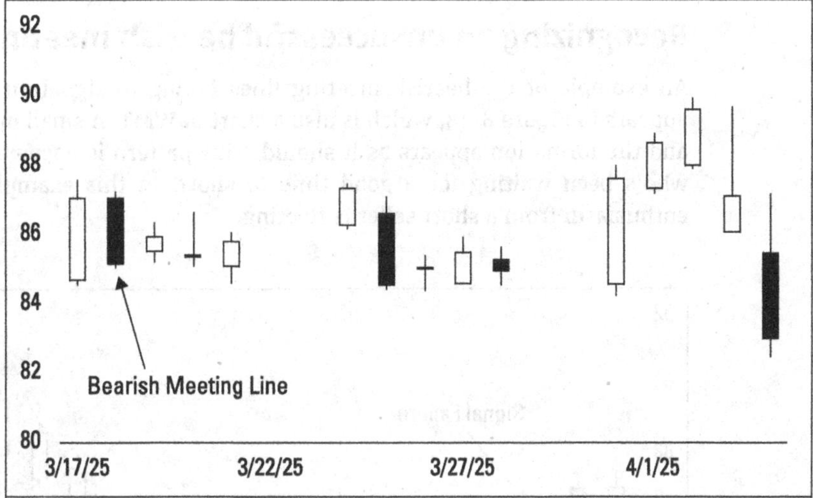

A definite uptrend exists in this chart — the first criterion for keeping an eye out for a bearish reversal signal. The setup day is a nice up day; then the signal day opens with a gap that's higher relative to the closing price the previous day. The bulls are ruling the trading activity, and the situation is perfect for a successful bearish meeting line pattern.

If you were watching this pattern develop, you'd be pleased to see that sellers come in to push prices lower than the previous day's close. Although the stock rebounds a little, the price settles on the signal day near where the stock closed on the setup day.

Then the trend reversal begins, and what a trend reversal it is! Five of the next six days have black candles, with the one up day being bearish in its own right, as there's a gap lower and little overlap with the previous day's activity. Any trader who wasn't prepared on the day the signal was completed missed out on a good part of the outstanding downtrend.

To get in on the close of a day when a pattern is completed, watch for the patterns as they develop during a trading day. Usually, with five to ten minutes left in a trading day, you can tell whether a pattern is forming. The problem for you, if you're a new or part-time trader, is that you probably have a job or other responsibilities that may prevent you from being available to trade during these important periods. Be sure to factor in your own availability when developing your trading strategy. Finally, many stocks are still quite liquid after the official trading day has ended, so with many stocks, you may have to wait until just after the official close to enter the trade.

Recognizing an unsuccessful bearish meeting line

An example of the bearish meeting lines failing to signal an uptrend reversal appears in Figure 8-18, which is also a chart of WMT. A small uptrend is in place, and the formation appears as it should. This pattern is encouraging for a trader who's been waiting for a good time to short. In this example, however, that enthusiasm from a short seller is fleeting.

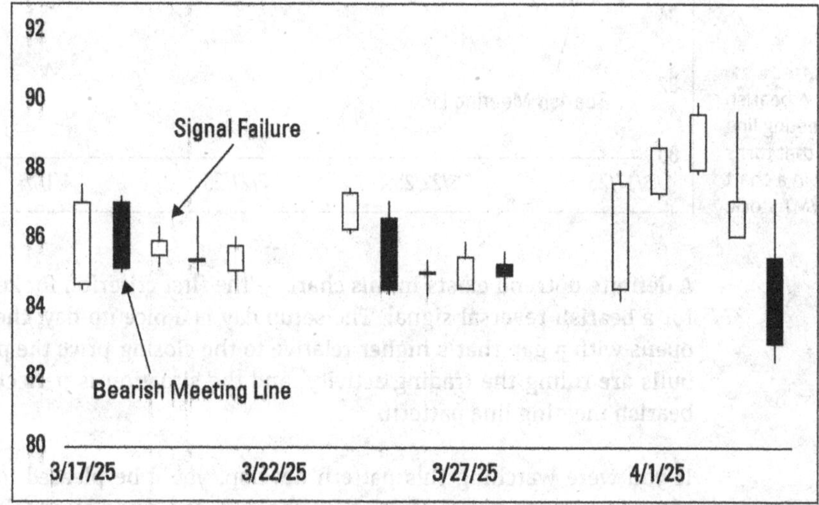

FIGURE 8-18: The bearish meeting line pattern failing in a chart of WMT stock.

The day that follows the pattern proves it to be invalid. Prices trade higher than both the open and the high of the pattern's signal day, making it clear that the pattern is a bust.

When we're shorting based on the bearish meeting line pattern, we usually place our stops on either the high of the signal day or the open of the signal day.

The bearish piercing line (or dark cloud cover pattern)

Another two-day bearish reversal pattern is the bearish piercing line (also known as the *dark cloud cover* because some people say that the signal day is an ominous dark cloud that hangs over the setup day). This pattern requires a little use of your imagination.

Identifying the bearish piercing line pattern

You can see a straightforward illustration of the bearish piercing line in Figure 8-19. Like all the bearish two-stick reversal patterns we describe in the preceding sections, this pattern must appear in an uptrend. Also, in keeping with the other bearish reversal patterns, the setup day for the bearish piercing line is a bullish day. The signal day is a long black candle with an opening that's higher than the setup day's high. The signal day indicates that some sellers came rushing in, pushing prices down through the setup day's opening price and below its midpoint.

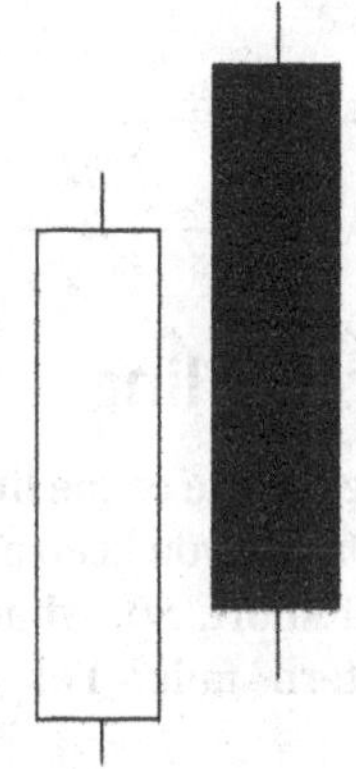

FIGURE 8-19: The bearish piercing line pattern.

Making trades based on the bearish piercing line

You can use a bearish piercing line pattern to put on a profitable short, as you see in Figure 8-20. This chart shows the bearish piercing line in a chart of Walmart (WMT).

The pattern occurs in what appears to be a push higher after a slowing uptrend. The price is still working higher, but not with as much momentum as it did where we've pointed out the first stage of the uptrend. This signal is a pretty solid one, as all of the next five days are down days, both on a day-over-day basis and on an intraday basis, with each of those signals being black candles.

If you see a reversal pattern when you believe that a trend is starting to lose steam, that pattern is more encouraging than one that appears during a strong trend. In Chapters 11, 14, and 15, we discuss how to use indicators to make these distinctions.

REMEMBER

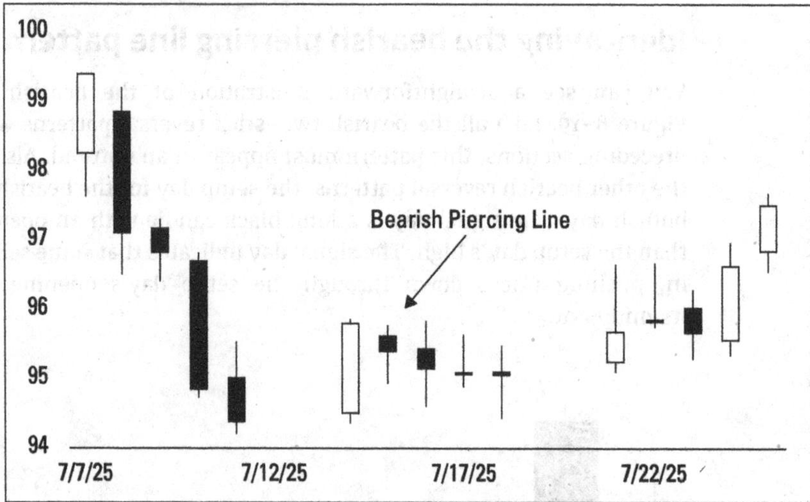

FIGURE 8-20: The bearish piercing line pattern working in a chart of WMT stock.

Falling short with the bearish piercing line

The WMT chart shown in Figure 8-21 is another example of the limited amount of time you may have for initiating certain trades. Unless you keep a close eye on the chart, you miss your chance to sell a successful short. So, what does a bearish piercing line pattern look like when the pattern fails? For an answer, see Figure 8-21.

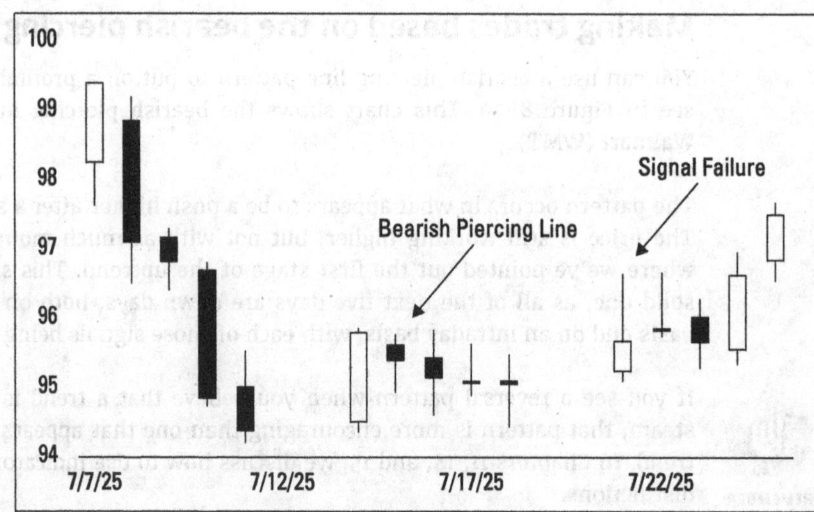

FIGURE 8-21: The bearish piercing line pattern failing in a chart of WMT stock.

Taking a closer look at Figure 8-21, you see seven white candles marching ever higher, indicating the kind of bearish piercing line that occurs during a strong uptrend. The uptrend continues and the failure of the pattern (and the appearance of higher prices) takes a few days. If you jump the gun on this pattern and sell a short without a smart stop, you see some losses.

Making a Profit with Bearish Trend Patterns

In addition to double-stick patterns that tell a trader it's time to sell or put on a short after an upward trending move, some patterns indicate that a downtrend continuation is on the horizon. These patterns can tell you when you still have room to profit on a short. You can also turn to them when you're looking to buy a stock that's been in a downtrend and looks to be getting cheap. A bearish double-stick trend continuation pattern can let you know that a stock will get cheaper and therefore can be had at an even lower price.

REMEMBER

All the two-day bearish trending patterns covered in this section require that the market or stock in question be in a down-trending mode. Determining the trend can be subjective and can also be a matter of the time frame in which you're trading. We go into great detail on determining trends in later chapters (especially Chapter 11), but for this section, just concentrate on the pattern; don't worry as much about whether you agree with our assessment of the prevailing trend.

The bearish thrusting lines

The first two-day pattern that indicates the continuation of a downtrend is the bearish thrusting lines pattern. We like this pattern because the signal day is an up day. You may scratch your head and wonder why we like an up day that indicates the continuation of a downtrend. At first blush, it does sound counterintuitive, but the presence of an up day on the signal day of this pattern means that a great opportunity exists to put on a short at prices higher than those on the previous day of the downtrend.

Spotting the bearish thrusting lines

Figure 8-22 shows you exactly what the bearish thrusting lines look like in a chart. Again, the prevailing trend should be down, and the setup day is a long black candle. On the signal day, prices open weak, but then the bulls come in, trying to reverse the trend and take over. They seem to be succeeding, but they're not quite strong enough to get prices to the upper half of the candlestick that was created by the setup day's trading. This activity means that although the bears don't completely control the day, they are still around and eager to reassert themselves in the coming days.

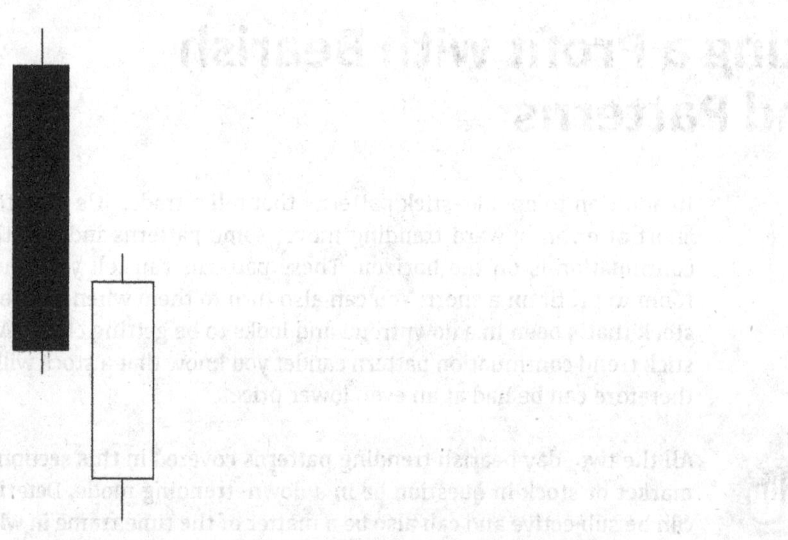

Trading on the bearish thrusting lines

For an example of the bearish thrusting lines working well, Figure 8-23 shows JPMorgan Chase (JPM).

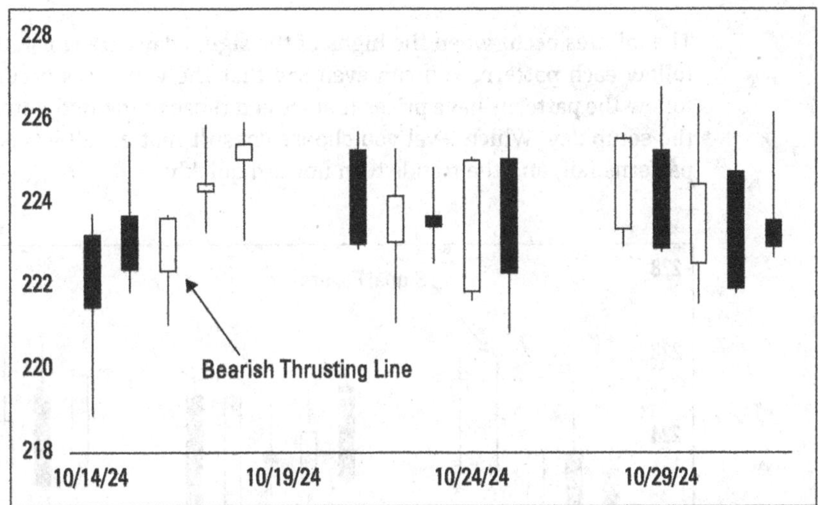

FIGURE 8-23: The bearish thrusting lines pattern working in a chart of JPM stock.

The bearish thrusting line shows up as JPM appears to be topping out as the uptrend starts to roll over. The open of the signal day is never violated, but it does take time for the pattern to work itself out. The pattern shows up nicely on the far right side of the chart, with six bearish days in a row finishing with a gap lower.

REMEMBER

A successful trade based on the bearish thrusting lines in this chart starts with the close of the first pattern's signal day. If you're short from the top of this downtrend, you definitely feel like a skilled trader. You can easily monitor the continuation patterns and follow the trend as it heads down. But where would you exit the short?

Making an exit would be prudent when the price trades over the trend. At that point, the downtrend has been broken, and the easy money on the short has been made, so be smart: Take your tidy profit and move on.

Recognizing a disappointing bearish thrusting line pattern

Want to see what happens when the bearish thrusting lines fail? Look no further than Figure 8-24, which is yet another JPM chart. Toward the end of this downtrend, you see a bearish thrusting line, which often indicates a continuation of a downtrend. In this case, however, the following day is a bullish day.

We hate to see the pattern in Figure 8-24 fail. They bearish thrusting lines start with so much promise! The pattern appears in downtrends and meets the criterion of having a long-black-candle setup day followed by an up signal day that retraces some of the preceding day's area but doesn't close higher than its midpoint.

The failures occur when the highs of the signal days are violated on the days that follow each pattern. You can even say that the violations occur when days that follow the patterns have prices that exceed those at the midpoint, open, or high of the setup day. Which level you choose doesn't matter; all levels get violated, the patterns fail, and the trends turn upward quickly.

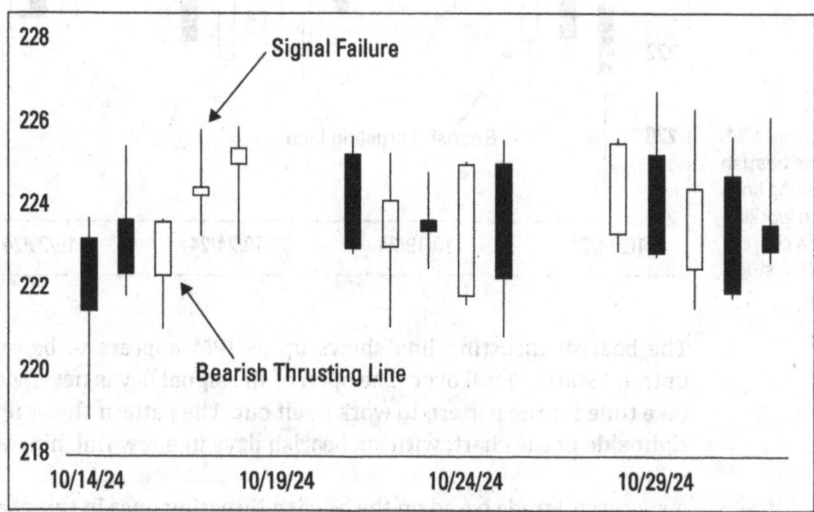

FIGURE 8-24: The bearish thrusting lines failing for JPM.

The bearish separating lines

The next continuation or trending pattern is the bearish separating lines pattern. (Chapter 7 discusses this pattern's bullish counterpart.)

Identifying the bearish separating lines

The setup day of the bearish separating lines pattern is a long white candle, which can make some bears or shorts a bit nervous when it appears in a downtrend. A little relief for those factions comes on the signal day, however, when the opening price is near the setup day's open. That price relaxes them a bit, and they decide that the up day wasn't justified, so they keep selling on the open of the signal day. But what happens to the bulls who had a ball on the setup day? They can't take the heat, so they sell their positions, and the price keeps trending lower. For a graphical representation, check out Figure 8-25.

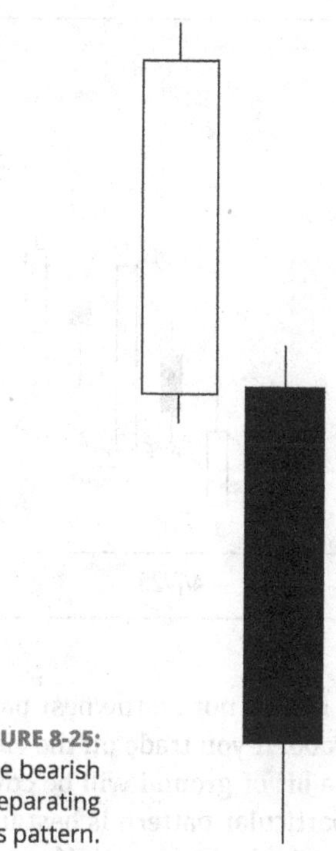

REMEMBER

This pattern is somewhat rare because it's unusual for the open of the signal day to be equal or near the setup day's open. It really amounts to a gap down opening, or having a quick price drop, with all the prices from the setup day not even trading on the signal day. Short-term buyers on the setup day hardly have a chance to get out with a profit on the signal day, which is a discouraging prospect for a buyer.

Knowing how to trade on the bearish separating lines

The example we use in Figure 8-26 to illustrate how you can use the bearish separating lines for your trading purposes.

The chart itself (yet another JPM chart) is a small picture of a longer-term downtrend that was in place, with a couple of bullish days in the midst of the downtrend. The setup day for this pattern is a white candle, which indicates a bullish day in a bearish trend, with the signal day indicating a resumption of the downtrend.

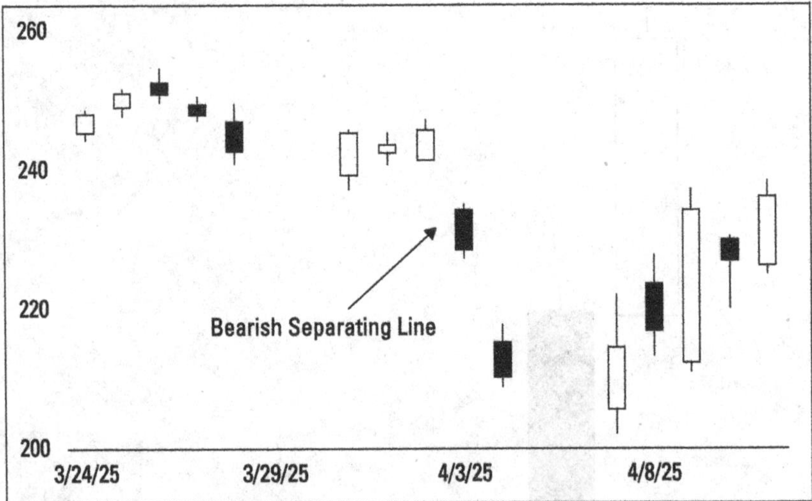

FIGURE 8-26: The bearish separating lines pattern working beautifully in a chart of JPM.

TIP

The pattern in Figure 8-26 is well formed, but it may not be the best pattern to rely on if you're interested in initiating a new trade. If you trade on the close, you sell at the bottom of a long black day, so quite a bit of ground will be covered in the direction in which you want to trade. This particular pattern is best used as a confirmation that the downtrend is intact, and you're lucky to see it if you want to hold on to a short position for a little while longer.

Recognizing a failing bearish separating line

Just when you thought you'd always love bearish separating lines, here's an example of what happens when this pattern goes bad. Figure 8-27 is another chart of JPM.

The downtrend on the chart in Figure 8-27 is a strong one, and when the pattern appears, it looks as though this downtrend will continue. The setup day of the pattern is an attempt by some buyers to pick a cheap place to buy. Then, on the signal day, the bears take over from the open and push prices lower. But notice that on the day immediately after the pattern, both the open and high of the signal day are violated — a pretty good sign that the pattern may not be indicating that the trend will continue.

Shortly after the pattern in Figure 8-27 is violated, a trend reversal occurs. If you're considering buying before you see the bearish separating lines, that pattern may keep you from doing so. If you're short when you see the pattern, you may have waited to cover, or protect, your position. Because the pattern didn't hold and the trend was broken, buyers can change their minds more easily and start buying. That's certainly the case here, and you can see that the price of JPM heads higher for a couple of days as a result.

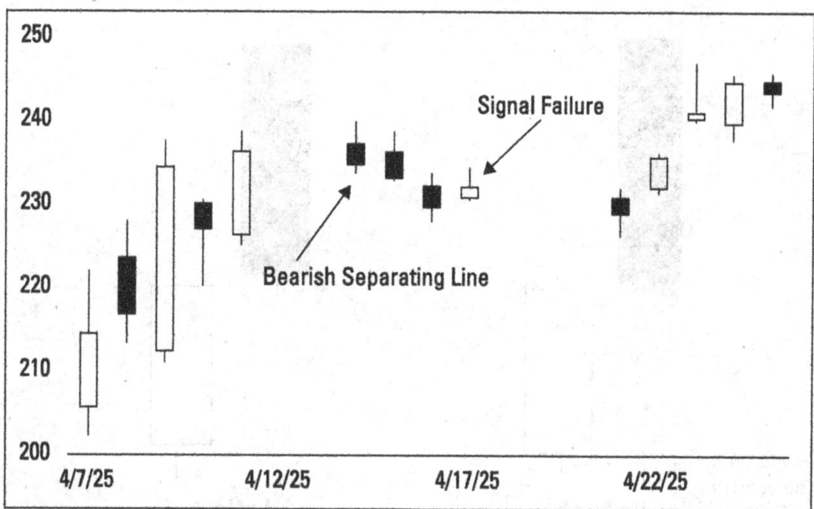

The bearish neck lines

The last bearish double-stick pattern in this chapter is bearish neck lines. Like its bullish counterparts in Chapter 7, this pattern is more a pattern classification than one single pattern.

Recognizing bearish neck lines

Bearish neck lines come in two types: bearish *on neck* lines and bearish *in neck* lines. The difference between the patterns is so small that you don't have to separate them into two sections.

Figure 8-28 includes both bearish in neck and bearish on neck patterns. The only difference is that the wick of the in neck setup day may overlap the signal day of the pattern. Both variations have a long black candle for the setup day, followed by a gap down and a rebound attempt that manages to trade back only to the close of the setup day. The bears hold their ground at this level.

Using the bearish neck lines for profitable trading

Figure 8-29 shows one more JPM chart. The bearish neck line on this chart is slightly in neck because the setup day overlaps with the signal day. The bulls try to put the price higher, but they're met with bearish resistance over the next two days. Finally, this reward is a gap lower, followed by lower prices over the next couple of weeks.

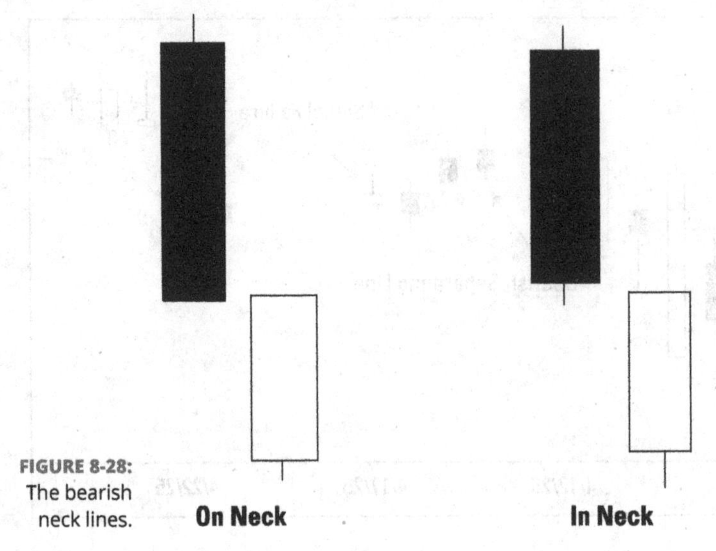

FIGURE 8-28:
The bearish
neck lines.

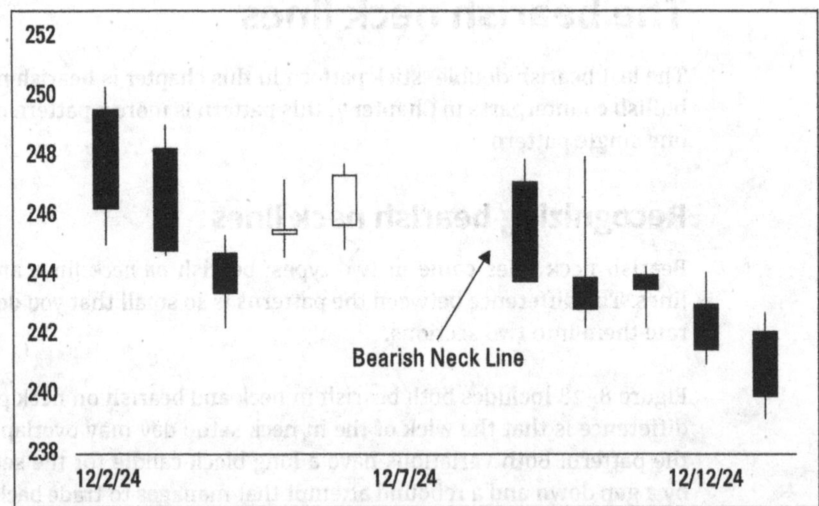

FIGURE 8-29:
The bearish neck
lines working in a
chart of the JPM.

REMEMBER

This pattern is valid even though prices don't continue down on the following day. The trend doesn't break, and the price levels of the long black day aren't violated. The next couple of days may be nerve-racking for bears, but those who hold their ground on a short are rewarded with lower prices.

Noticing an unsuccessful bearish neck line

Like the rest of the two-stick patterns in this chapter, the bearish neck lines can fail. Figure 8-30 is a chart showing the price action for JPM.

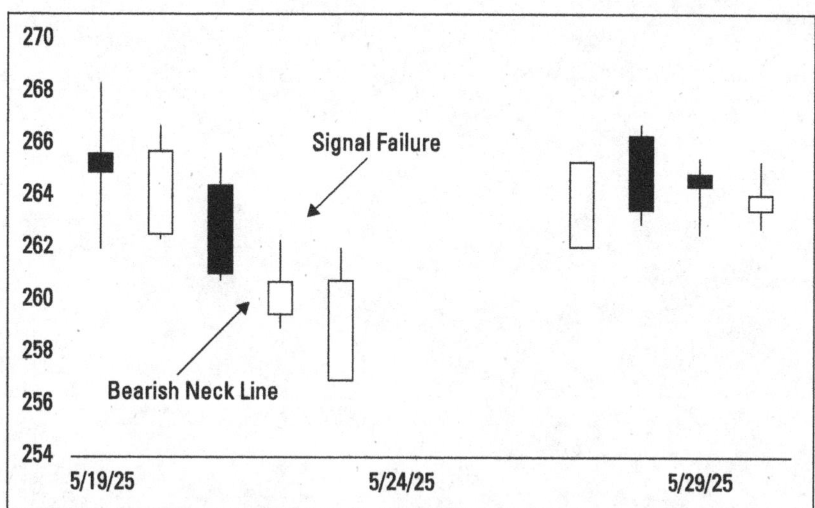

The bearish neck line appears during a downtrend, and the other criteria are in place; the setup day is represented by a long black candle, which is followed by a gap down. Then prices rebound, but the bears hold the price steady. All appears to be well, but a couple of days after the pattern appears, the bulls get rolling on a more successful run, and the trend changes. The following day is bullish for JPM. The price runs through any stop that you would have set based on the setup and signal day prices.

3
Making the Most of Complex Patterns

Acquire a working knowledge of complex patterns that emerge over three days of trading.

Find out how to spot these patterns as they emerge and know when it's time to act.

Get familiar with some basic technical indicators that are used to determine whether the market is trending or reversing.

Combine technical indicators with candlestick patterns for trade entries and exits.

Chapter **9**

Getting the Hang of Bullish Three-Stick Patterns

The addition of three-stick candlestick patterns to your trading arsenal makes your trading strategies more complicated, more interesting, and (we hope) more profitable. In this chapter, we cover some of the bullish three-stick patterns you can use to make effective and efficient trades.

Interpreting the three-stick patterns is a little more of a challenge than their single- and double-stick counterparts because each must follow several rules to emerge as a valid signal. Three-stick patterns can also be frustrating: You might watch the first two days of your favorite (and most reliable) pattern begin to emerge, for example, only to see it fizzle out on the third day. But if you're up to the challenge and willing to deal with the occasional annoyance, these patterns can be valuable tools for predicting trend reversals or confirming that a current trend will stay in place.

Understanding Bullish Three-Stick Trend Reversal Patterns

The three-stick patterns in this section offer you a heads-up whenever a downtrend is about to switch gears and turn into an uptrend. Many of these three-stick patterns exist, and in the pages that follow, we cover many of the most common ones. Because three days are needed to complete each pattern, you have time to watch as the patterns shape up. Your focus should be sharpest on the third day, after you've noticed the interesting developments on the chart during the two preceding days.

When working with three-day patterns, be prepared by closely monitoring days that follow two days of promising price action. If a pattern is completed as you'd hoped, you need to be ready to put on the appropriate trade and stop order near the close of the day on which the pattern is completed.

The three inside up pattern

The three inside up pattern is a good place to begin a discussion of the bullish three-stick patterns that let you know when a downtrend is about to be reversed. This pattern is a straightforward one that you can recognize with just a little practice.

Identifying the three inside up pattern

The three inside up pattern has a peculiar name, but a quick look at Figure 9-1 should give you a good idea of where the name originated. The *three* part comes from the three days involved in creating the pattern. There are three sticks, and the second day is an inside day relative to the first day, which is a long down day. *Inside* means that the price action for the second day traded within the high and low of the first day. The final day is an up day that closes higher than the open of the first day.

The trading activity that results in a three inside up pattern involves a gradual shift of power from the bears to the bulls. We like this pattern and the way it develops, because it usually gives a trader time to put on a trade before too much of the reversal has occurred. Traders can always buy high with the intention of selling higher, but it's nice when buying high doesn't mean buying *too* high.

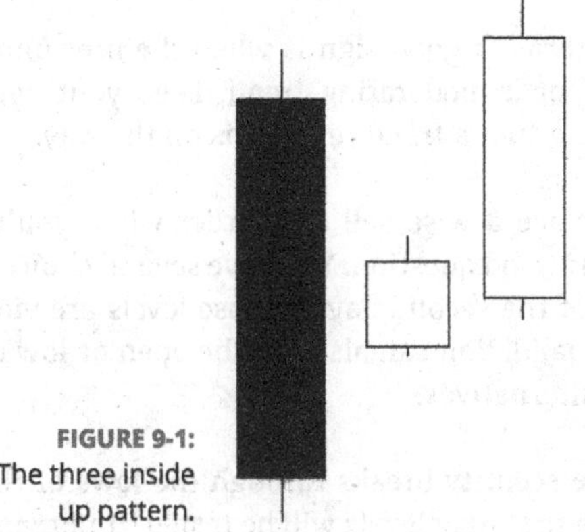

Making effective trades using the three inside up pattern

The chart in Figure 9-2 gives you a clear idea of how the three inside up pattern can tip you off on when to buy before a forthcoming uptrend. The figure shows a chart of trades based on Apple (APPL) stock.

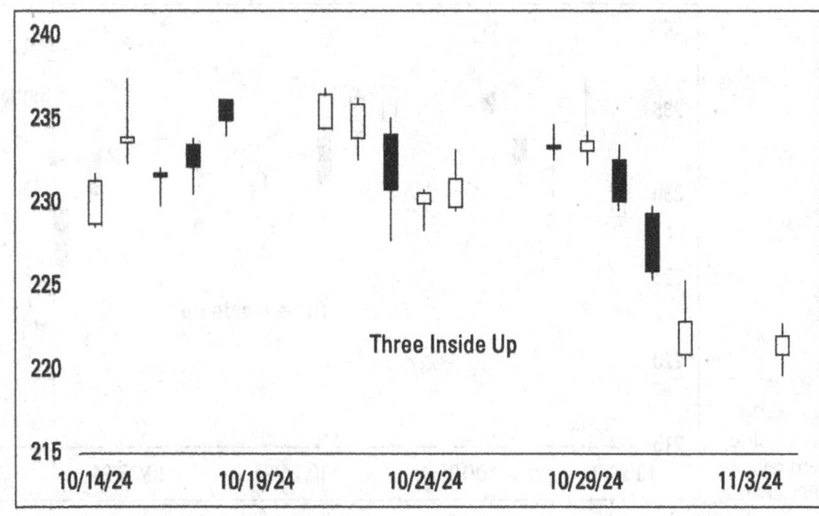

This chart shows a slight downtrend followed by a bearish day in the price of Apple stock (APPL). The trend reverses immediately to the upside after the pattern is completed.

If you're looking for trend reversal patterns, a good sign is when the prevailing trend starts to moderate. When you spot a moderating trend, keep your eyes peeled for a candlestick pattern indicating that a trend reversal is on the way.

Are you wondering where you might place a wise sell stop order when you're working with the three inside up pattern? Good question. You have several choices. In most cases, we use the open or low of the second day. If those levels are violated, we regard the pattern as being invalid. You can also use the open or low of the third day, both of which are viable alternatives.

Avoid using the first day because, if the security breaks through the lows of the first two days, there's a good chance the first-day levels will be tested, if not violated. Wouldn't you rather be out of the long trade before this situation occurs?

The three inside up pattern isn't working out well

This section gives you an example of what can happen when a three inside up pattern fails. Figure 9-3 shows a three inside up pattern that appears in a downtrend but doesn't signal a trend reversal. The figure shows a chart for APPL.

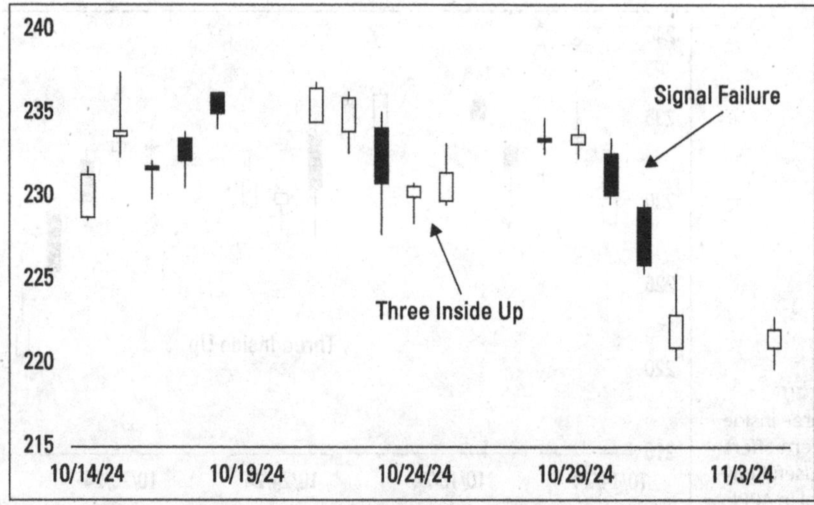

FIGURE 9-3:
The three inside up pattern failing in an APPL chart.

The first day of the pattern in Figure 9-3 is a down day, and the second day shows a gap up but doesn't have a low that violates the low of the first day. The second day's close is also higher than its open, but the second day's close stays between the open and close of the first day. And if you're thinking that the second day is an inside day, you're absolutely right! Finally, the third day is also an up day — a long white bar — with an open that's higher than the open of the second day. So where does the pattern go wrong?

The two days after the pattern are the culprits. The first day is a down day after Apple opened higher and then reversed during the day to close near the low. The following day, the signal is definitely a failure because Apple shares gap lower on the open, breaking through any areas that would be considered support.

The three outside up pattern

The three outside up pattern is another relatively simple three-stick reversal pattern that you can pick up on with a little patience and basic understanding of the necessary components. This section gives you the full scoop.

Spotting the three outside up pattern

Like all bullish reversal patterns, the three outside up should occur in the midst of a downtrend. Here's how the days play out:

Day 1: The pattern's first day is a down day, but a slight down day.

Day 2: The second day opens with a gap down from the first day, but prices don't stay down for long.

This day creates an outside day relative to the first day, with the high being higher and the low being lower than on the first day. Also, the open of the day is lower than the previous close, and the close of this second day is higher than the open of the first day.

The bulls take over at some point during the second day and push prices higher until the close is near the day's high. The second day is a long white bar; it's an outside day relative to the first day. *Outside* means that the price action for the second day traded outside the high and low of the first day.

Day 3: The third day completes the pattern with another up day.

On the third day, it's clear that the bulls aren't done, and the day closes higher than the high of the second day. The trend has definitely turned, and it's headed up, up, and away.

For a straightforward example of the three outside up pattern, see Figure 9-4.

Trading on the three outside up pattern

For a real-world example of the three outside up pattern, we use a chart of the stock for a company that helps its customers escape the real world. Figure 9-5 is a chart of APPL stock. (One of their products was used to write this chapter.)

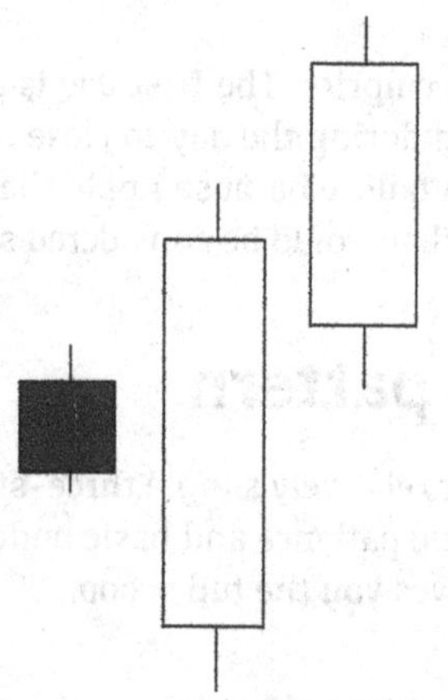

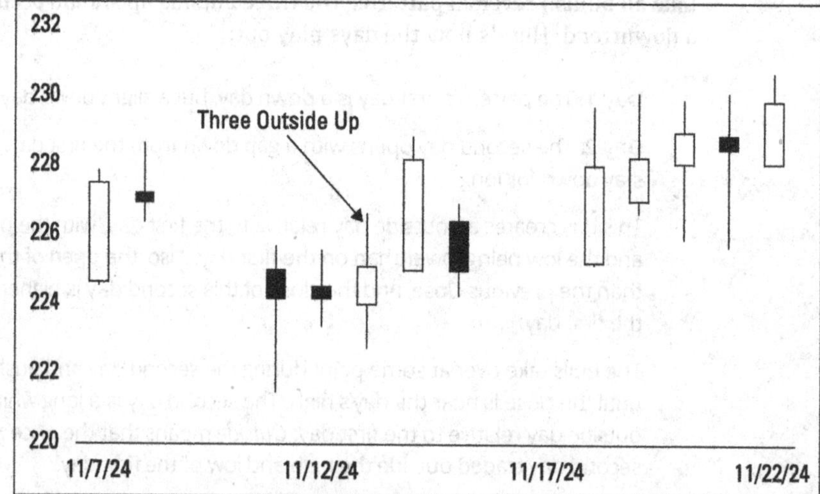

FIGURE 9-5:
The three outside
up pattern makes
for a winning
trading scenario
in a chart of
Apple stock.

In the chart, APPL appears to have found a bottom, and it looks as though an uptrend is on the horizon. When you're working with three-day reversal patterns, try to buy at the beginning of a trend when prices are relatively low compared with recent history. The pattern plays out fairly well. The trend is down, and a down day — albeit not a convincing one — occurs on the first day. The first day is followed by an outside up day, and the third day is an up day that outpaces the bullishness of the second day.

The three outside up pattern comes before more bearishness instead of bullishness

The three outside up pattern is a thing of beauty, but Figure 9-6 shows you the pattern's potential for ugliness when it goes bad. The chart is for Apple, a market that's sensitive to economic cycles and inflation. The pattern shows up in a down-trend, and the first day is indeed a down day. The second day is an up day, and it's an outside day relative to the first day, which is promising. The pattern is completed by an up third day that exhibits some bullish behavior.

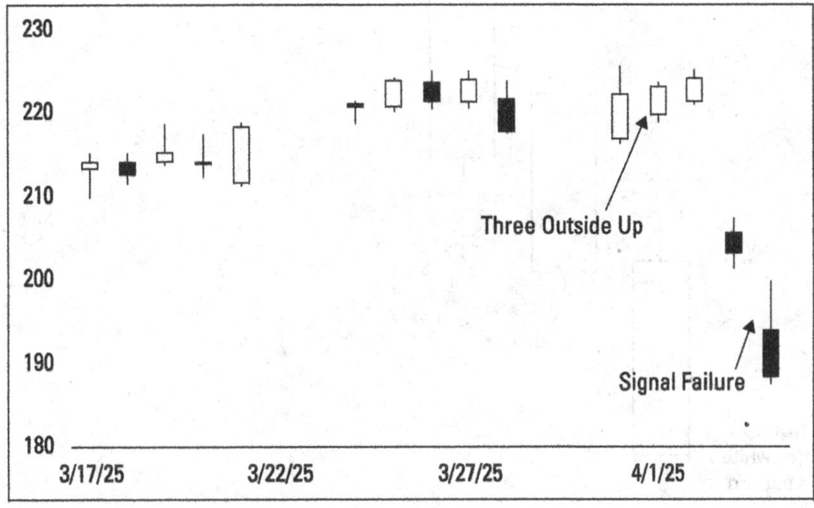

But the bullishness isn't meant to last. On the next trading day after the pattern appears, the stock never recovers over the previous day's closing price. The gap is filled quickly, and in a few days, anything that may be considered a support level is compromised. Easy come, easy go.

The three white soldiers pattern

The three white soldiers pattern includes three bullish candles in a row. If the pattern occurs with a downtrend in front of it, you can consider it a possible signal that the bulls have had enough and are buying in force.

Although it's a nice indication to buy, a small drawback to the three white soldiers is the amount of ground that's already been covered at the completion of the pattern.

Recognizing the three white soldiers

To locate the three white soldiers in a chart, look for three consecutive up days that occur in a prevailing downtrend. Then look closer. If the open, high, low, and close of the second day are higher than those of the first day, and those four points are also higher on the third day than the second, you're looking at the three white soldiers pattern. Make sense? Figure 9-7 shows a visual.

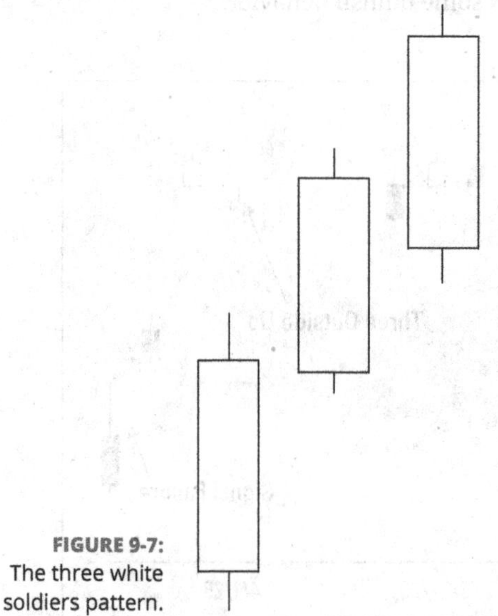

The price action behind these days is dramatic, and it normally indicates a quick shift from a downtrend to an uptrend. The three white soldiers mean that the bulls are in control for three straight days, beginning with the open of the first day.

Using the three white soldiers to make a profitable trade

The example we use to show you how to make trades based on the three white soldiers pattern is near and dear to our hearts. It's a chart of the futures contracts that trade on the level of Bitcoin, and we executed a successful trade based on this very pattern. Before spotting the pattern, we had been looking for an indication that the downtrend was coming to an end, so we were delighted to see the three white soldiers shown in Figure 9-8.

After such a dramatic move, you sometimes have the opportunity for a *pullback* (a small trend down from a higher level), but we bought the Bitcoin futures very close to the closing price of the third day of the pattern. We had a plan in place to buy Apple when it appeared that the downtrend was coming to an end, so we were a little more aggressive than necessary. With a little patience, we could have gotten a better price the next day, but we didn't want to risk missing the trade — something that sometimes feels worse than losing money.

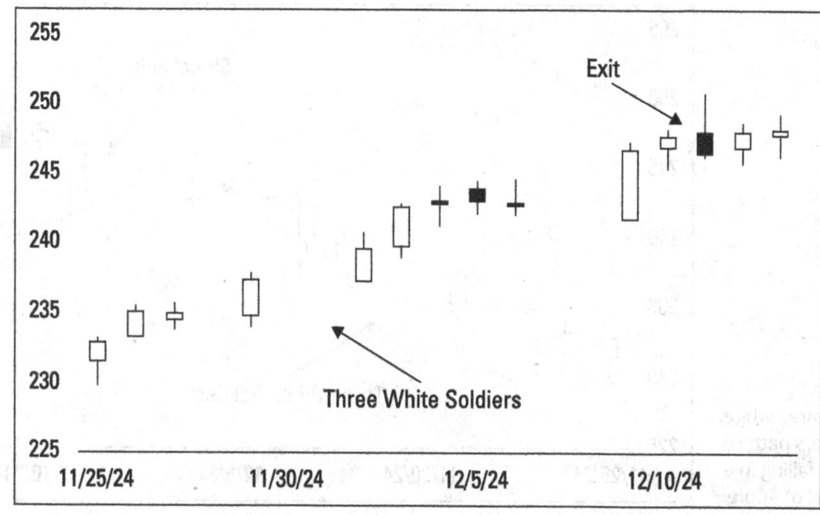

We also highlight on the chart in Figure 9-8 where we chose to exit the position. The trend had been in place for a few weeks, and the long black candle broke the low of the previous day. We had been using a sell stop order and continued to move the stop higher as the futures contract price increased. The stop was in place at the low of the day that came the day before the long black candle because we felt that this level indicated that the trend was starting to fade. We also kept an eye out for any problematic reversal formations, which you should do if you find yourself in a similar situation.

Although we exited the trade before the trend reversed again, we were still happy with this trade. We had a plan, executed it, and profited from it. Why can't all trades be as easy as this one?

The three white soldiers fail to signal bullishness

The three white soldiers pattern is a strong bullish trend reversal, but, like all other patterns, it has the potential for failure. Figure 9-9, which is a chart of APPL stock, shows you what can happen when the three white soldiers pattern doesn't fare so well in battle.

The three white soldiers pattern appears in the midst of a strong downtrend and even a gap lower, followed by some bearish candles. The pattern is encouraging because it ends with a strong upside move, but the first day after the signal may have foretold potential failure. Natural gas prices fluctuated for a few more days; then a new downtrend commenced.

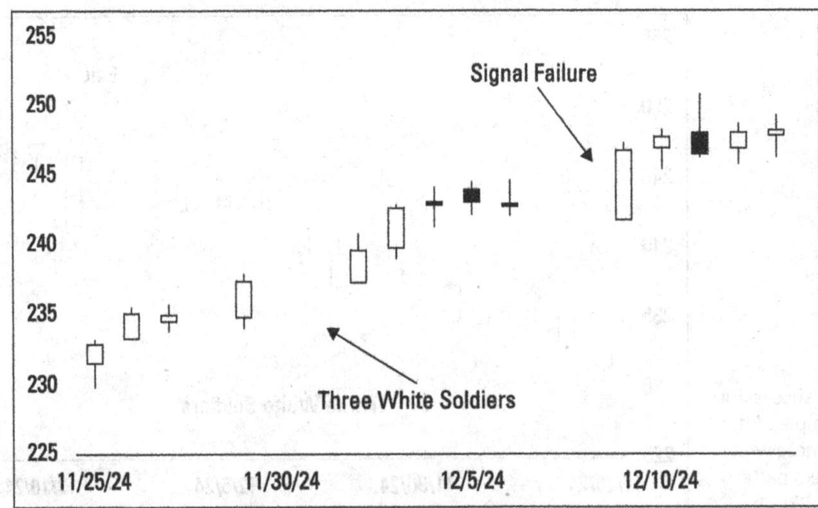

FIGURE 9-9:
The three white soldiers pattern failing in a chart of Apple.

The morning star and bullish doji star patterns

The morning star and bullish doji star are separate patterns, but because they have similar characteristics, we've grouped them together in this section.

Identifying the morning star and bullish doji star

You can see basic examples of the morning star and bullish doji star patterns in Figure 9-10. The only real difference between the two patterns is the second day: The second day of the bullish doji star is a true doji, whereas the second day of the morning star pattern is *almost* a doji.

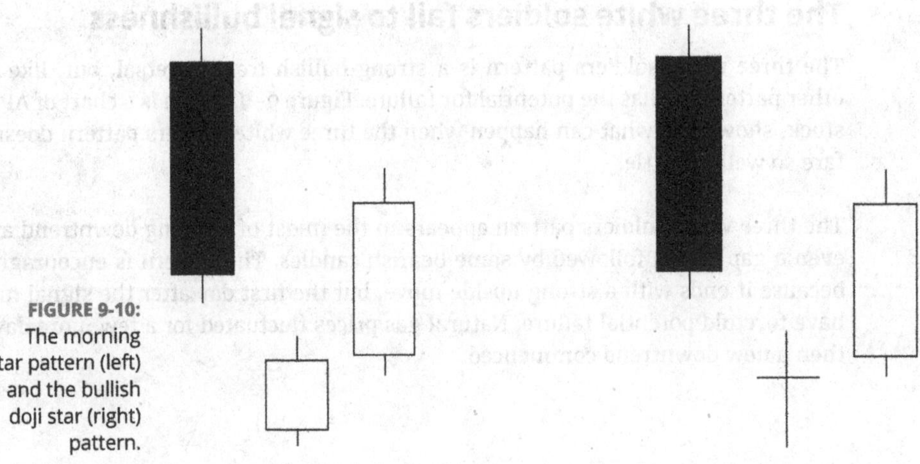

FIGURE 9-10:
The morning star pattern (left) and the bullish doji star (right) pattern.

The price action behind these two patterns is similar. The first day for both patterns is a down day, which is to be expected in a bullish reversal pattern. The second day for both patterns starts with a gap opening, indicating that the bears are continuing to push down the price. The rest of the second day is made up of very tight price action between the open and close. The third day is bullish, with prices rising to cover some or all of the ground from the down day. When you spot one of these patterns in a downtrend, it usually means that the trend is ready to reverse.

Trading on the morning star and bullish doji star patterns

Figure 9-11 is a chart of Nvidia (NVDA), one of the largest companies in the world, and it's a good example because the morning star pattern in the chart indicates that the trend has reached the bottom. Keep in mind that the morning star here could just as easily be a bullish doji star pattern, and the result would be the same.

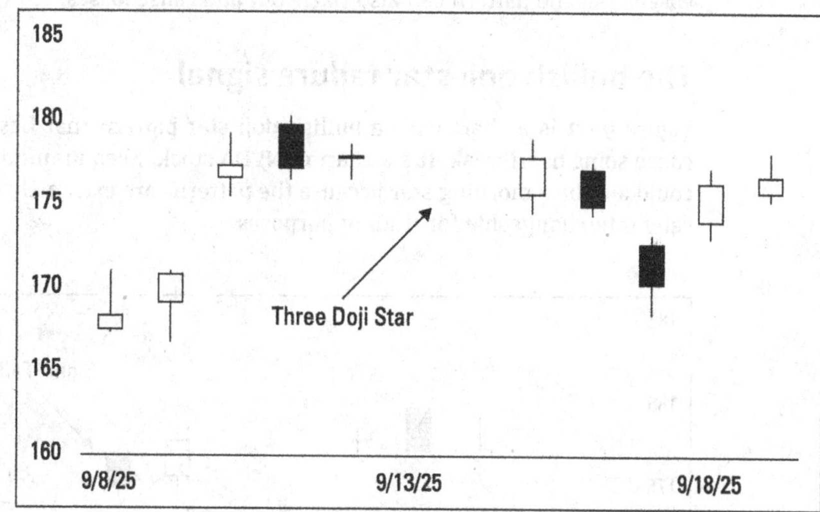

FIGURE 9-11: The morning star pattern performs favorably in a chart of NVDA stock.

The days play out in the following pattern:

Day 1: The first day of the pattern is the third of three bearish days.

Leading up to this pattern, the bears are ruling the price action.

Day 2: The second day features a gap opening that's lower than the low of the first day, and the day ends up forming a doji after some back-and-forth between the bulls and bears.

The doji has pretty long legs, indicating an intense battle for price action during the day.

Day 3: The third and final day of the pattern is a white candle, indicating that the bulls ruled the day.

The pattern closes high and into some of the range covered by the first day. The two days after the pattern see a bit of bearish price action, but no significant support levels are violated. Three days later, the bulls get rolling, and it's clear that an uptrend is in place. What an uptrend it is!

To take advantage of this type of bullish doji star pattern (or a morning star pattern in the same situation), try to buy near the end of the pattern or, possibly, attempt to put on a long position, or the purchase of the security, on any sort of near-term price weakness that doesn't violate a stop level.

As you can see, raking in a profit on a trade based on the bullish doji star or morning star is a definite possibility if you keep your eyes open and place your trades wisely. But the pattern can also fizzle out and cause losses.

The bullish doji star failure signal

Figure 9-12 is a chart with a bullish doji star pattern that has the potential to cause some heartbreak. It's a chart of NVDA stock. Keep in mind that this pattern could also be a morning star because the patterns are extremely similar and basically interchangeable for trading purposes.

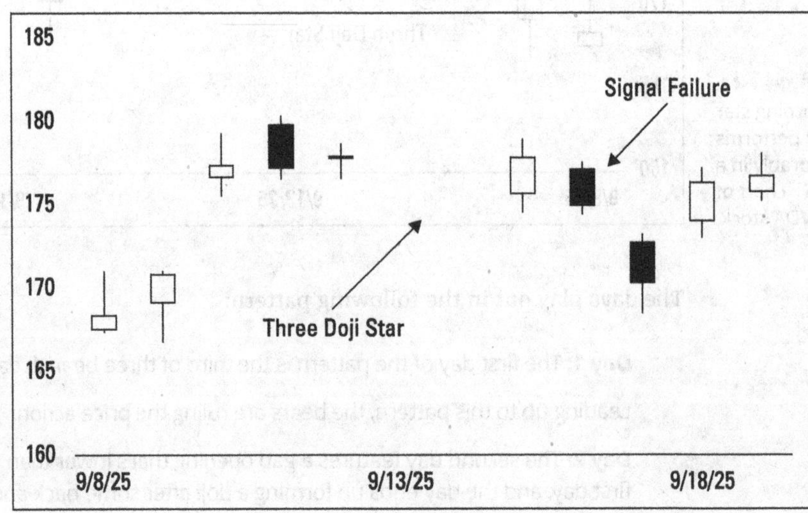

FIGURE 9-12: The bullish doji pattern failing in a chart of NVDA stock.

The morning star arrives after a downtrend has been in place for a few weeks. The trend appears to be moderating a bit — an encouraging sign if you're looking to buy a stock. The pattern is completed in textbook fashion, with just one exception: The stock doesn't change trend quickly. The price levels established by the pattern that you might use as stops are violated a few weeks after the pattern appears; you may want to bail out on this trade long before then.

REMEMBER

Another factor you can use to determine when to exit a trade is time. A violated price level isn't the only way a pattern can fail. You can also consider a pattern to be a failure due to the passage of time. If you see a promising pattern that doesn't fail, but the desired price action doesn't occur, feel free to call it a failure and get out. How long you wait before bagging the trade is up to you, but a time stop is a useful trading tool.

The bullish abandoned baby pattern

The next bullish three-stick trend reversal pattern we cover in this chapter is the bullish abandoned baby pattern, a close cousin of the morning star and bullish doji star patterns. Although its name sounds sad, you can end up quite happy with the results if you trade it wisely.

Identifying the bullish abandoned baby pattern

The bullish abandoned baby gets its name from the second day of the pattern, which kind of floats out on the chart by itself, as though it's been abandoned by the first and third days. Also, the second day's candlestick is smaller than the other two candlesticks. Figure 9-13 shows an example.

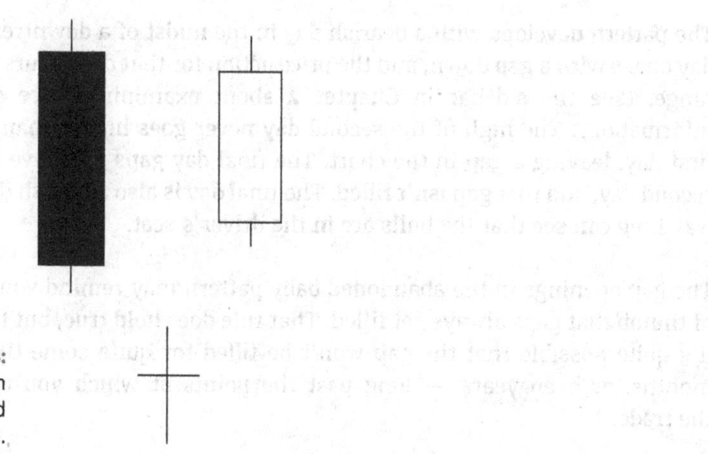

FIGURE 9-13: The bullish abandoned baby pattern.

The first day of the pattern is a bearish day. The second day gaps lower and has pretty tight price action, especially compared with the other two candlesticks in the pattern. Day 3 is a bullish day that gaps higher than the second day.

Making a trade based on the abandoned baby pattern

For a look at a bullish abandoned baby pattern that provides a buying signal, see Figure 9-14. The figure is a chart of NVDA stock, which is now dominating the entire economic system.

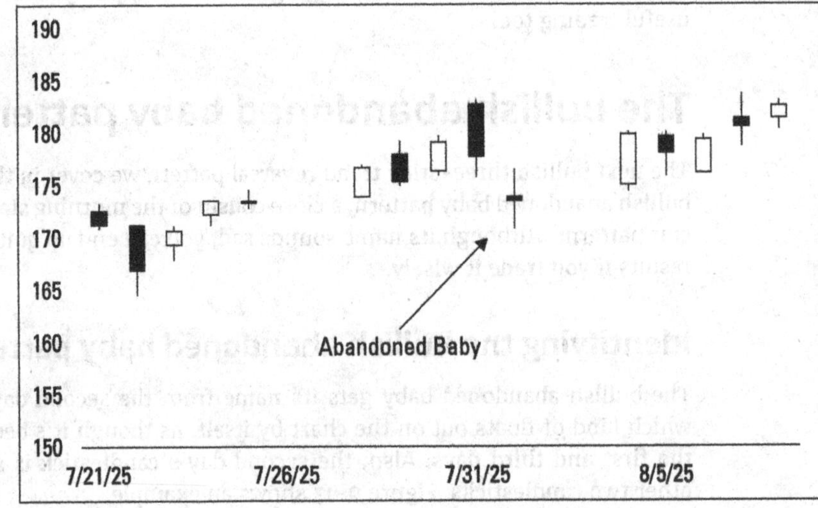

FIGURE 9-14: The abandoned baby pattern behaves as expected in a chart of NVDA stock.

The pattern develops with a bearish day in the midst of a downtrend. The second day opens with a gap down, and the price action for that day occurs in a fairly tight range. (See the sidebar in Chapter 2 about examining price gaps for more information.) The high of the second day never goes higher than the low of the first day, leaving a gap in the chart. The final day gaps up above the high of the second day, and that gap isn't filled. The final day is also a bullish day, and anyone watching can see that the bulls are in the driver's seat.

The gap openings in the abandoned baby pattern may remind you of the old rule of thumb that gaps always get filled. That rule does hold true, but for this pattern, it's quite possible that the gap won't be filled for quite some time. It can take months, or even years — long past the points at which you can profit from the trade.

The abandoned baby failure signal

The abandoned baby pattern sometimes signals a trend reversal, but in some cases, you'd be better off — well, just abandoning a trade involving this pattern. Figure 9-15 is an unusual chart, to say the least, but it's a good example of an abandoned baby that didn't work and probably shouldn't have been traded in the first place. This chart shows price action for NVDA stock.

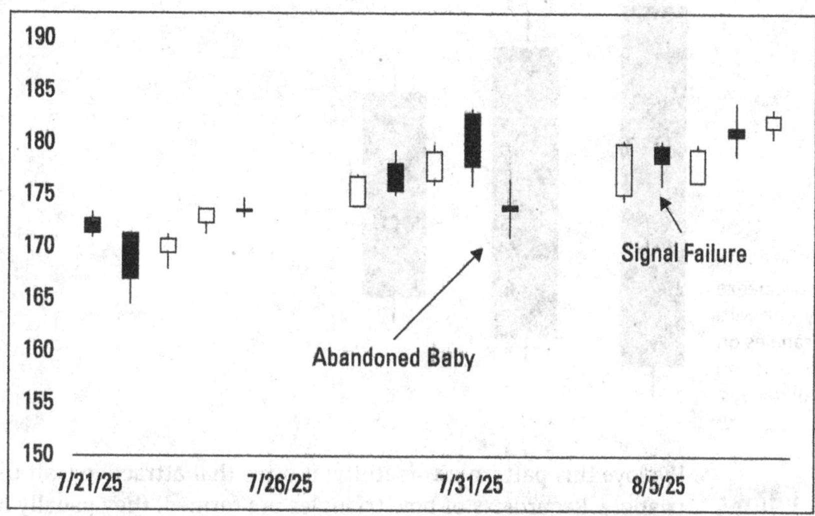

The pattern shows up as a textbook example of the abandoned baby with NVDA in a small downtrend. The day after the signal is complete, the market opened lower but traded higher — an encouraging start. The next couple of days are not very bullish, however, and NVDA rolls over, continuing the downtrend that was in place when the signal hit.

The bullish squeeze alert pattern

The bullish squeeze alert pattern is one of our favorite bullish patterns. It's a versatile three-stick pattern that pops up relatively frequently, so you'll have more opportunities to trade it than some of the other patterns we discuss.

Spotting the bullish squeeze alert pattern

The rules that govern the formation of a bullish squeeze alert allow a little wiggle room. The strictest rule is that the first day of the pattern must be a down day. After that, the second day has to be an inside day of the first, and the third an inside day of the second. Otherwise, the rules are flexible. The second and third days can be up days, down days, or a combination. The only strict criteria governing the second and third days are that they must be inside days and they have to form a triangle. Figure 9-16 shows a variation of the bullish squeeze alert that includes black candles for the second and third days.

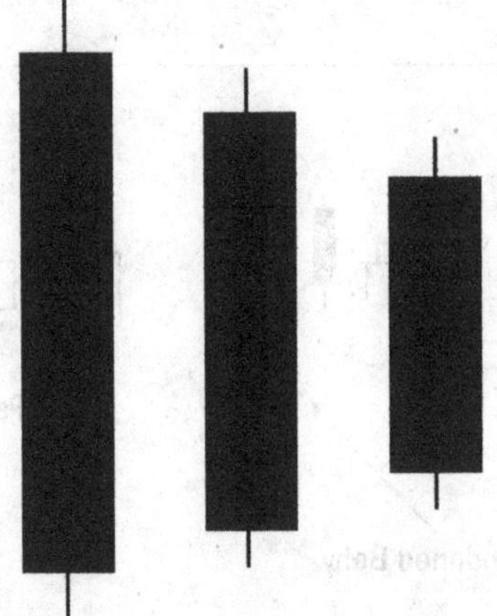

A bullish squeeze alert pattern with black candles on the second and third days.

REMEMBER

We love this pattern's versatility; it owes that attractive trait to the presence of a triangle. Regardless of how triangles are formed, they usually lead to some volatile moves. Be on the lookout for this triangle formation as you scan candlestick charts: A triangle in a chart shows that prices are coiling together and will soon be ready to spring in one direction or the other.

Executing trades with the bullish squeeze alert

You can see the bullish squeeze alert at its bullish best in Figure 9-17. The figure is a chart of Tesla (TSLA) stock.

TIP

Tesla stock has been volatile in the past.

The pattern appears during a downtrend, and the first day is a long black candle. The second day is an up day but also an inside day relative to the first day. The final day is a down day, but according to the rules, it's also an inside day relative to the second day. We chose this chart to show that the second and third days don't have to be specifically down or up, but they do have to be days that are inside days of the preceding day.

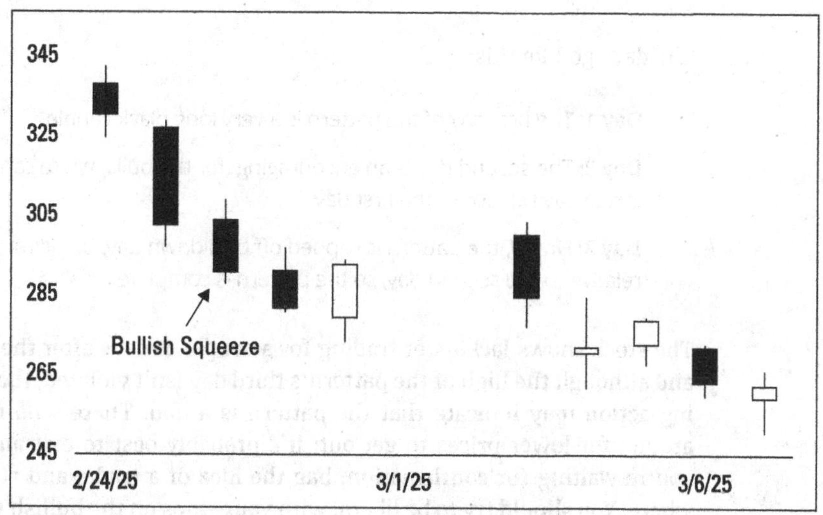

FIGURE 9-17: The bullish squeeze alert pattern performs well in a chart of TSLA stock.

The pattern forms a triangle, which means that you can expect quick price moves in either direction.

The bullish squeeze alert fails to bring on higher prices

If you want to see a bullish squeeze alert pattern in a failure situation, look no further than Figure 9-18. The figure features TSLA again.

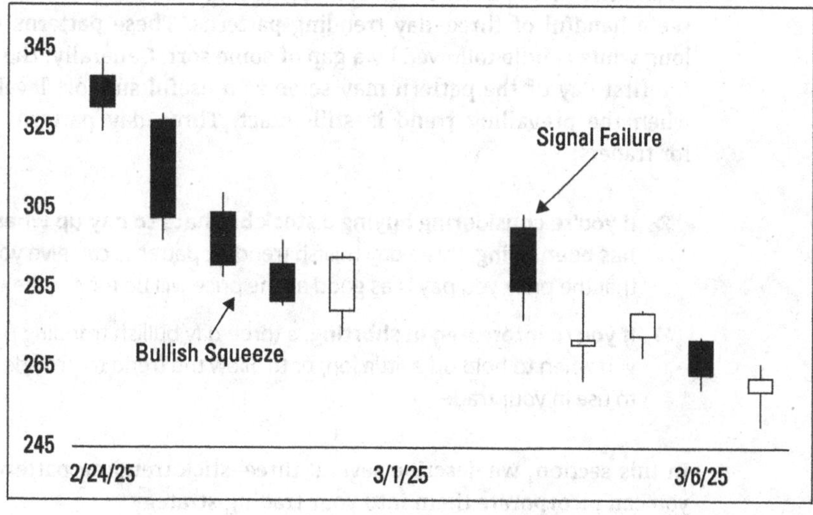

FIGURE 9-18: A bullish squeeze alert pattern failing in a chart of TSLA stock.

The days go like this:

Day 1: The first day of the pattern is a very long black candle.

Day 2: The second day is an encouraging (for the bulls) white candle, which is an inside day relative to the first day.

Day 3: Finally, the pattern is capped off by a down day, but it's an inside day relative to the second day, so the pattern is complete.

The stock shows lackluster trading for a couple of days after the pattern appears, and although the high of the pattern's third day isn't violated, the lack of uptrending action may indicate that the pattern is a dud. There's no real need to wait around for lower prices to get out; it's probably best to exit and move on. Or if you're waiting for confirmation, bag the idea of a trade, and start looking elsewhere. You should try to be liberal with your stops on the bullish squeeze alert, but sometimes it's best to require some confirmation that the squeeze is moving in the desired direction a couple of days after the pattern appears. If not, feel free to stop waiting and move on to your next trade.

Working with Bullish Three-Stick Trending Patterns

In addition to the trend reversal patterns that take three days to develop, you may see a handful of three-day trending patterns. These patterns usually include a long white candle followed by a gap of some sort. Generally, the gap or the low of the first day of the pattern may serve as a useful support level to let you know when the prevailing trend is still intact. Three-day patterns have three uses for traders:

>> **If you're considering buying a stock but hate to pay up when the price has been rising,** three-day bullish trending patterns can give you confidence that the price you pay is as good as the price will be for a while.

>> **If you're interested in shorting,** a three-day bullish trending pattern can tell you when to hold off a little longer to allow the trend to provide a better price to use in your trade.

In this section, we describe several three-stick trending patterns and show how you can incorporate them into your trading strategy.

The bullish side-by-side white lines pattern

The first bullish three-day trending pattern is the bullish side-by-side white lines pattern, which is about as bullish as patterns get. If you see this pattern in a chart, you can feel pretty confident that the prevailing uptrend will continue in grand fashion.

Spotting the bullish side-by-side white lines pattern

To locate the bullish side-by-side white lines pattern in one of your charts, look for a day with a long white candle that's followed by a gap opening on the second day. That second day should develop into an up day that never retraces prices down to the high of the first day. Finally, look for an up third day that covers the same ground as the second day and doesn't retrace to close the gap to the high of the first day. Sound confusing? The straightforward example in Figure 9-19 should clear things up.

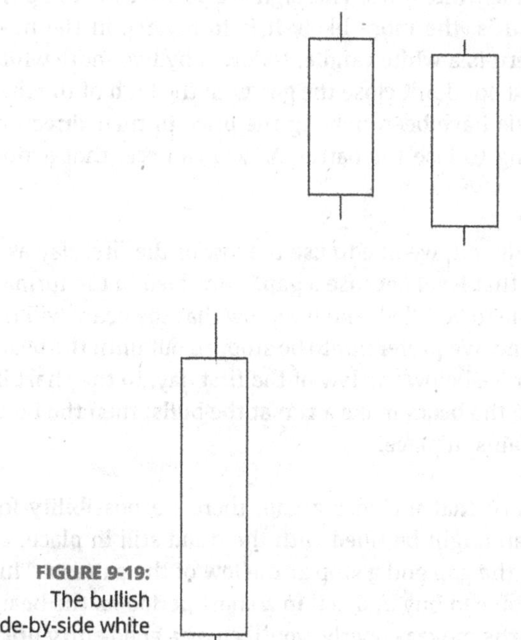

FIGURE 9-19: The bullish side-by-side white lines pattern.

Trading on the bullish side-by-side white lines

We provide a solid scenario for trading the bullish side-by-side white lines pattern in Figure 9-20, which is a chart of TSLA stock.

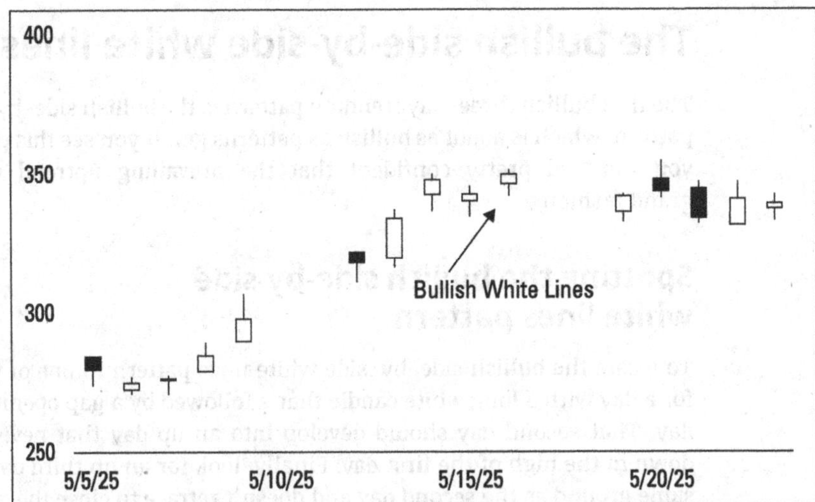

FIGURE 9-20:
The bullish
side-by-side white
lines pattern
works well in a
chart of
TSLA stock.

The pattern in Figure 9-20 emerges in a reversal that incorporates a white bar, gapping higher to the side-by-side white lines. This sign is a positive in our opinion because the longer the trend is, the more likely it is to reverse in the near future. The first day of the pattern is a white candle, followed by two more white candles that cover similar ground but don't close the gap with the high of the first candle. It's obvious that the bulls have been moving the price in their direction and that the bears are continuing to lose the battle. As you can see, that action continues for quite some time.

Although doing so may be a bit liberal, we like to use the low of the first day as a stop for this pattern. We choose that level because a gap is involved in the formation of the pattern. Gaps are made to be filled, and we know that the bears will try to make a run at a gap like this one. We prefer not to be stopped out until the bears have succeeded in running the price below the low of the first day. In the chart in Figure 9-20, we highlight where the bears make a run at the bulls; then the bulls push back, and the uptrend remains in place.

REMEMBER

When you spot a trending pattern that includes a gap, there's a possibility for some aggressive trading. The gap might be filled with the trend still in place, so you can place an order to buy in the gap and a stop at the low of the pattern. This strategy is aggressive because you can buy and sell in a short period as the bears take over. But if you can execute the move properly, you'll enjoy a good entry price in the midst of an uptrend.

The bullish side-by-side white lines fail to indicate more bullishness

Even though the bullish side-by-side white lines pattern is generally a bullish powerhouse, it's possible for the pattern to fail. To see an example, take a look at Figure 9-21.

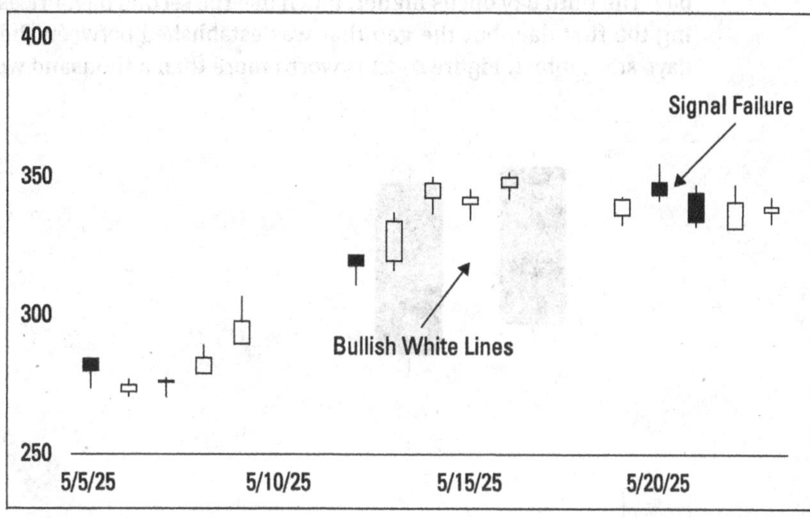

FIGURE 9-21: The bullish side-by-side white lines failing in a chart of TSLA stock.

Figure 9-21 is a chart of TSLA, one of the most volatile stocks available for trading. Something to keep in mind when trading volatile markets is that the trend can change quickly, so placing stops or quickly taking losses is suggested with TSLA stock.

The pattern in Figure 9-21 emerges during a solid but choppy uptrend. The pattern results in a gap that places the price at the highest levels in a few weeks. The day after, however, is a bearish day that doesn't fully negate the signal. The downtrend accelerates, and the signal is a bust a couple of days later.

The bullish side-by-side black lines pattern

The bullish side-by-side black lines pattern occurs during an uptrend. Although it includes some bearish trading, the pattern doesn't violate the uptrend's validity. It has some bearish undertones, but it's still a fairly bullish indication of a continued uptrend.

Recognizing the bullish side-by-side black lines pattern

The first day of the bullish side-by-side black lines is a long white candle that occurs during an uptrend. The second day opens with a large gap relative to the first day and then trades off some during the day. A gap is established between the first and second days, however, even though prices trade down during the second day. The third day opens higher, much like the second day. Prices trade lower during the first day, but the gap that was established between the first and second days stays intact. Figure 9-22 is worth more than a thousand words in this case.

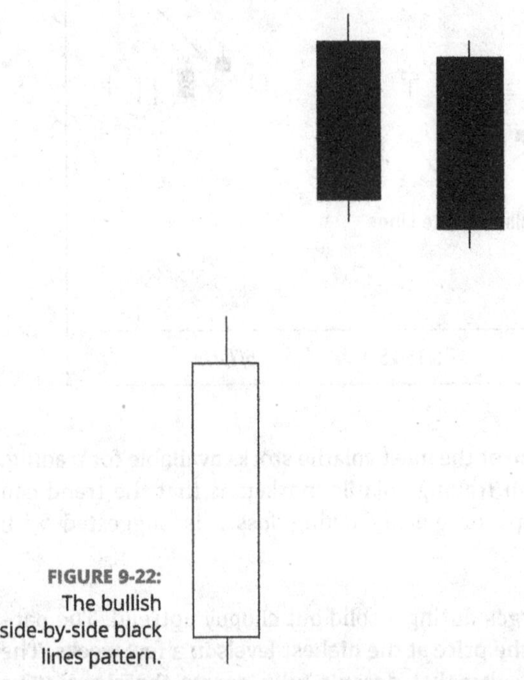

FIGURE 9-22:
The bullish side-by-side black lines pattern.

It may seem a bit odd that a three-day bullish pattern has two black candles as the final two days, but that's what it takes to create the bullish side-by-side black lines. This pattern works out because the bullishness of the prevailing uptrend and the first day of the pattern are strong enough to keep the bears from closing the price gap.

If you choose to enter on the completion of the side-by-side black lines pattern, your entry point will be a lower price point than if you made the same decision with the bullish side-by-side white lines.

REMEMBER

Using the bullish side-by-side black lines for a profitable trade

For an example of the bullish side-by-side black lines paying off in a real-world trading scenario, take a look at Figure 9-23. The figure is a chart of TSLA stock.

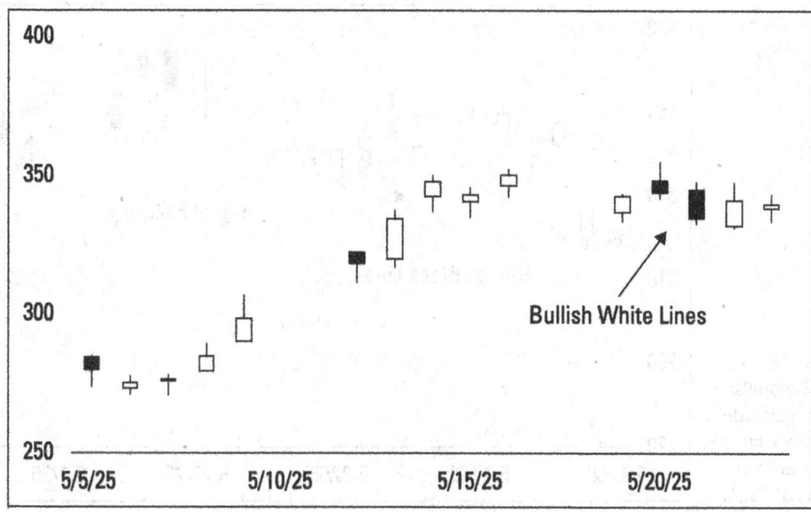

FIGURE 9-23: The bullish side-by-side black lines pattern pays off in a chart of TSLA stock.

The days play out as follows:

Day 1: The first day of the pattern is a white candle that occurs during a small downtrend.

The trend appears to remain intact, but it can be moderating.

Day 2: The second day has a gap opening and a little selling during the day.

A gap is established between the first and second days.

Day 3: The third day of the pattern has a slightly higher opening, and some selling takes place during the day.

The gap still exists, and the day closes slightly below the open. The process takes three or four days, but eventually, the uptrend is back in place, and the pattern in Figure 9-23 turns out to be a winner.

Failure of the bullish side-by-side black lines pattern

For an example of a failing bullish side-by-side black lines pattern, we turn back to natural gas futures in the chart in Figure 9-24.

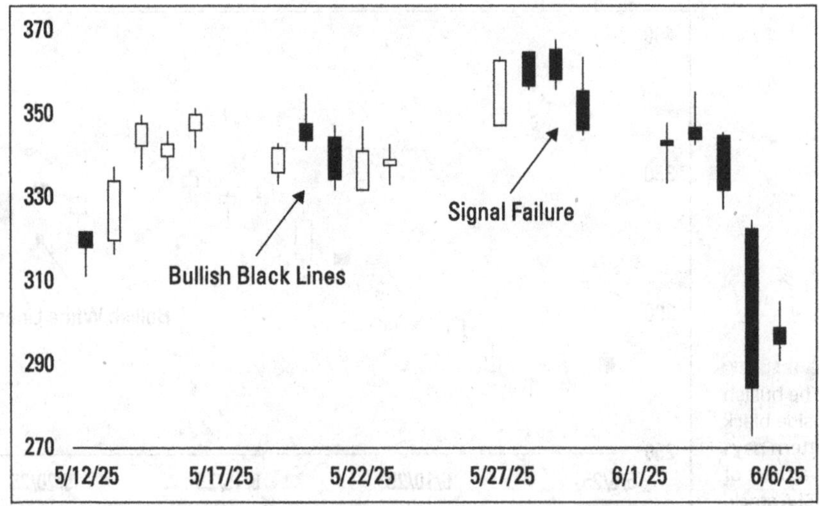

FIGURE 9-24: The bullish side-by-side black lines pattern failing in a chart of TSLA.

The first day of the pattern featured in Figure 9-24 is a bullish day at what appears to be the beginning of an uptrend. The second day has a gap opening with some weakness, but a close within the middle of the trading action for that day. The second day closes lower, but a gap between the first and second day is established. This signal doesn't hold on for long, as natural gas prices gapped lower the following day, filling that gap.

The upside tasuki gap pattern

The three-stick trending pattern in this section is a deviation from the patterns described in the preceding two sections. The upside tasuki gap can just as easily be called the upside white line beside black line pattern.

The name *tasuki* is a Japanese word for a sash that holds up a shirtsleeve. We have to be honest: We're not sure how that term relates to the pattern. But the word is fun to say, and the pattern can lead you to some great trades, so we won't question it.

Spotting the upside tasuki gap pattern

The upside tasuki gap starts with a white candle in an uptrend. The second day is much like the second day of the side-by-side white lines pattern, which we explain earlier in this chapter. The price gaps higher and closes higher for the day. The third day is much like the third day of a bullish side-by-side black lines pattern (described earlier in this chapter). There's an opening in the same range as the second day and then some lower trading, but the gap isn't completely filled. Figure 9-25 shows a visual representation.

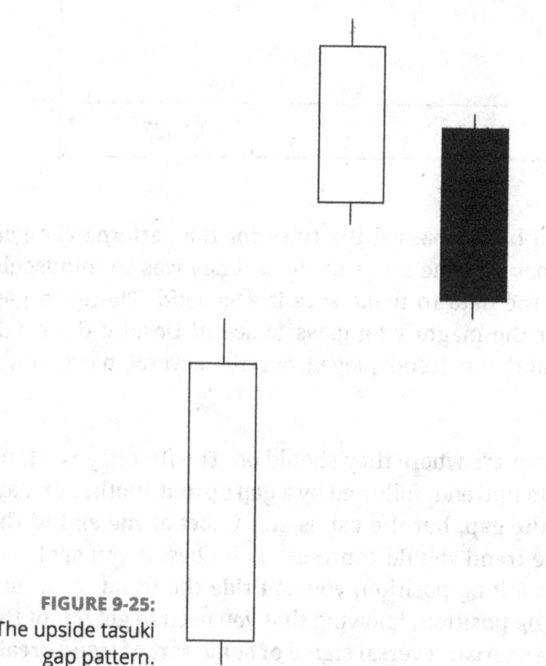

FIGURE 9-25:
The upside tasuki gap pattern.

We like this pattern because it offers an attractive entry point, especially compared with the side-by-side white lines pattern. Getting to buy on the low end of any candle when there's a bullish signal is fine with us.

Using the upside tasuki gap pattern for a successful trade

Figure 9-26 forms the basis of our explanation of how you can use the upside tasuki gap to make a profitable trade. The chart of Air Products (APD) shows a good example of the pattern.

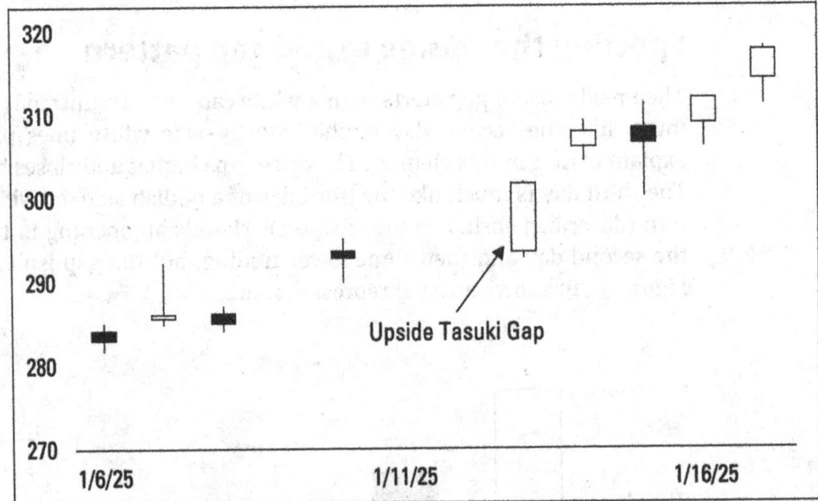

FIGURE 9-26: An upside tasuki gap pattern that provides a useful signal in a chart of APD stock.

The tasuki gap in Figure 9-26 barely passed the rules for the pattern. The gap between the high of the first day and the range of the last day was so minuscule that we had to double-check the data to make sure it was valid. There's a gap there, but you have to get out the magnifying glass to see it! Despite the small gap, the signal was strong and the trend played out for several more trading sessions.

The nuts and bolts of the pattern are where they should be. The first day is a long white candle in the middle of an uptrend, followed by a gap up and another up day. The third day encroaches on the gap, but the gap is still intact at the end of the day, offering evidence that the trend should continue, as it does. If you spot this pattern and choose to take on a long position, you can ride the trend for a nice profit. You can also put on a long position, knowing that you need to get out of the trade upon the appearance of a bearish reversal signal or some sort of trend break.

The tasuki gap fails to indicate more bullishness

We're fond of the upside tasuki gap pattern, but it certainly has a downside. Figure 9-27 shows what can happen when the upside tasuki gap turns out to be a dud.

Figure 9-27 is another chart of APD stock. The pattern shows up after a two-day uptrend or the possibility of the start of a new uptrend. Unfortunately, the stock opens lower the day after the signal, negating the buy signal.

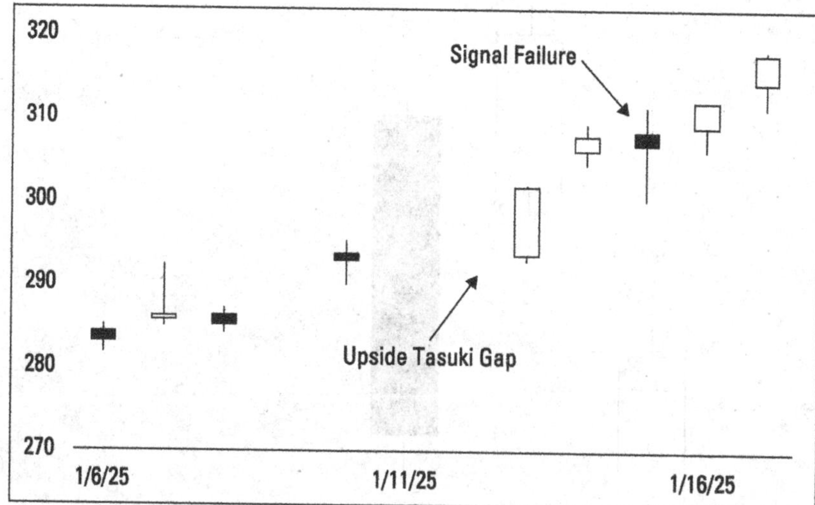

The pattern fails, but then the stock trades higher, falling into a pretty narrow trend for the balance of the days on the chart. Although the stock recovers after the signal failure, the signal failed, and you should consider the trade to be complete, even though a loss may have resulted from following the rules associated with the tasuki gap pattern.

The upside gap-filled pattern

The final bullish three-day pattern explored in this chapter is the upside gap-filled pattern. It offers bullish trend confirmation, but it's particularly nice because the gap that's created gets filled without violating the prevailing uptrend. Sometimes, gaps in charts are targets for longs, purchasing of the position, or shorts, selling an asset you don't own, to fill the gaps. But when this gap is filled, no gap is present to encourage the shorts to take action.

Recognizing the upside gap-filled pattern

The upside gap-filled pattern is aptly named, as you can see in Figure 9-28. The first day is a white candle that occurs in an uptrend. The second day is bullish, with a gap opening and a closing that establish a gap. The third and final day is bearish, and it closes the gap, but it doesn't violate the low of the first day.

A low level for entry on the final day makes this pattern attractive, in our opinion. Also, because the low of the first day would be considered to be a stop level, losses are typically minimal when the pattern doesn't work as planned.

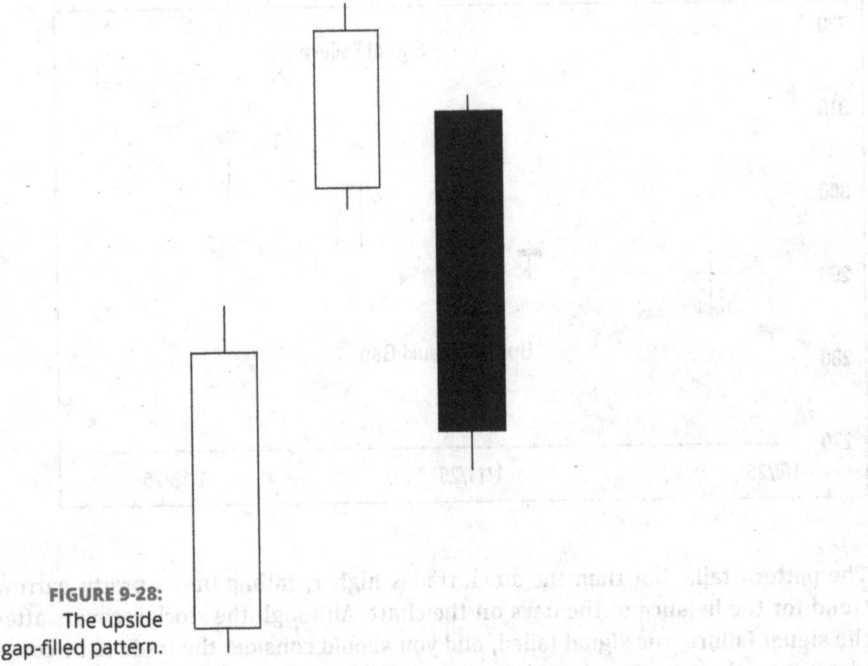

FIGURE 9-28:
The upside
gap-filled pattern.

Making wise trades using the upside gap-filled pattern

Examine the price action depicted in Figure 9-29 to see how you can profit from a trade by using the upside gap-filled pattern. This chart shows price action for APD.

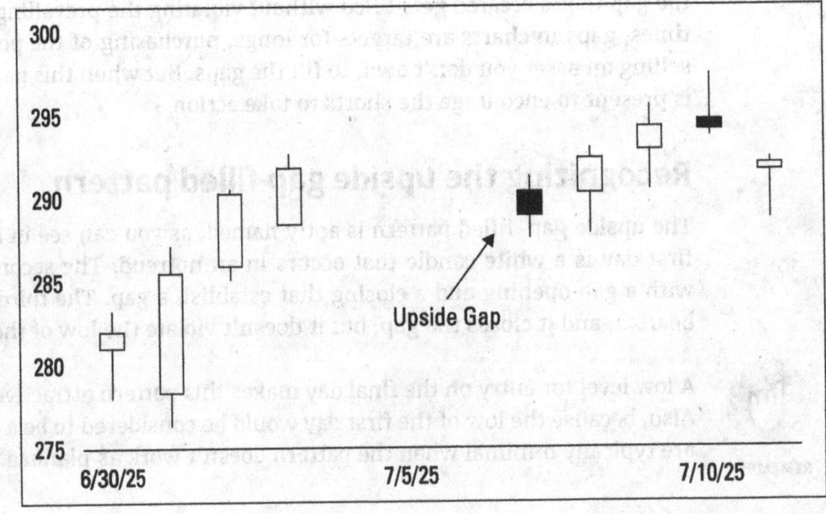

FIGURE 9-29:
The upside
gap-filled pattern
creates an
appealing trading
opportunity in a
chart of
APD stock.

The pattern in this chart emerges pretty early in an uptrend. The first day is an up day, and it's followed by a white candle for the second day, which gaps up. The third day is a down day that fills in the gap and closes in the range of the first day. The upside gap is filled!

The price action following the pattern is muted for a few days, and it even looks as though the pattern will fail, as prices come close to the low of the first day. But the bulls prevail, and the trend continues upward for some time.

The upside gap followed by lower prices

The bulls don't always prevail, of course. The upside gap-filled pattern can go wrong, and although failure is ugly, you need to know what it looks like. Figure 9-30 shows a pattern failure in a chart of APD again!

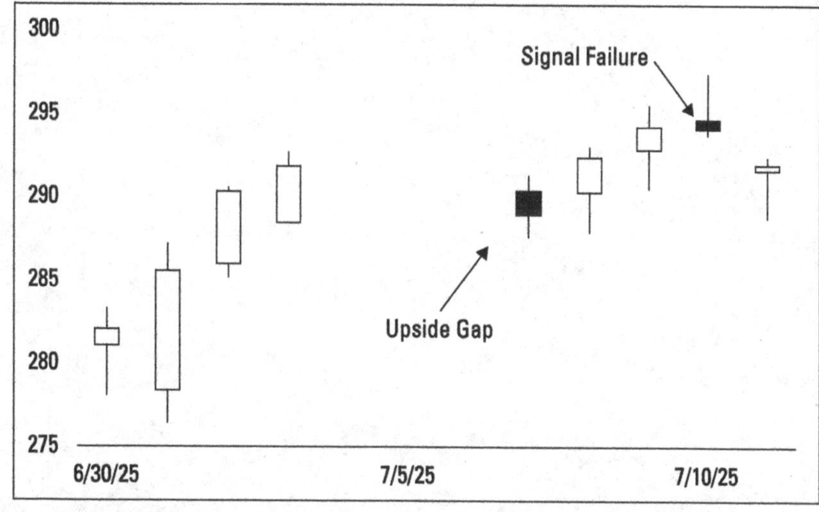

FIGURE 9-30: The upside gap-filled pattern fizzles out in a chart of APD stock.

The pattern in Figure 9-30 occurs at what would have been the beginning of an uptrend if the pattern had worked out. A few up days start to indicate that the trend is positive; the first day of the upside gap-filled pattern appears as a very long white candle, followed by an upside gap that closes, leaving that gap in place. The third day is a down day that closes the gap and closes within the first day's range.

This pattern takes a while to fail, and like several of the other examples in this chapter, it may illustrate a situation in which you'd be better served by bailing out of the trade because of time concerns than by exiting because of a clear price-level violation. After all, you can probably do more with your money in another trade than you can with it tied up for what seems like forever in a questionable upside gap-filled pattern trade.

Chapter **10**

Trading with Bearish Three-Stick Patterns

In this chapter, we focus on the biggest bearish formations included in this book: the three-stick bearish candlestick patterns. Three-stick patterns are pretty complex and also rare, but definitely powerful. Throughout the next few pages, we cover some of the most common bearish three-stick patterns that pop up in your charts.

If you turn back to Chapter 9, you can read about a variety of bullish three-stick patterns that can tell you when a downtrend is about to shift upward, as well as a few of those patterns that reveal when a downtrend will continue. This chapter features the bearish counterparts of those patterns, which can reveal when an uptrend is about to fall apart and head downward or when a downtrend is likely to continue. Use these patterns whenever you're looking to put on a short position or as sell signals if you've already established a long position, or purchasing the position.

Understanding Bearish Three-Stick Trend Reversal Patterns

Much like their bullish counterparts from Chapter 9, a host of three-day bullish patterns commonly indicate that a trend reversal is forthcoming. The patterns in this section tell you when an uptrend is nearing its end and when a downtrend is ready to begin. The bearish reversal patterns can be quite useful for shorts, but keep in mind that shorting — especially with stocks — when the trend is up can be a difficult undertaking.

The three inside down pattern

The three inside down pattern is a handy reversal pattern that shows up fairly regularly. The indecision implied by the pattern's second day (an inside day) provides useful insight into the action, telling you that the bears are starting to push against the trend.

Figuring out how to spot the three inside down

The three inside down always occurs in an established uptrend:

Day 1: The pattern is an up day. The bulls are in control on the first day of the three inside down.

Day 2: The second day is bearish, and it's also an inside day relative to the first day. The open is lower than the previous day's close, and the close is higher than the previous day's close. The high and low of the second day also fall within the high/low range established on the first day of the pattern. The bears take over on the second and third days.

Day 3: The pattern is completed on the third day with another down day that violates the low of the first day.

As you may guess, this formation is usually a helpful sign that an uptrend is set to fizzle out. For an example, see Figure 10-1.

Trading on the three inside down pattern

The preceding section shows how to identify the three inside down pattern, so now set your sights on Figure 10-2 for a real-world trading scenario in which the pattern may help you turn a profit. The chart in this figure is of Apple (APPL) stock.

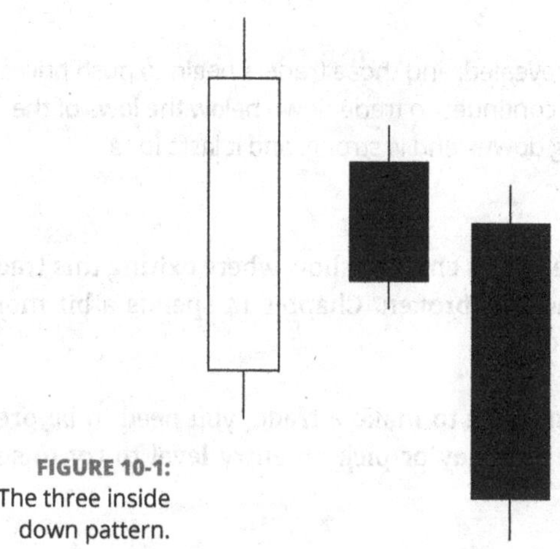

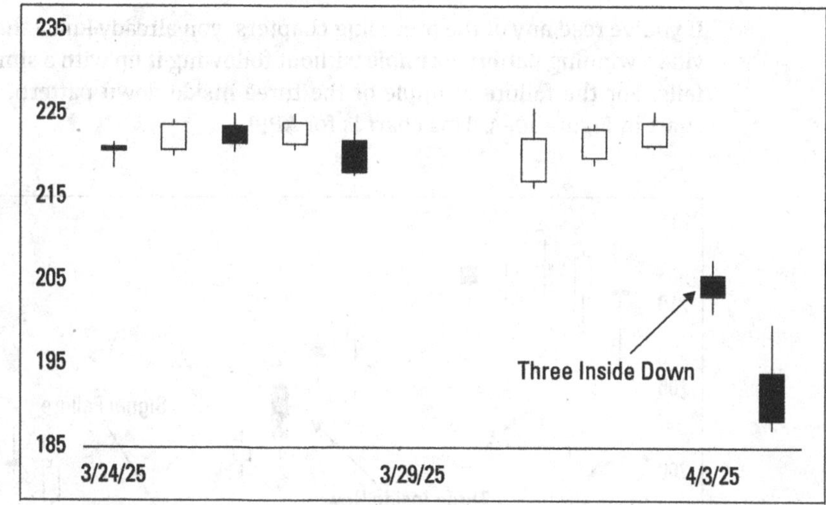

FIGURE 10-2:
The three inside
down pattern
precedes a trend
reversal in a chart
of APPL stock.

The three inside down pattern is the opposite of its bullish counterpart, discussed in Chapter 9. It starts with a bullish first day, but then things start to turn bearish. Here's how the pattern unfolds:

Day 1: A long white candle pattern occurs in the midst of a fairly strong uptrend.

Day 2: In textbook fashion, a down, inside day appears. The open of the second day is lower than the close of the first, and the close of the second day is higher than the first. Both the wick and the body are inside the first day's price action.

Day 3: A takeover by the bears is revealed, and those traders begin to push prices down. The stock opens lower and continues to trade down below the lows of the first and second days. The ensuing downtrend is strong, and it lasts for a few weeks.

Note: We decided to place a trend line in this chart to show where exiting this trade would make sense as the downtrend was broken. Chapter 14 spends a bit more time showing the usefulness of trend lines.

If you watch this pattern develop and look to make a trade, you need to be prepared to short near the close of the first day or pick an entry level to try to sell short on the second day.

Failing to give a good bearish signal

If you've read any of the preceding chapters, you already know that we never provide a winning pattern example without following it up with a similar pattern that fails. For the failure example of the three inside down pattern, we offer up the chart in Figure 10-3. This chart is for APPL.

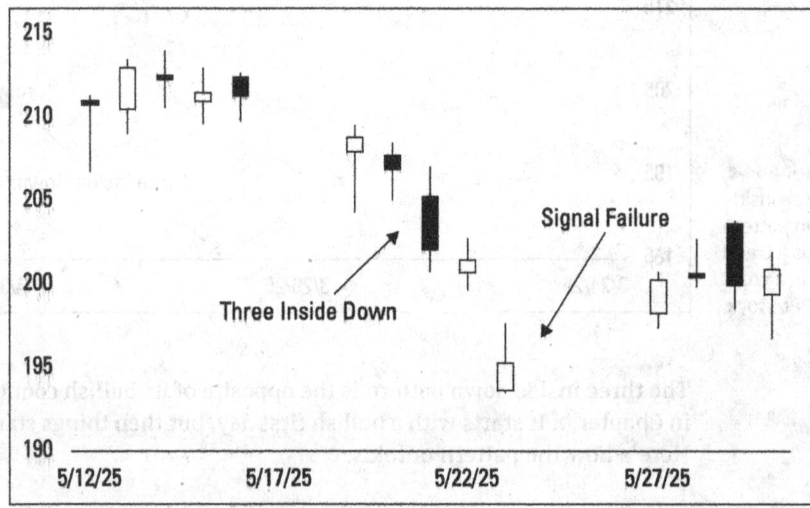

FIGURE 10-3: The three inside down pattern failing in a chart of APPL.

Figure 10-3 shows an inside down day for Apple, occurring a few days after a gap down in shares. The first day in the three inside down pattern is an up day, but not a terribly strong up day. The second day is an inside day, and the third day reveals a rally by the bulls that falls short when the day closes down. The price action that plays out shortly after the pattern is pretty encouraging for the bears. After just two days, the trend turns back up, and the pattern clearly fails. Astute chartists will notice that the first day after the completion of the pattern results in a long-legged doji, a common trend reversal pattern.

The three outside down pattern

Like the closely related three inside down pattern, the three outside down pattern should show up frequently in your charts. The pattern is a solid three-stick bearish trend reversal, and if you know how to identify it, you can rely on it for some lucrative trades.

Spotting the three outside down

This pattern shows up during an up trend and commences with another up day in the bullish run. On the second day, the bulls get started again with a gap opening, but they don't control the price action long. The bears find a selling point above the previous day's close and go to work driving down the price. As a result, the second day has a close lower than the first day and a low that's lower that the first day. The second day, therefore, is an outside day relative to the first day.

On the third day of the three outside down pattern, the bears call the shots from open to close. The day produces a black candle with the open, high, low, and close all lower than the previous day's levels. The bears are firmly in control. For an illustration, check out Figure 10-4.

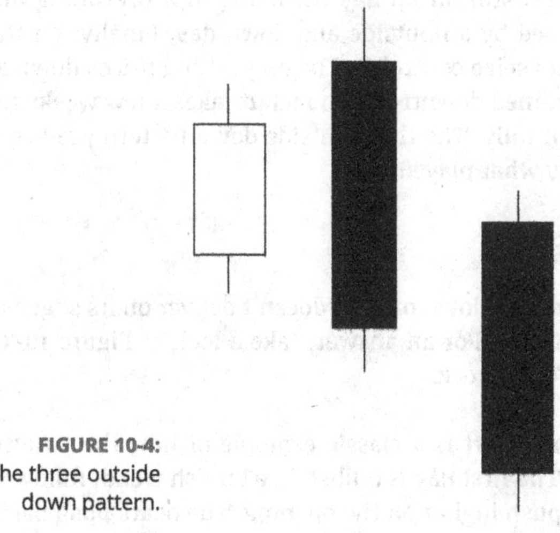

FIGURE 10-4:
The three outside down pattern.

Making trades with the three outside down pattern

The three outside down pattern does an outstanding job of picking up a change in trend and offering a useful sell or short opportunity, and you can see it sing in Figure 10-5. This chart is of Apple stock, whose programming is seen by millions.

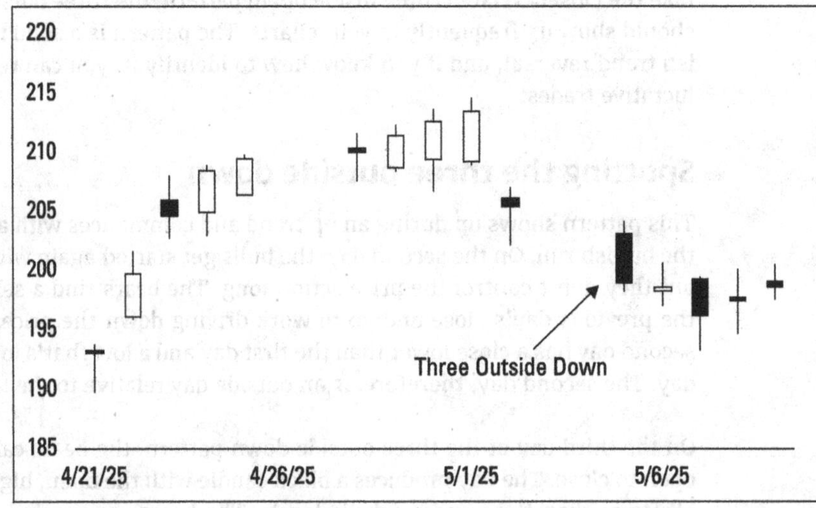

FIGURE 10-5: The three outside down pattern offers a sound signal in a chart of APPL stock.

The first day of the pattern featured in Figure 10-5 is an up day, and although it's nothing to write home about, it's still an up day occurring in a prevailing but slowing uptrend. Day 1 is followed by an outside and down day. Finally, on the third day of the pattern, the bears seize control and begin pushing prices down at the start of what becomes a sustained downtrend. In fact, it takes a few weeks for the bulls to attempt some sort of rally. The three outside down pattern predicted a trend reversal, which is exactly what played out.

Offering a failing signal

What happens when the three outside down pattern doesn't deliver on its suggestion that a downtrend is on the way? For an answer, take a look at Figure 10-6, which displays price action for APPL stock.

The outside down pattern in this chart is a classic example of how the pattern appears as it gives a sell signal. The first day is bullish in a bullish trend, followed by a second day when the bulls push higher on the opening. The bears push back, creating a down day that's outside compared with the first day. The bears are in control on the final day as they push prices even lower.

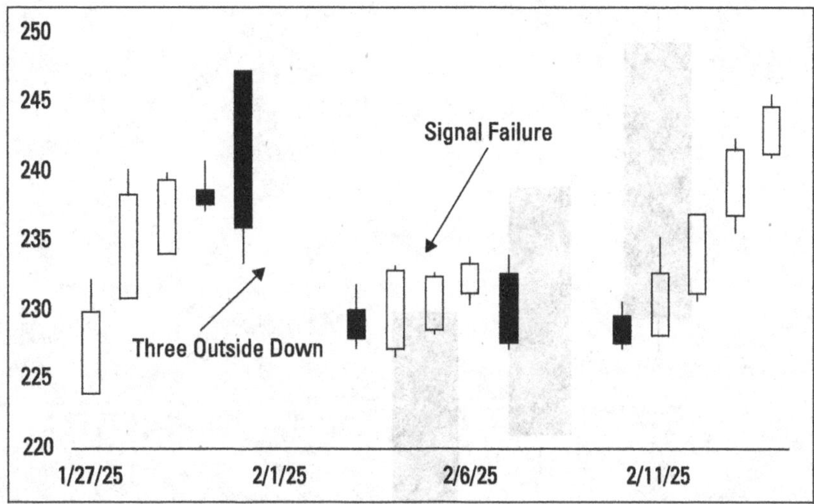

FIGURE 10-6: The three outside down pattern offers a failing signal in a chart of APPL stock.

After the pattern, a reversal day in the form of a hanging man appears in the chart. The hanging man alone may be a reason to cover the short position and move on to the next trade. (Refer to Chapter 6 for information on the hanging man pattern.) Slowly, Apple that eventually breaches any price level considered to be a stop, an acknowledgment that the short signal has failed.

REMEMBER

Splitting hairs on candlestick pattern formations can cost you a profitable trade. Just because a small price difference seems to disqualify a pattern, don't be too quick to disregard the formation. The psychology behind the pattern that almost panned out is the same as what drives a by-the-book pattern, and you may be able to make a successful trade if you aren't too strict in your pattern evaluations.

The three black crows pattern

The pattern featured in this section looks just plain ugly. The three black crows pattern certainly isn't much to look at, but it can benefit your trading activities if you can spot it and then use it to trade wisely.

Identifying the three black crows pattern

If you're into the kind of bird-watching that can lead to profits in the stock market, be on the lookout for the three black crows. This pattern includes three down days in a row, and it must occur during an uptrend to be valid. Figure 10-7 shows an example.

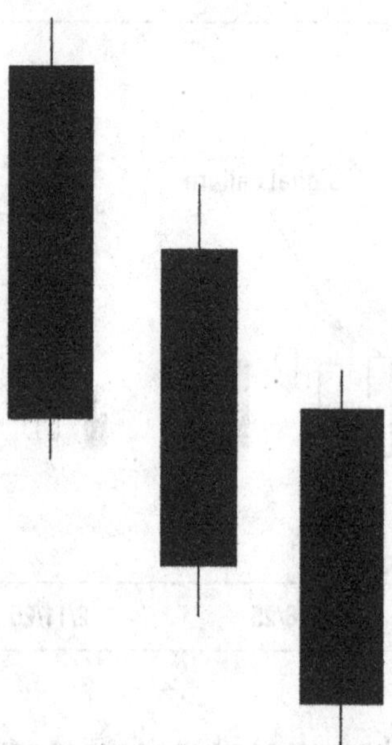

REMEMBER

The first day of the pattern may actually include a gap opening compared with the previous day, but even if the bulls are in charge at the start of the day, that trend doesn't last long. The bears push prices lower, and the result is an obvious down day. The next two days see lower price levels across the board. Both the second and third days are black candles with lower opens, highs, lows, and closes. The bears have definitely taken over.

Making trades with the three black crows pattern

This example of a successful three black crows pattern is based on a chart of a stock that's closely tied to the stock market. It's APPL stock, so we decided to stick with this market for the chart in Figure 10-8.

The three black crows pattern shows up shortly after a few bullish days. The black crows fill the gap, which we consider to be an encouraging sign. As you can see, each day of the pattern is a black candle, and each level is lower than the previous day's levels.

It's safe to say that this sign is bearish. After all, sellers are putting pressure on a stock for three straight days. The pattern also indicates lots of downward price movement in a short period — an indication of an opportunity to make a sale a little higher than the close of the pattern. That's the case with the pattern in Figure 10-8, and for the next few days, the pattern holds, despite a weak attempt by buyers to resume the uptrend. A patient trader who sold even the day after the pattern would be rewarded by a nice entry point.

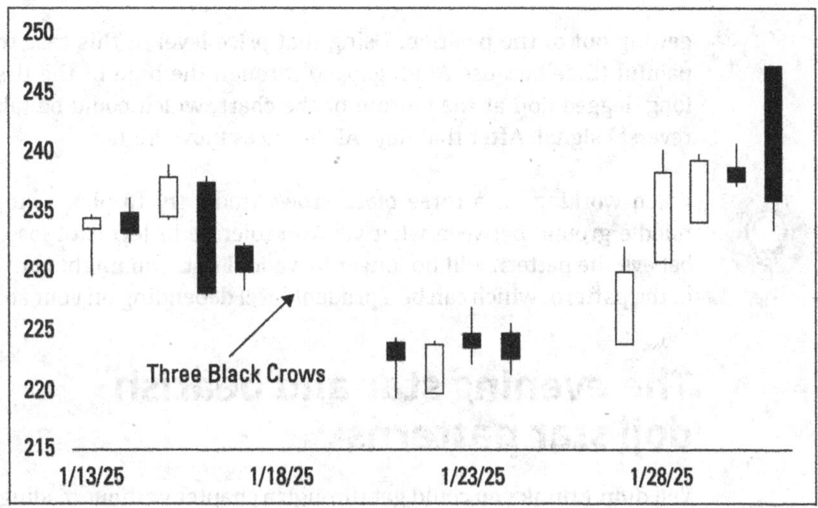

FIGURE 10-8: The three black crows pattern predicts a trend reversal in a chart of APPL stock.

Failing to signal lower prices ahead

If you're the kind of trader who insists that this pattern always works out when it appears, you may end up eating crow. The three black crows pattern can fail, as you can plainly see in Figure 10-9.

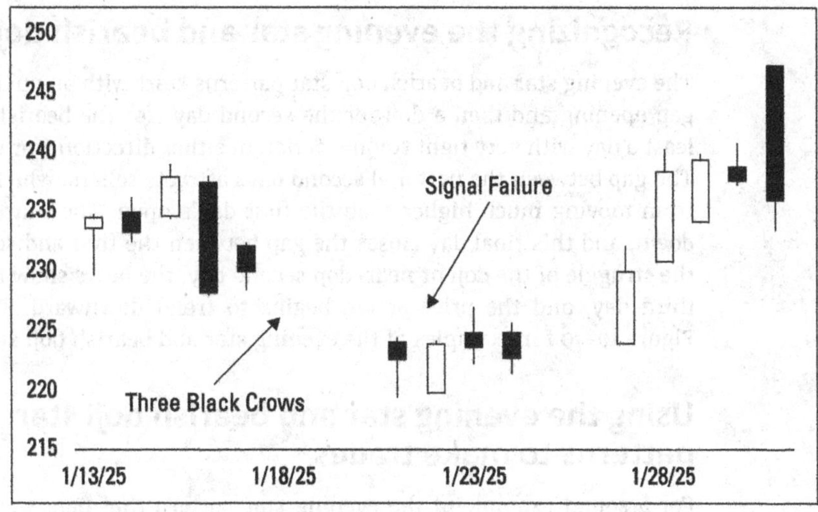

FIGURE 10-9: The three black crows pattern failing in a chart of APPL stock.

Figure 10-9 is a chart of the company formerly known as Apple. The three black crows pattern covers lots of ground on the down side, and placing a stop at the high of the first day leaves you with lots of room to accumulate losses before getting out of the position. Using that price level in this case would have been a painful trade because APPL gapped through the high of the first day. Notice the long-legged doji at the bottom of the chart, which could be taken as a potential reversal signal. After that day, APPL prices move higher.

When working on a three black crows trade, try to pick a stop that achieves a middle ground between what you can tolerate in terms of losses and where you believe the pattern will no longer be valid. First, you might consider the midpoint of the pattern, which can be a prudent level depending on your ability to take a loss.

The evening star and bearish doji star patterns

You didn't think you could get through a chapter without reading about a doji pattern, did you? We confess our love for the doji several times in this book, and we're happy to report that the two patterns described in this section make us grow even fonder of dojis and the trading opportunities they present.

The evening star and bearish doji star patterns are technically two different patterns, but they're so close — and the trading psychology behind them is so similar — that we lump them together in this section.

Recognizing the evening star and bearish doji star

The evening star and bearish doji star patterns start with an up day, followed by a gap opening and then a doji for the second day (for the bearish doji star), or at least a day with very tight trading action in either direction (for the evening star). The gap between the first and second days attracts sellers, which keeps the stock from moving much higher than the first day's open. The third and final day is down, and this final day closes the gap between the first and second days. After the struggle of the doji or near-doji second day, the bears show their teeth on the third day, and the price action begins to trend downward. Take a gander at Figure 10-10 for examples of the evening star and bearish doji star patterns.

Using the evening star and bearish doji star patterns to make trades

For a sound example of the evening star pattern that pans out in a real-world trading environment, check out Figure 10-11. The chart in that figure is of Nvidia (NVDA) stock, one of the largest traded stocks globally.

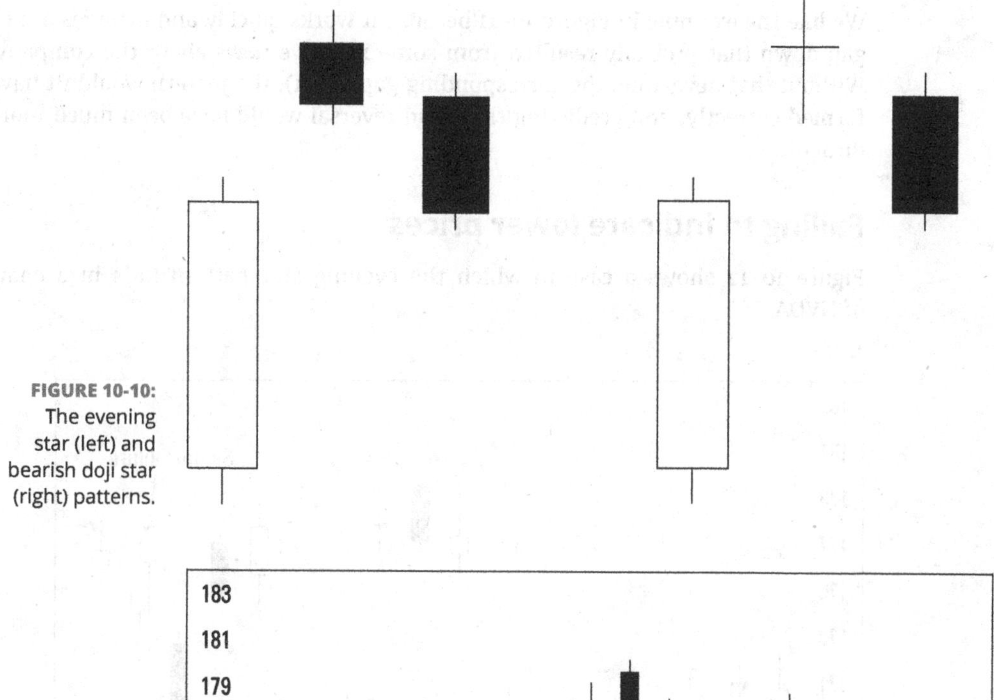

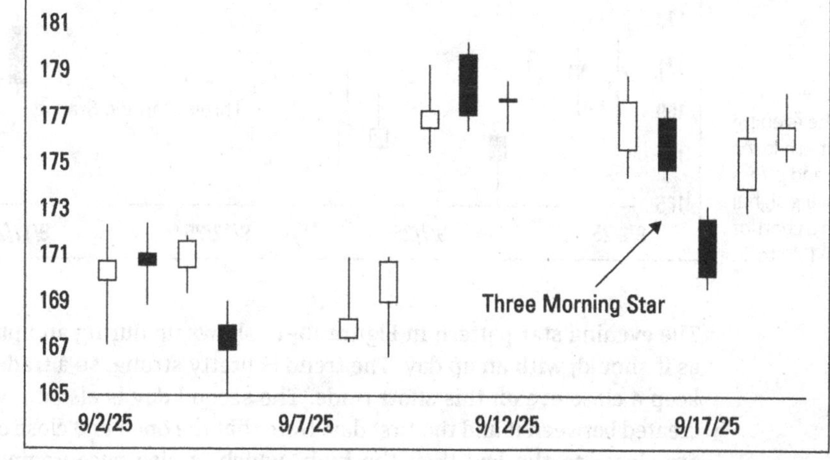

FIGURE 10-11:
The evening star
pattern works in
a chart of
NVDA stock.

As you look at the chart, notice that the first day is just another up day in a very long uptrend. The second day adheres to the price action that occurs on the second day of a doji or evening star pattern, with a small gap up and a tight trading range between the open and close. The pattern isn't quite a doji, but it's certainly enough to qualify as the second day of an evening star pattern. (If the pattern were a bona fide doji, it would be a bearish doji star pattern, but the price action and result would be the same.) The third day is a down day, and the pattern is complete.

We like the example in Figure 10-11 because it works quickly and includes a nice gap down that probably resulted from some negative news about the company. Without that news (and the corresponding gap down), the pattern wouldn't have formed correctly, and predicting the trend reversal would have been much more difficult.

Failing to indicate lower prices

Figure 10-12 shows a case in which the evening star pattern fails in a chart of NVDA.

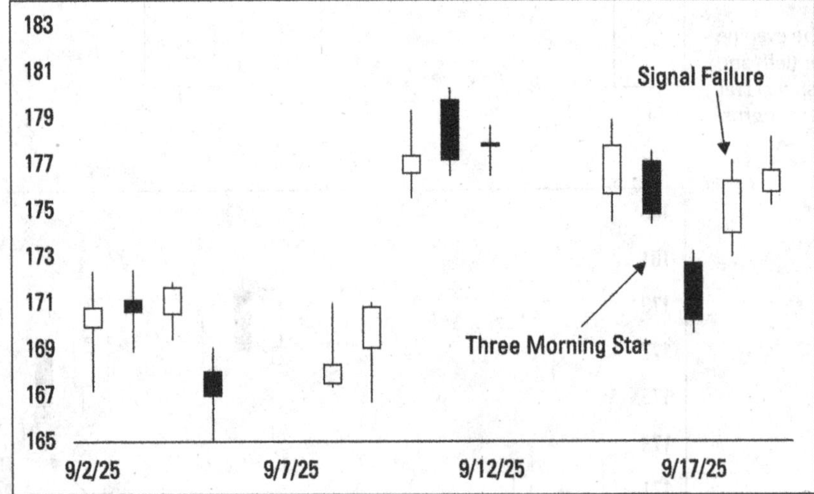

FIGURE 10-12: The evening star pattern loses pep and offers a failing signal in a chart of NVDA stock.

The evening star pattern in Figure 10-12 shows up during an uptrend and begins as it should, with an up day. The trend is pretty strong, so a trader would want to keep a close eye on this short trade. The second day is also up, with a small gap created between it and the first day. Note that the open and close of the second day are closer to the low than the high, which is also encouraging as the pattern develops. The third day is a down day, and it appears that a downtrend is commencing. Looking good!

WARNING But then disaster strikes. The downtrend is short-lived, and anyone who's trying to short the signal is out of luck. Just a couple of days after the pattern emerges, the stock starts to trade higher again. Then, with a gap opening and a strong bullish day, the pattern fails.

The bearish abandoned baby pattern

The bearish abandoned baby pattern is fairly rare, but when it pops up, it can be a powerful indication that a quick trend change is in the works. In fact, the abandoned baby pattern examples in this book — both the bullish examples in Chapter 9 and the ones we present in this section — were some of the most difficult patterns to find when we were gathering chart examples. It was especially hard to find examples in which the pattern failed.

Spotting the bearish abandoned baby pattern

A bearish abandoned baby pattern starts with an up day in an uptrend. That day is followed by a day that sticks way out by itself on the chart, often a doji with a gap opening that isn't filled in. The third day is down and includes a gap down opening between the second and third days. You can see a bearish abandoned baby in Figure 10-13, but please don't call child services; it's only a candlestick, after all.

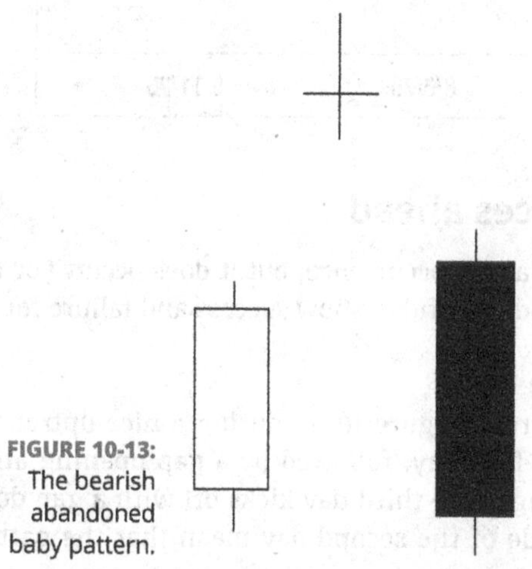

Trading on the bearish abandoned baby pattern

We're fond of the bearish abandoned baby example in Figure 10-14, showing the stock for Apple (APPL), the iPhone creator. Because the trend is rolling over — showing that the price action on a chart has been strong but is starting to top out — at the same time that the pattern shows up, this chart is a useful example of the pattern at work. The first day is clearly bullish, and the uptrend is in place, even though it looks to be rolling over. There's a gap between the first and second days, and the open and close of the second day are in a tight range. That range falls near the low end of the wick, which serves as a bearish indicator. The third day is up, but only after a very large gap down opening. Even though the bulls make a run on the third day, the close is discouraging for them because it falls near the low of the first day. After the final day, a sustained downtrend kicks in, and anyone who was working a clever short would be in for some profits.

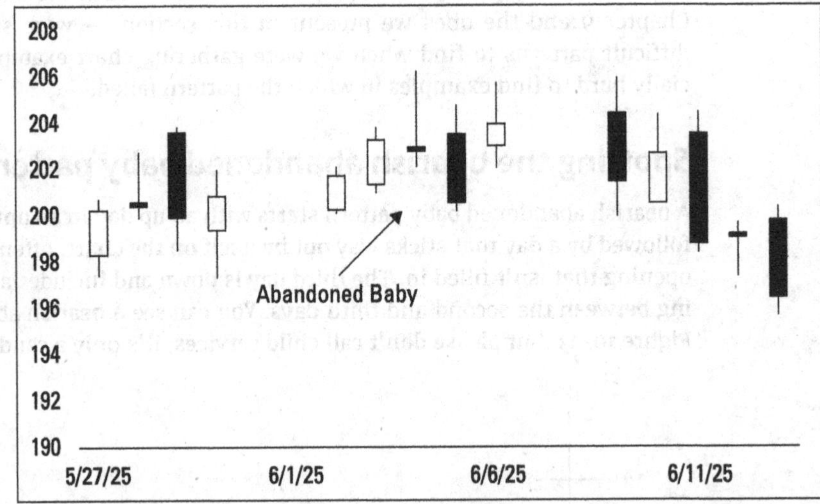

FIGURE 10-14: The bearish abandoned baby pattern comes out a winner in a chart of APPL stock.

Failing to signal lower prices ahead

A failing bearish abandoned baby is a rare occurrence, but it does occur. For this example, we stick with Apple. We find it useful to show success and failure for the same signal in the same security.

The bearish abandoned baby appears in Figure 10-15 during a nice uptrend in the market. The pattern has an up first day, followed by a gap opening and a second day with a fairly narrow range. The third day kicks off with a gap down opening, and the gaps on either side of the second day mean that the pattern is in place.

The signal doesn't hold up long because the stock gaps higher two days in a row. Shorts would be stopped out, and sellers would be disappointed because the price is headed higher in the short term.

The bearish squeeze alert pattern

We're fond of the bearish squeeze alert. (See its bullish counterpart in Chapter 9.) This signal either works or doesn't work quickly, and it appears frequently because the criteria for the pattern are relatively flexible.

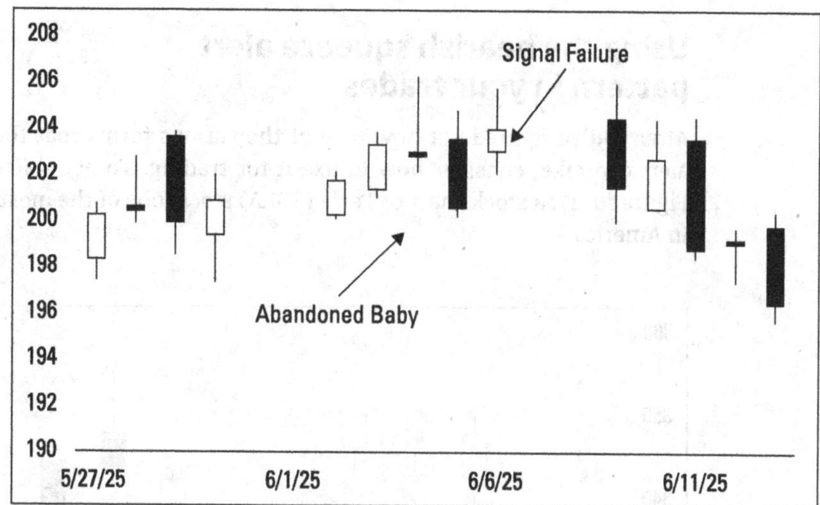

FIGURE 10-15: The bearish abandoned baby pattern failing in a chart of APPL stock.

Familiarizing yourself with the bearish squeeze alert pattern

The bearish squeeze alert pattern can take a few forms, and you can get a feel for one of them by reviewing Figure 10-16. The first day of the pattern has to be a down day, and the longer, the better. The second and third days can be up or down as long as they're inside days relative to the previous day. Both days must have a high that's lower than the previous high and a low that's higher than the previous low. In other words, the body of each candle has to have a range that doesn't exceed the upper or lower ends of the body of the previous day's candlestick.

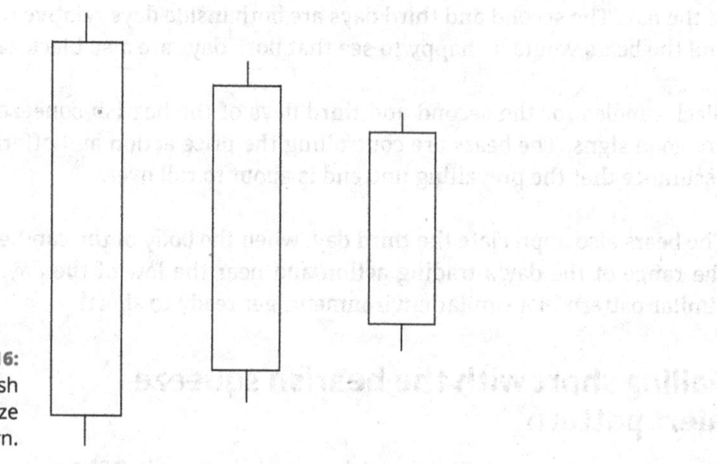

FIGURE 10-16: The bearish squeeze alert pattern.

Using the bearish squeeze alert pattern in your trades

After you've figured out how to spot the various forms that the bearish squeeze alert can take, consider how to use it for trading. To get started, take a look at Figure 10-17, a stock chart of Tesla (TSLA) stock, one of the most infamous brands in America.

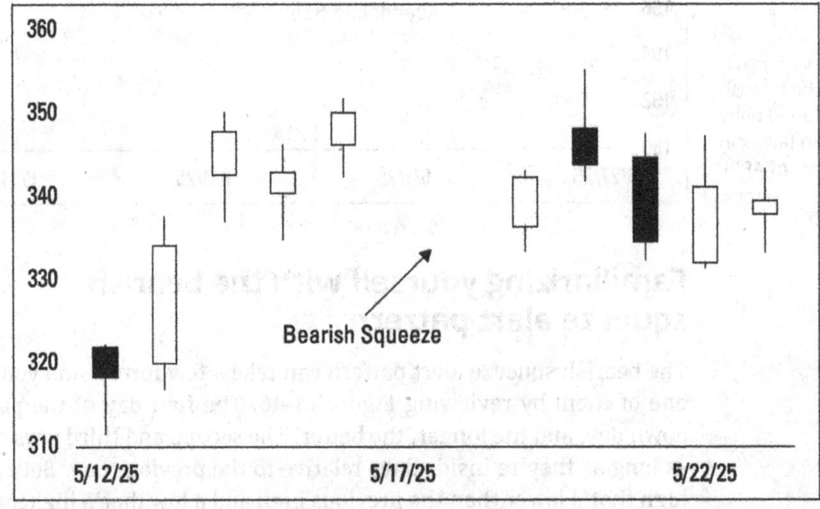

FIGURE 10-17: The bearish squeeze alert pattern comes through with a useful signal in a chart of TSLA stock.

The bearish squeeze alert in this chart occurs as TSLA shares are gapping higher. The first day is a strong up day with a gap opening and a close very near the high of the day. The second and third days are both inside days relative to the first day, and the bears would be happy to see that both days are also black candles.

Black candles for the second and third days of the bearish squeeze alert pattern are good signs. The bears are controlling the price action and offering additional assurance that the prevailing uptrend is about to roll over.

The bears also appreciate the third day, when the body of the candlestick is low in the range of the day's trading action and near the low of the day. If you spot a similar pattern in a similar environment, get ready to short!

Falling short with the bearish squeeze alert pattern

Figure 10-18 shows a failing bearish squeeze pattern in TSLA.

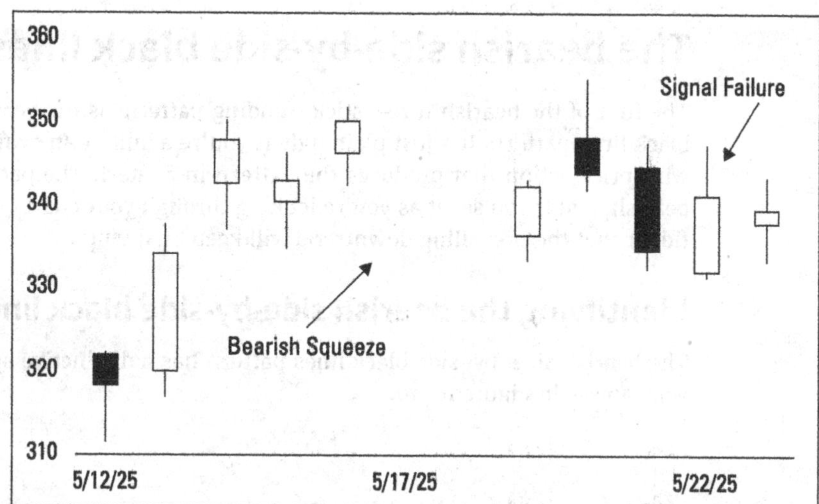

FIGURE 10-18: The bearish squeeze alert pattern doesn't work out well in a chart of TSLA stock.

This pattern emerges in Figure 10-18 as it appears that an uptrend is already rolling over — a good sign for a short trade. A long white candle shows up on the first day, followed by two inside days, both of which are black candles. The pattern is complete, but the bears have only one day to feel good about their short position before the pattern is proved to be invalid. The day after the pattern is a bearish day, and it really does appear that the trend will turn. But the bulls show up on the second day after the pattern and violate any level that can be considered to be resistance.

Forecasting with Bullish Three-Stick Trending Patterns

Like the patterns described in the preceding pages of this chapter, the bearish three-stick patterns that foreshadow the continuation of a downtrend are mirror images of their bullish counterparts, which you can read about in Chapter 9. The patterns in this section are useful, but more so as confirmations for trades that are already on than as inspiration to initiate a new trading position.

REMEMBER

You can initiate new positions by using bearish three-stick continuation patterns, but keep in mind that with trending signals, there's already been some price movement in the direction in which you'll be trading (sometimes considerable price movement). Trends are your friends, but they don't last forever.

The bearish side-by-side black lines pattern

The first of the bearish three-stick trending patterns is the bearish side-by-side black lines pattern. It's just plain ugly if you're a bull or an owner of the security with price action that produces the pattern in a chart. The pattern is extremely bearish, and if you see it as you're looking through your charts, you can feel confident that the prevailing downtrend will keep on diving.

Identifying the bearish side-by-side black lines

The bearish side-by-side black lines pattern has a distinctive appearance, which you can see in Figure 10-19.

The first day of this pattern is a down day that comes on the heels of a downtrend. The second day has a gap down and also trades bearishly. Note that the gap between the high of the second day and the low of the first day isn't filled. On the third and final day, the bears have their way again, and as on the second day, there's a lasting gap. The bears are definitely in charge.

Using the bearish side-by-side black lines pattern

You can harness the bearish power of the bearish side-by-side black lines pattern to give yourself confidence that a downtrend will continue. For an example, see Figure 10-20, a chart of TSLA stock. Tesla has given the world lots of technological innovations.

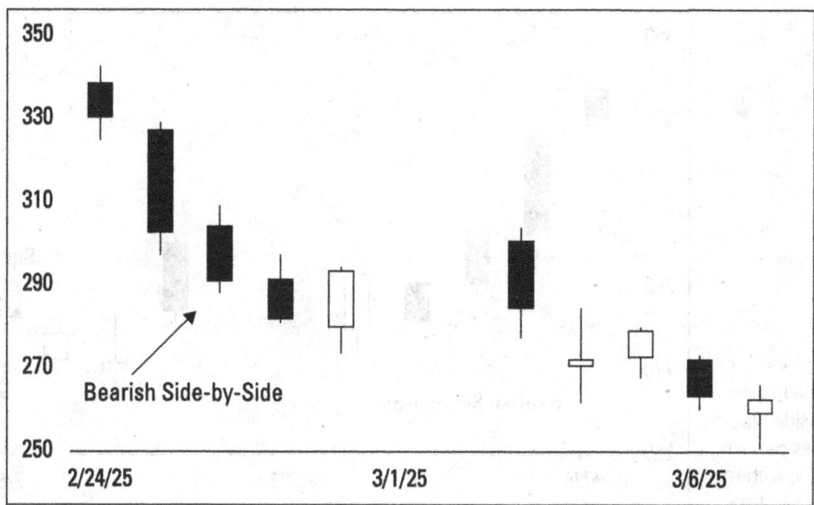

It's also worth noting that JPM is a good stock to trade based on macro trends — those economic and political factors that affect the world — because it's exposed to most areas of the global economy.

As you can see in Figure 10-20, the stock is already in the early stages of a downtrend when the bearish side-by-side black lines pattern starts to develop. The first and second days are down, with a substantial gap between them. The third day is also a bearish day, so the pattern is complete; the downtrend continuation is verified.

Failing to confirm a downtrend

Although some rebounding normally occurs shortly after the appearance of a trending pattern like the side-by-side black lines, that's not the case with the pattern in Figure 10-21. You can spot a little bit of bullishness a few days after the pattern shows up, but there's no real move into the gap.

You may ask yourself whether an ultra-bearish pattern like the bearish side-by-side black lines can ever fail. The answer is a resounding *yes*. By the way, the answer is the same for all patterns.

The chart in Figure 10-21 is a fun one because the pattern includes a big gap lower in the price. It can be difficult to sell short when a market is already moving lower. In this example, the failure to confirm the downtrend prevented getting into a trade that went nowhere fast.

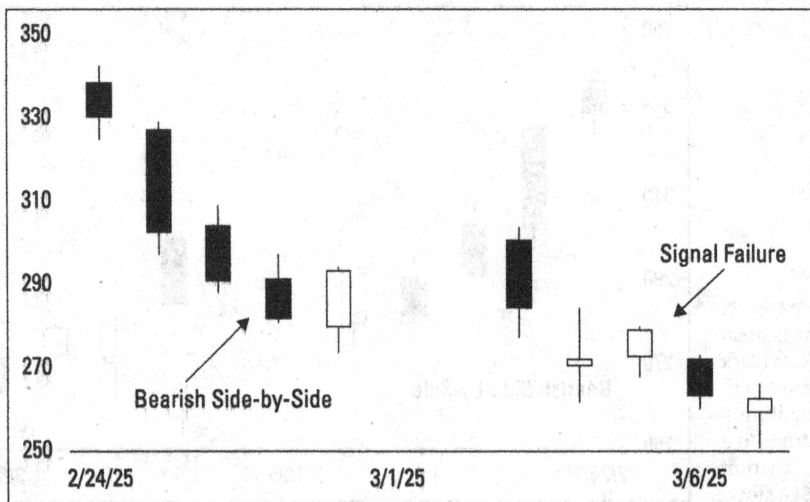

FIGURE 10-21: The bearish side-by-side black lines pattern failing in a chart of TSLA stock.

The bearish side-by-side white lines pattern

The bearish side-by-side white lines pattern is similar to the pattern in the preceding section, but its second and third days are white candles rather than black ones. The pattern is still a bearish one, but not quite as bearish.

Spotting the bearish side-by-side white lines pattern

The first day of this pattern is a long black candle in a downtrending market or stock. The second day kicks off with a gap down opening, and throughout the course of the day, the bulls push prices higher. The bulls try hard, but they're unable to push prices over the low of the first day, and this failure results in a gap.

The final day of the pattern once again sees a lower opening and a push at higher prices, and once again, the first day's low isn't reached. After two days of effort from the bulls, a gap remains in the chart. You can see what we mean in Figure 10-22.

Working with the bearish side-by-side white lines

Figure 10-23 offers a look at a successful occurrence of the bearish side-by-side white lines pattern. The figure is a chart of TSLA stock.

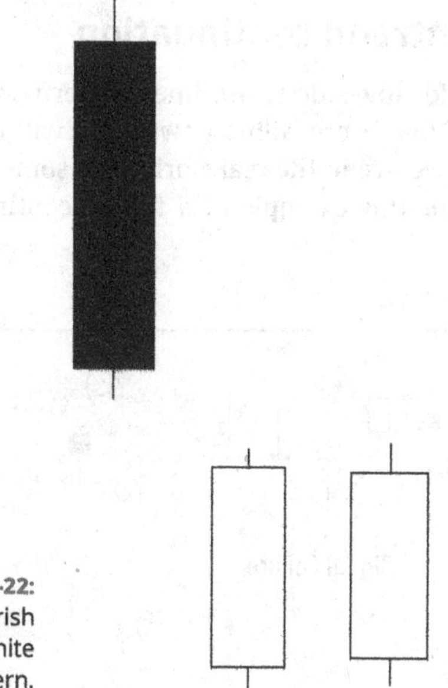

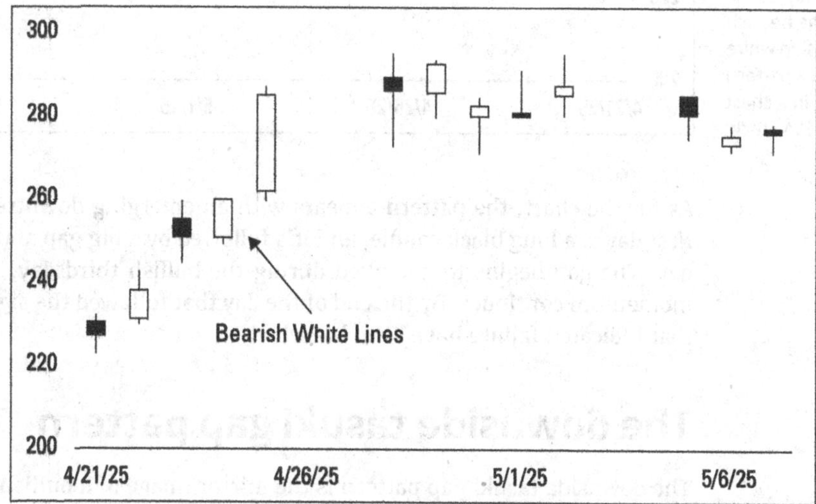

FIGURE 10-23:
The bearish
side-by-side
white lines
pattern predicts
a downtrend
continuation
in a chart of
TSLA stock.

The bearish side-by-side white lines pattern shows up in Figure 10-23 in a downtrend, and the first day is a down day. The second day opens with a gap down, but the bulls go to work and TSLA trades up a little. But a fairly substantial gap is left between the first and second days. The third day opens lower, and once again, the bulls give it a go, but they don't do much to move the price into the gap between the first and second days. The result is a bearish side-by-side white lines pattern. Then the price action of the next few days results in lower prices.

Failing to predict a downtrend continuation

In a perfect world, the bearish side-by-side white lines pattern would always provide a safe, comforting signal that a prevailing downtrend will continue for days, weeks, or even months. But we live in the real world, and sometimes, these things fail. We stick with TSLA for this example of a failing continuation of a downtrend (see Figure 10-24).

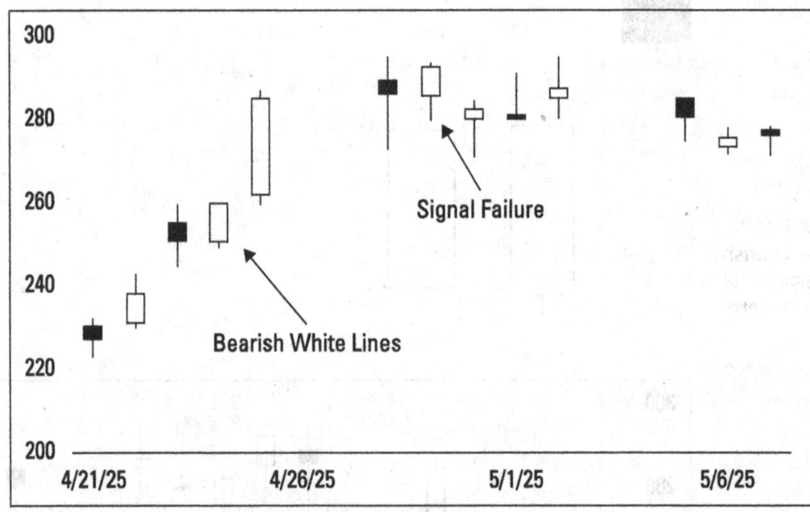

FIGURE 10-24: The bearish side-by-side white lines pattern failing in a chart of TSLA stock.

As for the chart, the pattern appears with an emerging downtrend in place. The first day is a long black candle, and it's followed by a big gap and a bullish second day. The gap begins to get filled during the bullish third day, and that upward momentum continues. By the end of the day that followed the signal, all the levels that indicated failure have been breached.

The downside tasuki gap pattern

The downside tasuki gap pattern is the mirror image of a bullish version that you can read about in Chapter 9. Compared with the other bearish three-stick trending patterns in this chapter, this pattern is more useful for you if you're looking to put on a new trade because of the higher closing price that occurs when the close of the third day moves into the gap between the first and second day.

Understanding how to identify the downside tasuki gap pattern

The downside tasuki gap begins with a black candle that appears during a down-trend. The second day sees a gap opening downward and bearish trading that result in a lower closing. When the third day rolls around, however, the bulls show up to push prices higher. The bulls push enough to make the third day an up day, with a closing price that's higher than the high of the second day. But don't count on the bullish behavior to continue. The bears are willing to sell within the gap between the first and second days, and they soon stop the bulls in their tracks. Want to see an example? Check out Figure 10-25.

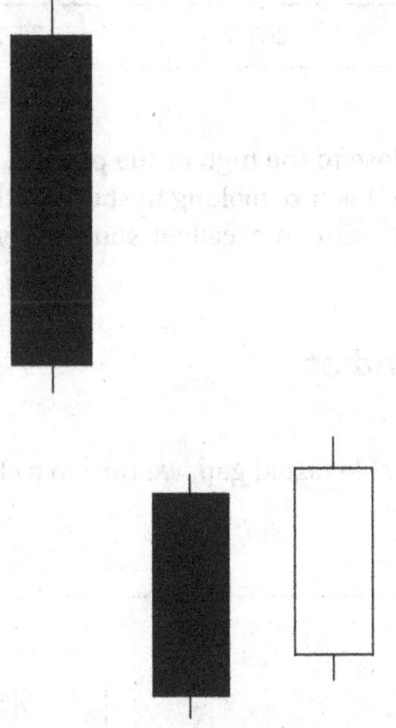

Making a trade with the downside tasuki gap pattern

The downside tasuki gap is one of the bearish three-stick trending patterns that makes for a good candidate when you're looking to initiate a short position. Figure 10-26 is a chart of Air Products (APD).

The second day of the downside tasuki gap pattern sees a gap down that isn't filled. The third day is an attempt by the bulls to move the price higher, and it stalls very low in the gap between the first and second days. The pattern is followed by a downtrend, including several consecutive bearish days.

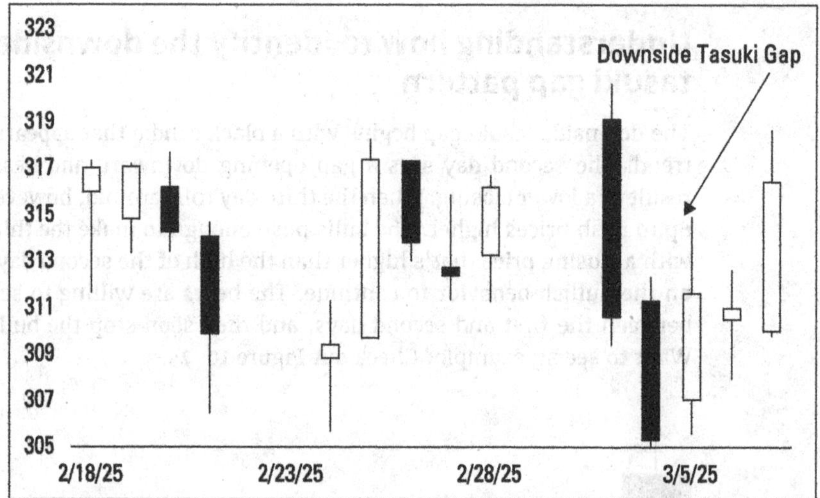

FIGURE 10-26:
The downside tasuki gap pattern works in a chart of APD stock.

TIP

Because the tasuki gap finishes close to the high of the pattern, you may want to enter on the close of the third day if you're looking to short. In this example, that strategy would have provided you with an excellent short entry before the continuation of the downtrend.

Catching the failing trend at the end of the pattern

For a failure example of the downside tasuki gap, we turn to a chart of APD stock once again, in Figure 10-27.

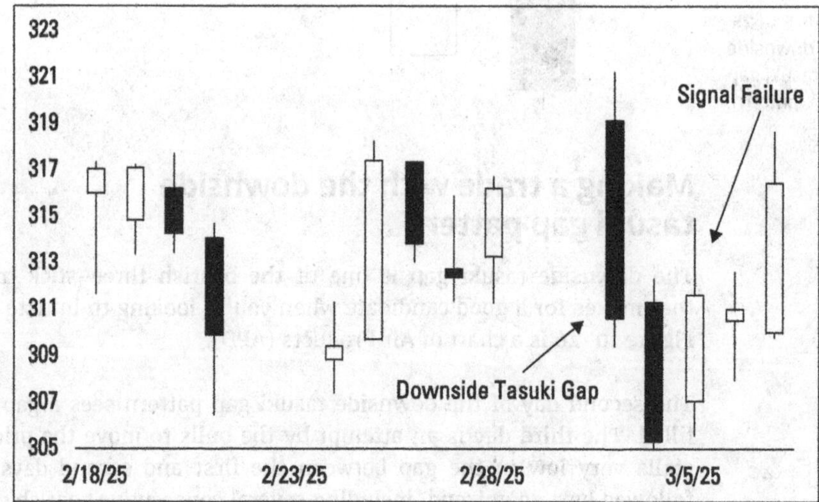

FIGURE 10-27:
The downside tasuki gap pattern (kind of) fails in a chart of APD stock.

Figure 10-27 is a fun example of the downside tasuki gap. If you've read about any of the other patterns in this chapter, you're probably expecting an outright pattern failure, but in this case, a signal to exit shows up before the pattern fizzles out. An astute user of candlestick patterns may have caught this signal before the trend changed and taken a profit instead of being stopped out for a loss.

The first day is a down day at the upper end of the downtrend. This day is followed by a gap down that isn't filled during the day and a down second day. Finally, on the third day of the pattern, a small rally occurs, and prices trade inside the gap, but the gap isn't filled.

Trading after the pattern in Figure 10-27 is interesting, with a few attempted rallies that get into the gap but don't trade over the high of the first day. There's also a drop to new lows, so the price action is quite varied. After the drop, a bullish reversal pattern shows up!

Look for one more thing in Figure 10-27: We highlight an outside up day — a bullish reversal pattern — that precedes a change to an uptrend. A wise candlestick pattern user would use that pattern as a signal to exit or even a chance to buy the futures, thus putting on a long position. On the flip side, a short who isn't looking out for candlestick patterns wouldn't see the writing on the wall and would probably be stopped out in the next few days as prices exceed the pattern's highs.

The downside gap-filled pattern

The downside gap-filled pattern rounds out our discussion of the bearish three-stick trending patterns. It's the most trade-worthy of all the patterns in this main section because its close is higher than the others. It also calls for some pretty tight stops, so you'll know quickly whether the pattern will succeed or fail.

Recognizing the downside gap-filled pattern

As you can see in Figure 10-28, the downside gap-filled pattern starts with a down day in a downtrend. As with the other trending patterns in this chapter, the second day is a gap down, and it's bearish. At first, the gap between the first and second days isn't filled and remains in the chart. On the third and final day, there's a lower open, but the bulls push the price higher over the course of the day. The gap between the first and second days is filled. At some point, however, the bears decide that it's time to take over again, and the rise in prices stops, usually in the lower half of the first day's trading range. The downtrend is still in place.

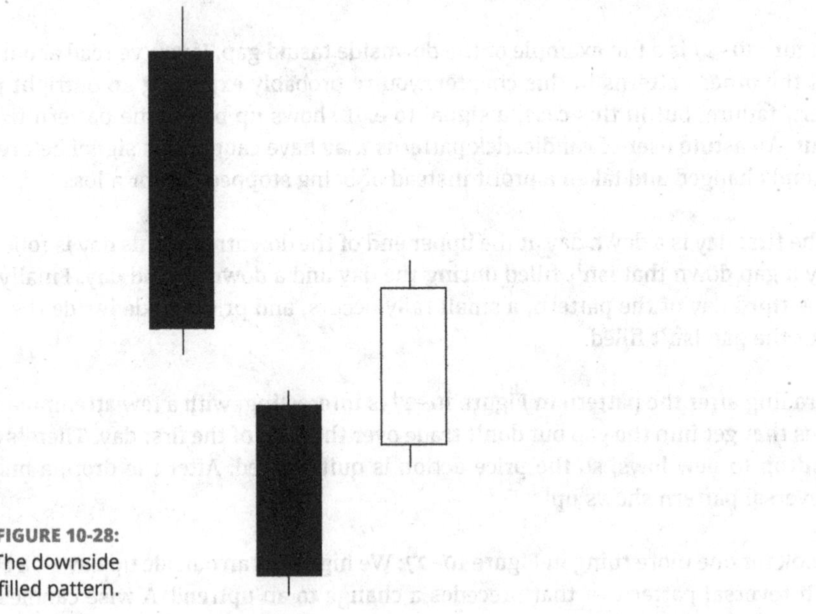

Trading the downside gap-filled pattern

To give you an idea of how you can trade the downside gap-filled pattern, we provide the example in Figure 10-29: a chart of APD stock.

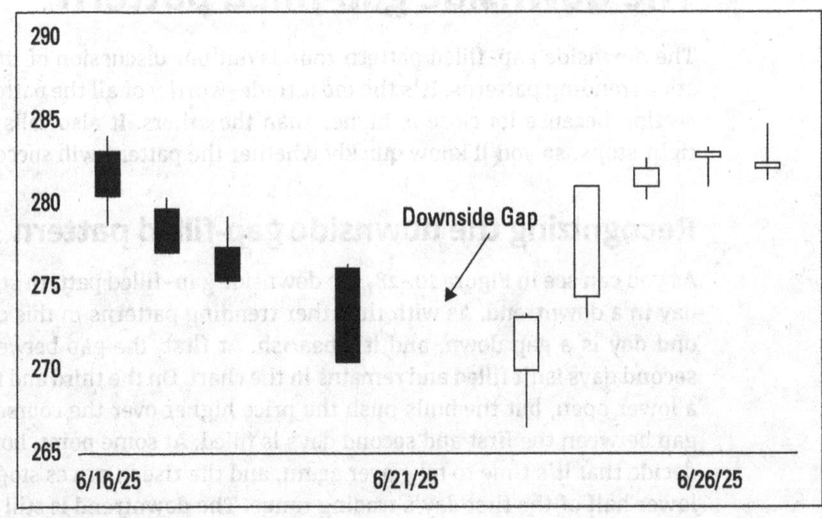

FIGURE 10-29:
The downside gap-filled pattern predicts a downtrend continuation in a chart of APD stock.

The downside gap-filled pattern appears at the upper end of the downtrend, beginning with a black candle for the first day. On the second day, APD gaps lower, and the bears control the day, so the gap isn't filled as the day progresses bearishly. The third day completes the pattern with an up day that fills in the gap, and the downtrend continues.

If you shorted by using this pattern, you'd be pleased to see some bearish action that continues for a while after the pattern is complete. After a few weeks, however, a bullish reversal pattern emerges. There's a doji followed by an up day in a downtrend, which usually indicates that prices have reached a bottom. That pattern would mean it's time to exit your short position and walk away with your profits.

Failing to signal a continuing downtrend

We hate for the last example in this chapter to be a down note, but we feel obligated to present a failing example of the downside gap-filled pattern. For that purpose, turn to Figure 10-30, a chart of APD stock.

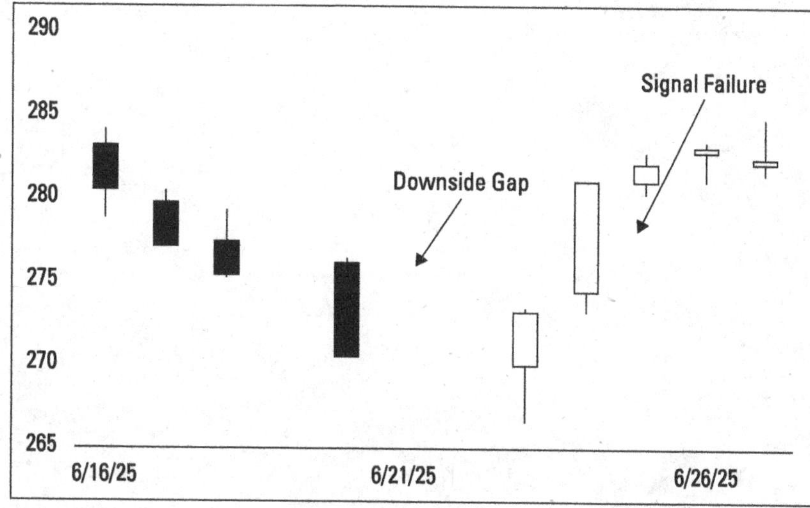

FIGURE 10-30: The downside gap-filled pattern providing a dud signal in a chart of APD stock.

The pattern emerges in a downtrend, with a black candle that's followed by a gap down, which is eventually filled on the third day. All is as it should be in terms of pattern formation, but if you look closely, you can see an indication that the pattern may not hold up long. AAPL was rolling over, but the downtrend was never really established. The high of the pattern was violated, rendering it null, void, and more than a little annoying.

4
Combining Patterns and Indicators

Chapter **11**

Using Technical Indicators to Complement Your Candlestick Charts

You can use nothing but candlestick patterns when trading, and some traders have proved that route to be a profitable one. But don't think twice about combining candlesticks with other technical indicators. You can take advantage of a wide range of indicators to confirm the conclusions you draw from your candlestick charts, and your results are often more reliable and profitable than they were before you learned this. You may well find that you can't live by candlesticks alone!

Many candlestick patterns — from single sticks to complex multiple-stick formations — depend on the market context in which they appear. A bullish signal in a bearish market, for example, sparks skepticism and may even be ignored. But what constitutes a bull or bear market? (As we write this chapter, one of us has a financial TV show on in the background, and two market professionals are vigorously debating whether we're in a bull or bear market. If these market pros can't agree on the nature of the market, how are individual traders supposed to figure it out?) The answer is simple: Use technical analysis! More specifically, use indicators that attempt to define the market trend.

Traders use many types of technical indicators to enhance and complement their trading styles. Traders are always trying to come up with the perfect combination of indicators and signals. (Russell confesses to always having a pen and a small notebook on his desk for use whenever the light bulb goes off with a new approach to trading.) You never know when inspiration will strike! That brilliant new way to incorporate candlestick charting into a new trading scheme may reveal itself at any moment.

Technical indicators share one of a couple of purposes. The first is to define the current trend, whether up, down, or even sideways (more on that topic in the next section). To quote a popular trading saying, "The trend is your friend." The other indicators try to identify market extremes or reversals. That information allows a trader to "fade the market" — go against the trend in the hope that the trend will soon fade out and reverse. Traders have heated arguments about whether trading with the trend or trying to profit from reversals is the key to success, but as long as traders are still making a living (and losing their shirts) by using both styles, the debate will continue.

There are more complex indicators than you can shake a (candle)stick at. In fact, *Technical Analysis For Dummies*, 4th Edition, by Barbara Rockefeller (Wiley) covers them extensively. In this chapter, we clue you in on a few tried-and-true indicators you can use to determine the trend of the market and make your candlestick-based decisions even more reliable: trend lines, moving averages, relative strength index, stochastics, and Bollinger bands.

Using Trend Lines

Trend lines can be the most basic of all technical indicators. A *trend line* is exactly what it sounds like: a line in a chart that shows the general direction in which a stock is trending. If a stock is moving up in price, its trend line slopes upward from left to right. If a stock is trending down in price, its trend line slopes downward from left to right.

In this section, you can see how to draw a trend line on a chart. Also, you find out how to determine the direction (up or down). Finally, you see how a computer can draw trend lines for you.

Drawing trend lines

Trend lines seem to be pretty straightforward, but drawing a trend line can be tricky. Based on how you think a stock is performing, you draw a line of support (in a bullish case) or a line of resistance (in a bearish case).

You can construct a trend line with nothing more than a printed chart, a ruler, and a pencil. If you can't find a ruler, just close this book (if you bought the print version) and use its spine. Anything that allows you to draw a straight line between two points will do. To draw a trend line, simply draw a line that connects two or more low price points (for an upward trending line) or two or more high price points (for a downward trending line). Figure 11-1 shows a prime example of a trend line.

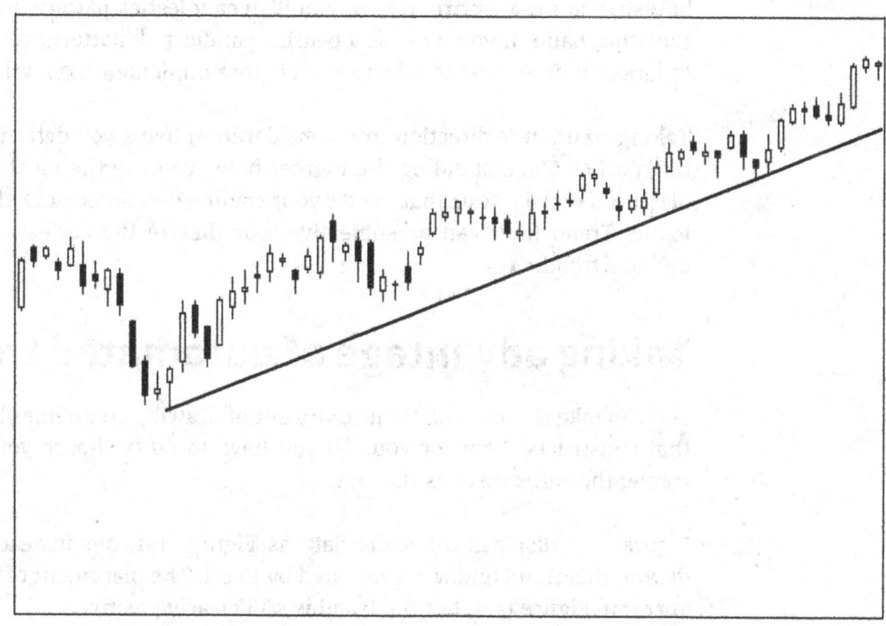

FIGURE 11-1:
A chart showing a trend line with a positive trend.

WARNING

Don't let the ease of constructing trend lines fool you into thinking that trend lines are simple or cut-and-dried. In fact, it's difficult to refer to a trend line in a chart as a technical indicator because drawing the line is a subjective task. Much like market experts debating on TV, two traders are likely to come up with completely different lines when they're asked to draw what they consider to be the most significant trend line on a chart. If a trader happens to be biased against a certain stock, that trader may be more inclined to look at a chart and find a downtrend.

Despite all the subjectivity involved in drawing trend lines, some hugely successful traders rely heavily on them for their buy and sell decisions. When Russell began his career as a runner in the cattle-trading pits back when there still were trading pits, a successful trader he knew based decisions on nothing more than daily charts and trend lines that he'd drawn during his train ride every morning. It worked for him.

Considering trend line direction

Although different trend lines drawn on the same chart may differ a bit, you'll usually find that at least the directions of the trend lines are the same. Trend lines can trend up, down, or not at all. For simplicity's sake, Figure 11-1 shows an obvious up (bullish) trend. (We say the trend is obvious, but we wonder how many of our colleagues would insist that we're wrong!) After you determine that a trend is bullish, you may confirm it with a bullish candlestick pattern and look to buy. On the other hand, if you witness a bearish candlestick pattern, you may be inclined to ignore it or at least to take caution before implementing a sell signal.

Taking trend-line direction into consideration helps you determine the status of the market. Understanding the market helps you use the most appropriate candlestick pattern — one that makes your trading decisions more effective and profitable. Trend lines can be subjective, but they're the easiest, quickest ways to define a trend.

Taking advantage of automated trend lines

You can take some of the subjectivity out of drawing trend lines by using software that constructs them for you. All you have to do is choose your preferred time frame; the software does the rest.

Figure 11-2 displays the same data as Figure 11-1, but instead of being hand-drawn, this trend line was generated by Excel. The placement of the line is different from Figure 11-1, but the trend is still clearly positive.

Using software reduces the subjective nature of trend lines, but it doesn't remove subjectivity; software-drawn trend lines still have a subjective component. The user still determines the time frame for the trend line, which can have a definite effect on the type of line that's generated. As with any computer program that involves user input, the data you get out is only as good as what you put in.

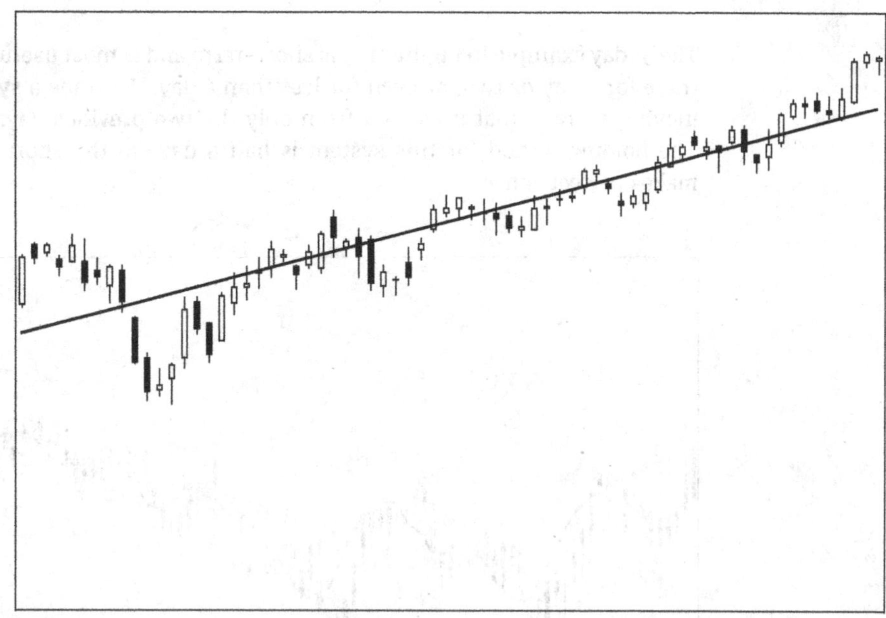

Using Moving Averages

Technical analysis doesn't get much easier than drawing a trend line. But what if you're in need of a slightly more complex indicator? The next step up from drawing trend lines is calculating moving averages. Put simply, a *moving average* is the average of the closing prices of a stock over a certain period. You can compare a closing price with a moving average to determine a trend.

Like most technical indicators, moving averages come in several types, and we explain a few in this section. First, though, you must understand how to make good choices about the time frames you use when calculating your moving averages.

Selecting appropriate moving average periods

The time frames of your moving averages are determined by the number of closing prices you include. To decide on that number, consider the types of trading decisions you make based on your moving average. Pick a time frame that's appropriate for the amount of time you intend to have a trade on. For a trade to be held for only a day or two, a 5- to 10-day moving average will suffice.

The 5-day example in Figure 11-3 is short-term and is most useful for traders who trade for a day or two, or even for less than a day. We trade a system based on a moving average that uses data from only the two previous days' closing prices. The holding period for this system is half a day, so the short moving average makes perfect sense.

The range of moving averages we've seen used in charts varies from 2 to 200 days (over six months). A 200-day moving average is very long-term, but in many circles, it's considered to be significant for determining a stock's long-term trend. In fact, one common description of a long-term bull or bear market is whether an index is trading above (bull) or below (bear) its 200-day moving average.

Using simple moving averages

The most basic type of moving average is the simple moving average, which is also the easiest to calculate and the most common — so common, in fact, that the word *simple* is often left off when a simple moving average is displayed in a chart. In Figure 11-4, a 5-day simple moving average is calculated by using the closing prices from five previous days. The calculation can't be much easier: The five closing prices are added up and divided by five. If you keep the number of closing prices in your simple moving averages low, you can easily work them out with a calculator.

The 5-day simple moving average in Figure 11-4 comes out at 114.20, and the closing price on the fifth day is 113.87. Some technical analysts would say that this pattern indicates a downtrend because the close on the final day is lower than the moving average — useful information if you're working on a short-term trade.

Day	Close
1	114.70
2	114.73
3	114.14
4	113.56
5	113.87
Total	571.00
Total / 5	114.20

But if you have a longer-term trade in mind, it wouldn't make much sense to fret because a closing price dipped below a 5-day moving average. There just aren't enough data points (closing prices, in this case) involved, so a relatively minor change in a closing price can have a sizable effect on the average. A moving average calculated over a longer period with many more closing prices — say, 100 days or more — is less likely to reveal any closing prices that cross the average.

REMEMBER

The longer your time horizon for a trade (or even an investment), the longer the moving average you need. A trade for a day or two should use a 5-day moving average, whereas a position to be held for several months may use a 50- or 200-day moving average.

The A and B parts of Figure 11-5 contain the same pricing data, but A has a 5-day moving average, and B uses a 20-day moving average. Notice the extreme differences in trends between the two charts.

Using other types of moving averages: What have you done for me lately?

Two fairly common deviations on the simple moving average are the *weighted* moving average and the *exponential* moving average. These types of moving averages are calculated in different ways, but both have the same goal: to place more emphasis on recent prices.

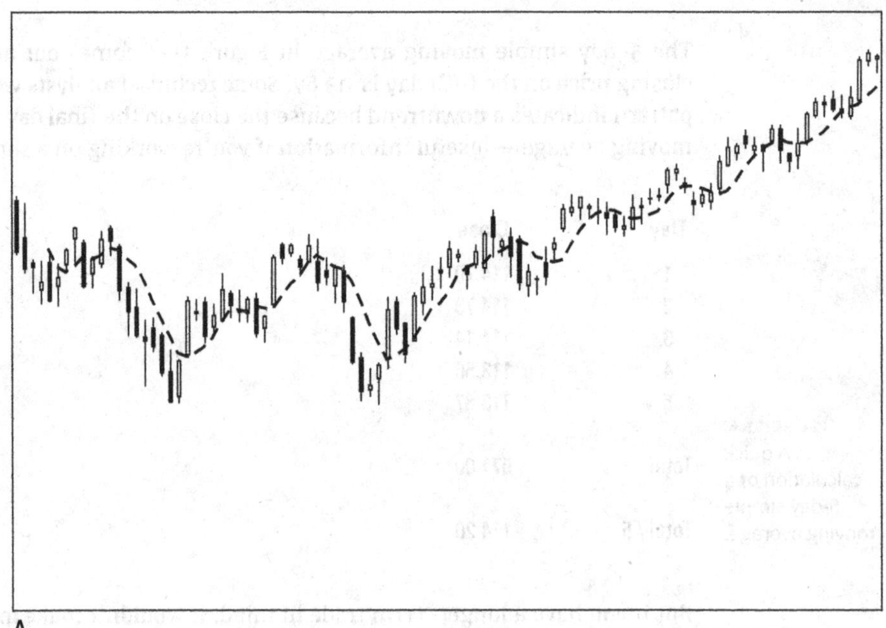

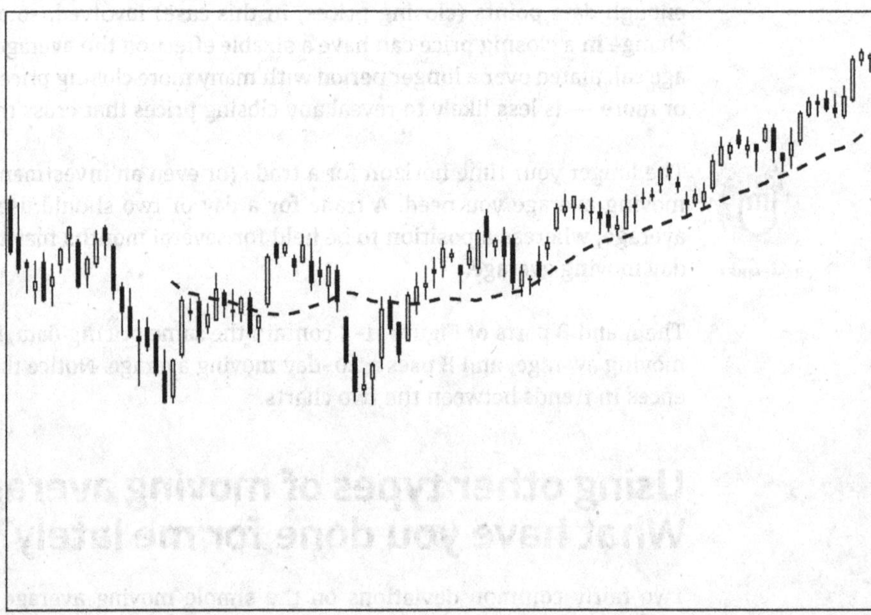

FIGURE 11-5:
A 5-day (A) and 20-day (B) moving average comparison.

Why would a trader want to explore more complex moving averages? Well, the major advantage of one of these more complicated moving averages over the simple moving average is that it's better at more quickly revealing a change in trend. Being able to detect trend changes faster makes you a more agile trader. Also, traders (especially short-term traders) have short memories. Ask us what the market did yesterday, and we're pretty sure we can give you a quick answer. Ask us what the market did two Fridays ago, however, and we'd have to pull up a chart (a candlestick chart, of course!) to give you an answer. Because a short-term trader places more emphasis on recent price action, using a charting method that does the same thing typically works better for shorter-term styles of trading. Both weighted and exponential moving averages emphasize recent price action; the only substantial difference is the method of calculation.

REMEMBER

If you were to rank the three most commonly used types of moving averages — simple, weighted, and exponential — according to their emphasis on recent price action, exponential moving averages, which place *lots* of emphasis on recent prices, would top the list. Weighted moving averages would be a close second, and simple moving averages would finish a distant last.

Calculating a weighted moving average

To calculate a weighted moving average, multiply the most recent stock price by the total number of prices in your chosen time frame. Then multiply the second-most-recent stock price by the total number of prices *minus one*, and work your way back to the first price in your time frame, using the same method.

For Figure 11-6, we've taken the same 5-day data used for the simple moving average in Figure 11-4 and calculated a weighted moving average. *Note:* For Day 5, the weighted close is equal to 5×113.87 or 569.35, whereas the weighted close for Day 1 is simply the closing price $\times 1$ (114.70). To determine the weighted moving average, we added the weighted closing prices and divided them by the sum of the weights. In this case, that number is

$$[(1 \times \text{Day 1 closing price}) + (2 \times \text{Day 2 closing price}) + (3 \times \text{Day 3 closing price}) +$$
$$(4 \times \text{Day 4 closing price}) + (5 \times \text{Day 5 closing price})] \div 15.$$

Figure 11-4 and Figure 11-6 show the difference between the simple moving average and the weighted moving average — a pretty significant difference! The lower recent prices mean that the weighted moving average is quite a bit lower.

Day	Close	Weighted Close
1	114.70	114.70
2	114.73	229.46
3	114.14	342.42
4	113.56	454.24
5	113.87	569.35
15 Total		1710.17
Total / 15		114.01

FIGURE 11-6:
A calculation of a 5-day weighted moving average.

Calculating an exponential moving average

You can calculate an exponential moving average in a handful of ways, and we suggest that you use, believe it or not, none of them. The math involved in the calculations is a bit complex, and for your purposes, we recommend leaving the hard work to a charting program. (See Chapter 4 for more info on popular charting software.)

Combining two moving averages

Comparing closing prices with moving averages is a helpful way to use moving averages to determine a trend, but it's not the only way. You can also combine and compare two moving averages to define the current trend. You might calculate both a 5- and 20-day moving average for a stock, for example, and then compare them to spot a trend. To do so, work your way through these steps:

1. **Calculate the two moving averages, using the process described in the earlier section "Using simple moving averages."**

2. **Determine which of your two moving averages is fast and which is slow.**

   The *fast-moving average* is always the one with the fewest data points (closing prices). It's labeled *fast* because its small number of data points makes it likely to change much more quickly. The *slow-moving average* is slower to change because of its heftier number of data points.

3. **Compare your moving averages to spot a trend.**

   If the fast-moving average is higher than the slow-moving average, it indicates an uptrend. The logic is exactly the same as comparing a closing price with a moving average to determine trend, but the fast-moving average takes the place of the closing price.

If you notice this type of trend, be more inclined to follow a bullish candlestick pattern and consider buying. If the fast-moving average is lower than the slow-moving average, it indicates a downtrend, in which case you should follow a bearish candlestick pattern and look to sell.

Figure 11-7 contains the same price data as Figure 11-1, but overlays both a 5- and 20-day moving average. The 5-day moving average is represented by the solid line, and a dashed line is used for the 20-day moving average. You can clearly see the higher volatility of the 5-day moving average compared with the 20-day moving average, and you can also see that the chart indicates an uptrend!

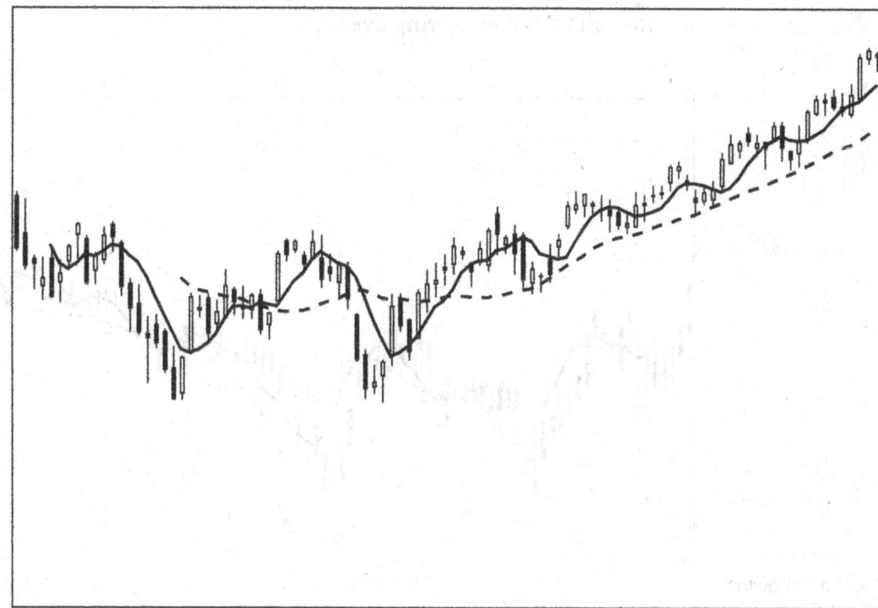

FIGURE 11-7:
A chart with 5-day and 20-day moving averages.

Experts often use a combination of 5-day and the longer 200-day moving averages to define a long-term bull or bear market. These choices may seem somewhat arbitrary, but they've been cemented as rules of thumb in the market.

Combining three moving averages

Two moving averages can be useful company, but is three a crowd? Who really needs to use three moving averages? Believe it or not, some successful longer-term trading systems make comparisons by using three moving averages. The technique is useful because it allows the market to be defined as having no trend, as opposed to an uptrend or downtrend.

REMEMBER

You may be thinking, "No trend? The market and stock prices change daily! There *has* to be a trend." But some markets (and individual stocks in particular) have long periods with no uptrend or downtrend. You often refer to this market or stock as being stuck in a range, or *range-bound*. Identifying a market without a trend can be extremely helpful because it's difficult to make money trading when there isn't much price movement. With that fact in mind, combining three moving averages is certainly worth your time.

Comparisons that use three moving averages identify each average as fast, medium, or slow. As in comparisons of two moving averages, the one considered to be fastest has the fewest data points. The slow-moving average has the most data points, and the medium one is somewhere in the middle. Figure 11-8 shows 5-, 10-, and 20-day moving averages.

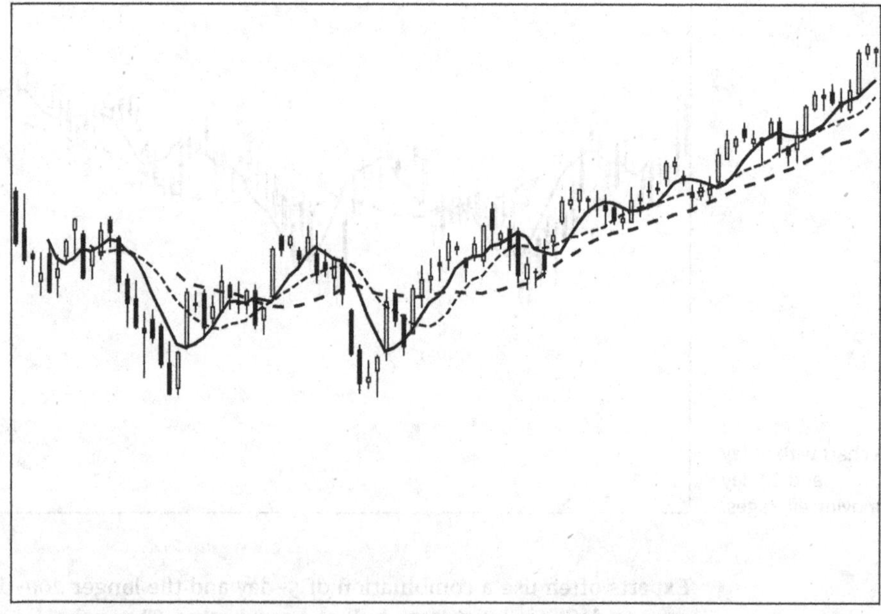

In Figure 11-8, the moving averages are represented by different lines:

>> **Fast:** The 5-day moving average is represented by the solid line.

>> **Medium:** The line with long dashes is the 10-day moving average.

>> **Slow:** The 20-day moving average is the line with the short dashes.

In any chart containing three moving averages, you can pick out an uptrend when the fast-moving average is higher than the medium one and the medium one is higher than the slow one. You can see an uptrend on the right side of this chart, where all three moving averages are in order and trending together.

You can identify a downtrend when the fast-moving average is lower than the medium one and the medium one is lower than the slow one. If the fast, medium, and slow-moving averages aren't lined up fast to slow or vice versa, you can safely say that the market has no trend.

Knowing the type of market you're dealing with is the key to using many candlestick patterns correctly, so you may need to use three moving averages, especially for longer-term trading. The more certain you can be about a trend, the more likely you are to identify a bullish or bearish candlestick pattern properly and trade on it effectively.

Examining the Relative Strength Index

Our favorite indicator is the relative strength index (RSI), which compares the strength of a stock's up days with the strength of its down days. RSI proponents believe that as a result, the RSI can cut through erratic changes to confirm price movement. This index is considered to be a leading indicator because you can usually count on the direction of a security's RSI to change ahead of its price action.

The RSI is classified as a *momentum oscillator*. The *momentum* part of that term comes from the fact that as a security is in an uptrend or downtrend, the RSI's trend should correspond, and it's an *oscillator* because RSIs fluctuate between 0 and 100 percent.

Another attractive feature of RSIs is that they include levels indicating when a security is overbought or oversold. When the security reaches one of these levels, savvy traders should be on their toes, waiting for a corresponding change in the trend of the RSI — or, even better, some sort of revealing bullish or bearish candlestick pattern that lets them know it's time to buy or sell.

Calculating the RSI

Calculating an RSI is fairly complex, even when you use a spreadsheet program. Rather than spend several pages describing the steps for calculating an RSI, we give you a brief overview of the formulas that drive it:

1. **Add up the price change on up days and the price change on down days for the number of periods (usually, 14) in your look-back range.**

2. **Divide those individual sums by 14.**

3. **Calculate the relative strength (not the RSI) by dividing the up-day average by the down-day average:**

   RS = Average up days ÷ Average down days

The RSI plugs the data from the up and down days into a fairly complex formula, resulting in a reading between 0 and 100. The following equation explains the math behind the RSI:

RSI = 100 – (100 + Relative Strength)

Reading an RSI chart

Like many technical indicators, RSIs are much easier to digest in chart form. Figure 11-9 is a daily price for Air Products (APD). The top section of the chart is a basic candlestick chart depicting the price action in APD stock. Numerous bullish and bearish candlestick formations are charted, but for now, focus on the RSI component.

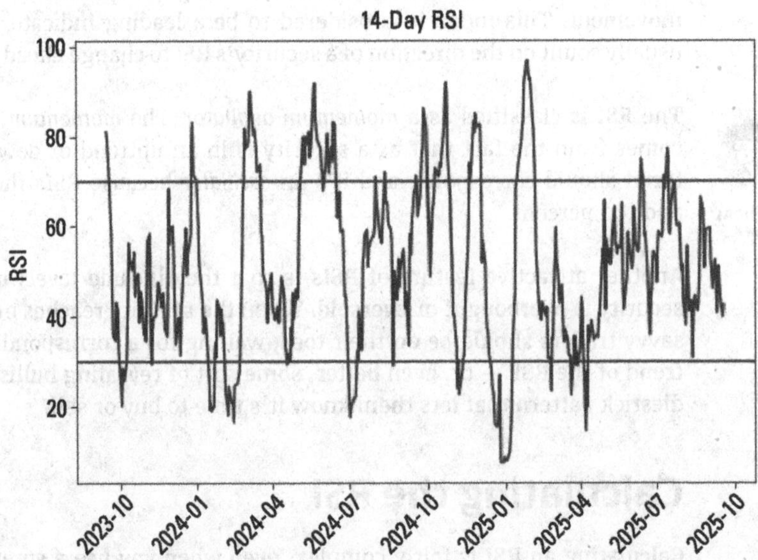

FIGURE 11-9:
A chart of APD stock with the RSI.

The bottom quarter of the chart contains a slow-moving line that depicts the RSI. Normally, this line is how an oscillator is depicted on a chart. Unlike a moving average, which is imposed on top of a chart's price component, the RSI (or any similar indicator) appears *below* the price component. Notice that the RSI seems to flow along and mirror the movements of the closing prices. At times, however, the RSI flattens while the price continues to move or even moves in the opposite direction. This change is called a *divergence*.

Divergence is the key to using the RSI. A divergence combined with a candlestick pattern that matches the direction of the divergence can provide a profitable trade signal.

But the usefulness of RSIs doesn't end with their role as a momentum indicator. RSIs may also be used as signals that reveal when the price of a security has reached a level that's too high or too low for the near term, or where a reversal of trend is likely.

This simplicity may sound too good to be true, and of course, it is. Using the RSI strictly by buying when it hits 30 or selling when it hits 70 is a disastrous strategy. It does make for a good rule of thumb, however, when you consider it alongside a signal from a candlestick pattern or a divergent move in the RSI relative to the price chart.

Combining a divergent RSI with a candlestick pattern is a smart move. Adding the overbought or oversold levels to the equation is even smarter, providing much more reliable buy and sell signals. The strength of the RSI as a momentum and oscillating signal is why it's one of our favorite indicators.

THE ORIGIN OF OVERBOUGHT AND OVERSOLD LEVELS

You may be wondering how overbought and oversold levels were established. Those benchmarks came from of renowned technical analyst J. Welles Wilder, who introduced the RSI in his 1978 book *New Concepts in Technical Trading Systems* (Trend Research Publishing). In the book, he recommends using 30 as an oversold level (an attractive area to buy) and 70 as an overbought level (an area to exit or sell short). In Figure 11-9, the oversold level of 30 and the overbought level of 70 are indicated by lines along the bottom of the chart. Wilder also suggests using 14 as the standard number of price periods for calculating RSIs, which is the input used for the chart in Figure 11-9.

Cashing In on Stochastics

Another useful indicator with an extremely clumsy name is the *stochastic oscillator*. This momentum indicator considers the current closing price of a security in relation to a high-low range of prices over a set number of look-back periods, usually 5 or 14 days, depending. This oscillator can be useful when used in tandem with candlestick charts. The stochastic oscillator can also be used as an overbought or oversold indicator when readings are at extreme levels: 30 percent for oversold and 70 percent for overbought (see "Examining the Relative Strength Index," earlier in this chapter).

Grasping the math behind the stochastic oscillator

George Lane developed the stochastic oscillator in the late 1950s. The math behind it is pretty remarkable for an indicator that is more than 60 years old. Two readings for a stochastic oscillator are combined in a chart. These readings are referred to as *slow (%D)* and *fast (%K) stochastics*. The slow one is generally a moving average of the fast one.

These are the formulas for the slow and fast stochastic oscillators:

» **Fast stochastic:**

- %K = 100 × (Recent Close – Lowest Low(n) – Highest High(n) – Lowest Low(n))

- N = Number of periods used in calculation

» **Slow stochastic:**

- %D = 3-period moving average of %K

Interpreting the stochastic oscillator

Luckily, most (if not all) charting software calculates the stochastic oscillator for you, so you don't need to memorize or even fully understand the formulas behind it. (Whew!) You really just need to know how to interpret the lines in a chart. Figure 11-10 shows how the stochastic oscillator shows up in a chart. This chart contains the same APD data as in Figure 11-9, but the RSI has been removed, and a stochastic indicator has been inserted.

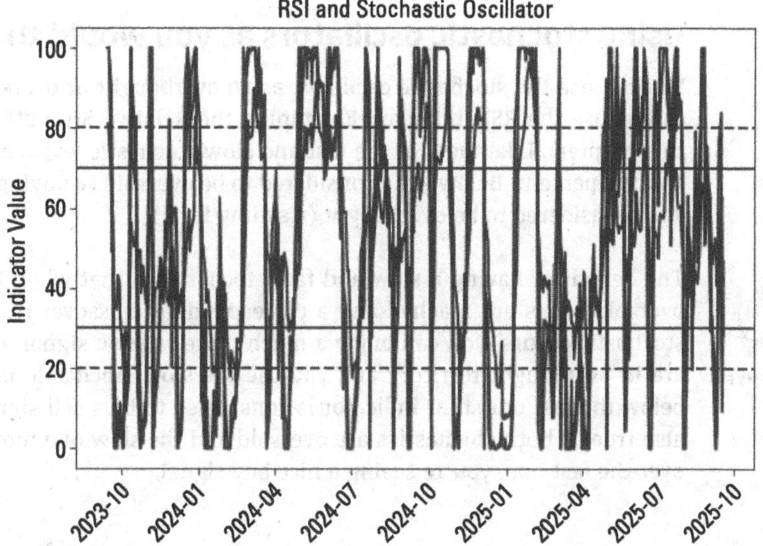

FIGURE 11-10:
A chart of INTC
stock with the
stochastic
oscillator.

REMEMBER

When interpreting the stochastic oscillator, you use methods similar to those used to interpret the RSI and moving averages.

Using stochastic oscillators as you would two moving averages

Knowing how to use two moving averages is helpful for interpreting stochastic oscillators. For defining a trend, if both the fast (%K) and slow (%D) stochastics are trending higher and the fast line is higher than the slow line, you're looking at an uptrend. For example, if you're using two moving averages, and the moving average with the shorter look-back period is above the moving average with the longer look-back period, the trend is considered to be up.

Another situation where using stochastics is similar to using two moving averages is that a change in trend may be signaled when the fast stochastic changes from being over or under the slower stochastic. Keep an eye out for those important changes.

The rule is that if the fast stochastic is above the slow one, an uptrend is in place; if the fast one is below the slow one, a downtrend is in place; and when they cross, a trend change is occurring. When the indicators are in overbought territory and the fast one crosses below the slow one, that pattern may represent a good selling opportunity. Conversely, when the indicators are in oversold territory and the fast one crosses over the slow one, they may show a good buying opportunity.

Using stochastic oscillators as you would the RSI

You can use the stochastic oscillator as an overbought or oversold indicator, just as you use the RSI (refer to "Examining the Relative Strength Index" earlier in this chapter). Like the RSI, the fast and slow stochastic levels oscillate between 0 and 100 percent. Below 30 is considered to be oversold (a buying level), and above 70 is considered to be overbought (a selling level).

REMEMBER

The benefit of having a slow and fast stochastic is that when the overbought or oversold levels are reached and a corresponding crossover of the fast and slow stochastic occurs, you can enjoy a much more reliable signal. If both stochastics are in overbought territory and you see the slow stochastic move from over to below the fast one, that indicator is considered to be a sell signal. The reverse is also true: If both stochastics are oversold and the slow one moves from below to over the fast one, you're seeing a nice buy signal.

Buddying Up with Bollinger Bands

The idea behind Bollinger bands is that when the price of a security gets too high above or below a moving average, that security is considered to be overbought or oversold. Bollinger bands look like moving averages in a price chart (refer to "Using Moving Averages," earlier in this chapter), but they're positioned a certain distance above and below the real moving average in a chart. The bands mark the areas where a security is considered to be overbought or oversold.

(Bollinger bands are named for the renowned technical analyst John Bollinger.)

You may do well to leave the necessary calculations of Bollinger bands to charting software, but the process starts simply enough, with the calculation of a simple moving average of a price series. (For details on that process, refer to "Using simple moving averages," earlier in this chapter.) Bollinger suggests a 20-day moving average, which many charting software programs use as the default, so that's always a good place to start.

After the 20-day moving average is calculated, things get a bit trickier. The bands that run above and below the moving average are based on a statistical measure known as *standard deviation.* The bands are placed a certain number of standard deviations higher and lower than the moving average. Without delving into too much detail, the distance of the bands from the moving average is determined by the amount of volatility in the market. The more the market is moving around, the wider the bands are spread.

As the standard deviation rises and falls with the level of market volatility, the overbought and oversold levels tend to adjust for the market environment. Figure 11-11 shows an excellent example of a Bollinger band chart. The data is the same that's used in Figure 11-9 and Figure 11-10, but now the only indicators in the chart are the Bollinger bands.

Bollinger bands make for useful overbought and oversold indicators. Broadly speaking, when the price of a security is higher than the top Bollinger band in a chart, you're in a sell area, and when the price is lower than the bottom Bollinger band, you're in buy territory. As you can see in Figure 11-11, these bands highlight plenty of buy and sell opportunities. But not every one of those opportunities is worth acting on immediately, so combining them with your handy candlestick charts can be an ideal way to minimize risk and separate the excellent signals from the mediocre ones.

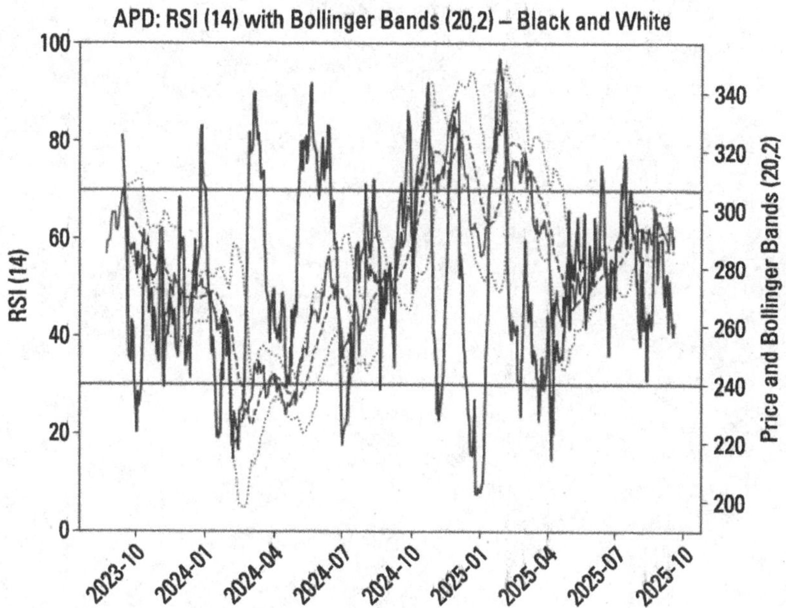

FIGURE 11-11: A chart of INTC stock with Bollinger bands.

Chapter **12**

Buy Indicators and Bullish Reversal Candlestick Patterns

This chapter clues you in on ways in which you can begin combining your trading tools to make your trades even more efficient and profitable. More specifically, the strategies we describe in the next few pages help you understand how you can use two buy indicators — the relative strength index (RSI) and stochastics — in tandem with bullish trend reversal candlestick patterns to pick the best times and situations for entering and exiting long trades.

We've found the two technical indicators we discuss in this chapter to be reliable and relatively easy to combine with candlestick patterns. But please don't think for a second that the RSI and stochastic indicators are the only ones that work well with candlesticks. Several other indicators also work well; we strongly encourage you to research those indicators and find some that work best with your trading style.

Buying with the RSI and Bullish Reversal Candlestick Patterns

The RSI is a fairly reliable indicator that can tell you whether a stock or market is overbought or oversold. The RSI fluctuates between 0 and 100 percent, although it hardly ever reaches either of those levels. You can choose the levels between 0 and 100 percent that you think indicate that a stock is overbought or oversold, but for the sake of analysis in this chapter, we use 30 percent as the oversold level and 70 percent as the overbought level. Therefore, RSI readings below 30 tell you that a bottom could be coming soon and that you should be ready to buy; readings over 70 should lead you to consider putting on a short or selling a long. (For more of the nitty-gritty details on the RSI, check out Chapter 11.)

The RSI has two potential uses when you're working on candlestick analysis:

>> You can combine the information from an RSI with reversal patterns to further confirm that a reversal is imminent and that it's time to take a long position.

>> You can use the RSI to select your exit levels, whether they're stops to prevent losses or exits that allow you to walk away with a tidy profit.

Using the RSI to pick a long entry point

Figure 12-1 provides a solid example of the type of situation that calls for using the RSI in combination with a bullish reversal pattern. This chart is of the iShares Russell 2000 ETF (IWM), which is an exchange-traded fund and one of the best ways for investors to gain exposure to small-capitalization stocks.

The reversal signal for this IWM chart is the ever-popular doji. Notice that the RSI is in oversold territory for a while and even pops up once before moving lower again. The oversold RSI signal moves over the 30 level (the line between oversold and neutral, the shaded space in the middle), coinciding with the appearance of the doji on the chart.

What RSI is doing in this case is confirming the bullish signal. When a bullish pattern and bullish signal from the RSI happen simultaneously, a trader may consider the signal to be a bit stronger than a stand-alone pattern. When the RSI is in oversold territory, a trader should be prepared to take action if a bullish signal also pops up in the chart.

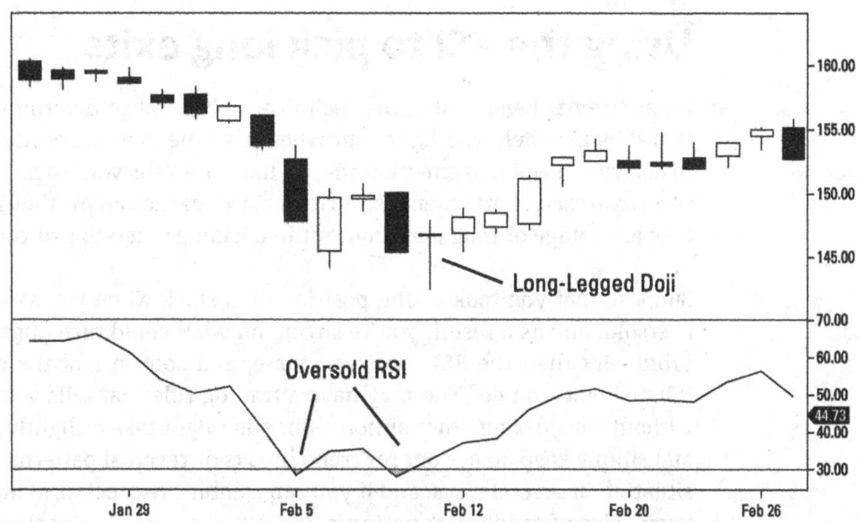

FIGURE 12-1: A combination of the RSI and a long-legged doji in a chart of IWM.

Figure 12-2 offers one more example of how you can use the RSI in combination with a bullish reversal pattern. This figure features a chart of Chipotle Mexican Grill (CMG) stock, representing the fast-casual restaurant. The RSI in the chart in Figure 12-2 spends some time trading around the oversold level of 30, dipping below and then rising above that level on two occasions. What's the difference between these two instances? The second (and successful) move was accompanied by a bullish reversal pattern.

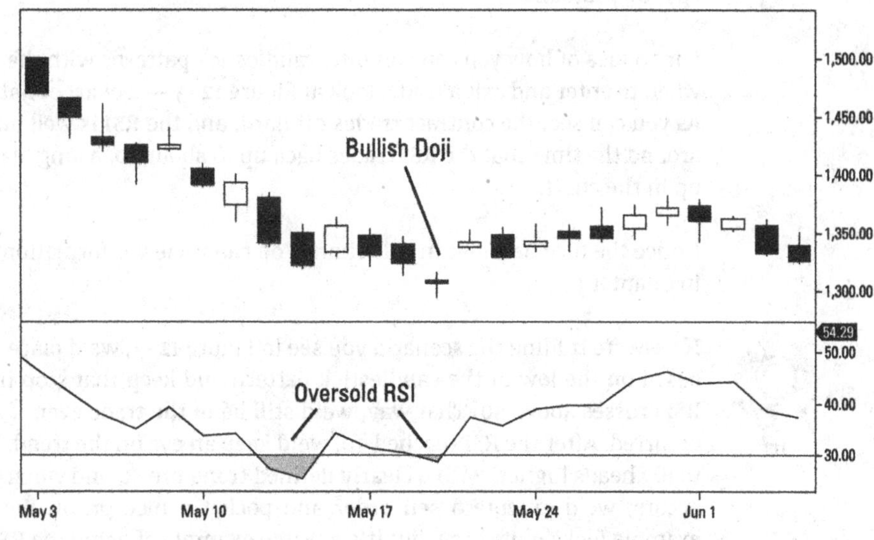

FIGURE 12-2: An RSI and trend reversal pattern indicate where to buy in a chart of CMG stock.

Using the RSI to pick long exits

An additional benefit of using technical indicators to determine entry points is that they may help you figure out when it's time to exit a position. Used properly to determine when to enter a trade, an indicator tells you when to buy an oversold security or sell short when a security's price reaches an overbought level. You can take advantage of that same concept in deciding when to exit trades.

Suppose that you took a long position on a stock when you saw that its RSI was oversold, and as a result, you're sitting on what could turn out to be a handsome profit. But then the RSI changes course, and soon it's at the overbought level. What should you do? You may have a trading rule that tells you to exit the trade without considering other options. But you might take a slightly more liberal tack and simply keep an eye out for trend breaks or reversal patterns. You can play the situation in several ways, and if you can combine the technical indicator with your knowledge of candlestick patterns, you stand a much better chance of exiting the trade at the most opportune moment.

For short-term long trades involving the RSI, we begin to look for an exit point when the RSI trades over 50. Until that level is reached, we stick to the stop level prescribed by the candlestick pattern we used to enter the trade. After the RSI reaches 50, we start to watch for a reversal or trend break. You may think that we're potentially leaving too much profit on the table, but just because a stock has traded higher and the RSI is above 50 doesn't mean that we're out; it just means we're more cautious if we think things are going to turn. Consider a similar strategy for yourself.

For an idea of how you can combine candlestick patterns with the RSI to figure out when to enter and exit a trade, look at Figure 12-3 — a chart of natural gas futures. As you can see, the contract trades off hard, and the RSI is well under 30. Then, at around the time that the RSI trades back up to about 50, a long black candle shows up in the chart.

Notice the nice hammer in this chart. You can review information about hammers in Chapter 6.

If we were trading the scenario you see in Figure 12-3, we'd place a stop loss order based on the low of the candlestick pattern and keep that stop in place until the RSI crosses above 50. That way, we'd still be in the trade even if a small pullback occurred. After the RSI reached 50, we'd keep an eye on the trend. The trend eventually heads higher, with a clearly defined trend break, and when that trend break occurs, we'd execute a sell order and pocket a nice profit. We know that this example looks quite easy, but it's a prime example of using the RSI in conjunction with candlestick patterns — particularly, bullish reversal patterns.

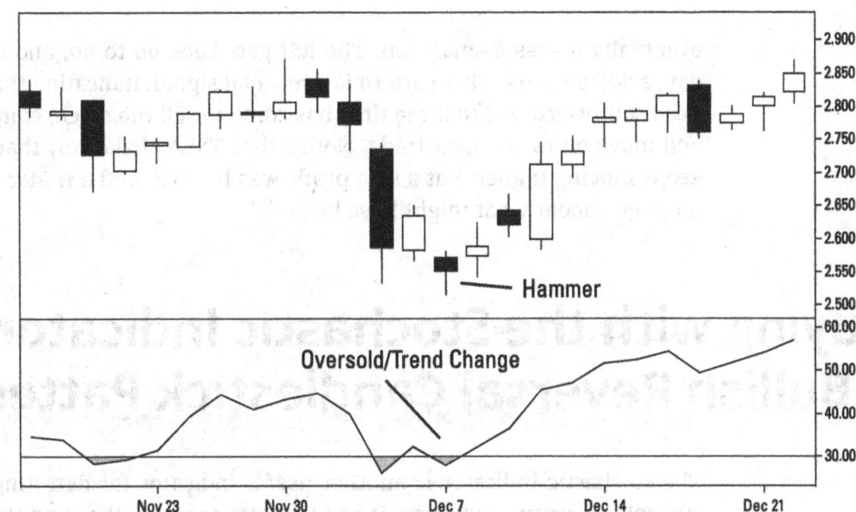

Still not convinced? We offer another example in Figure 12-4. That figure features Tesla (TSLA), the electric-car manufacturer. You can see that the ideal entry point is when the RSI is below 30. Then a bullish thrusting line pattern appears, indicating that the trend is headed upward, so you need to buy and take on a long position. Also, the RSI crosses from below 30 to neutral territory.

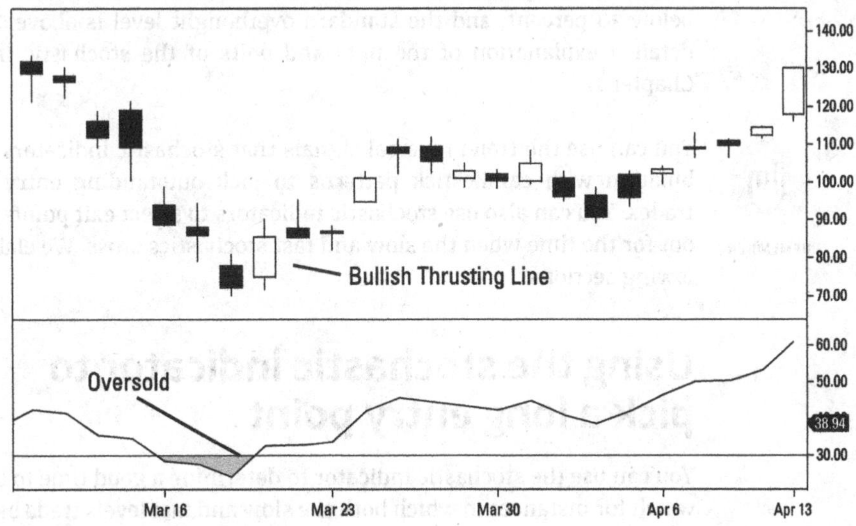

After a promising start, the stock stalls, and things look a bit disappointing. The trading is essentially trendless for a couple of weeks. The support level isn't broken, and an uptrend doesn't develop. If you stay patient, though, the stock eventually makes a small run. The RSI gets back up to 50, and on the following day, a doji appears. That pattern is a reversal signal, indicating that the trend may head southward and that the time has come to sell the stock, enjoy a small profit, and move on to the next trade. Notice that TSLA shakes off that doji signal and keeps moving higher, but a safe profit was booked, and a trader shouldn't worry too much about what might have been.

Buying with the Stochastic Indicator and a Bullish Reversal Candlestick Pattern

The stochastic indicator is another useful indicator for detecting overbought or oversold security conditions. It has two components: the slow stochastic and the fast stochastic. When the fast is below the slow, a downtrend is in place, and when the fast is higher than the slow, an uptrend is occurring. The slow and fast stochastic indicators oscillate between 0 and 100 and have fairly complex look-back periods, much like the RSI. (Refer to "Buying with the RSI and Bullish Reversal Candlestick Patterns," earlier in this chapter, for more info on RSI.)

For simplicity's sake, we use the 14-day look-back period, which is a standard level in charting software. The standard oversold level for a stochastic indicator is below 30 percent, and the standard overbought level is above 70 percent. For a detailed explanation of the nuts and bolts of the stochastic indicator, turn to Chapter 11.

You can use the trend reversal signals that stochastic indicators provide in combination with candlestick patterns to pick outstanding entry points for your trades. You can also use stochastic indicators to select exit points; just keep an eye out for the time when the slow and fast stochastics cross. We elaborate in the following sections.

Using the stochastic indicator to pick a long entry point

You can use the stochastic indicator to determine a good time to buy a stock if you watch for instances in which both the slow and fast levels trade below the oversold level of 20 and then the fast stochastic crosses over or goes higher than the slow stochastic. We've always felt confident in the stochastic indicator because of that feature; even though the levels are technically oversold, the signal isn't truly a buy signal until the trend moves a bit higher. And a stochastic indicator is even more comforting when you combine it with a bullish reversal candlestick pattern. You can see what we mean in Figure 12-5, which is another chart of IWM. IWM is a favorite exchange-traded fund (ETF) of traders because it's a bit more volatile than funds that focus on the Standard & Poor's (S&P) 500.

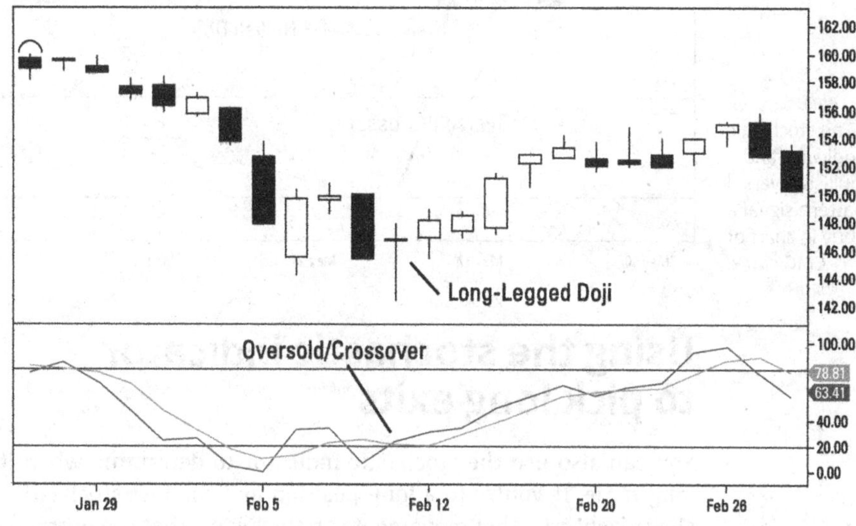

FIGURE 12-5: The stochastic indicator and a bullish reversal candlestick pattern signaling a buy in a chart of IWM.

The chart begins with a downtrend. The slow and fast stochastic levels trade below the oversold level of 20. Then a long-legged doji reversal pattern appears in the chart when the stochastic levels are emerging from below the significant level of 20. The fast stochastic also crosses over the slow line and maintains that position for several trading days. Notice that on the right side of the chart, the fast line crosses below the slow one while both are over 80, a clear indication that it's time to exit the long position.

Figure 12-6 shows another example of combining the stochastic indicator with a bullish reversal pattern. The chart in this figure is of the stock CMG.

The stock has clearly been in a downtrend. The stochastic readings reach the oversold level, and a bullish doji develops. At just about the same time, the fast stochastic moves above the slow one, signaling a change in trend from down to up. The uptrend after the entry signal isn't terribly strong, and about ten days after the entry, the fast line crosses below the slow line, indicating that it may be time to move on to the next trade.

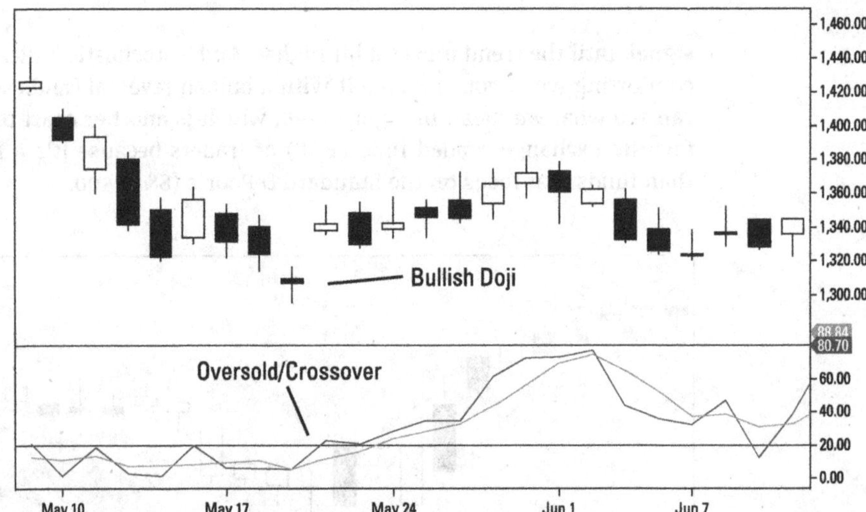

FIGURE 12-6: The stochastic indicator and a bullish reversal pattern signal a buy in chart of CMG stock.

Using the stochastic indicator to pick long exits

You can also use the stochastic indicator to determine when it's time to exit a long trade. If you're in a long position and the fast stochastic moves below the slow stochastic, that movement can tip you off that the uptrend may be changing to a downtrend; the time for getting out of your long position is probably drawing near.

REMEMBER

Stochastic indicators can signal a trend change even when the stochastic readings haven't yet reached an overbought or oversold level. To see an example, check out Figure 12-7, which depicts natural gas futures.

Notice the bullish doji in the chart. Just keep in mind that with your exits, you may need to act and get out of a trade when the fast and slow stochastics cross, whether they're in overbought or oversold territory. The trend is fairly strong, but toward the end of the chart, you see a very overbought level for the stochastic indicators along with a crossover, which may indicate that it's time to exit.

Figure 12-8 is an excellent example of combining the stochastic indicator with a candlestick pattern to identify a successful entry point and profitable exit. This chart of TSLA stock shows why someone might stick with a trade by using stochastics.

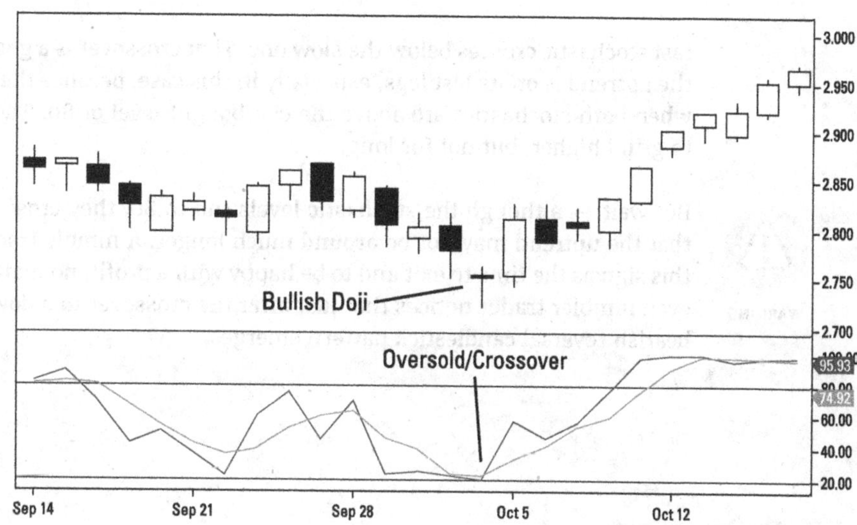

FIGURE 12-7: The stochastic indicator signaling a trend change in a chart of natural gas futures.

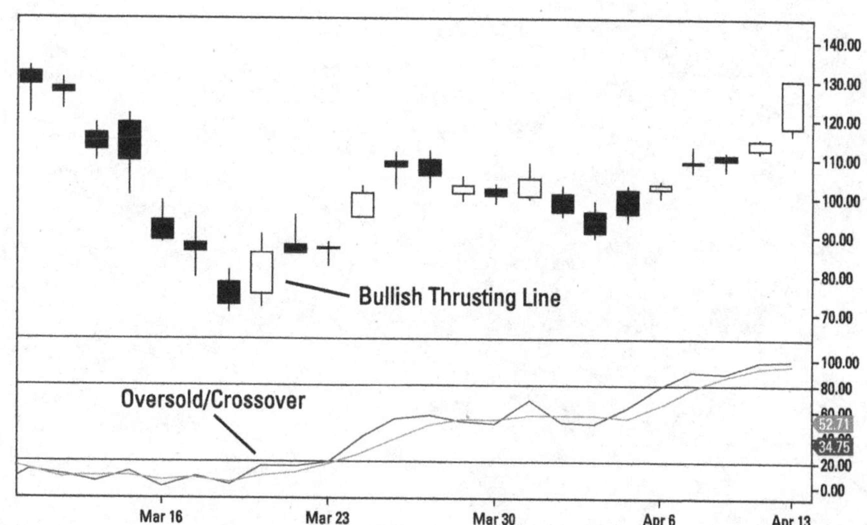

FIGURE 12-8: The stochastic indicator and a bullish thrusting line pattern in a chart of TSLA stock.

You can see that the entry point appears after a downtrend, when the stochastic levels make an upward break after spending some time below the 20 buy level. The break coincides with a bullish thrusting line pattern, and that combination of factors is a crystal-clear indication that it's a good time to get in on a long trade. Then the uptrend gets going quickly.

The stock trades higher, and both the slow and fast stochastic readings move up with it. Both stochastics reach an overbought level, and as the trend dwindles, the fast stochastic crosses below the slow one. That crossover is a good indication that the uptrend is on its last legs, especially in this case, because the crossover occurs when both stochastics are above the overbought level of 80. The stock continues to grind higher, but not for long.

But wait — although the stochastic levels run to 80, they cross again, indicating that the uptrend may not be around much longer. A nimble trader can recognize this sign as the time to exit and to be happy with a profit, no matter how small. An even nimbler trader notices that just after the crossover to a downtrend occurs, a bearish reversal candlestick pattern emerges.

Chapter **13**

Sell Indicators and Bearish Reversal Candlestick Patterns

Technical indicators are useful in many trading situations, and as we describe in the other chapters in Part 4, you can use them in tandem with candlestick patterns to conduct some outstanding trades. In this chapter, we fill you in on how to combine a couple of common technical indicators with bearish candlestick patterns to make wise decisions about short trades.

We focus much more on the prospects for shorting than on the opportunities to use candlesticks and indicators to decide when to exit a long trade because realizing when to exit a long position is relatively easy: If it looks like a trend is ready to tank, sell and get out!

We know that some people are resistant to short selling, but it's part of the game, and not using the short side of trading puts you at a disadvantage. Risks are involved, but if you employ the methods we describe in this chapter, you can minimize those risks. With any luck, after reading Chapter 13 in this book, you won't have to file Chapter 13!

Shorting with the RSI and Bearish Candlestick Patterns

The *relative strength index* (RSI) is an indicator that can reveal an oversold or overbought security. The RSI typically appears below a chart; visually, it's represented by a line that moves up and down between 0 and 100. It's up to you to choose which levels in that range will be considered to be overbought and oversold, but in this chapter, we use 30 as our oversold level and 70 as our overbought level. Those levels mean that an RSI reading below 30 indicates that a bottom is forthcoming. Be ready to buy when that situation presents itself. Using 70 as an overbought level means that an RSI above 70 should alert you to put on a short trade or sell a long position because the trend is about to head south. You can read all about the nuts and bolts of the RSI in Chapter 11.

When combined with candlestick patterns, the RSI can provide an even stronger indication of when the situation is ripe to execute short trades or sell on long positions. In this section, we discuss the ways in which you can combine your candlestick charts with the RSI to make some clever, profitable trades.

Picking short entry points with the RSI and candlesticks

When using the RSI combined with a candlestick pattern to pick a good time to enter a short position, you want to see an RSI reading above 70 (or your personal overbought level) that coincides with the formation of a bearish candlestick pattern. If you have your eye on a chart and see those two things come together, put your short pants on! (That's just a figure of speech, of course; we encourage everyone to wear pants of an appropriate length while trading.)

There's no better way to master these scenarios than to see them in a chart, so please take a gander at Figure 13-1. This example combines the RSI with a bearish reversal candlestick pattern to help you figure out when to put on a short trade. The chart is of Chipotle (CMG), the fast-casual restaurant that's featured frequently in this book. In fact, this figure is a repeat of Figure 6-28 in Chapter 6, in which the hanging man was confirmed by the down day after the signal. (The candlesticks look a little shorter in Figure 13-1 than in Figure 6-28 to accommodate the different price range on the charts.)

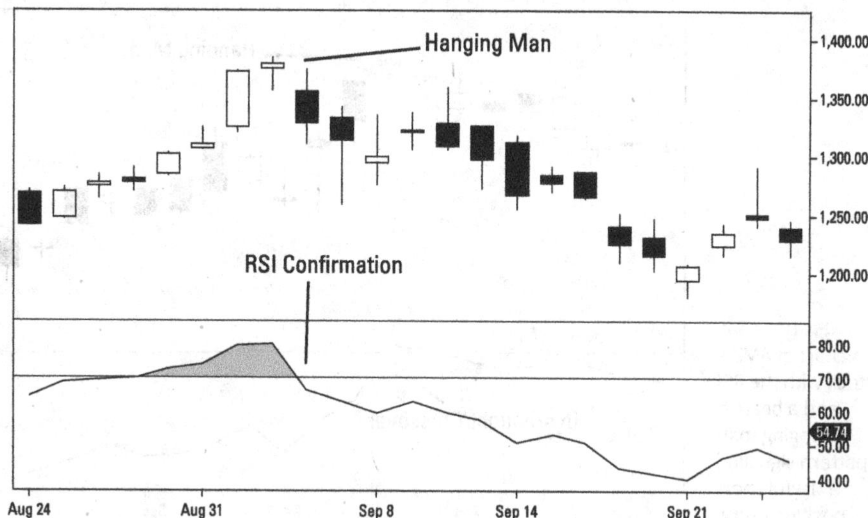

FIGURE 13-1: An overbought RSI reading and a hanging man signal in a chart of CMG stock.

The RSI in Figure 13-1 goes into the overbought range about five days before the hanging man signal. The hanging man can indicate a reversal in either direction, but in this case, there's an established uptrend. The RSI reading has been overbought for some time, so it's safe to say that this particular hanging man is signaling a bearish reversal. Notice that the drop from above 70 on the RSI occurs the day after the trade. In Chapter 6, we point out that the price action is a confirmation signal; you can also think of the drop in the RSI to neutral territory as confirmation.

REMEMBER

If you keep an eye on this overbought RSI and spot the hanging man, you'd put on a short position because the hanging man shows that the bears are taking control of the price action after a run by the bulls. The pattern is followed by a small downtrend that lasts a couple of weeks. You wouldn't be able to go out and start shopping for yachts if you trade this pattern successfully, but it's certainly worth studying because it's a fairly reliable indication of bearishness.

Perhaps it's most important to note that this example shows you how the RSI (or other technical indicators, for that matter) can be useful when you spot a reversal signal that doesn't tell you definitively which way the trend will go. You have to be certain of the market environment in those cases, and the RSI can tell you what you need to know.

Good things do come in pairs, so Figure 13-2 provides another example of how you can combine the RSI with a bearish candlestick pattern. This figure shows a chart of shares of Amazon (AMZN). In this example, a hanging man candlestick is followed by a drop in RSI from above 70 to below 70.

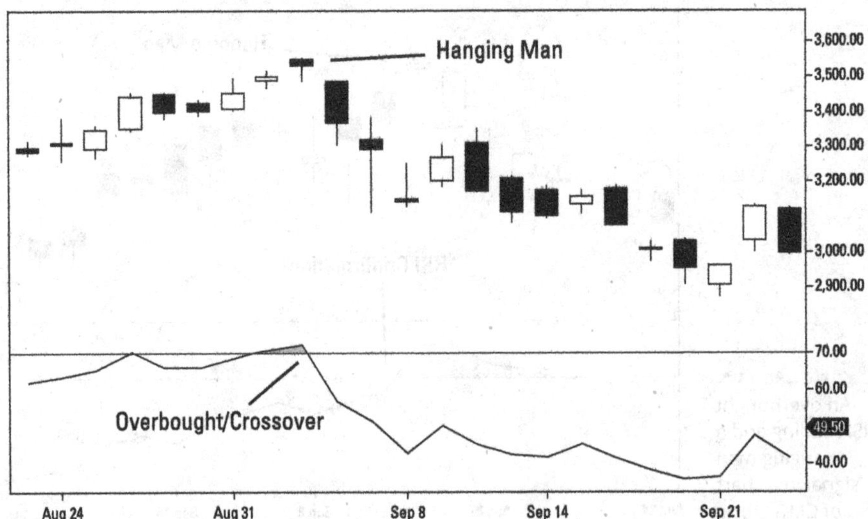

FIGURE 13-2: A chart of AMZN stock with the RSI and a bearish hanging man pattern signaling a useful short position entry.

The hanging man pattern appears to be preceded by a doji. That doji signal isn't confirmed the following day by a drop in the RSI. In this case, combining RSI with a bearish pattern allows a trader to be a bit more patient about getting into the trade.

Using the RSI to help pick short entry and exit points

You can combine the RSI with your candlestick patterns to pick wise entry points for a short trade. But that option isn't the whole story. You can use that same combination of trading tools to decide when you should exit a short.

Figure 13-3 presents a situation in which a combination of the RSI and a bearish candlestick pattern shows you when to get in *and* out of a short position. This chart shows the SPDR Gold Shares (GLD), an exchange-traded fund (ETF), which, in our opinion, is one of the best ways to get exposure to the price of gold.

The chart in Figure 13-3 doesn't cover the whole period when GLD's RSI is in overbought territory. Also, several of the daily candlesticks that come before a confirmation in RSI (dropping from overbought to neutral territory) appear to hint that a trend change is in the works.

RSI confirmation is combined with a gap lower in GLD. The price tries to recover but doesn't manage to fill the gap; neither does RSI return to overbought. Toward the right side of the chart, RSI reaches oversold and then crosses back into neutral territory, perhaps indicating a good time to take profits and move on to the next trade. Or it might be a signal to cover the short and possibly even go long!

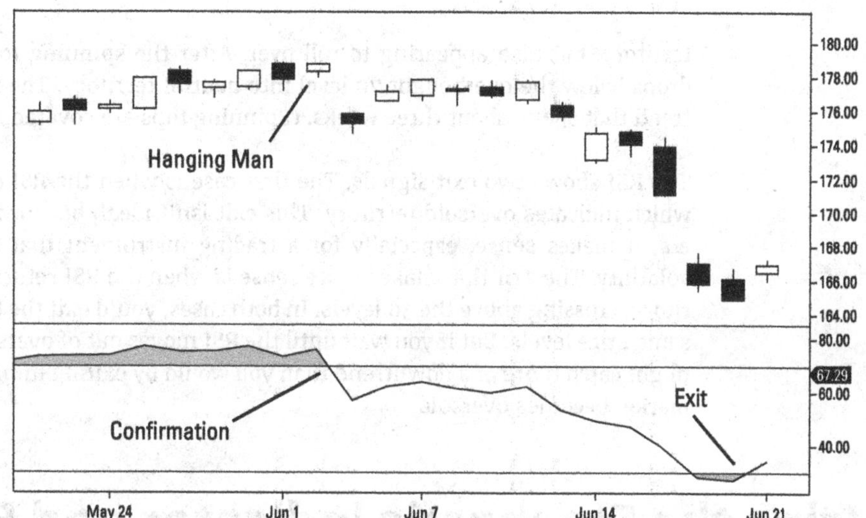

FIGURE 13-3: A chart of GLD in which a combination of the RSI and hanging man indicates a short entry and exit point.

Figure 13-4 shows candlestick patterns combined with the RSI in a chart of the iShares Russell 2000 ETF (IWM), an ETF of small-capitalization stocks. We note earlier in this book that this market is a bit more volatile than other broad-based index ETFs. The more volatile the market, the more likely it is to be overbought *and* oversold, making an indicator like RSI a good tool to use for trading in that market.

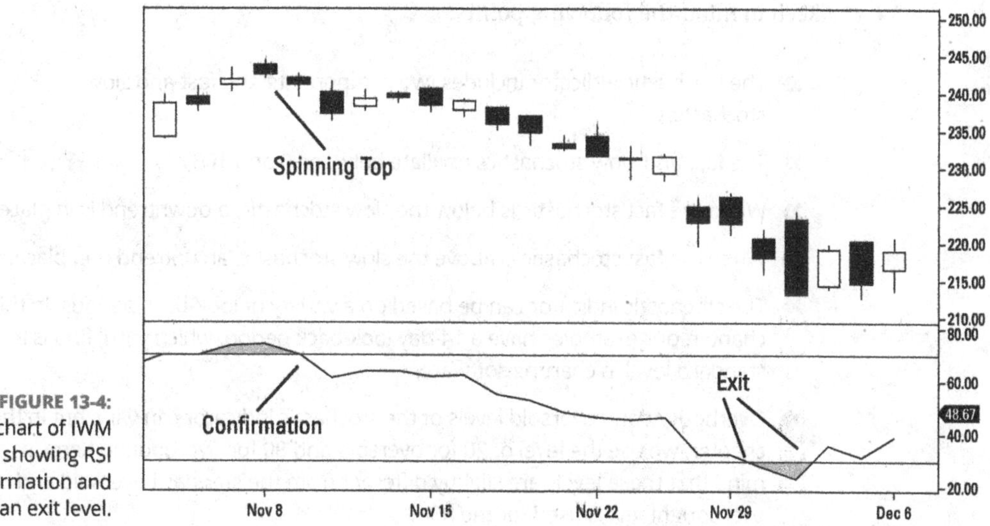

FIGURE 13-4: A chart of IWM showing RSI confirmation and an exit level.

The entry for this trade combines a reversal signal when IWM is already experiencing a slowing uptrend. The signal shows up with the RSI in overbought territory, but also appearing to roll over. After the spinning top signal, the RSI drops below the overbought 70 level into neutral territory. The result is a downtrend that spans about three weeks. (Spinning tops are covered in Chapter 6.)

The RSI shows two exit signals. The first case is when the RSI crosses below 30, which indicates oversold territory. This exit isn't ideal, but for risk-averse traders, it makes sense, especially for a trading instrument that experiences high volatility. The exit that makes more sense is when the RSI returns to neutral territory, crossing above the 30 levels. In both cases, you'd exit the trade at about the same price levels. But if you wait until the RSI moves out of oversold territory, you might catch more of a downtrend than you would by exiting immediately after the market becomes oversold.

Using the Stochastic Indicator and Bearish Candlestick Patterns for Shorting

If you're interested in another reliable technical indicator that you can combine with bearish candlestick patterns to help you in your short trades, look no further than the stochastic indicator. The stochastic indicator can be a useful trading tool when you're trying to determine when a security is overbought or oversold. You can read all about the stochastic indicator in Chapter 11, but for this discussion, keep in mind the following points:

>> The stochastic indicator includes two components: the fast and slow stochastics.

>> The fast and slow stochastics oscillate between 0 and 100.

>> When the fast stochastic is below the slow stochastic, a downtrend is in place.

>> When the fast stochastic is above the slow stochastic, an uptrend is in place.

>> The stochastic indicator can be based on a variety of look-back periods. In this chapter, our examples have a 14-day look-back period, which you'll find is a standard level in charting software.

>> Overbought and oversold levels of the stochastic indicator can vary, but in this chapter, we use the level of 20 for oversold and 80 for overbought. Keep in mind that these levels are slightly different from the standard oversold and overbought levels used for the RSI.

This section focuses on how to use the stochastic indicator alongside your candlesticks in shorting situations. You can use the same information to figure out when to get out of a long position. The rule is fairly simple: If you have a long position and the trend looks as though it will head downward, exit and take your profit!

Picking short entry points

Picking the best entry point for a short can be a difficult undertaking, but using the stochastic indicator as a supplement to your candlestick patterns can make the task much easier. For a prime example of how the stochastic indicator can be used with a bearish candlestick pattern to pick a short entry, take a look at Figure 13-5.

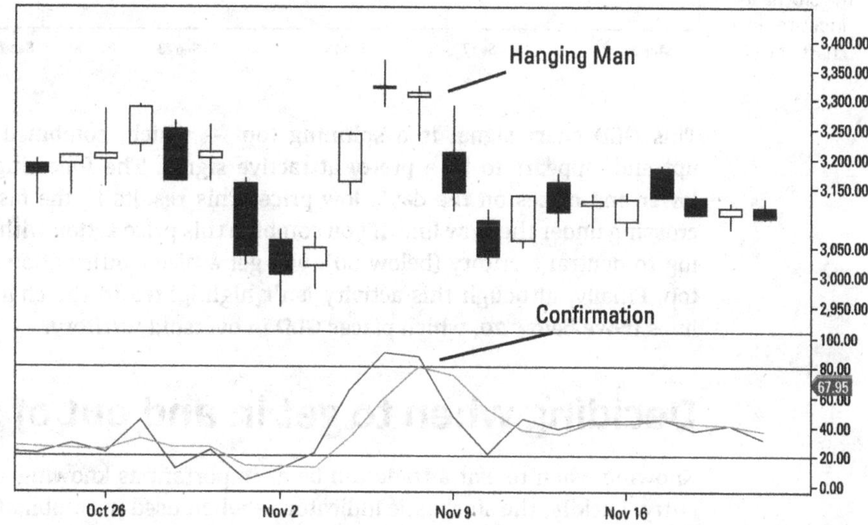

FIGURE 13-5: A bearish hanging man pattern and the stochastic indicator reveal a short entry in a chart of AMZN.

In the figure, you see another chart of AMZN stock, which demonstrates waiting for confirmation from the stochastics. Like Figure 13-2, this AMZN chart has a doji in it, but the reversal isn't confirmed by the stochastic indicators until the following day. The following day is a hanging man, and the fast stochastic line drops from overbought and crosses below the slow line.

The AMZN chart is followed by a quick drop, and the fast stochastic line hits the 20 level, followed by a crossover of the slow line. Although this activity may not be an exit signal that's set in stone, it may be a warning to keep a close eye on AMZN to lock in profits. For a second example, see the chart of the GLD ETF in Figure 13-6.

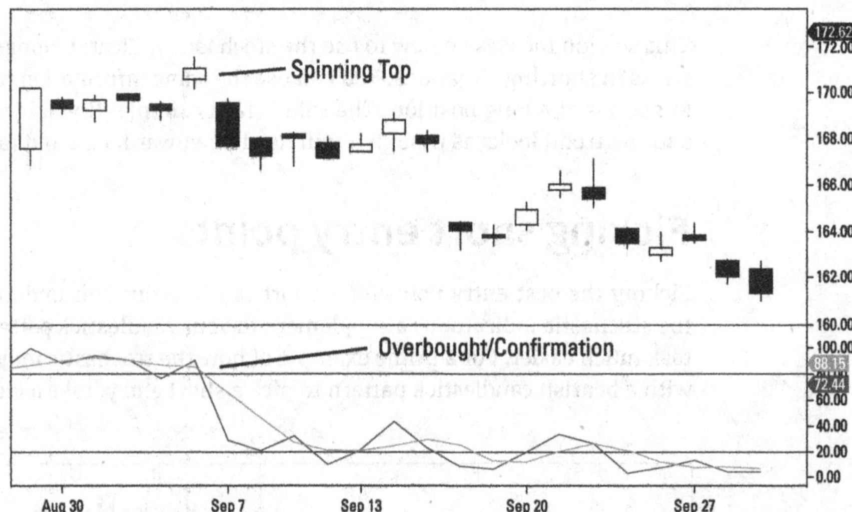

This GLD chart signal is a spinning top — which, combined with a slowing uptrend, appears to be a pretty attractive signal. The following day, GLD gaps lower and closes on the day's low price. This results in the fast stochastic line crossing under the slow line. If you combine this price action with both lines moving to neutral territory (below 80), you get a nice confirmation of that spinning top. Finally, although this activity isn't highlighted in the chart, the stochastic lines move below 20, which places GLD in oversold territory.

Deciding when to get in and out of shorts

Knowing when to exit a trade can be as important as knowing when to make an entry. Luckily, the stochastic indicator — when used in combination with bearish candlestick patterns — can provide you guidance on covering a short. Truth be told, the stochastic indicator does a decent job on its own, but when you use this indicator with candlestick patterns correctly, the odds of success are in your favor. To close this chapter, we present a couple of examples of using the stochastic indicator with bearish candlestick patterns to determine when to get in and out of a short.

The first example is Figure 13-7, a chart showing CMG stock and stochastic readings moving from overbought to oversold very quickly.

The stochastic readings in Figure 13-7 have been in overbought territory for a while. Astute traders, who like to trade reversals, would be following CMG's price action closely. A doji pattern shows up, and the following day, you see a defined drop in the stochastic readings and a move to neutral territory. These lines trend down to the oversold range, and an oversold buy signal appears on the right side of the chart, forming your exit signal.

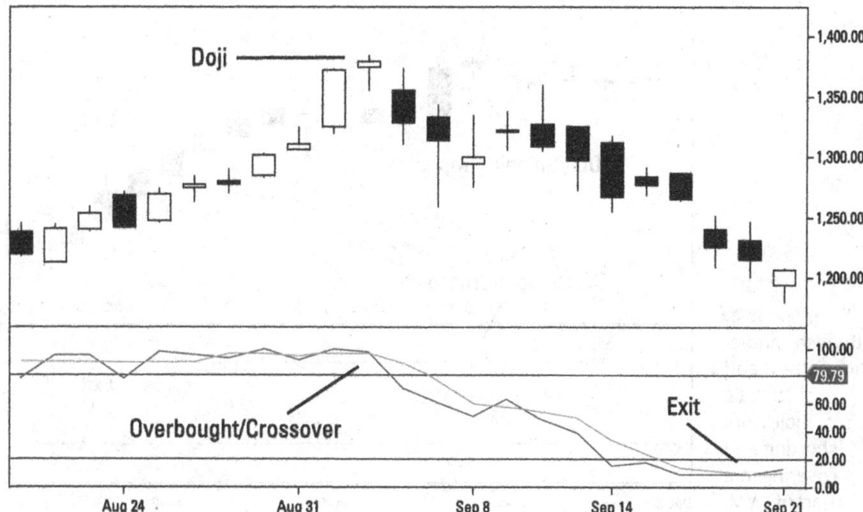

REMEMBER

Generally speaking, you can forgo a revealing candlestick pattern and rely on another technical indicator to pick a spot to exit a trade. Exits are usually a little less precise, and often, one technical indicator is enough to go on. It's best to have a candlestick pattern for confirmation, but it isn't absolutely necessary.

WARNING

You'd need to get out of the short in Figure 13-7 quickly because the next day gaps higher, and the gap isn't filled. Prices just keep moving up, which is pretty scary for a short in this position. Not exiting quickly when a stop-loss signal is hit can result in worse losses. Figure 13-7 is a prime example.

Figure 13-8 is an excellent entry and exit example of using stochastics with candlestick patterns. The chart shows the IWM ETF.

The candlestick signal is so close to a doji or spinning top that we decided to label it as both. The idea behind these reversal signals is a tug-of-war between bulls and bears, where the close is near the open of the day. Whether you see a doji or a spinning top doesn't matter because both are bearish indicators. Combined with the stochastics crossing over and moving below 80, it represents a solid short sell signal.

The signal turns out to be a profitable one because IWM trends lower over the next two to three weeks; nothing that could be considered to be an exit signal comes until the stochastic lines cross in oversold territory. Notice that both lines enter oversold territory about halfway through the downtrend and stay there for several days. This scenario is a useful example of a market staying oversold and continuing to trade lower even when it's oversold.

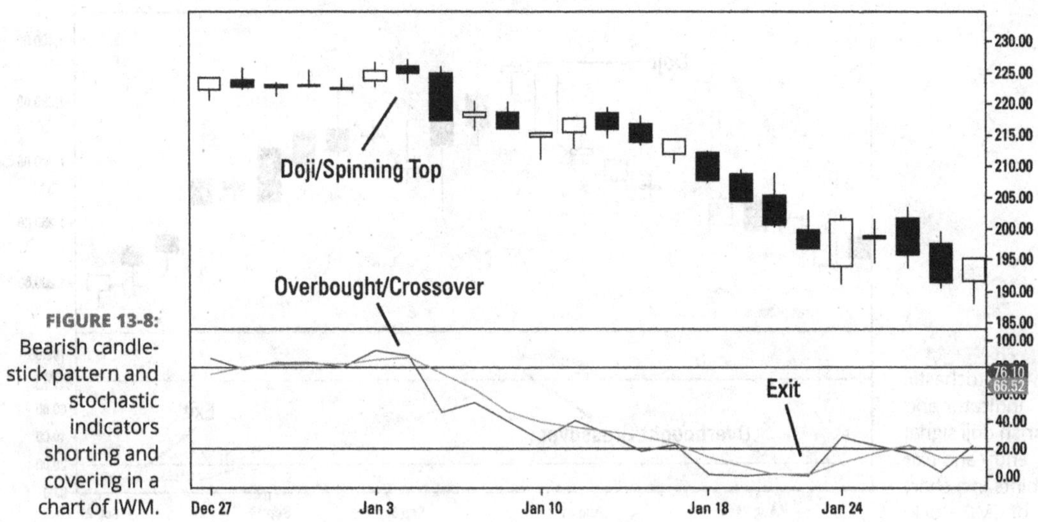

FIGURE 13-8: Bearish candlestick pattern and stochastic indicators shorting and covering in a chart of IWM.

Chapter **14**

Using Technical Indicators Alongside Bullish-Trending Candlestick Patterns

You can combine candlestick patterns effectively with a variety of technical indicators to produce information that helps you decide when to put on and get out of trades. Like candlestick patterns, many technical indicators tell you when a trend is about to reverse, but several others can let you know that a prevailing trend continues. These indicators are powerful weapons that can add to the versatility of your trading arsenal.

If you understand how to use technical indicators in tandem with bullish-trending candlestick patterns, it's easier to spot situations in which buying to enter a long position is a wise move. You can also use technical indicators to confirm market or individual security predictions that you've made based on candlestick patterns.

We cover all those topics and more in this chapter, focusing our discussion on two of the most common technical indicators: trend lines and moving averages. Both indicators are covered in Chapter 11. If you have a basic understanding of how these indicators are created and how they work, read on, and get trading!

Using Trending Patterns for Buying and Confirmation

The trend line is one of the oldest and easiest to understand of all the technical indicators. You'd be hard-pressed to find any current charting software that won't draw a trend line for you automatically, but you can hark back to the good ol' days and draw a trend line yourself with nothing more than a chart, a ruler, and a pencil. Trend lines are covered in Chapter 11.

Trend lines have a positive, upward slope during an uptrend and a negative, downward slope during a downtrend. These simple signals can be useful when you're trying to confirm your opinion of the market trend.

In this section, we show you how to use the confirmation that trend lines provide in combination with bullish-trending candlestick patterns, which signal that a trend in place will continue. You can use the combinations to decide when it's time to buy to enter a long position or stick with a trade to realize additional profits.

Buying trend lines with bullish candlestick patterns

Because trend lines are so useful for trend confirmation, you can trade with confidence when you combine bullish trend lines with bullish candlestick patterns. That tandem can help you decide when to stick with a position or initiate a new one.

It's pretty obvious where a trend line should be drawn on a chart, but sometimes, you may question its placement. Don't stress about placement too much because, as a trend goes along and changes, you can always alter the trend line accordingly. In the following sections, we present a couple of examples of combining positive trend lines and bullish-trending candlestick patterns.

A trend line and bullish pattern in a chart

Figure 14-1 is a chart of the Energy Select Sector SPDR (XLE), which is an exchange-traded fund (ETF). The figure shows a defined trend line along with a trend-confirmation signal about halfway through the chart.

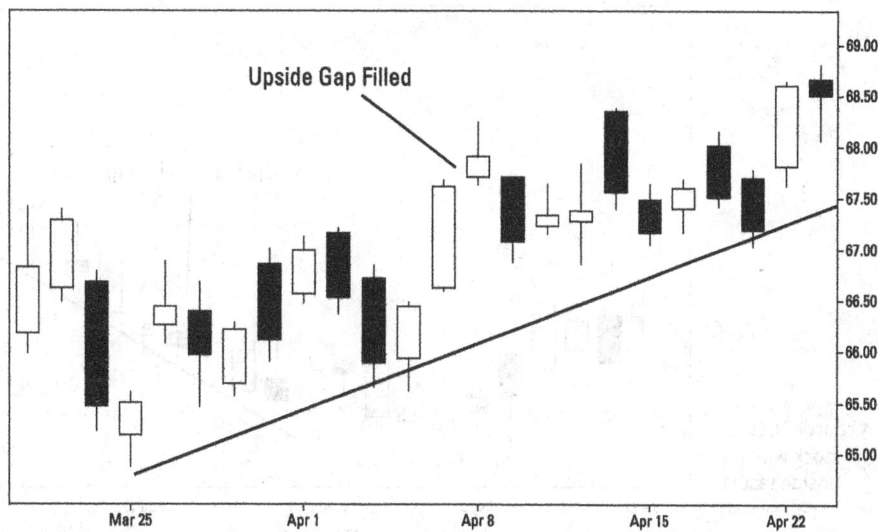

FIGURE 14-1:
A chart of XLE showing a defined uptrend and an upside gap-filled pattern.

Commodities tend to trade in trends, and XLE follows this characteristic because the performance of energy stocks is closely related to that of oil and other energy-related commodities. This chart shows a trend line that is put in place based on two low prices that appear before the upside gap-filled pattern. This pattern is an indication that a bullish trend is expected to continue.

The line would actually be drawn after the pattern shows up. This is a pattern that confirms an uptrend. But if you take a long position based on this pattern, you also need a method of determining when that trend is coming to an end (and then you sell). Placing this trend line in the chart and continuing to extend the line until it's broken is a primary use of trend lines.

Another example of a trend line working with a bullish pattern

Our second example of bullish candlestick patterns and trend lines working together is present in Figure 14-2. This chart shows daily price action for Alphabet (GOOG), formerly known as Google.

A trend line is drawn after an upside tasuki gap is noted, indicating a bullish trend in the chart. Again, the line is drawn after the signal appears, so you can get an idea when the trend is coming to an end and exit the long position. This trend line extends to the end of the chart on the right side, but the uptrend can't last forever. In the next section, you see how a trend line can help you exit a trade.

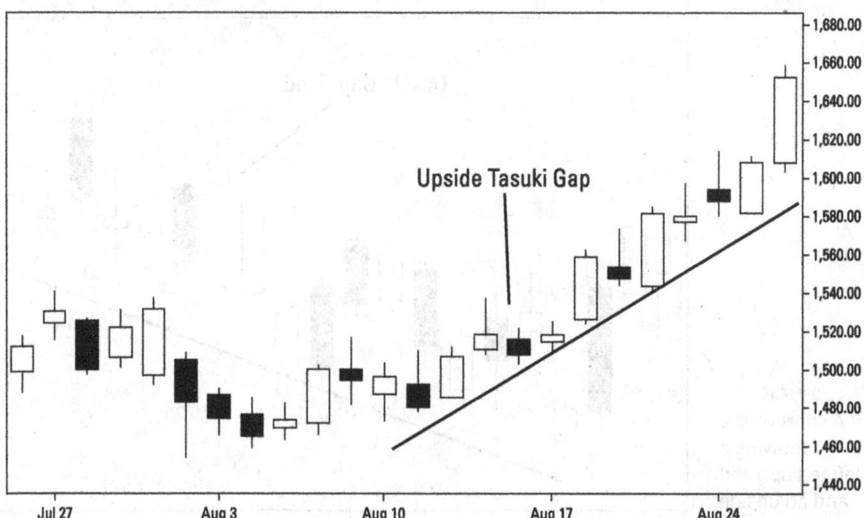

FIGURE 14-2: A chart of GOOG stock with an upside tasuki gap signal.

Determining sales and stop levels with trend lines

In addition to confirming trends and letting you know when to get in on a long trade, trend lines can help you decide when to exit a trade. Put simply, a bullish trend line may serve as an exit point when it occurs in a bullish trend. Finding an exit point isn't always easy because trend lines are constantly changing, but that can also be a plus because the trend line is moving in the same direction as your position (higher). Sound confusing? We clear things up with a couple of examples in the following sections.

Trend line and patterns for entries and exits

Figure 14-3 is the same chart of GOOG stock that you see in Figure 14-2, but the trend line has been expanded a bit to include a level where you would exit a long trade if you use the trend line to define the prevailing uptrend.

Once again, an uptrend is in place due to the upside tasuki gap pattern. The line is tested several times, but the trend break doesn't occur for almost four weeks, and at much higher price levels. A disciplined trader who uses trend lines would use this moment to sell the GOOG stock, take some profits, and look for the next trading signal.

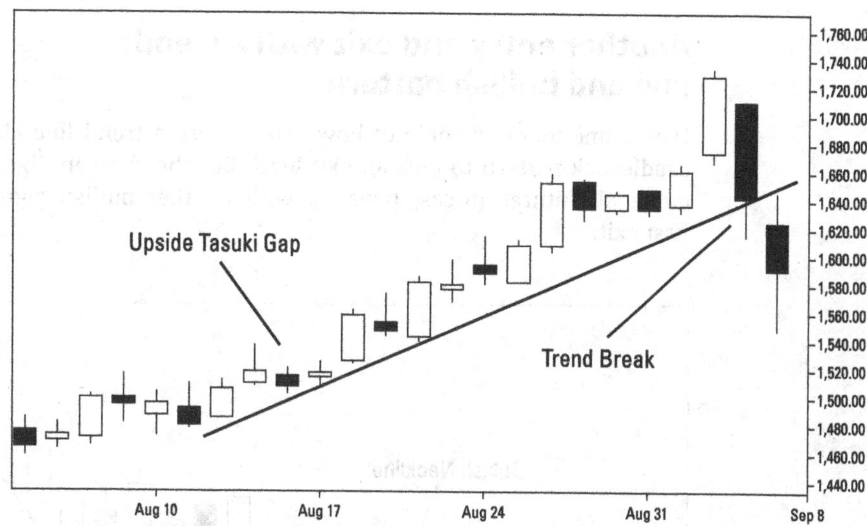

FIGURE 14-3: A chart of GOOG stock with a trend line break.

EXITING WITH A TREND LINE

You may be wondering how it's possible to use a trend line as an exit stop level, because it moves every day. That concern is a valid one! Unlike the set points associated with candlestick patterns, a trend line's level in a chart changes daily. You can deal with that challenge in either of two ways:

- **Determine the level of the support trend line every day, and place an appropriate stop order that's good only for the day.** This strategy works well because the line moves with the trend, and your exit point moves accordingly daily. On the downside, you do have to commit to making the change every day, which can be tough for some busy amateur traders.

- **Exit the trade only if the closing price is lower than the trend line.** This strategy keeps you from having to place trades every day, but it requires you to check your chart toward the close of each day. This approach is attractive because it can keep you from getting stopped out of a potentially valid trade if the price happens to take a slight dive. On the flip side, the price can fall dramatically below the trend line during the day and close at a low level as well, so your exit would be far lower than if you went with the first stop level strategy.

Another entry and exit with a trend line and bullish pattern

Here's one more example of how you can use a trend line alongside a bullish candlestick pattern to pick an exit level. But the chart in Figure 14-4, showing crude-oil futures prices, pops up with another bullish signal just after the first exit.

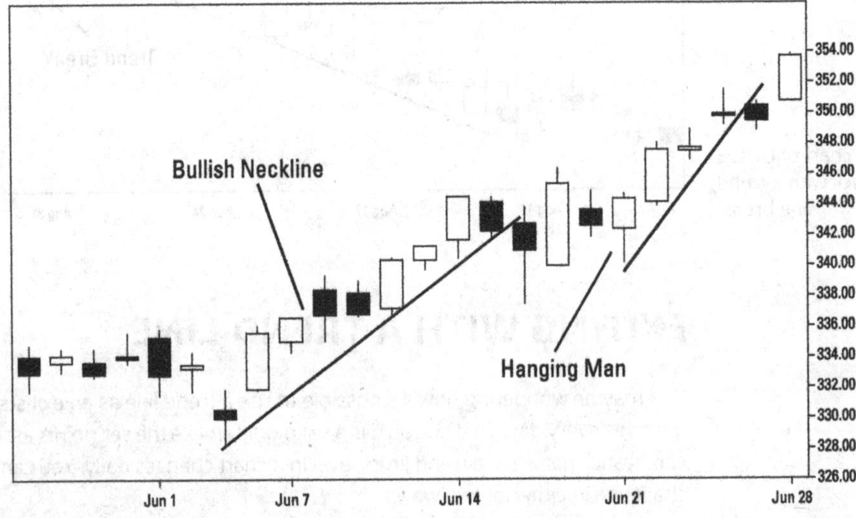

FIGURE 14-4: A bullish candlestick pattern and two trend lines in crude-oil futures.

The chart in Figure 14-4 is interesting because one uptrend is established after a bullish neckline pattern emerges. This trend line is pretty steep, but commodities trend hard in both directions. Also, commodities prices can turn quickly, so using some sort of stop that is set close to the current price or trend line makes sense with oil. This trend is broken later, but then something interesting happens: After a few days of trendless price action, a hanging man pattern shows up. This pattern could indicate that a new uptrend is in place. The white candle on the following day confirms this interpretation, so a new trend line is in place. A couple of days later, however, the trend is broken again at slightly higher prices.

There's nothing wrong with getting back into a trade. In the example shown in Figure 14-4, you'd be buying at a slightly higher price. Don't worry about the previous trade — only the new one — and don't worry about selling and then buying back a bit higher.

Combining Moving Averages and Bullish-Trending Candlestick Patterns

The moving average is reliable and easy to understand, at least as far as technical indicators go. See Chapter 11 for more info on moving averages.

In basic terms, a *moving average* is the average of the closing prices of a security over a certain period. Moving averages can be helpful when you're looking to confirm a trend, so you can rely on them to boost your confidence in the trading decisions you make based on bullish-trending candlestick patterns.

Using moving averages with bullish-trending candlestick patterns to confirm trends

If you haven't yet made your way through our discussion of technical indicators in Chapter 11, the first rule of thumb in using moving averages as trend indicators is if a security's price is above the moving average, an uptrend is in place. With that rule in mind, take a gander at our first example of combining moving averages with bullish-trending candlestick patterns.

Charting the moving average and a bullish-trending pattern

Figure 14-5 is a chart of the Invesco QQQ Trust Series 1, an ETF representing ownership in the Nasdaq 100. This chart includes a 10-day moving average, which is a pretty common average for short-term traders.

In Figure 14-5, the trend is changing as the price is moving over the 10-day moving average. At the same time, a doji pops up in the chart. The combination of a trend change relative to the moving average and the doji pattern is a powerful buy signal.

The example in Figure 14-5 uses only one moving average, but don't feel that you have to stick to using only one. You may well want to add more moving averages to your charts, and using two or more can be revealing if you can keep up with them all.

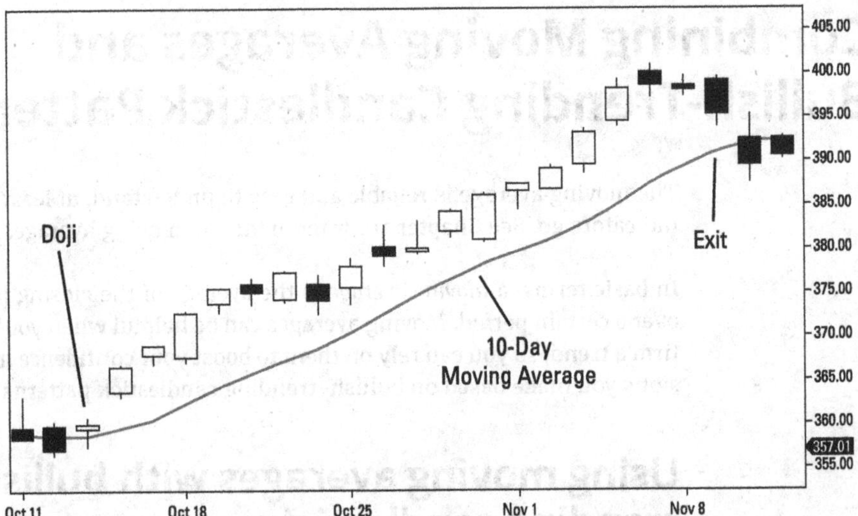

FIGURE 14-5: A chart of QQQ confirming an uptrend in combination with a doji.

Using a couple of moving averages and a bullish-trending pattern

When you use two moving averages in a candlestick chart, the trend is defined by the location of one moving average relative to the other moving average. When the moving average with the lower number of days is trading higher than the one with more days, the trend is positive. For the examples in this chapter that include two moving averages, we use 10- and 20-day moving averages. So when the 10-day moving average is higher than the 20-day moving average, the trend is positive. Sound simple enough? We dive right in with an example.

Figure 14-6 is another chart of GOOG stock. This chart includes both a 10-day and a 20-day moving average, and for much of the chart, the former is higher than the latter, which means that an uptrend is in place. After you look at the chart, it's hard to argue for another trend.

A reversal signal shows up in the chart and is confirmed when the 10-day moving average crosses above the 20-day moving average. After the inside-up signal and the crossover dip a bit, the uptrend is still in place if you use the 10-day versus the 20-day moving average. The goal is to determine the trend you want to see to stay in the trade and be rewarded with much higher levels as an exit.

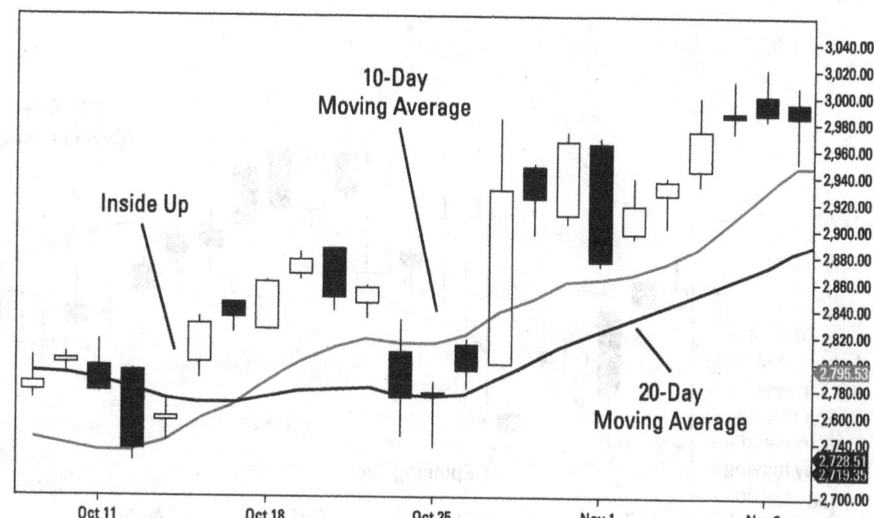

FIGURE 14-6: A chart of GOOG stock with 10- and 20-day moving averages and a bullish-trending candlestick pattern that confirm a reversal.

Setting stops with the moving average and bullish-trending candlestick patterns

Making a wise decision in picking an exit point or a stop level for a long trade can be the difference between booking a tidy profit and suffering a frustrating loss. In the preceding section, we explain how you can use moving averages when you're deciding when to get in on a long trade, but you can just as easily use moving averages when you're trying to figure out when to exit a trade. If you're in a long position and a moving-average reading tells you that the trend is headed for a reversal, be prepared to sell and get out. Allow us to elaborate with a couple of examples.

An entry and exit with a single moving average and bullish pattern

Figure 14-7 is a chart of Microsoft (MSFT). A spinning top signal shows up, but the pattern is below the 10-day moving average.

After the buy signal, MSFT takes off to the upside and moves above the 10-day moving average. This signal is a good all-clear signal for future bullishness, but the pattern ends up not paying off well because the moving average is violated less than two weeks later. Finally, notice the right side of the chart, which shows a doji below the 10-day moving average and then a quick move over the line. It may be time to take another shot at buying MSFT.

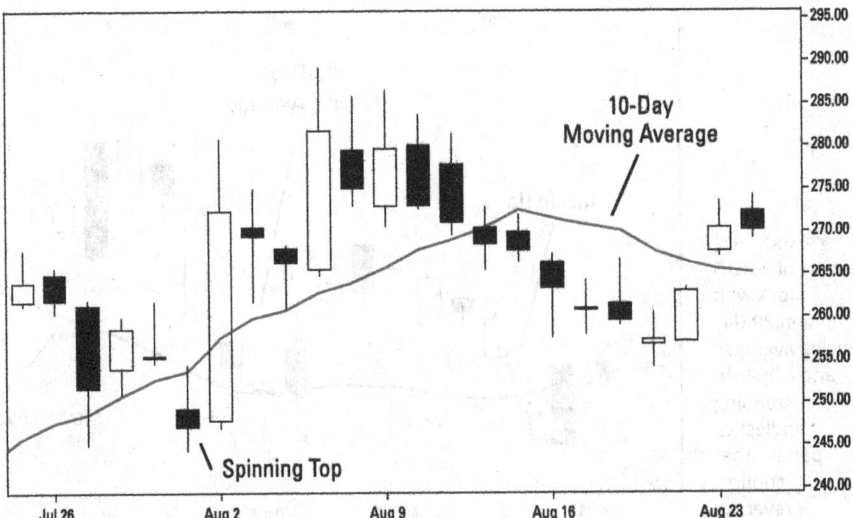

FIGURE 14-7: A chart of MSFT stock in which a spinning top pattern and a 10-day moving average provide an exit signal.

REMEMBER

Setting stops is trickier with moving averages than it is with trend lines. You can anticipate the level of a trend line because it's the slope of the line moving forward by a day (or another time period). The moving average level changes more erratically, however, depending on the price action.

TIP

If you can't monitor your trading positions, use the previous day's moving average as a stop. If a security dips below the previous day's moving average, initiate a sell.

In the case of the MSFT trade, a stop should have been in place because the price continued to fall and settled below the moving average on the day it broke this support level.

Letting two moving averages keep you out of a bad trade

One of the best fully quantifiable trend indicators involves combining two moving averages. When the one based on the shorter time frame is higher than the one with a longer time frame, this indicator shows an uptrend. What about a bearish candlestick signal when the trend is bullish? Figure 14-8, which uses MSFT shares, is a perfect example.

A bearish reversal signal in the form of a spinning top shows up in the MSFT chart. But the 10-day moving average is well below the price level, as is the 20-day moving average. The day after the spinning top shows up in the chart, the 10-day moving average moves above the 20-day average, even though the price is lower that day. The 10-day average continues to move higher than the 20-day, indicating that a short trade isn't advisable at this time. Moving averages and other trend indicators help you get into and out of trades, and they also may keep you from getting into trades that are doomed from the start.

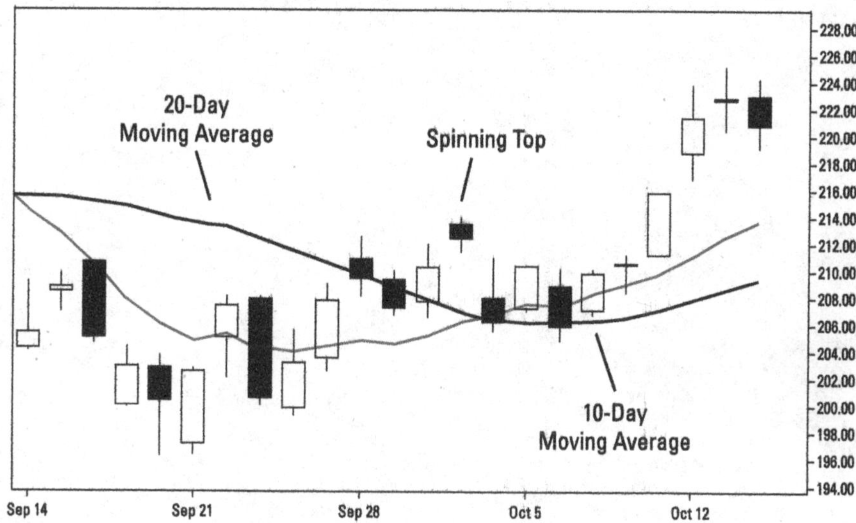

FIGURE 14-8: Bullish trend combined with bearish spinning top candlestick.

Chapter **15**

Combining Technical Indicators and Bearish-Trending Candlestick Patterns

I n this chapter, we explore the ways you can use trend lines and moving averages with bearish-trending candlestick patterns to uncover promising trading opportunities. Those two versatile types of technical analysis methods are useful for detecting downtrends, and when you pair them with bearish-trending candlestick patterns, you may find it much easier to pick the best spots for entering short-selling trades. And as though that weren't enough, you can use that potent combination to determine when it's time to cover your short position and (ideally) pocket a profit.

Combining Lines with Candles for Confirmation

Trend lines are among the most straightforward technical indicators. If an uptrend is in place, a trend line has a positive slope. If a downtrend is the order of the day (or week or month), a trend line has a negative slope. This concept sounds simplistic, but it can be hugely helpful when you're trying to determine a market's trend. If that trend turns out to be down, you can use a downward-sloping trend line alongside bearish-trending candlestick patterns to inform your short trading decisions.

If you're blanking on trend lines, turn to Chapter 11, where we discuss them in detail.

Analyzing short trades with trend lines and bearish patterns

Selecting the most appropriate time to get into a short trade can be a trying task. Timing is critical, and any decision-making help can be a real blessing. Luckily for you, considering trend lines and bearish-trending candlestick patterns together can provide just that type of help. We show you what we mean in this section with a couple of real-world examples.

A short trade with a bearish trend line and candlestick pattern

You can find the first example in Figure 15-1, a chart of the Energy Select Sector SPDR Fund (XLE), an exchange-traded fund (ETF). This chart shows a downtrend that is confirmed about halfway through with a bearish neckline pattern.

The downtrend in the chart in Figure 15-1 is about as convincing as you can find, which is common among commodities and extends to energy stocks. When the bearish neckline shows up, a trend line can be drawn to define the speed of the downtrend. In this case, the line extends back to the recent high and incorporates the high of the bearish neckline pattern. The downtrend for XLE extends for a few more weeks, but, like all good things, it comes to an end.

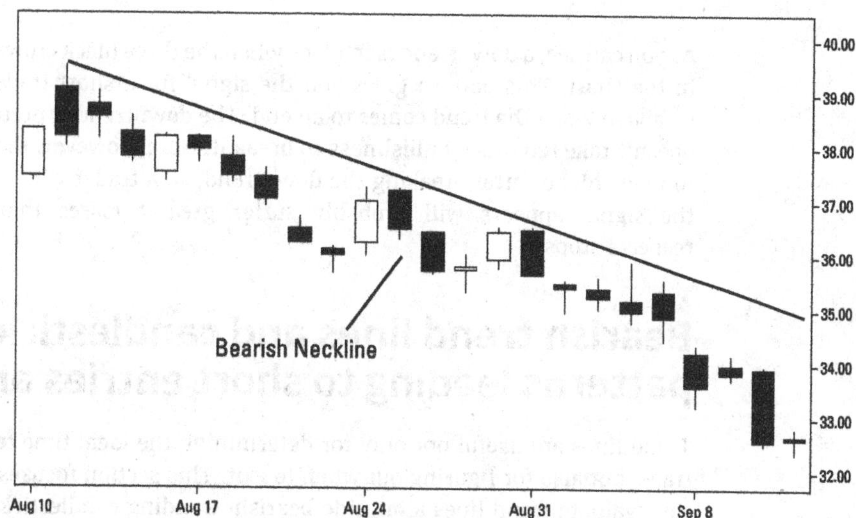

FIGURE 15-1:
A chart of XLE
showing a
downtrend line
confirming a
bearish neck-
line pattern.

Another bearish trend line and bearish pattern leading to a short trade

One more example of how you can combine a bearish trend line and a bearish-trending candlestick pattern is on display in Figure 15-2, which is a chart of the Nasdaq 100 ETF QQQ.

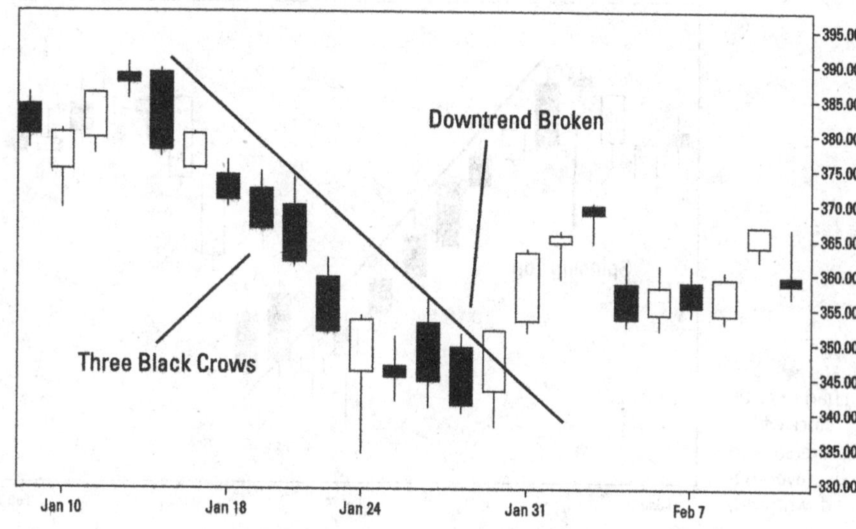

FIGURE 15-2:
A chart of QQQ
with three
black crows, a
downtrend line,
and an exit based
on breaking
the trend.

As you can see, a downtrend is in place when the three black crows pattern appears in the chart. This pattern gives you the signal for a short trade. Draw a line to establish when the trend comes to an end. The downtrend is pretty dramatic, so it doesn't take too much bullishness to break it. Note, however, that QQQ continues to move higher after breaking the downtrend, so a trader who doesn't exit when the signal appears will probably suffer greater losses than a trader who respects stops.

Bearish trend lines and candlestick patterns leading to short entries and exits

Trend lines are useful not only for determining the ideal time to get into a short trade, but also for figuring out when to exit. This section focuses on the ways you can evaluate trend lines alongside bearish-trending candlestick patterns to pick the best time to cover a short.

Shorting and covering using a trend line combined with a reversal candlestick pattern

Figure 15-3 features a chart of Apple (AAPL), showing a reversal and the subsequent downtrend after the reversal signal.

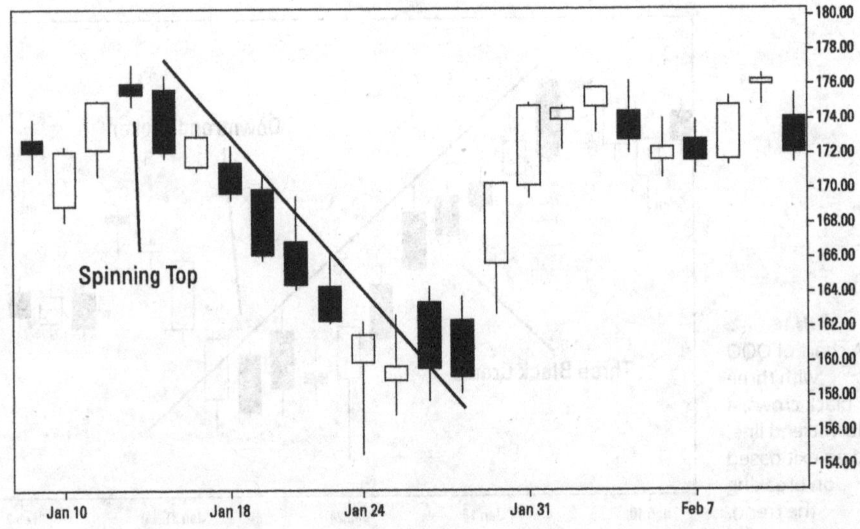

FIGURE 15-3: A chart of AAPL stock with a reversal and eventual downtrend.

A spinning top, indicating a bearish reversal, shows up and is confirmed by a long black candle the following day. This pattern gives you an opportunity to follow the trend, which is consistently lower for about two weeks.

Eventually, this downtrend is broken, and an argument could be made that a day or two before the trend meets its end, a bullish reversal signal appears. Those two signals combined should be enough to cover your AAPL short.

One final note on the chart in Figure 15-3 before we move on: An astute chart observer will notice a bullish reversal pattern at the bottom of the downtrend. Did you catch it? It's the *bullish three outside up* pattern, which signals that the downtrend is about to change directions and head up. You can always use a reversal pattern as an exit when it shows up in a chart; in this case, the pattern helps you lock in just a little more profit on the short trade. Also, if you're so inclined, you can use this bullish pattern to establish a long position.

Exiting one trade doesn't mean you have to stop working with a particular security for any period of time. If you're in a trade and riding a prevailing trend and you spot a trend reversal candlestick pattern, don't rule out the possibility of exiting the current trade and jumping back in with a trade that rides the trend in the opposite direction!

DETERMINING TRADING LEVELS WITH TREND LINES

Trend lines are helpful indicators for many reasons, but one slightly tricky feature is figuring out how to use them as exit stop levels. This judgment is difficult because the lines move every day. How can you deal with that movement? You have a couple of choices:

- Draw a new trend line every day to keep up with the changing price action. This method works because your line moves consistently with the trend, and you can place corresponding stop orders that are good for that day only. But that method can also be taxing because you have to commit to changing the trend line every day.

- Set up a stop that gets you out of the trade only if the close for a day is above your trend line. That strategy eliminates the need for a daily trend line change, but it does require you to check your chart toward the close of each day.

Some traders like the second option because it keeps them from getting stopped out of a trade if the price makes a little run above the trend line. Other traders contend that the price can rise dramatically (and close quite a bit higher), erasing profits or even causing losses before the stop takes effect. It's up to you to decide which method works best with your trading strategy and style.

Shorting and covering with a downtrend line and bearish pattern

We offer one more example before we wrap up this explanation. Figure 15-4 is a chart of spot Bitcoin prices (that is, the current exchange rate). Two bearish neckline patterns show up, and the trend is defined as down after the second pattern appears.

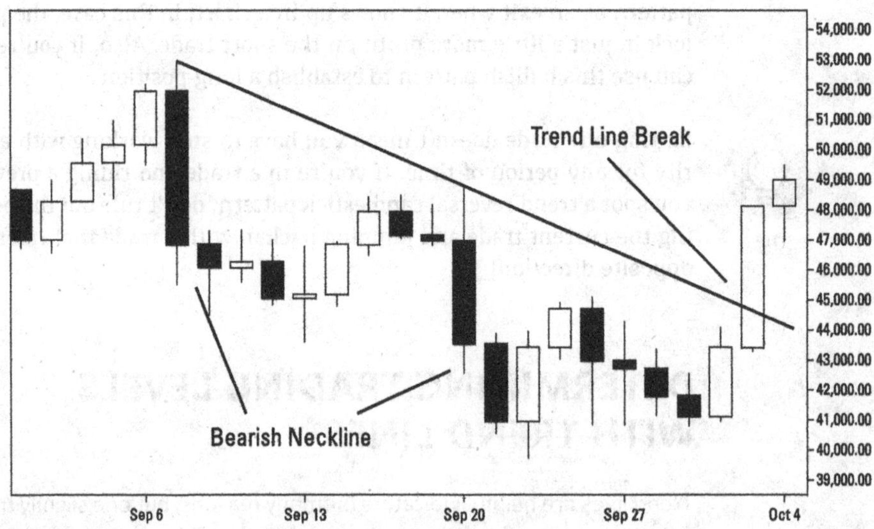

FIGURE 15-4: Two bearish necklines in a chart of Bitcoin prices.

The second bearish neckline allows you to define the trend as lower. Using the highs of both patterns, you can place a justifiable downtrend line on the chart and use a violation of this line as an exit signal. Bitcoin is *volatile,* and it doesn't take long for this downtrend to be broken with a couple of highly bullish days. Again, note that after the trend is broken, prices move higher quickly. When an exit signal shows up, take it. Your first trade is always your best trade when a trend is broken.

Combining Moving Averages and Bearish Patterns for Shorts

The moving average is another technical indicator you can combine with bearish-trending candlestick patterns to figure out when to enter and exit your short trades. You can read all about moving averages (and several other technical indicators) in Chapter 11, but broadly speaking, a *moving average* is the average of the closing prices of a security over a certain period.

Moving averages are useful for confirming trends, and that functionality makes them good bearish-trending candlestick pattern partners. Read on to find out more.

Pinning down short entry points and confirming trends

You can use one moving average or multiple moving averages to determine trends in a chart. In this section, we present a real-world example of each approach.

A short trade using a signal moving average and bearish pattern

Figure 15-5 is another chart of the QQQ ETF. In this example, a couple of days after a bearish reversal signal shows up, the 10-day moving average is violated by the QQQ price action.

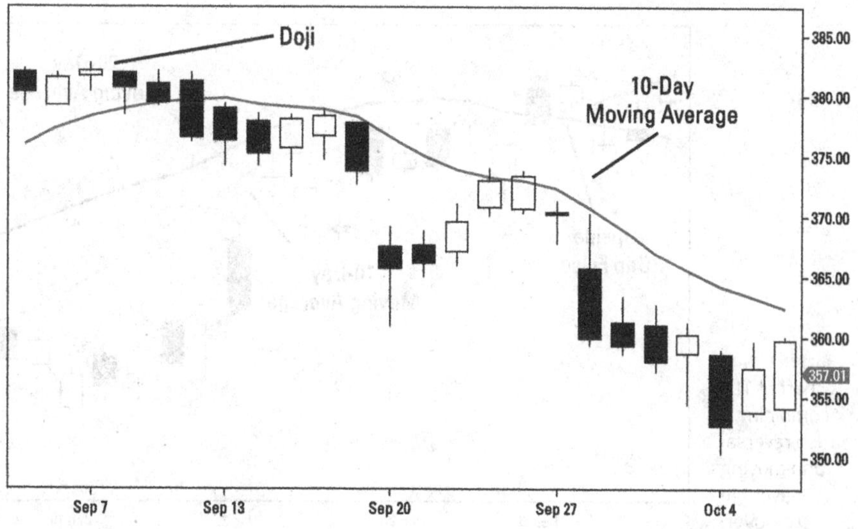

The doji shows up when QQQ is still in an uptrend. If a trader took the initial signal, they would be rewarded by lower QQQ prices in a short period. A more cautious trader who uses moving averages to establish a trend, however, wouldn't enter the trade until three days later, when QQQ closes below the moving average. In both cases, the trader would be happy as QQQ gaps lower and tries to recover, but never truly violates the 10-day moving average.

If one moving average is good, are two moving averages great? That's often the case because you can compare the two moving averages to glean even more information about the nature of the price action and the prevailing trend.

When you're using two moving averages in a chart, you can detect a bearish trend when the moving average that uses fewer days in the calculation (the fast one) is below the moving average calculated with more days (the slow one).

Two moving averages and a bearish pattern giving a short signal

You can see a helpful example of combining two moving averages with bearish-trending candlestick patterns in Figure 15-6, which is a chart of iShares 20+ Year Treasury Bond (TLT), an ETF that gives you exposure to the bond market. This chart is dominated by a bearish trend, revealed by a 10-day moving average that mostly stays below the 20-day moving average.

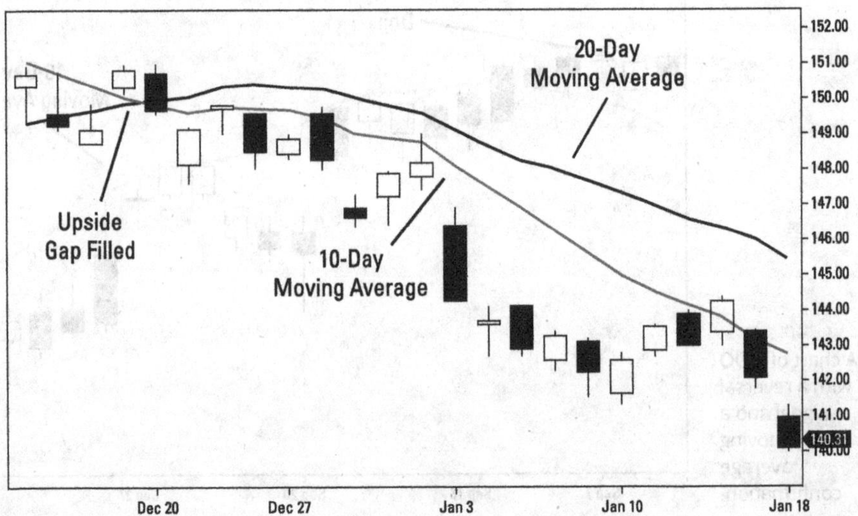

FIGURE 15-6: A chart of TLT combining a bearish reversal and moving average crossover.

A complex pattern — upside gap-filled — kicks off this chart. This example is perfect because on the day the pattern is complete, the 10-day moving average moves below the 20-day moving average. A bearish moving average signal plus a bearish candlestick pattern results in a sustained move lower for TLT.

Picking shorts with moving averages and candlesticks

Moving averages can be a huge help when you combine them with bearish-trending candlestick patterns to pick short trade entry points, but you can also use that dynamic duo to determine stop levels and exit points. We wrap up this chapter with a couple of examples that show you how to do just that.

A single moving average and bearish pattern for a short trade and trade exit signal

Figure 15-7 features a chart of the iShares Silver Trust (SLV), an ETF that is an efficient method of gaining exposure to the price of silver. This chart is similar to Figure 15-6, in which a bearish signal shows up and is confirmed a few days later by a cross below the 10-day moving average.

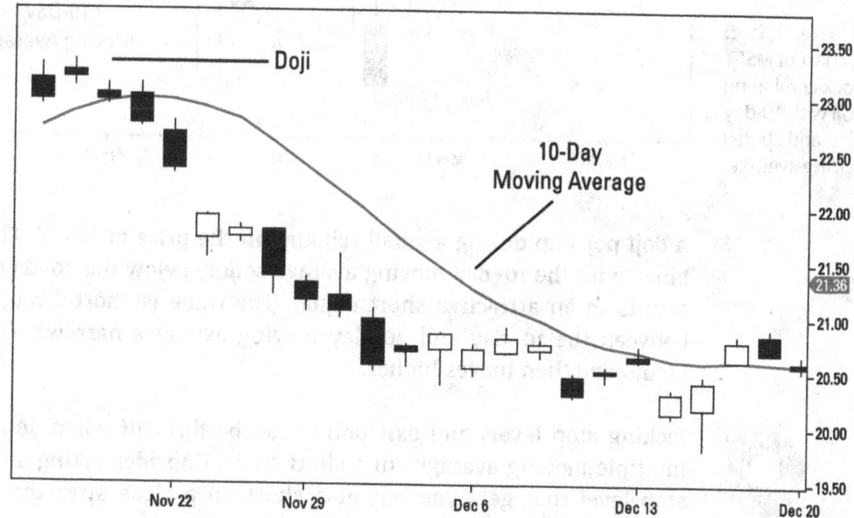

FIGURE 15-7:
A 10-day moving average and bearish doji in an SLV chart.

The ETF closes below the moving average two days after the doji appears, and a couple of days later, it gaps lower. Eventually, the trend flattens and SLV closes above the 10-day moving average. Note that the day before SLV moves from below to above the 10-day moving average, a hanging man appears. This pattern is another reversal signal that may be an early indication that it's time to take profits on the short SLV trade.

Two moving averages along with a bearish pattern for a short sale and an exit trade

Figure 15-8 is a Microsoft (MSFT) chart showing how a trend and a doji can be in sync.

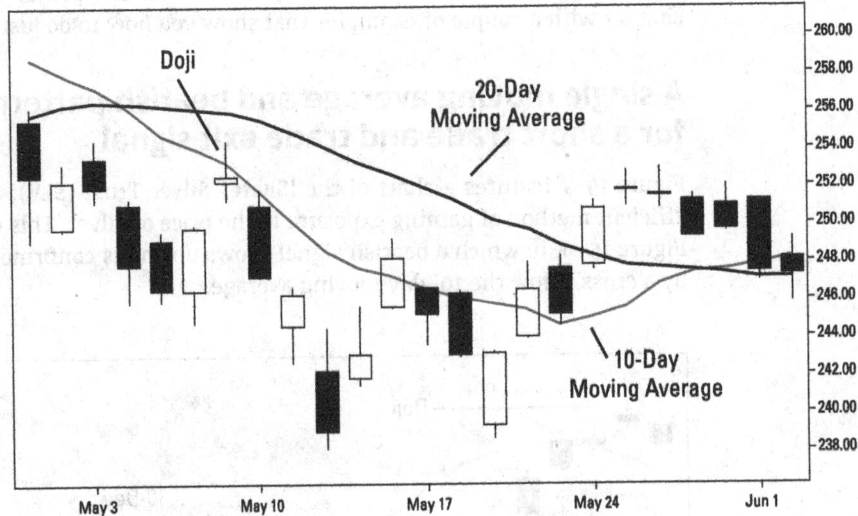

FIGURE 15-8: A chart of MSFT stock combining a doji with 10-day and 20-day moving average.

A doji pops up during a small rebound in the price of MSFT. This pattern, combined with the 10-day moving average solidly below the 20-day moving average, results in an attractive short signal. The trade is short-lived, though; the gap between the 10-day and 20-day moving averages narrows as MSFT is range-bound and then moves higher.

Picking stop levels and exit points can be difficult when you're working with multiple moving averages in a short trade. Consider taking an easy route: Set a stop level that gets you out of a short on a close after the moving averages have crossed.

It's also worth noting in Figure 15-8 that the price trades above the 10-day moving average several times and even over the 20-day moving average on a few occasions, even though the downtrend stays in place and the 10-day average stays below the 20-day average. Using these two moving averages together keeps you in the trade longer, making it much more profitable.

Chapter **16**

Combining Economic Indicators and Bullish-Trending Candlestick Patterns

Traders can combine candlestick charts with economic indicators to combine fundamental and technical analysis to make trading decisions. This combination allows traders to not only understand the direction of the economy but also gain better insight into the timing of the economy. The combination of fundamental and technical analysis then becomes a one-two punch to better trading.

Fundamental analysis looks at the overall market with regard to whether the economy is growing or contracting. During periods of growth, the economy tends to increase in value or expand. Stock prices tend to have small, positive gains. Prices of goods and services are stable. And finally, unemployment is low. Those who want to work can find gainful employment and can afford their lifestyle.

Fundamental analysis can also depict an economic contraction, or bearish conditions, which we explore in Chapter 17.

Let's take a look in this chapter at the gross domestic product (GDP), interest rates, unemployment rate, consumer price index (CPI), and volatility index (VIX) as economic indicators. As with all economic indicators, these can be used to evaluate whether the economy is *bullish* (growing) or *bearish* (contracting). Traders use these signals as a gauge for the overall health of the economy.

Gross Domestic Product

The gross domestic product (GDP) represents the total goods and services sold by firms in the United States of America. The increase in GDP represents growth or expansion in the overall economy. Most cyclical stocks also increase in value during these expansionary periods, resulting in a rise in their stock prices. An increasing GDP is a bullish signal to traders. A normal market is often indicated by way of small increases in the GDP.

The St. Louis Federal Reserve has a free database (named FRED) that contains historical GDP data, which can be downloaded for free. Figure 16-1 demonstrates the GDP between 2000 and 2024.

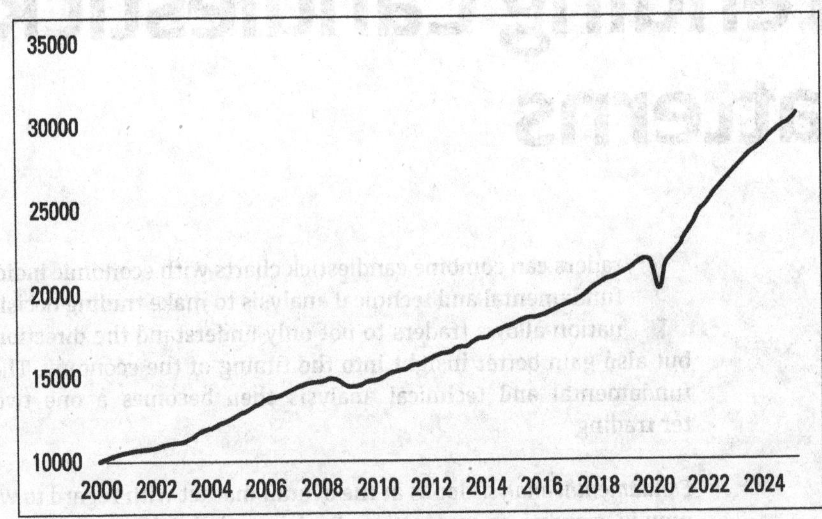

FIGURE 16-1:
The US GDP between 2000 and 2024.

The GDP consistently expanded from 2000 to 2024. The economy took a few downturns during that period, but overall, it expanded. Recently, in 2025, the economy had a bifurcation of the overall population, causing some of the population to believe that the US is in an expanding period, and the other portion of the population to believe that the economy is contracting. However, the GDP indicates that the economy has been growing. Because of this growth, traders would expect to look for bullish candlestick chart patterns.

Looking at Cedar Fairs (FUN), which operates amusement parks such as Cedar Point and, recently, Six Flags, you can find bullish trends during the recent economic expansion, as shown in the bullish chart in Figure 16-2.

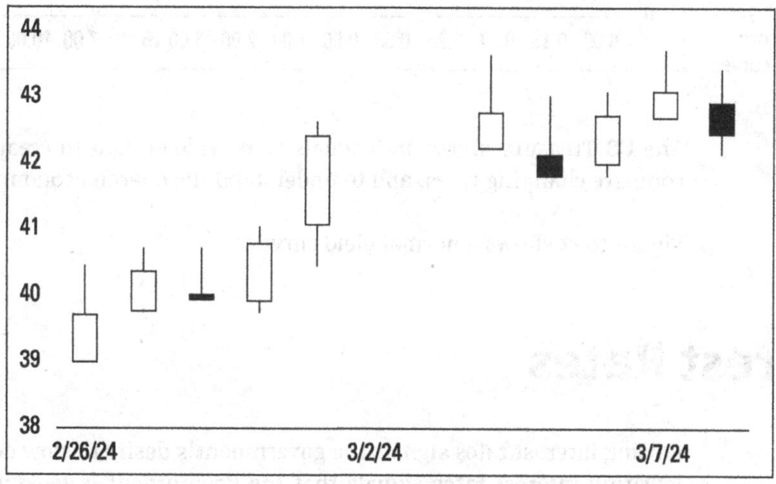

FIGURE 16-2:
A bullish chart for
Cedar Fairs.

Using Cedar Fairs as an example, you can apply several different bullish techniques to the chart, such as bullish engulfing, bullish harami, bullish harami cross, and bullish meeting line.

Another bullish indicator includes the term structure in Treasury instruments. A normal *term structure*, which plots the yield-to-maturity of the instruments against their maturity, consists of lower rates in the short term and higher rates in the long term because of longer-dated securities having more risk than shorter-dated securities. Yield curves can have various shapes, including inverted, twisted, and flat.

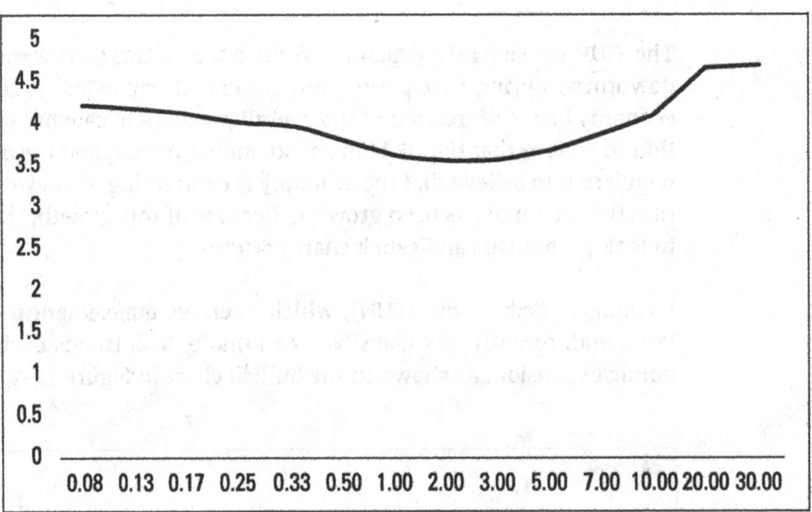

FIGURE 16-3: A normal yield curve.

The US Treasury allows individuals to download data to create yield curves, to compare changing rates, and to understand the overall economy in depth.

Figure 16-3 shows a normal yield curve.

Interest Rates

Raising interest rates signals the government's desire to slow down the economy; lowering interest rates signals that the government is looking to speed up the economy. Raising interest rates doesn't necessarily signal a bearish indicator; similarly, lowering interest rates doesn't necessarily signal a bullish indicator. Traders use these pieces of fundamental information to analyze whether to buy or sell a security.

Figure 16-4 shows today's yield curve. Notice that it lacks the smooth hump shape of a normal curve. Rather, this yield curve has higher rates for shorter periods, lower rates for the middle of the curve, and higher rates for longer-dated maturities at the end of the curve. This is an indication that the markets perceive more risk in the short run than in the long run.

A rapid increase in GDP followed by a quick decrease in interest rates would be a bearish signal; a slow increase in GDP followed by a slow decrease in interest rates would not be a bearish signal.

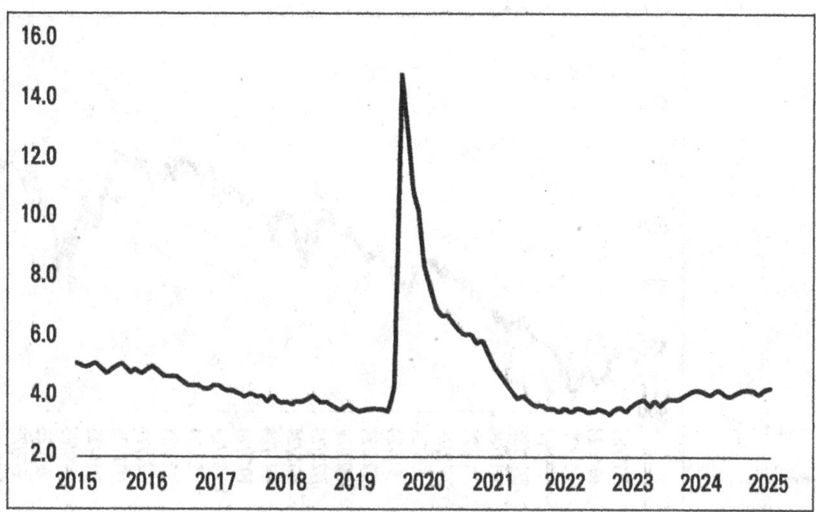

FIGURE 16-4: Today's yield curve.

Unemployment Rate

Unemployment is another economic indicator. Low unemployment indicates an expanding economy and overall positive news. This positive news will help boost the economy and overall stock prices. Traders utilize this news to gain insight into the overall direction. Candlestick charts give better guidance for when to enter into a trade and when to exit the trade.

The US Treasury allows individuals to download historical unemployment data. Allowing the trader to do this allows for the trader to have a better understanding of whether the new unemployment data is "good" (bullish) or "bad" (bearish). Without the historical context, a trader would be lost in determining whether the signal is positive or negative.

Figure 16-5 shows unemployment numbers throughout the past decade. Comparing the unemployment number with the overall stock price of the S&P 500 demonstrates that these two economic indicators follow the same pattern. During periods of low unemployment, the stock market increases in price. Conversely, during periods of high periods of unemployment, the stock market decreases in price.

Figure 16-6 demonstrates the performance of the overall market — specifically, the S&P 500 over the past three years' worth of unemployment data. The SPY is an exchange traded fund (ETF) that follows the S&P 500 index.

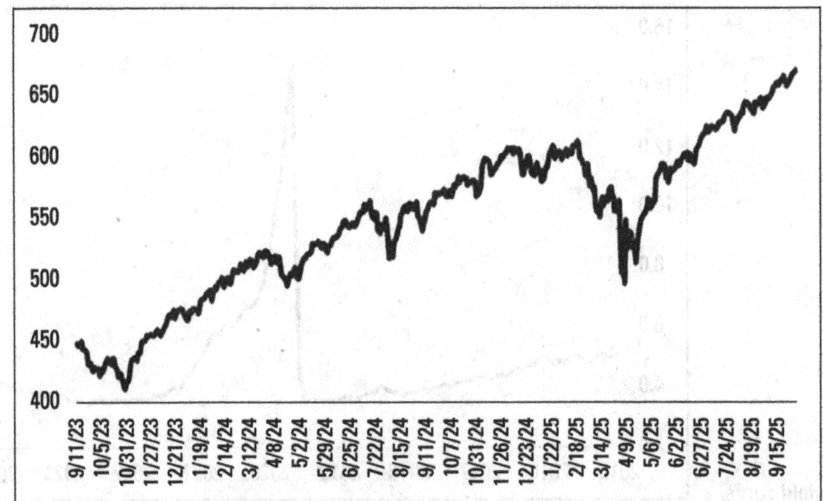

FIGURE 16-5: An unemployment graph.

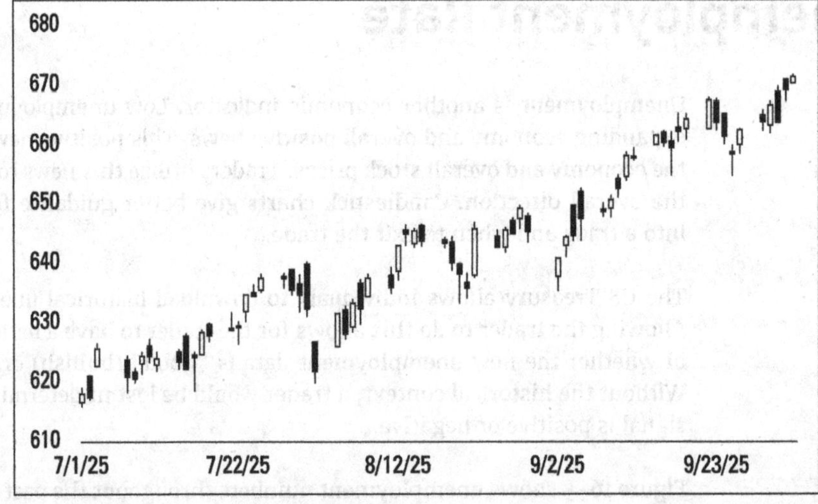

FIGURE 16-6: The performance of the overall market.

Using SPY as an example, you can apply several different bullish techniques to the chart, such as bullish engulfing, bullish harami, bullish harami cross, and bullish meeting line. You can use SPY directly because it's an ETF, which is traded like a stock. Investors can purchase the stock and sell the stock whenever they want. Because of the way shares of the ETF are created and redeemed, the share price of the ETF is always in line with the value of the underlying index — in this case, the S&P 500.

Consumer Price Index

The *consumer price index* (CPI) represents the price of a basket of goods and services used by Americans. The basket was initially designed to represent a typical household's essential goods, such as bread and eggs. The items in the basket have changed dramatically over the years — for example, Internet service wasn't included in the basket 30 years ago.

Now the basket of goods and services is much broader and includes housing, energy, and other items essential to live. Pricing of these goods demonstrates how quickly essential goods have changed. When salaries are increasing at a higher rate than the CPI, individuals have more disposable income for making decisions. This is a positive signal to the markets because it traditionally implies higher sales from consumers buying more goods and services. On the other hand, if wages don't keep up with CPI, individuals have to limit their spending, causing the economy to have a contraction.

The St. Louis Federal Reserve has a free database (known as the FRED) that contains historical CPI data, which can be downloaded for free. The FRED allows the user to choose not only the region from which the data is collected but also the timeframe in which the data exists. Data categories include essential items required for living in the United States, such as used cars, food, energy, apparel, electricity, medical care, motor vehicle maintenance, water and sewer, and trash collection. The FRED also includes some nonessential items such as new vehicles, food away from home, airline fares, alcoholic beverages, transportation services, lodging away from home, recreation, candy and chewing gum, toys, nonalcoholic beverages, personal care, and recreational books.

During times of high price increases, the market sees a jump in the CPI, which is often associated with periods that may be recessionary or bearish. Times in which the CPI simply increases at a slow pace represent a healthy growing economy. When unemployment is low and the CPI is slowly increasing, individuals have disposable income that they can either consume by spending money on nonessential items or save for another period.

Traders often use the announcement of the CPI to indicate the overall health of the economy. Low growth in CPI represents an expansion, or a bullish market. Periods of high growth in CPI represent a period of contraction, or a bearish market.

Figure 16-7 demonstrates the CPI over the past ten years. CPI had low, slow growth from the beginning of the period until 2020, representing the beginning of the COVID pandemic. During this period, the economy saw substantial inflation caused by a lack of productivity, unemployment, and supply chain issues.

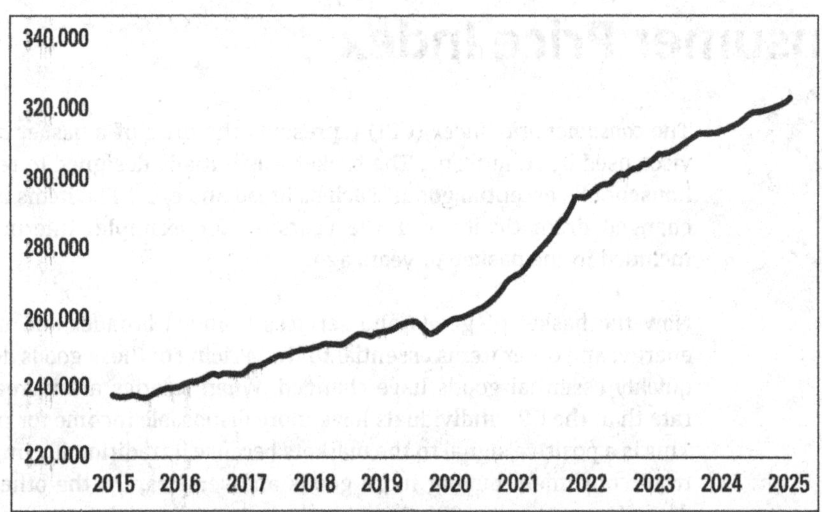

FIGURE 16-7:
CPI data over the
past decade.

Figure 16-8 demonstrates the candlestick chart for Target (TGT), a seller of many
different types of products. During the bullish period of CPI, Target did very well.
Using the bullish indicators allows the trader to know when to get into the trade
and when to get out of the trade.

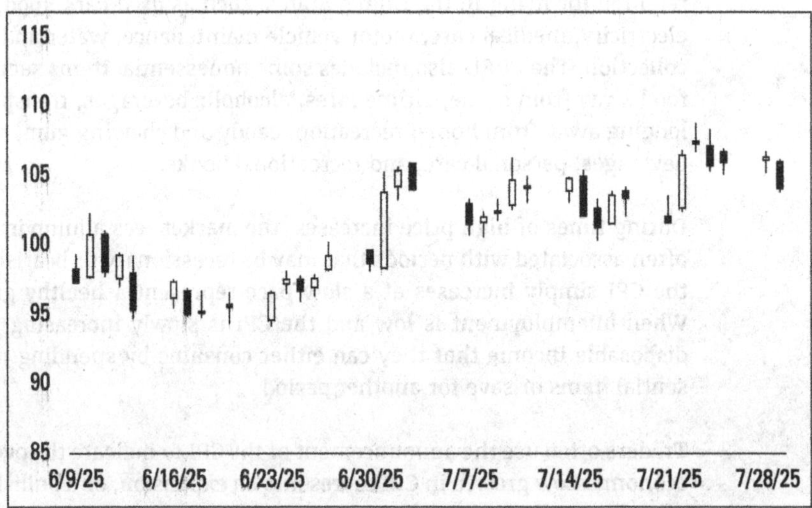

FIGURE 16-8:
Target, during a
bullish period.

Volatility Index

The *Volatility Index* (VIX) is a consistent measure of S&P 500 volatility related to
index price options. The higher the volatility, the greater the chance of a major
market downturn, making the VIX a valuable economic indicator. (This index is

near and dear to Russell's heart because he worked for the Chicago Board Options Exchange for many years, writing several books about the VIX.)

Figure 16-9 demonstrates the historical prices of the VIX between 2010 and 2020. A higher VIX indicates higher volatility; a lower VIX indicates lower volatility, which is shown as small increasing prices in the overall S&P 500 market.

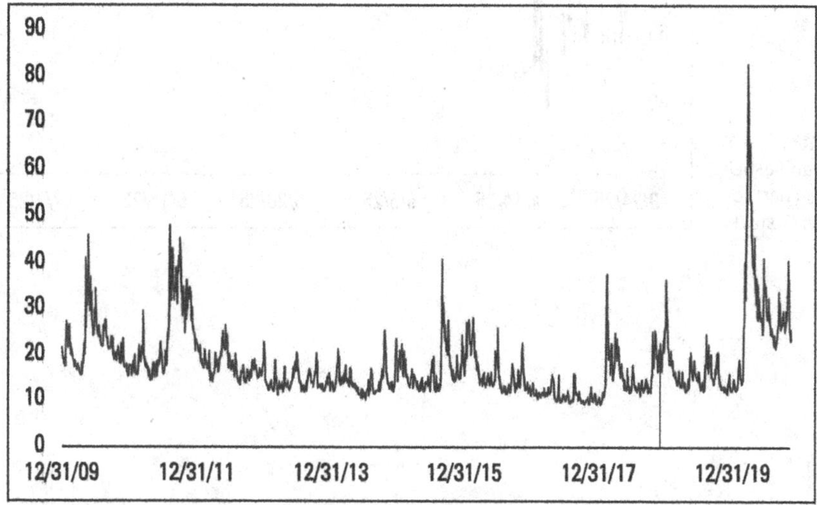

VIX typically stays between 15 and 20. Between January 2010 and August 2020, the index had an average value of 19.54. The maximum value occurred on March 18, 2020, with a value of 85.47, during the initial peak and uncertainty of the pandemic. VIX broke through the 50 level 24 times during this almost 10-year period, representing 0.63% of all occurrences. The majority of the high 24 data points in daily VIX were from 2020, the pandemic, representing 21 out of 24 of the data points, or 87.5%. August 24, 2015, depicts the flash crash of the financial markets. On this day, the Dow Jones declined by 9% in 5 minutes and then bounced back. On February 16, 2018, the Dow Jones declined by 4%, causing a spike in volatility.

Figure 16-10 demonstrates the candlestick chart for Walmart (WMT), a seller of many different types of products. During low periods of volatility, the company did very well. Using the bullish indicators allows the trader to know when to get into the trade and when to get out of the trade.

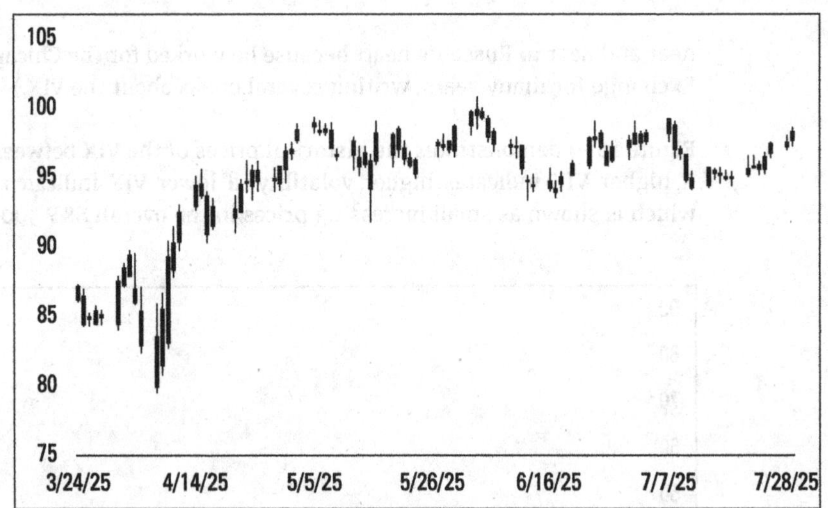

FIGURE 16-10:
A candlestick chart for WMT stock.

Chapter 17

Combining Economic Indicators and Bearish-Trending Candlestick Patterns

As we discuss in Chapter 16, traders can combine candlestick charts with economic indicators to combine fundamental and technical analysis to make trading decisions. The combination of these two factors allows the trader to better understand whether they should be looking for a bearish or bullish indicator. As a trader, you can easily see both bullish and bearish patterns in the data, so knowing what to look for when evaluating your data will make you a better trader.

Fundamental analysis gives an idea of the overall health of the economy. Bullish investors are looking for periods of higher prices in the overall market. Conversely, bearish investors are looking for signs that the economy is weakening, that prices are lowering, or that a recession is possibly near.

Fundamental analysis can also depict an economic growth, or bullish conditions, which is explored in Chapter 16.

Let's take a look next at the gross domestic product (GDP), interest rates, unemployment rate, consumer price index (CPI), and Volatility Index (VIX) as economic indicators. Like all economic indicators, these can be used to evaluate whether the economy is growing (bullish) or contracting (bearish). Traders use these signals as a gauge for the overall health of the economy.

Gross Domestic Product

The *gross domestic product* (GDP) represents the total goods and services sold by firms in the United States of America. The increase in GDP represents growth or expansion in the overall economy. Most cyclical stocks also increase in value during these expansionary periods, resulting in a rise in their stock prices. An increasing GDP is a bullish signal to traders. A normal market is often indicated by way of small increases in the GDP.

The St. Louis Federal Reserve has a free database (known as FRED) that contains historical GDP data, which can be downloaded for free. Figure 17-1 demonstrates the GDP between 2000 and 2024. Because the data can be downloaded for free, traders can be on the lookout for either bullish or bearish trends.

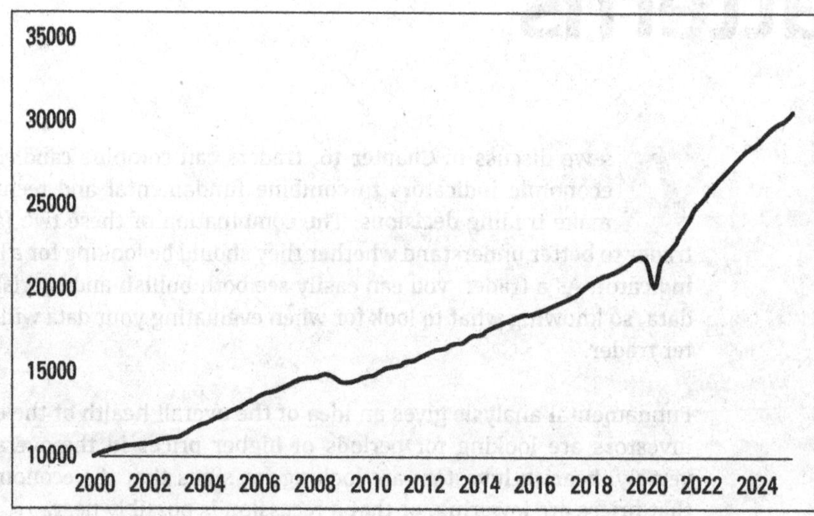

FIGURE 17-1: The US GDP between 2000 and 2024.

The GDP has consistently expanded from 2000 to 2024. There were a few down-turns during the period, but overall, the economy has expanded. Recently, in 2025, the economy has had a bifurcation (branching) of the overall population, causing some to believe that the economy is in an expanding period and others to believe that the economy is contracting. However, the GDP indicates that the economy has been growing. Due to this growth, traders would expect to look for bullish candlestick chart patterns.

Walmart (WMT), as you undoubtedly know, is a firm that sells just about any-thing, in a format known as *big box store*. Prices are thought to be generally lower at Walmart relative to its competitors. Some theories state that it's a countercycli-cal firm that tends to do better during recessionary periods. Looking at the WMT chart during the beginning of the COVID-19 global pandemic, you can see bearish indicators (see Figure 17-2).

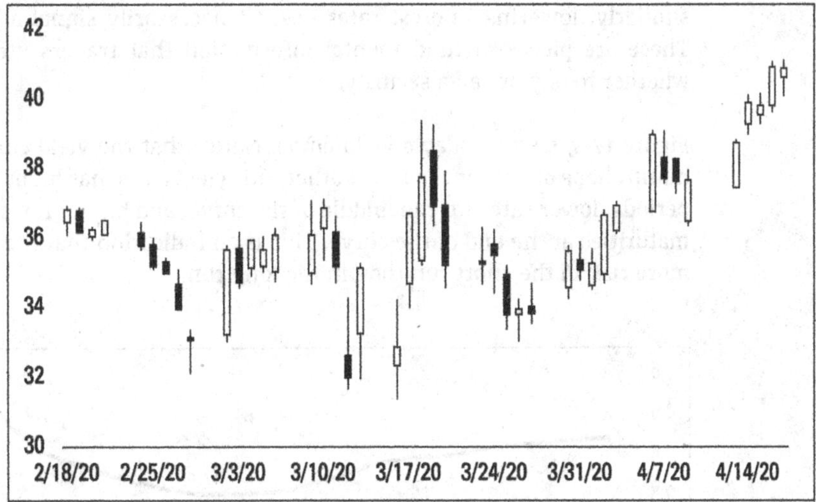

FIGURE 17-2: Walmart, at the beginning of the pandemic.

Interest Rates

Another bearish indicator includes the term structure in Treasury instruments. A normal term structure, which plots the yield-to-maturity of the instruments against their maturity, consists of lower rates in the short term and higher rates in the long term. This is due to longer-dated securities having more risk than shorter-dated securities. Yield curves can have various shapes, including inverted, twisted, and flat.

Figure 17-3 shows a normal yield curve.

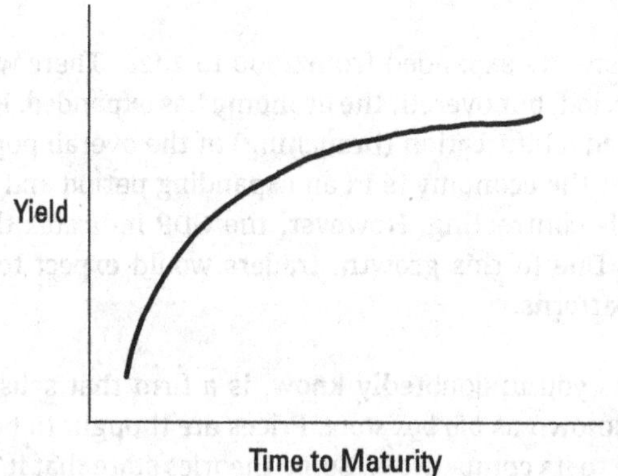

FIGURE 17-3:
A normal
yield curve.

Raising interest rates signals the government's desire to slow down the economy. Lowering interest rates signals that the government is looking to speed up the economy. Raising interest rates does not necessarily signal a bearish indicator; similarly, lowering interest rates doesn't necessarily signal a bullish indicator. These are pieces of fundamental information that traders utilize in analyzing whether to buy or sell a security.

Figure 17-4 shows today's yield curve. Notice that the yield curve lacks the nice hump shape of a normal curve. Rather, this yield curve has higher rates for shorter periods, lower rates for the middle of the curve, and higher rates for longer-dated maturities at the end of the curve. This is an indication that the markets perceive more risk in the short run than in the long run.

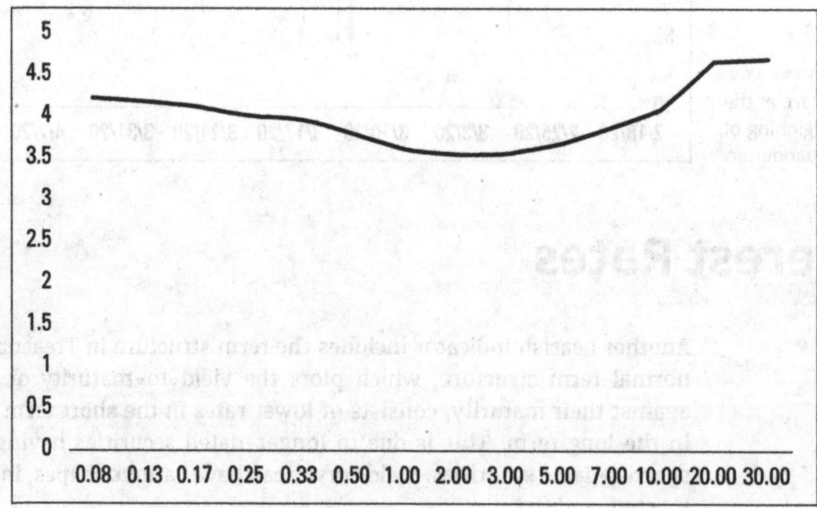

FIGURE 17-4:
Today's
yield curve.

A rapid increase in GDP followed by a quick decrease in interest rates would be a bearish signal; a slow increase in GDP followed by a slow decrease in interest rates would not be a bearish signal. The higher short-term rates indicate to the market that there's more uncertainty in the short term than the long term.

During recessionary periods or bearish periods, Target (TGT) often declines in value. (Target is a direct competitor of Walmart, mentioned in the previous example.) During the summer and early fall of 2025, the economy became a bit bearish, which is reflected in the company's stock price (see Figure 17-5). Using the term structure allows the trader to become more focused on looking for bearish candlestick patterns.

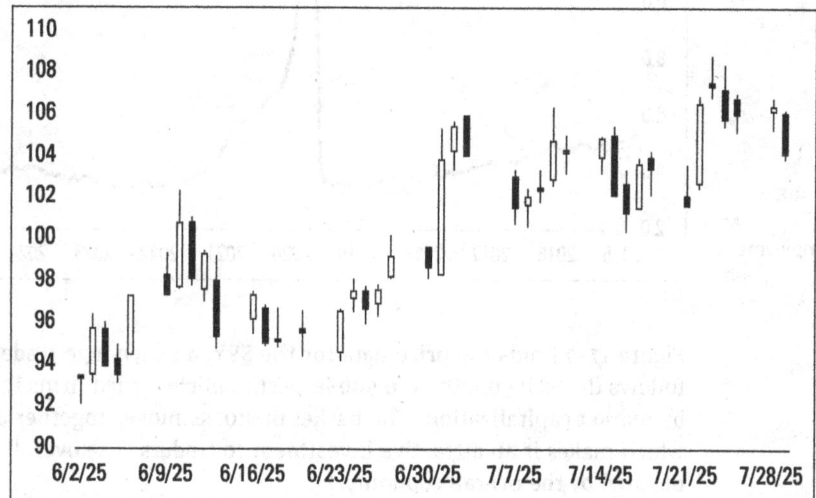

FIGURE 17-5: Target's stock price mid-2025.

Unemployment

Unemployment is another economic indicator. Low unemployment indicates an expanding economy and overall positive news. This positive news helps boost the economy and overall stock prices. Traders utilize this news to gain insight into the overall direction. Candlestick charts give better guidance on when to enter into a trade and when to exit the trade.

The US Treasury allows individuals to download historical unemployment data. Allowing traders to do this allows them to better understand whether the new unemployment data is "good" (bullish) or "bad" (bearish). Without the historical context, a trader would be lost in determining whether the signal is positive or negative.

Figure 17-6 shows the unemployment numbers throughout the past decade. Comparing the unemployment number with the overall stock price of the S&P 500 demonstrates that these two economic indicators follow the same pattern. During periods of low unemployment, the stock market increases in price. Conversely, during periods of high periods of unemployment, the stock market decreases in price.

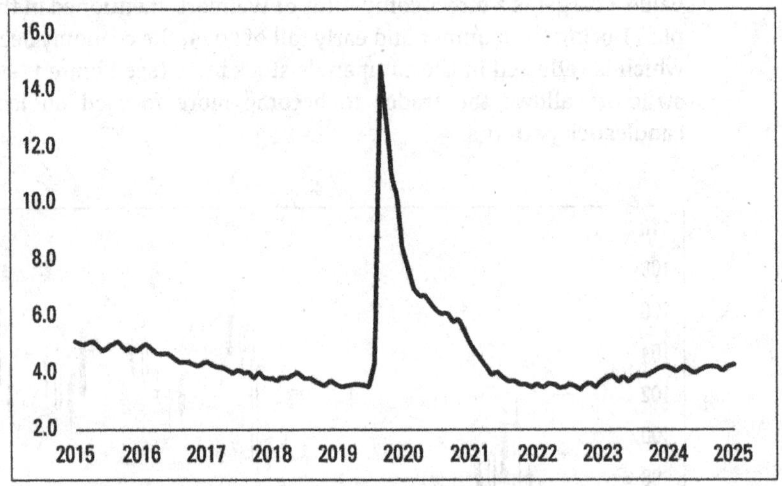

FIGURE 17-6: An unemployment graph.

Figure 17-7 holds the price data for the SPY, an exchange traded fund (ETF) that follows the S&P 500, the top 500 largest publicly traded firms in the United States by market capitalization. The basket of stocks moves together as a singular unit, which makes it an attractive investment to traders. The overall price changes are dictated by the overall economy.

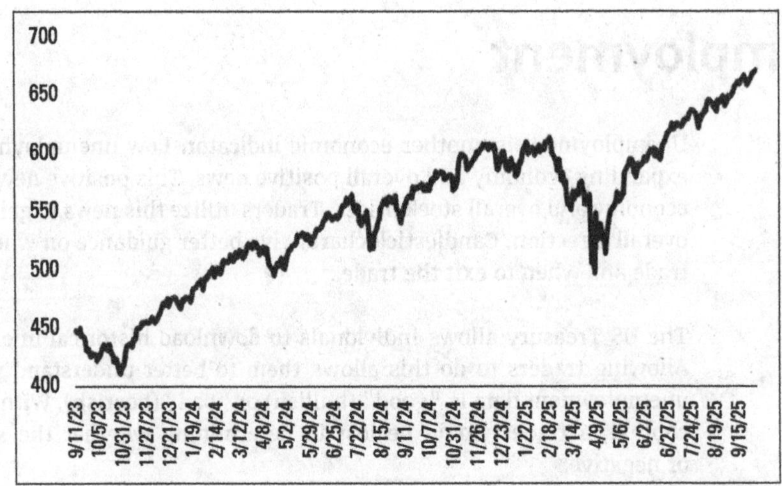

FIGURE 17-7: SPY, an ETF that follows the S&P 500.

Consumer Price Index

The *consumer price index (CPI)* represents the price of a basket of goods and services that are used by Americans. The items placed in the basket have changed dramatically over the years. The goods that are placed in the basket change throughout the years, depending on which goods Americans use on a daily basis. The CPI can be controversial because it measures the change in prices from period to period. What it does measure is how expensive these items are relative to a person's ability to buy them.

Now the basket of goods and services is much more broad and includes housing, energy, and other items that are essential to live. Pricing of these goods demonstrates how quickly essential goods have changed. If salaries are increasing at a higher rate than the CPI, individuals will have more disposable income to be able to make decisions with. This is a positive signal to the markets because it traditionally implies higher sales from consumers buying more goods and services. On the other hand, if wages haven't kept up with CPI, individuals will have to limit their spending, causing the economy to have a contraction.

The St. Louis Federal Reserve has a free database (known as FRED) that contains historical CPI data, which can be downloaded for free. The FRED allows the user to choose not only the region from which the data is collected but also the timeframe when the data exists. Data categories include essential items required for living in the United States, such as used cars, food, energy, apparel, electricity, medical care, motor vehicle maintenance, water and sewer, and trash collection. The FRED also includes some nonessential items, such as new vehicles, food away from home, airline fares, alcoholic beverages, transportation services, lodging away from home, recreation, candy and chewing gum, toys, nonalcoholic beverages, personal care, and recreational books.

During times of high price increases, the market will see a jump in the CPI. This is often associated with periods that may be recessionary or bearish. Times in which the CPI simply increases at a slow pace represent a healthy growing economy. As unemployment is low, and the CPI is slowly increasing, individuals have disposable income, which they can either consume by spending money on nonessential items or save for another period.

Traders often use the announcement of the CPI to indicate the overall health of the economy. Low growth in CPI represents an expansion or a bullish market. Periods of high growth in CPI represent a period of contraction or a bearish market.

Figure 17-8 shows the CPI over the past decade. CPI had low slow growth from the beginning of the period until 2020, representing the beginning of the COVID pandemic. During this period, the economy saw substantial inflation caused by lack of productivity, unemployment, and supply chain issues.

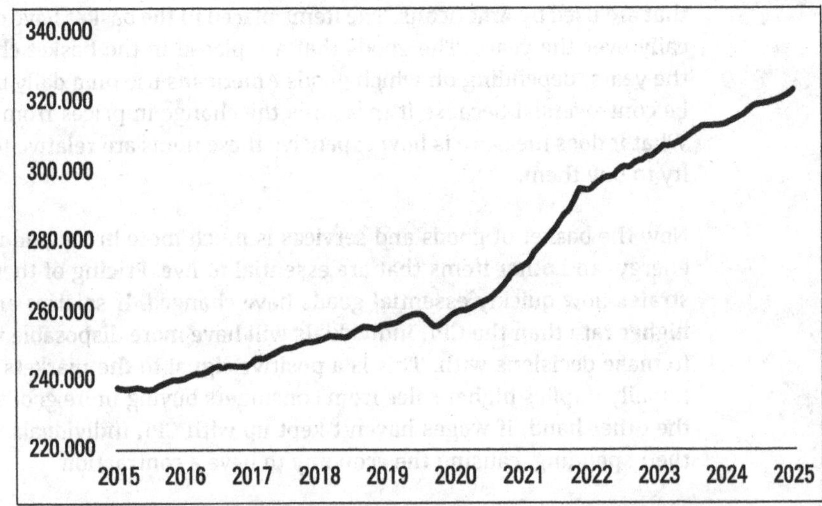

FIGURE 17-8: CPI data over the past decade.

Figure 17-9 represents Cedar Fairs (FUN), an amusement park company. The firm operates both the Cedar Point suite of amusement parks and Six Flags. CPI data demonstrates higher inflationary pressure on spending on vacations, and spending money outside of the home on food. The FUN data demonstrates similar downward pressures on its price.

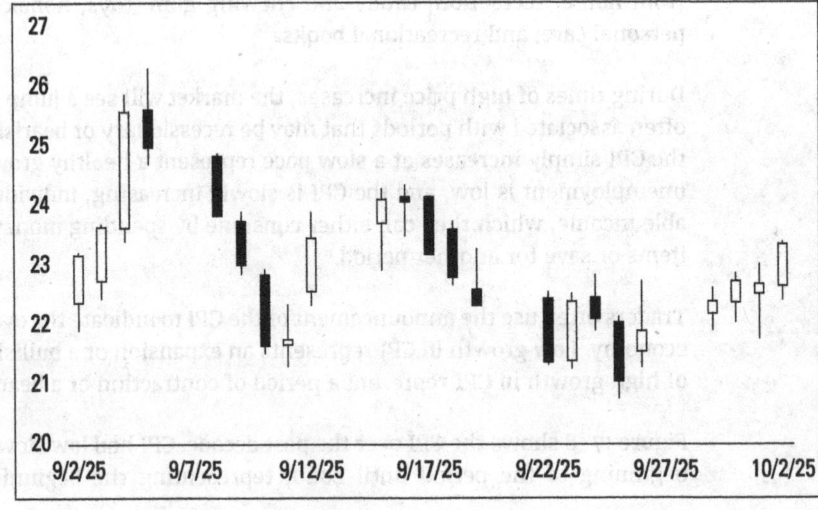

FIGURE 17-9: Bearish movement for Cedar Fairs.

Volatility Index

VIX is a consistent measure of S&P 500 volatility related to index price options. The higher the volatility, the greater the chance of a major market downturn, making the VIX a valuable economic indicator. (The Volatility Index, or VIX, is near and dear to Russell's heart because he had worked for the Chicago Board Options Exchange for many years, writing several books about the VIX.)

Figure 17-10 demonstrates the historical prices of the VIX between 2010 and 2024. A higher VIX indicates higher volatility; a lower VIX indicates lower volatility, which is seen as small increasing prices in the overall S&P 500 market.

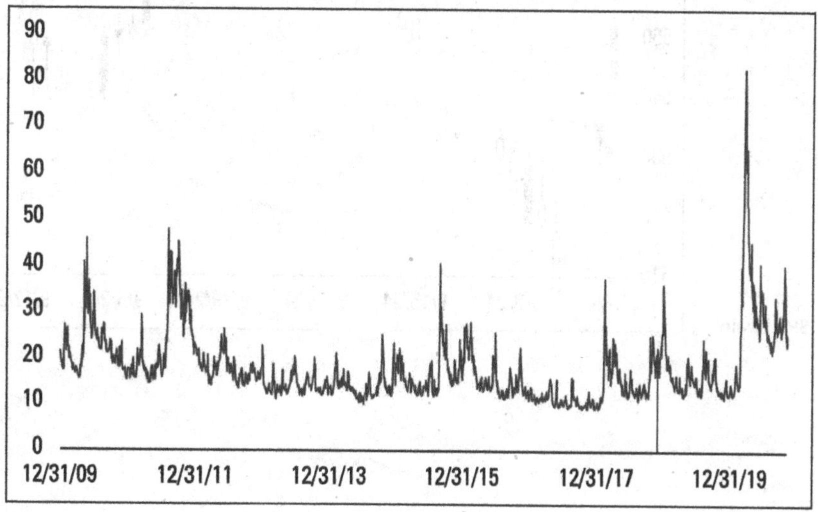

FIGURE 17-10: A VIX graph showing both higher and lower volatility.

VIX typically stays between 15 and 20. Between January 2010 and August 2024, the index had an average value of 19.54. The maximum value occurred on March 18, 2020, with a value of 85.47, during the initial peak and uncertainty of the pandemic. VIX broke through the 50 level 24 times during this almost 14-year period, representing 0.63% of all occurrences. The majority of the high 24 datapoints in daily VIX were from 2020, the pandemic, representing 21 out of 24 of the datapoints, or 87.5%. August 24, 2015, depicts the flash crash of the financial markets. On this day, the Dow Jones declined by 9% in 5 minutes and then bounced back. On February 16, 2018, the Dow Jones declined by 4%, causing a spike in volatility.

During August 2024, there was a crash in the carry trade market with the Japanese yen. The *carry trade* is a type of foreign exchange trade in which the trader shorts the expensive interest rate and goes long on the cheap interest rate. The trader makes the difference between those two interest rates. This trade typically does well, generating small positive returns. In August 2024, the trade unwound, disrupting the overall market. There was a huge spike in VIX as a result. Using this information, a trader can then see a downturn in the S&P 500, causing bearish economic conditions. You can see this in Figure 17-11 as the SPY follows the S&P 500 in performance.

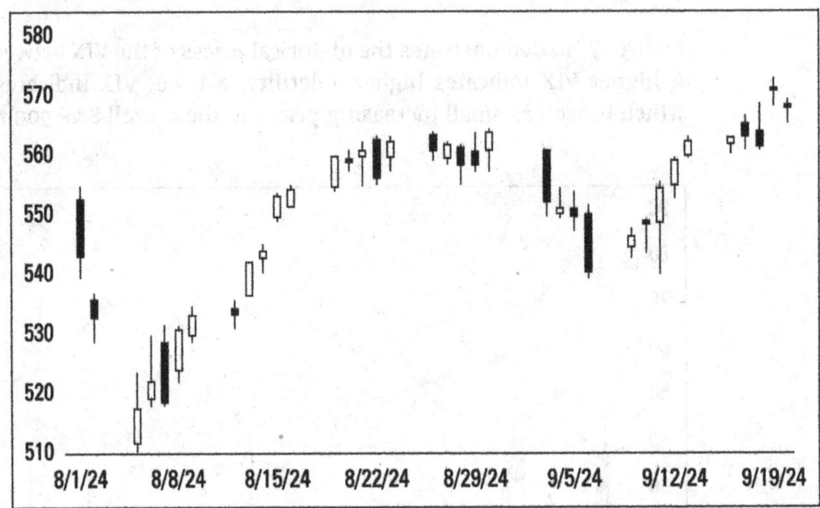

FIGURE 17-11: SPY, again.

The Part of Tens

Chapter **18**

Ten Myths about Charting, Trading, and Candlesticks

Throughout this book, we reveal how charting techniques — especially candlestick charts — are a path to making money in the markets. But our views on the subject aren't unanimous among those who are interested in the markets. Many folks are critical of technical analysis in general. Also, some traders say that there's no benefit in keeping an eye out for candlestick patterns. (We know — unthinkable!) If you attended business school, you may have heard professors (not professional investors or traders) argue that the markets are efficient and that nothing can be done long-term to outperform this efficiency. But rest assured that the reverse is true: We've worked with some smart people who did just what these professors say can't be done, and they did it well.

In this chapter, we dispel ten common myths and misconceptions about trading and candlestick charts to set your mind at ease and keep you confident in your trading pursuits.

There's No Difference between Candlesticks and Bar Charts

If you've already read some of the material in this book, we hope you'll roll your eyes when you see or hear this myth. Candlestick charts are far superior to ordinary bar charts, for a whole host of reasons:

» Candlestick charts are aesthetically appealing.

» Candlestick charts feature patterns that can be easily discerned and used as the basis of profitable trading decisions.

» Although the same price action shows up in bar charts, the dull presentation makes it difficult for you to pick up on the intricacies of the price movement.

» Bar chart patterns don't have exotic names. After you're used to marubozus and dojis and haramis, how can you go back?

Market Efficiency Makes It Impossible to Beat the Market over the Long Run

Professors may have drilled the myth of market efficiency into your brain in college and perhaps again in graduate school. As educators, we teach about the theoretical background of efficient markets, but we also describe instances in which it's possible to generate alpha (that is, a return greater than expected for the amount of risk taken) or make money in the markets beyond owning an index fund.

Looking back, why, oh, why was Russell trying to earn a degree in finance to break into the investment field if it was impossible to make any money at it? Why were all his classes full of people who wanted to move on to careers picking stocks, making investments, or trading securities? Well, some people do make good money as investors and traders. Also, everyone believes that America is the land of opportunity and that with hard work, you can achieve some level of success.

Market efficiency is the belief that all investors have access to the same information and are making informed investing decisions. Some people say that because these decisions are well-informed and rational, current market prices reflect the proper value of a stock or commodity. But that statement simply isn't true. Traders make impulse purchases, and prices are always moving. Prices do get out of line, and it's possible to profit from the results.

Only a Full-Time Professional Can Make Money in the Markets

Plenty of professionals make money as traders or full-time investors. If this game is truly made up of winners taking money from losers, how can a part-time amateur with a small account and limited time for analysis be expected to profit? The answer is easy: focus.

One of the most successful traders we know of trades nothing but Apple (AAPL) — specifically, AAPL stock and options. They know the company inside and out; they know how the stock has historically reacted to various pieces of news, such as earnings announcements and new-product rollouts. Even though this person isn't a professional, their focus on one company and a few strategies results in consistent profits.

REMEMBER

If you work in a particular industry, focus on the stocks in that industry. You already have a leg up on the competition because you have a fundamental knowledge of the industry through experience, which is something that many traders will never gain. If you work for a regional bank, for example, find a few similar banks to focus on; if you work for a construction company, focus on the companies that supply to builders. By narrowing your focus, you may find a small niche in which you can profit while professionals spread themselves too thin looking at multiple stocks and industries.

Technical Analysis Is Nothing More than Reading Tea Leaves

This myth gets us every time, probably because we just love it when charting is compared with psychic or supernatural activities. Ludicrous! Quite a bit of upper-level math goes into various methods of charting and trading. Also, when back-testing is conducted on technical trading methods, the statistical measures used are similar to those used to check for errors in other hard sciences. Finally, charting can offer insight about times when traders step up to buy or sell aggressively. Those price points become significant for traders who use charts as well as for those who don't.

If you're still convinced that technical analysis is serious, tell it to the members of the Market Technicians Association (MTA). The MTA is a professional society with a professional designation called Chartered Market Technician (CMT), which requires hours of study and the successful completion of three levels of tests to obtain. Loads of extremely smart people who make a living using technical analysis belong to this organization; they all argue vehemently against the idea that technical analysis isn't a hard science; and you'd be hard-pressed to find an owner of Tarot cards or a crystal ball anywhere in the group.

Charting Is for Short-Term Traders Only

Charts are wonderful for short-term trading: They depict the emotion behind what the market is doing and allow more-rational traders to pick points to buy and sell. We can't imagine trading over the short term without these charts. But long-term charts are also useful, despite what you may hear from naysayers.

Those of you who have full-time jobs outside trading probably can't trade full-time. If you still want to get involved with trading, one solution is to trade by using longer holding periods. You simply need to work with longer time periods in your charts (weekly rather than daily, for example) and plan to hold your trades a bit longer.

One of the most successful technical traders is William O'Neil, the founder of *Investor's Business Daily*. O'Neil has a long-term charting methodology that he highlights in his newspaper and through his charting service. If you're interested in longer-term trading, you can find more info on his strategies at www.investors.com.

You Must Be Rich to Start Trading

Don't get us wrong: No one should be speculating with money they can't afford to lose. If you're interested in day-trading stocks, you must open an account with at least $25,000, which is more than most people can lose without suffering major repercussions. You shouldn't take out a second mortgage or bet the kids' college fund on a trading strategy, regardless of how confident you are in your abilities. Trading is stressful enough without worrying about the potentially devastating effects of losing money if you lack the appropriate means.

That said, you can open a small account with a discount broker for a few thousand dollars and trade lower-priced stocks or futures contracts. To trade futures with a small account, concentrate on futures contracts that aren't terribly volatile, or follow a strategy that employs stops to limit losses. You can get started with a small account, but you should be prepared to expect limited returns or use very tight stops.

Trading Is an Easy Way to Get Rich Quick

Trading isn't easy. We can't emphasize that point enough. Imagine working on something for a while, and then, rather than reap monetary rewards for your hard work, you end up losing money. If trading were easy, all of us would do it for an hour a day and live lives of luxury. Becoming consistently profitable requires quite a bit of hard work and consistency in putting in the effort.

Hard work does pay off in trading, but don't expect to strike it rich with a half-hearted or lackadaisical effort. It took Russell a few years of working on systems (and losing some money) before he became consistently profitable trading for himself. His beautiful wife can attest to the amount of work he continues to put into his personal trading endeavor, which is almost like a second full-time job. But he has noticed a direct correlation between how much time he devotes to trading preparations and how well he's doing.

Candlestick Charts Require In-Depth Data and Are Difficult to Create

If you're drawing your charts by hand, yes, candlestick charts are tougher to create than other kinds. But with few exceptions, candlestick charts are widely available, and you can create them by using the same information you'd used to make bar charts. For more info on all the electronic resources you can tap into to view and build candlestick charts, refer to Chapter 3.

The Trading Game Is Stacked against the Small Trader

This myth may have been true years ago, when almost all trading took place by way of a trading pit or floor specialists. Now that the Internet has transformed trading into a mostly electronic medium, no professionals stand between you and the execution of a trade. Technology has leveled the playing field.

Also, professionals used to pay much lower commissions than individual traders, but no longer. Heck, at many brokers, commissions are close to zero. Several discount brokers charge individual traders the same low rates that institutions and large traders pay to trade. Small traders have many versatile tools at their disposal and can more than fend for themselves in most markets.

Selling Short Is for Professional Traders Only

Selling short can be a difficult and nerve-racking business, especially when you're working with stocks. Extra fees may be involved, and if your broker is unable to borrow a particular stock, you may not even be able to put on the desired short position. Also, keep in mind that the overall long-term trend of the stock market is for prices to move higher, so you're always trying to buck the long-term trend when selling a stock short. Finally, in theory, the potential loss on a short is unlimited, whereas buying a stock limits your losses to your initial investment.

Despite all the downsides associated with shorting, we can honestly say that it's silly to assert that selling short is for professionals only. Not many small traders consider shorting, so there's ample opportunity to make money.

If you're interested in trying your hand at shorting, consider selling futures contracts short as an initial effort. The barriers for shorting futures contracts aren't quite as high as those for shorting stocks. Further, a futures contract never needs to be borrowed; you just short and wait for a price drop to buy back.

Chapter **19**

Ten Tips to Remember about Technical Analysis

A debate continues to rage about the validity and usefulness of technical analysis in security trading. We're firm believers that when it's used correctly, technical analysis is an outstanding trading and investing tool. Other methods of investing and trading exist, but for our purposes, technical analysis combined with candlestick charting has worked quite well. As you begin or continue your trading efforts, you'll almost certainly encounter differing opinions on technical analysis, and we use this chapter to set out ten points on the topic that you should remember as you get down to the business of trading.

Charts Can Give False Signals

We're the first to admit that sometimes — in some cases, up to 50 percent of the time — signals can be wrong. If all signals were reliable, you could see A and do B time after time, and you (and all your trading peers) would rake in the profits.

But the reality is that charts do give false signals, and it's up to you to use proper money management to limit the losses that can occur when good signals go bad. Always use wise stops when you put on a trade, and remember that when a signal fails, you must get out and move on.

You Will Run into Skeptics

Some people regard charting and trading as being nothing more than glorified gambling or guessing at the future. Let them talk. Smile, bite your tongue, and think about the profit you just earned after closing out a winning position.

Plenty of successful traders make a comfortable living using technical analysis as a primary trading tool; one of them even owns a professional baseball team. Who's gonna try to ridicule you when you're buying a sports franchise? Okay, your trading goals may not be that lofty, but you see our point.

There's No Definite Right or Wrong Opinion of a Chart

Because charting combines many factors and approaches, two traders or analysts can view a chart and have completely different opinions about whether the chart is bullish or bearish. If you don't believe me, get on Twitter sometime and search the stock symbol for Tesla, $TSLA. (The $ sign in a stock symbol is called a *cash tag*.) As in politics, the differing opinions can be nasty and personal.

The reason for the differing points of view may be as simple as the time frame that each trader has in mind for a trade, or it can be that one of the traders is biased for or against a particular stock or market depicted in a chart. Regardless of the reasons, both opinions have some measure of validity. Also, keep in mind it takes a buyer and seller to make a market, so when you make a trade, the other side of that trade has a different opinion from you.

Wrong opinions don't exist — just those that don't pan out in a specific scenario. You want people to be open-minded about your use of charts for trading and investing, right? You should offer them the same level of respect and consideration. After all, differing opinions are crucial components of an active market!

A Single Chart Doesn't Tell a Whole Story

Multiple factors affect the prices of securities, from the health of the overall economy to industry-specific concerns to individual company events. People trade specific stocks daily, all with a variety of goals and time frames.

One solitary chart can't provide insight into what all the various players and influ-ences hope to accomplish as they buy and trade a security over a given period. Keep this fact in mind as you develop your trading strategy, and be sure to look at charts with time frames that don't necessarily match the ones you use for your trades.

You may be looking for a trade that lasts two or three days — a pretty short time frame. It certainly doesn't hurt to look at charts with a longer time frame as you search for a good environment for your trade. In fact, it may be a confidence-booster to find that traders with a longer time horizon are going to be on the same side as you! Retrieving and studying additional charts is well worth the small amount of extra time and effort.

Charting Is Part Science, Part Art

Although higher math is crucial for technical analysis, there's also what we like to refer to as the art component. Some people have a knack for looking at charts and getting an instant — and profitable — feel for how future trading action will develop for a stock or market. We think that these few talented people have a sixth sense, much as traditional artists have natural artistic talent. These abilities are rare, but we've seen them in action (unfortunately, not while looking in the mirror).

That said, we've been able to take the natural talents we do have for analyzing charts and enhance them with study and practice. You can do the same! Keep reading up on your patterns, and maintain a watchful eye on your charts, and you can develop the ability to analyze and trade quickly and efficiently.

You Can Overanalyze

In "A Single Chart Doesn't Tell a Whole Story" earlier in this chapter, we state that you should consider varying time frames when putting together your trading ideas. But make sure you don't overdo your analysis!

How can you overdo it? You can look at so many time frames and indicators that you end up seeing both bullish and bearish features in every security you analyze. You can end up with so much information influencing your opinion in both direc-tions that you develop analysis paralysis, and you can't make a decision.

Don't overcomplicate your trades. Look at a few charts, draw your conclusions, and then make a reasonable move. Don't forget to place your stops wisely! (For more information on placing stops or exiting when a pattern doesn't play out, see Chapters 7 through 15.)

Develop a Backup System

Whatever system you choose for your charting and data needs — whether it's a high-end system that charges hundreds of dollars a month or a free website — make sure to have a backup plan. No matter how costly or clever they are, systems go down, and problems usually strike just when you need the systems most. Make sure that you have a backup you can rely on when you face a system failure.

You should also have a backup system that you can use for confirmation when something just doesn't look right in a particular chart (or when it looks too good to be true). Data errors are part of the game, and using a backup to check on what seems like a sure thing can save you some heartache and losses. Have an online backup system or use an external backup drive to keep your data protected so that you can access it if you need it.

Also, brokerage firms periodically have system issues. If doing so makes sense, you might consider having accounts at more than one firm.

Error-Free Data Doesn't Exist

We can't emphasize the fact enough that error-free data isn't possible. If you start to back-test your trading theories with historical data, keep in mind that errors occur in almost all data. We use two sources of data and compare them before performing tests, but we enjoy the luxury of having some programming knowledge and access to several data sources.

If you're on a limited budget, compare charts from two sources or use free data from two sources, and make sure that everything matches up. If you spot discrepancies, find a third data source, and see which of the first two sources is correct.

No System Is Silly as Long as It Works

The world is filled with outrageous money-making theories. But if you have an idea of what works in the market, and you can test and execute it properly to make consistent profits, your idea is worth incorporating into your strategy. We don't care if you say, "When it rains on Wall Street on a Friday, it's time to short the Dow Jones Industrial Average." If your system works consistently, don't discount it, no matter how ridiculous it may seem. If something works historically for you in real money situations, keep an open mind when you're considering whether to keep doing it.

Past Results Don't Always Predict Future Performance

Sometimes, the best-laid trading plans just don't work. You can come up with a logical plan that worked in the past and execute it while following all the right rules, and still fail to make money (or even lose it).

The market environment can change in erratic ways, and predicting what your trading peers will do all the time is very difficult. If you trade long enough, you're bound to get knocked down when you expected to leap ahead. What's the best thing to do? Dust yourself off, chalk up the loss to experience, and begin looking for your next promising trade.

Index

A

abandoned baby pattern, bearish
  failure of, 210, 211
  identification of, 209
  trading based on, 209–210
abandoned baby pattern, bullish, 179
  failure of, 181
  identification of, 179–180
  trading based on, 180
AI. *See* artificial intelligence
Air Products, 98–100, 102–104, 106–108, 191–193, 219–223, 240–241
Alphabet, 38, 39, 86–87, 91, 92, 94, 269–271, 274–275
Amazon, 259–260, 263
Apple, 84, 125, 169–170, 172–173, 175–176, 198–200, 202–206, 209–210, 282–283, 313
artificial intelligence (AI), 49
  ChatGPT, 50–56
  Claude, 56–59
automated trend lines, 230–231

B

back testing, 50, 313
bar charts, 8, 26–28, 312
bearish candlesticks, 10–11
bearish days, 20–21

bearish double-stick patterns, 137–138
  doji star, 147–149
  engulfing pattern, 138–140
  harami, 141–143
  harami cross, 143–145
  inverted hammer, 145–147
  meeting line, 150–152
  neck lines, 161–163
  piercing line, 152–155
  separating lines, 158–161
  thrusting line, 156–158
bearish market, 86
bearish single-stick patterns
  belt holds, 100–101, 103–105
  gravestone doji, 81–84
  hanging man, 105–108, 259–261, 263, 272
  long black candle, 75–81
bearish three-stick patterns, 197
  abandoned baby pattern, 209–211
  downside gap-filled pattern, 221–223
  downside tasuki gap pattern, 218–221
  evening star and doji star patterns, 206–208
  side-by-side black lines pattern, 214–216
  side-by-side white lines pattern, 216–218
  squeeze alert pattern, 210–213
  three black crows pattern, 203–206, 281–282
  three inside down pattern, 198–201
  three outside down pattern, 201–203

bearish-trending patterns, combining economic indicators with, 299–298

consumer price index, 305–306

gross domestic product, 300–301

interest rates, 301–303

unemployment rate, 303–304

Volatility Index, 307–308

bearish-trending patterns, combining technical indicators with, 279

analyzing short trades with trend lines, 280–281

picking short entry points, 287–288

pinning down short entry points and confirming trends, 285–286

trend lines for covering a short, 282–284

belt holds, 100

bearish, 100–101, 103–105

bullish, 100–103

failure of, 103–105

long, 102–103

Bitcoin, 284

black marubozu, 77

Bollinger bands, 244–245

bullish candlesticks, 10–11

bullish days, 20–21

bullish double-stick patterns, 109–110

doji star, 122–124

engulfing pattern, 110–114

harami, 114–116

harami cross, 117–119

inverted hammer, 119–122

meeting line, 123–126

neck lines, 134–136

piercing line, 126–128

separating lines, 131–134

thrusting line, 129–131, 255

bullish market, 86

bullish reversal patterns, buying with, 248–256

bullish single-stick patterns

belt holds, 100–103

dragonfly doji, 70–74

hammer, 105–107

long white candle, 64–70

bullish three-stick patterns, 167

abandoned baby pattern, 179–181

morning star and doji star, 176–179

side-by-side black lines pattern, 187–190

side-by-side white lines pattern, 185–187

squeeze alert pattern, 181–184

three inside up pattern, 168–171

three outside up pattern, 171–173, 283

three white soldiers pattern, 173–176

upside gap-filled pattern, 193–195, 269

upside tasuki gap pattern, 190–193, 269–271

bullish-trending patterns, combining economic indicators with, 289–290

consumer price index, 295–296

gross domestic product, 290–292

interest rates, 292–293

unemployment rate, 293–294

Volatility Index, 296–298

bullish-trending patterns, using technical indicators alongside, 267–268

buying trend lines, 268–269

determining sales and stop levels with trend lines, 270–272

setting stops with moving average, 275–277

using moving averages for trend confirmation, 273–275

buy stop, 79, 84, 149

C

candlestick charts/charting, 7–8, 17, 32. *See also* technical indicators

advantages of, 9, 312

bearish and bullish days, 20–21

benefits of, 18–25

closing price, 37–38

comparison with alternative charting methods, 26–30

components of, 9–11

fundamental information in, 43–47

gap opening, 22

high and low prices, 35–37

history of, 18

myths about, 312, 315

opening price, 32–35

open interest, 40–42

readability of charts, 19–20

risks of, 25–26

technical analysis, 12–13, 313–314, 317–321

using AI with, 49–59

volume, 39–40

candlestick patterns, 11, 23–25. *See also specific patterns*

complex, 12

sell pattern, 23–24

simple, 11–12

carry trade market, 307–308

Cedar Fairs, 291, 306

Chartered Market Technician (CMT), 313

charting methods, 8–9, 26–30

ChatGPT

history of, 50

limitations of, 51

working with, 51–56

Claude, 56–59

closing long black candle/closing black marubozu, 77, 78

closing long white candle/closing white marubozu, 69

closing price, 37. *See also* moving average(s)

pinning down, 38

recording on candlestick, 37–38

closing white candle. *See* opening long white candle

CMT. *See* Chartered Market Technician

complex candlestick patterns, 12

consumer price index (CPI), 295–296, 305–306

CPI. *See* consumer price index

D

dark cloud cover pattern. *See* piercing line, bearish

data errors, 320

divergence (relative strength index), 241

dividend dates, 43–44

dojis, 273

  definition of, 88

  dragonfly doji, 70–74

  gravestone doji, 81–84

  long, 94, 95

  long-legged doji, 88–93, 249, 253

  short, 94–96

  variety of, 93–94

doji star, bearish (three-stick), 206

  failure of, 208

  identification of, 206

  trading based on, 206–208

doji star, bearish (two-stick), 147

  failure of, 148–149

  identification of, 148

  trading based on, 148

doji star, bullish (three-stick)

  failure of, 178

  identification of, 176–177

  trading based on, 177–178

doji star, bullish (two-stick), 122

  failure of, 123, 124

  identification of, 122–123

  trading based on, 123, 124

dot.com bubble, 138

double-stick patterns. *See* bearish double-stick patterns; bullish double-stick patterns

downside gap-filled pattern, 221

  failure of, 223

  identification of, 221–222

  trading based on, 222–223

downside tasuki gap pattern, 218

  failure of, 220–221

  identification of, 219

  trading based on, 219–220

dragonfly doji, 70–71

  recognition of, 71–73

  trading based on, 73–74

E

earnings dates, 44–45

earnings season, 38

ECN. *See* electronic communication network

economic indicators, 289–290, 299–300

  consumer price index, 295–296, 305–306

  gross domestic product, 290–292, 300–301

  interest rates, 292–293, 301–303

  unemployment rate, 293–294, 303–304

  Volatility Index, 296–298, 307–308

electronic communication network (ECN), 19, 33

Energy Select Sector SPDR ETF, 268–269, 280–282

engulfing pattern, bearish, 138

  failure of, 140

  identification of, 138–139

  trading based on, 139

engulfing pattern, bullish, 110

  failure of, 113–114

  identification of, 111–112

  trading based on, 112–113

entry point(s)

long, using RSI for picking, 248–249

long, using stochastic indicator for picking, 252–254

short, using moving average for picking, 287–288

short, using moving average for pinning down, 285–286

short, using RSI for picking, 258–262

short, using stochastic indicator for picking, 263–266

evening star, bullish

failure of, 208

identification of, 206

trading based on, 206–208

exit point(s)

long, using RSI for picking, 250–252

long, using stochastic indicator for picking, 254–256

short, using RSI for picking, 260–262

short, using stochastic indicator for picking, 264–266

exponential moving average, 233, 235, 236

F

false signals of charts, 317

fast-moving average, 236, 238–239

fast stochastics, 242, 243, 252

fundamental analysis, 289–290, 299–300

futures, 79, 272–273, 314

example of, 34–35

high and low prices of, 36–37

opening price for, 33–34

open interest, 40–42

G

gap opening, definition of, 22

GDP. *See* gross domestic product

gravestone doji, 81

failure of, 84

identification of, 81–82

trading based on, 83–84

gross domestic product (GDP), 290–292, 300–301

H

hammer, 105. *See also* inverted hammer, bullish

going long with, 106–107

identification of, 105–106

hanging man, 105, 259–261, 263, 272

failure of, 108

identification of, 105–106

shorting with, 107–108

harami, bearish, 141

failure of, 142–143

identification of, 141

trading based on, 142

harami, bullish, 114

identification of, 114–115

trading based on, 115–116

harami cross, bearish, 143

failure of, 144–145

identification of, 143

trading based on, 143–144

harami cross, bullish, 117
  buy signal from, 118
  failure of, 118–119
  identification of, 117
  trading based on, 118
high price, 35–37
Homma, Munehisa, 18

I

inside day, definition of, 141
insider trading, 46–47
interest rates, 292–293, 301–303
inverted hammer, bearish, 146
  failure of, 146–147
  identification of, 146
  trading based on, 146
inverted hammer, bullish, 119
  failure of, 121–122
  identification of, 120
  successful, 121
  trading based on, 120–121
Invesco QQQ Trust Series 1 ETF,
    273–274, 285
iShares 20+ Year Treasury Bond ETF, 286
iShares Russell 2000 ETF, 248–249, 253,
    261, 265–266
iShares Silver Trust ETF, 287

J

Japanese yen futures, 34
JPMorgan Chase, 130–131, 133–134,
    156–158, 160–163

L

Lane, George, 242
legal insider trading, 46–47
line charts, 8, 26–27
long black candle
  bearish signal from, 79–80
  black marubozu, 77
  closing, 77, 78
  failure as a short signal, 80–81
  in intraday chart, 75–76
  opening, 77, 78
  trading based on, 78–81
long-legged doji, 88, 249, 253
  as buy signal, 90
  failure of, 91
  giving a buy signal, 90–91
  identification of, 88–90
  as sell signal, 92
  sell signal failure of, 92–93
  short signal on, 92
long white candle, 64–66
  closing, 69
  failure as a long signal, 67–68
  in intraday chart, 64, 65
  opening, 69–70
  signaling an uptrend, 66–67
  white marubozu, 68
low price, 35–37

M

market efficiency, 312
market environment, 86, 321

Market Technicians Association (MTA), 313

market trend, 86–87

medium-moving average, 238–239

meeting line, bearish
 failure of, 152
 identification of, 150
 trading based on, 150–152

meeting line, bullish, 123
 failure of, 125, 126
 identification of, 124–125
 trading based on, 125, 126

Microsoft, 38, 275–278, 288

morning star, bullish
 failure of, 177–178
 identification of, 176–177
 trading based on, 177–178

moving average(s), 231
 definition of, 231
 exponential, 233, 235, 236
 for picking short entry points, 287–288
 for pinning down short entry points and confirming trends, 285–286
 setting stops with, 275–277
 simple, 232–233, 235
 and stochastic oscillator interpretation, 243
 three, combining, 237–239
 time frames of, 231–232
 two, combining, 236–237, 274–277, 286
 using for trend confirmation, 273–275
 weighted, 233, 235–236

MTA. *See* Market Technicians Association

N

neck lines, bearish
 failure of, 162–163
 identification of, 161
 trading based on, 161–162

neck lines, bullish, 134
 failure of, 135, 136
 identification of, 134
 trading based on, 134–136

New York Stock Exchange (NYSE), 19, 32

Nison, Steve, 18

Nvidia, 177–181, 206–208

NYSE. *See* New York Stock Exchange

O

O'Neil, William, 314

opening long black candle/opening black marubozu, 77, 78

opening long white candle, 69–70

opening price
 pinning down, 33–34
 recording on candlestick, 32

open interest, 40–42

overbought level (relative strength index), 241, 248, 250, 258–262

oversold level (relative strength index), 241, 248, 250, 252, 258, 260–262

P

paper trading, 14

P&F. *See* point and figure charts

piercing line, bearish, 152
  failure of, 154–155
  identification of, 153
  trading based on, 153–154
piercing line, bullish, 126
  failure of, 128
  identification of, 126–127
  trading based on, 127–128
point and figure (P&F) charts, 8, 26, 28–30
price gaps, 22, 23

R

range-bound market, 86, 238
range trading, 73
reactionary trading day, 25
readability of candlestick charts, 19–20
relative strength index (RSI), 42–43
  calculation of, 239–240
  chart, reading, 240–241
  as momentum oscillator, 239
  overbought and oversold levels, 241, 248,
      250, 258, 260–262
  for picking long entry point, 248–249
  for picking long exits, 250–252
  for picking short entry points, 258–262
  for picking short exit points, 260–262
  and stochastic oscillator
      interpretation, 244
resistance, 9, 29, 80
RSI. *See* relative strength index

S

sell stop orders, 68
separating lines, bearish

failure of, 160–161
  identification of, 158–159
  trading based on, 159–160
separating lines, bullish, 131
  failure of, 133–134
  signaling out, 132
  trading based on, 132–133
setup day, 109, 137
short selling/shorting, 24–25, 316
  using moving averages for, 284–288
  using RSI for, 258–262
  using stochastic indicators for,
      262–266
  using trend lines for, 280–284
short-term trading, 314
side-by-side black lines pattern,
      bearish, 214
  failure of, 215–216
  identification of, 214
  trading based on, 214–215
side-by-side black lines pattern,
      bullish, 187
  failure of, 190
  identification of, 188
  trading based on, 189
side-by-side white lines pattern,
      bearish, 216
  failure of, 218
  identification of, 216
  trading based on, 216–217
side-by-side white lines pattern,
      bullish, 185
  failure of, 187
  identification of, 185
  trading based on, 185–186

signal day, 109, 137

simple candlestick patterns, 11–12

simple moving average, 232–235

single-stick patterns, 63–64
  belt holds, 100–105
  dojis, 88–96
  dragonfly doji, 70–74
  gravestone doji, 81–84
  hanging man and hammer, 105–108
  long black candle, 75–81
  long white candle, 64–70
  spinning tops, 96–100, 276, 277, 282

slow-moving average, 236, 238–239

slow stochastics, 242, 243, 252

SPDR Gold Shares ETF, 260–261, 263–264

specialists (stock market), 33

spinning tops, 96–97, 276, 277, 282
  failing, 98–100
  identification of, 97
  recognition of buy signal with, 98
  short signal from, 99

SPY ETF, 112–113, 116, 139–140, 142–143, 293–294, 304, 308

squeeze alert pattern, bearish, 210
  failure of, 212–213
  identification of, 211
  trading based on, 212

squeeze alert pattern, bullish, 181
  failure of, 183–184
  identification of, 181–182
  trading based on, 182–183

standard deviation, 244–245

St. Louis Federal Reserve, 290, 295, 300, 305

stochastic oscillators, 242
  interpretation of, 242–244
  math behind, 242
  for picking long entry point, 252–254
  for picking long exits, 254–256
  for picking short entry points, 263–266
  for picking short exit points, 264–266

stock market, 32–33

stock splits, 45–46

stop orders, 68

support, 9, 29, 67

T

Target, 118–119, 121–122, 124, 143–147, 149, 296, 303

technical analysis, 12–13, 313–314, 317
  art component of charting, 319
  backup system, 320
  charts with longer time horizon, 318–319
  data errors, 320
  differing opinions about charts, 318
  false signals of charts, 317
  overanalysis, 319–320
  prediction based on past results, 321
  skepticism about, 318

technical indicators, 42–43, 227–228
  Bollinger bands, 244–245
  combining bearish-trending patterns with, 279–288
  moving averages, 231–239, 273–277
  relative strength index, 239–241
  stochastic oscillator, 242–244
  trend lines, 228–231, 268–272
  using alongside bullish-trending patterns, 267–277

term structure, 291, 301

Tesla, 182–184, 186–187, 189–190, 212–218, 251–252, 254–255

three black crows pattern, 203, 281–282

  failure of, 205–206

  identification of, 203–204

  trading based on, 204–205

three inside down pattern, 198

  failure of, 200–201

  identification of, 198, 199

  trading based on, 198–200

three inside up pattern, 168

  failure of, 170–171

  identification of, 168–169

  trading based on, 169–170

three outside down pattern, 201

  failure of, 202–203

  identification of, 201

  trading based on, 202

three outside up pattern, 283

  failure of, 172–173

  identification of, 171

  trading based on, 171–172

three-stick patterns. *See* bearish three-stick patterns; bullish three-stick patterns

three white soldiers pattern, 173

  failure of, 175–176

  identification of, 173–174

  trading based on, 174–175

thrusting line, bearish, 156

  failure of, 157–158

  identification of, 156

  trading based on, 156–157

thrusting line, bullish, 129, 255

  failure of, 130, 131

  recognizing, 129

  trading based on, 129–131

trading

  creating and adhering to rules for, 14–15

  day, 19

  earnings season, 38

  money management, 13

  myths about, 312–316

  paper, 14

  part-time, 313

  platforms, 59–60

  preparation for, 13, 315

  short-term, 314

  and technology, 315–316

trend confirmation

  bearish double-stick patterns, 155–163

  bearish three-stick patterns, 213–223

  bullish double-stick patterns, 129–136

  bullish three-stick patterns, 184–195

  using moving averages for, 273–275, 285–286

  using trend lines for, 268–270, 280–282

trend followers, 129

trend lines

  analyzing short trades with, 280–281

  automated, 230–231

  for buying and confirmation, 268–270

  definition of, 228

  determining sales and stop levels with, 270–272

  determining trading levels with, 283

  direction of, 230

drawing, 229–230

for shorting entries and exits, 282–284

trend reversal

bearish double-stick patterns,
137–155

bearish three-stick patterns, 198–213

bullish double-stick patterns, 110–128

bullish three-stick patterns, 168–184

buying with bullish reversal
patterns, 248–256

selling with bearish reversal
patterns, 257–266

U

unemployment rate, 293–294,
303–304

upside gap-filled pattern, 193, 269

failure of, 195

identification of, 193–194

trading based on, 194–195

upside tasuki gap pattern, 190, 269–271

failure of, 192–193

identification of, 191

trading based on, 191–192

V

VIX. *See* Volatility Index

Volatility Index (VIX), 296–298, 307–308

volume data, in candlestick chart, 39–40

W

Walmart, 125–128, 150–154, 297–298, 301

weighted moving average, 233, 235–236

white marubozu, 68

Wilder, J. Welles, 241

Y

yield curves, 291–293, 301–302

About the Author

Larissa J. Adamiec, PhD, is an academic and a financial markets practitioner. She has worked in various asset classes, founding Stuart Investments (equities), working at the Federal Home Loan Bank of Chicago (fixed income), PEAK6 (derivatives), and her dissertation work (foreign exchange). She has taught at the Chicago Board Options Exchange (CBOE), Financial Markets Education (FME), and the Kelley School of Business. She is currently a clinical professor at Purdue University.

Larissa has taught finance and economics at both undergraduate and graduate levels. She holds a BS in finance from the University of Pittsburgh, an MS in financial engineering from Illinois Institute of Technology, and a PhD in management science from Illinois Institute of Technology in Chicago.

Dedication

For my children, our number-one fan, and of course, the VIX.

Author's Acknowledgments

The Wiley editorial team has been phenomenal to work with. I have especially enjoyed working with Tracy Boggier, Nina Hook, and Paul Levesque. I would like to thank Dr. Russell Rhoads, for allowing me to continue his fine work in candlestick charting.

I could not have written this book without the support of the entire team at Academic Market Insights, my family (John, Sandy, Joe, Karly, Adam, John, Lindsay, Eleanor, Owen, Luke, Nicholas, Skadi, Wrigley, Hopper, Adayla, Artemis), my mentors (Irene, Deb, Sandra, John, Joe, Russell), my friends (Jodi, Rebekah, Bethany, Petra, Michael, Katie, Deb, Kathy, Merribeth, Jackie, Jaime, Carla, Joan, Dr. Hubka, Aaron, Jenna, Ally, Jean, Josan, Yvonne, Maria, Melissa, Gina, Simon, Rebecca), the College of Human Health & Science, and the department of Hospitality Tourism and Management at Purdue University (Ceridwyn, Barclay, Rod, Amanda, Julie, Dan, Jiong, Susan).

Publisher's Acknowledgments

Executive Editor: Tracy Boggier
Development Editor: Paul Levesque
Copy Editor: Becky Whitney
Technical Editor: Russell Rhoads, PhD

Managing Editor: Murari Mukundan
Production Editor: Tamilmani Varadharaj
Cover Image: © pookpiik/stock.adobe.com